CAMBRIDGE ENGLISH CLASSICS

The English Writings
of
Abraham Cowley

ABRAHAM COWLEY

Born 1618
Died 1667

ABRAHAM COWLEY

ESSAYS, PLAYS

AND

SUNDRY VERSES

THE TEXT EDITED BY
A. R. WALLER, M.A.

CAMBRIDGE :
at the University Press
1906

CAMBRIDGE UNIVERSITY PRESS WAREHOUSE,

C. F. CLAY, Manager.

London: FETTER LANE, E.C.

Glasgow: 50, WELLINGTON STREET.

Leipzig: F. A. BROCKHAUS.

New York: G. P. PUTNAM'S SONS.

Bombay and Calcutta: MACMILLAN AND CO., Ltd.

NOTE.

THE first volume of this edition of the English writings of Cowley contained the whole of the poems that were collected for the folio which appeared the year after his death. The present volume contains the poems not included in the folio, its prose contents and Cowley's English plays.

The earlier writings have been printed from a copy of the third edition of 1637, preserved in the University Library, Cambridge ; but, as that copy is imperfect, transcripts of the missing portions have been made from two other copies and the deficiencies supplied thereby. The collation of these similarly dated copies has shown that they differ in a few passages. In the notes I have printed the variants noted in a collation of the first and second editions of 1633 and 1636. It may, perhaps, be permitted me to remind the reader that, of these earlier writings, *Pyramus and Thisbe* was written at the age ' of ten yeeres,' *Constantius and Phile-tus* when 'two yeeres older' and that the volume entitled *Poeticall Blossomes* was first published when Cowley was but fifteen.

The *Satyre* called *The Puritan and the Papist* seems entitled to a definite place among the works of Cowley and I have therefore printed it as part of the present text. By the kindness of the authorities of Bodley's Library, Oxford, it has been set up from photographs of the very rare first edition of 1643.

The English play *The Guardian,* and its later recension *Cutter of Coleman-Street,* follow the first editions of

v

NOTE

1650 and 1663 respectively. They were apparently written in 1641 and 1658 respectively. Pepys (ed. Wheatley, ii, p. 155) records in 1661 that he went 'after dinner to the Opera, where there was a new play ("Cutter of Coleman Street"), made in the year 1658, with reflections much upon the late times, and it being the first time, the pay was doubled, and so to save money, my wife and I went up into the gallery, and there saw very well; and a very good play it is.'

The *Proposition For the Advancement Of Experimental Philosophy* was printed in 1661. I am indebted to Mr W. Aldis Wright for the loan of a copy of that year for the purpose of reproduction. The essay was included in the prose miscellanies of the folio of 1668 referred to above, but the important *Preface* was omitted. The tract is given here, therefore, as it was published in 1661.

The *Discourse By way of Vision, Concerning the Government of Oliver Cromwell*, published also in 1661, has been printed from the folio of 1668 and so have the *Several Discourses by way of Essays, in Verse and Prose.*

At the end of these (see p. 462) I have added a poem which was printed in the ninth edition of Cowley's works (folio, 1700, Printed for *Henry Herringman*, etc.). Attention is drawn to this poem on the title page of the ninth edition by the words ' To which are added, some Verses by the *AUTHOR* | Never before Printed.' And I have ventured to add, also as part of the text, the unfinished poem on the Civil War first printed in 1679 (see Cowley's reference to this in the first volume of the present edition, p. 9).

I have not included *The Four Ages of England, or The Iron Age*, 1648, as it was specifically disavowed by Cowley in the Preface to the folio edition of his works

NOTE

referred to above (see the first volume of the present edition, p. 4): I have not been able to find any reason why his statement should be doubted. Nor have I included *A Satyre against Separatists*, 1642, also attributed to Cowley.

A few verses attributed to Cowley are printed in the appendix and notes : of these, the lines *Upon the Happie Birth of the Duke* may be regarded as certainly his, although he never included them in his works ; and probably the verses beginning ' Come, *Poetry*, and with you bring along' (p. 489) are his also : the edition in which they are to be found appeared during the lifetime of his literary executor (Bishop Thomas Sprat, 1635—1713).

As previously announced it is not intended to print Cowley's Latin poems as part of the present edition.

Material for a Supplement of Notes, biographical, bibliographical and critical, is being collected and will be published, it is hoped, at no very distant date.

A. R. WALLER.

University Press,
 Cambridge.
  12 *September*, 1906.

CONTENTS

POETICALL
BLOSSOMES.

The third Edition.

Enlarged by the Author.

——*fit surculus Arbor.*

London.

Printed by E. P. for Henry Seile,
and are to bee sold at his shop at the signe
of the Tygers-head in Fleet-street
between the Bridge and
the Conduit
1637.

2

To the Reader.

READER (I know not yet whether Gentle or no) Some, I know, have beene angrie (I dare not assume the honour of their envie) at my Poeticall boldnes, and blamed in mine, what commends other fruits, earliness: others, who are either of a weake faith, or strong malice, have thought me like a Pipe, which never sounds but when 'tis blowed in, and read me, not as *Abraham Cowley*, but *Authorem anonymum*: to the first I answer, that it is an envious frost which nippes the Blossomes, because they appeare quickly: to the latter, that he is the worst homicide who strives to murther anothers fame; to both, that it is a ridiculous follie to condemne or laugh at the starres, because the Moone and Sunne shine brighter. The small fire I have is rather blowne then extinguished by this wind. For the itch of Poesie by being angered encreaseth, by rubbing, spreads farther; which appeares in that I have ventured upon this third Edition. What though it be neglected? It is not, I am sure, the first booke, which hath lighted Tobacco, or been imployed by Cooks, and Groacers. If in all mens judgements it suffer shipwracke, it shall something content mee, that it hath pleased My selfe and the Bookseller. In it you shall finde one argument (and I hope I shall need no more) to confute unbelievers: which is, that as mine age, and consequently experience (which is yet but little) hath encreased, so they have not left my Poesie flagging behind them. I should not bee angrie to see any one burne my *Pyramus*, and *Thisbe*, nay I would doe it my selfe, but that I hope a pardon may easily bee gotten for the errors of ten yeeres age. My *Constantia* and *Philetus* confesseth mee two yeeres older when I writ it. The rest were made since upon severall occasions, and perhaps doe not belie the time of their birth. Such as they are, they were created by mee, but their fate lies in your hands, it is onely you, can effect, that neither the Booke-seller repent himselfe of his charge in printing them, nor I of my labour in composing them. Farewell.

A. C.

To his deare Friend and Schoole-fellow *Abraham Cowley*, on his flourishing and hopefull Blossomes.

Nature *we say decayes, because our* Age
      Is worse then were the Times of old: The Stage
And Histories *the former times declare:*
In these our latter Dayes what defects are
Experience *teacheth, What then? shall wee blame*
Nature *for this? Not so; let us declame*
Rather against our Selves: 'tis we Decay,
Not She: Shee is the same every way
She was at first. Cowley, *thou prov'st this truth.*
Could ever former Age brag of a Youth
So forward at these yeeres? Could Naso *write*
Thus young such wittie Poems? Tulli's *mite*
Of Eloquence, *at this age was not seene.*
Nor yet was Cato's *Judgement, at Thirteene*
So great as thine. Suppose it were so; yet
He Cic'ro's *Eloquence,* Tully *the Wit*
Of Ovid *wanted:* Ovid *too came farre*
In Judgement behind Cato. *Therefore are*
None of all equall unto Thee, so pretty,
So Eloquent, Judicious, and Witty.
Let the world's spring time but produce and show
Such Blossomes *as thy Writings are, and know,*
      Then (not till then) shall my opinion be,
      That it is Nature *faileth, and not* wee.

Ben. Masters.

To his Friend and Schoole-fellow ABRAHAM COWLEY, on his Poeticall BLOSSOMES.

*M*Any, *when* Youths *of tender* Age *they see*
   Expressing CATO, *in their Gravity,*
Judgement, *and* Wit *will oftentimes report,*
They thinke their thread of Life *exceeding short.*
But my opinion is not so of Thee,
For thou shalt live, to all Posterity.
These gifts will never let thee *dye, for* Death
Can not bereave thee of thy fame, *though breath.*
Let snarling Criticks *spend their braines to find*
A fault, though there be none; This is my mind;
Let him that carpeth with his vipers Tongue,
Thinke with himselfe what he could doe as young.
    But if the Springing Blossomes, *thus rare bee,*
   What ripen'd Fruit *shall we hereafter see?*

ROB. MEADE,

Condiscipulus.

To the Reader.

I.

I call'd the buskin'd *Muse* Melpomene,
  And told her what sad Story I would write:
Shee wept at hearing such a Tragedie,
Though wont in mournefull Ditties to delight.
If thou dislike these sorrowfull lines ; Then know
My Muse with teares, not with Conceits did flow.

II.

And as shee my unabler quill did guide,
Her briny teares did on the paper fall,
If then unequall numbers bee espied,
Oh Reader ! doe not that my error call,
    But thinke her teares defac't it, and blame then
    My Muses griefe, and not my missing Pen.

Abraham Cowley.

CONSTANTIA

AND

PHILETUS.

1.

I Sing two constant Lovers various fate,
  The hopes, and feares which equally attend
Their loves: Their rivals envie, Parents hate;
I sing their sorrowfull life, and tragicke end.
    Assist me this sad story to rehearse
    You Gods, and be propitious to my verse.

2.

In *Florence*, for her stately buildings fam'd,
And lofty roofes that emulate the skie;
There dwelt a lovely Mayd *Constantia* nam'd
Renown'd, as mirrour of all *Italy*.
    Her lavish nature did at first adorne,
    With *Pallas* soule in *Cytherea's* forme.

3.

And framing her attractive eyes so bright,
Spent all her wit in studie, that they might
Keepe th'earth from *Chaos*, and eternall night;
But envious Death destroy'd their glorious light.
    Expect not beauty then, since shee did part;
    For in her Nature wasted all her Art.

4.

Her hayre was brighter then the beams which are
A Crowne to *Phœbus*, and her breath so sweet,
It did transcend *Arabian* odours farre,
Or th'smelling Flowers, wherewith the Spring doth greet
    Approaching Summer, teeth like falling snow
    For white, were placed in a double row.

7

ABRAHAM COWLEY

5.

Her wit excell'd all praise, all admiration,
And speech was so attractive it might be
A meanes to cause great *Pallas* indignation,
And raise an envie from that Deity.
    The mayden Lillyes at her lovely sight
    Waxt pale with envie, and from thence grew white.

6.

She was in birth and parentage as high
As in her fortune great, or beauty rare,
And to her vertuous mindes nobility
The gifts of Fate and Nature doubled were;
    That in her spotlesse Soule, and lovely Face
    Thou might'st have seene each Deity and grace.

7.

The scornefull Boy *Adonis* viewing her
Would *Venus* still despise, yet her desire,
Each who but saw, was a Competitor
And rivall, scorcht alike with *Cupid's* fire.
    The glorious beames of her fayre Eyes did move,
    And light beholders on their way to Love.

8.

Amongst her many Sutors a young Knight
Bove others wounded with the Majesty
Of her faire presence, presseth most in sight;
Yet seldome his desire can satisfie
    With that blest object, or her rarenesse see;
    For Beauties guard, is watchfull Jealousie.

9.

Oft-times that he might see his *Dearest-faire*,
Vpon his stately Jennet he in th'way
Rides by her house, who neigh's, as if he were
Proud to be view'd by bright *Constantia*.
    But his poore Master though to see her move
    His joy, dares show no looke betraying love.

CONSTANTIA AND PHILETUS

10.

Soone as the morne peep'd from her rosie bed
And all Heavens smaller lights expulsed were:
She by her friends and neere acquaintance led
Like other Maids oft walk't to take the ayre;
    Aurora blusht at such a sight unknowne,
    To see those cheekes were redder then her owne.

11.

Th'obsequious Lover follows still her traine
And where they goe, that way his journey feines.
Should they turne backe, he would turne backe againe;
For where his Love, his businesse there remaines.
    Nor is it strange hee should be loath to part
    From her, since shee had stolne away his heart.

12.

Philetus hee was call'd sprung from a race
Of Noble ancestors; But greedy *Time*
And envious *Fate* had labour'd to deface
The glory which in his great Stocke did shine;
    His state but small, so Fortune did decree,
    But *Love* being blind, hee that could never see.

13.

Yet he by chance had hit his heart aright,
And on *Constantia's* eye his Arrow whet,
Had blowne the Fire, that would destroy him quite,
Unlesse his flames might like in her beget:
    But yet he feares, because he blinded is,
    Though he have shot him right, her heart hee'l misse.

14.

Unto *Loves* Altar therefore hee repayers,
And offers there a pleasing Sacrifice;
Intreating *Cupid* with inducing Prayers,
To looke upon, and ease his Miseries:
    Where having wept, recovering breath againe,
    Thus to immortall *Love* he did complaine:

ABRAHAM COWLEY

15.

Oh Cupid! *thou whose uncontrolled sway,*
Hath oft-times rul'd the Olympian *Thunderer,*
Whom all Cœlestiall Deities obey,
Whom Men and Gods both reverence and feare!
    Oh force Constantias *heart to yeeld to Love,*
    Of all thy Workes the Master piece 'twill prove.

16.

And let me not Affection vainely spend,
But kindle flames in her, like those in me;
Yet if that guift my Fortune doth transcend,
Grant that her charming Beauty I may see:
    And view those Eyes which with their ravishing light,
    Doe onely give contentment to my sight.

17.

Those who contemne thy sacred Deity,
And mocke thy power, let them thine anger know,
I faultlesse am, nor can't an honour be
To wound your slave alone, and spare your Foe.
    Here teares and sighes speake his imperfect mone,
    In language farre more dolorous than his owne.

18.

Home he retyr'd, his Soule he brought not home,
Just like a Ship whil'st every mounting wave
Tost by enraged *Boreas* up and downe,
Threatens the Mariner with a gaping grave;
    Such did his case, such did his state appeare,
    Alike distracted betweene hope and feare.

19.

Thinking her love hee never shall obtaine,
One morne he goes to th'Woods, and doth complaine
Of his unhappy Fate, but all in vaine,
And thus fond *Eccho*, answers him againe.
    So that it seemes *Aurora* wept to heare,
    For th'verdant grasse was dew'd with many a teare.

CONSTANTIA AND PHILETUS

THE ECCHO.

1.

OH! *what hath caus'd my killing miseries?*
    Eyes, Eccho said, What hath detain'd my ease?
Ease, straight the resonable Nymph replyes,
That nothing can my troubled minde appease :
    Peace, Eccho answers. What, is any nigh?
    Quoth he : at which, she quickly utters, I.

2.

Is't Eccho answers? tell mee then thy will :
I will, shee said. What shall I get (quoth he)
By loving still? to which she answers, ill.
Ill? shall I void of wisht for pleasure dye?
    I ; shall not I who toyle in ceaselesse paine,
    Some pleasure know? no, she replyes againe.

3.

False and inconstant Nymph, thou lyest (quoth he)
Thou lyest, shee said, And I deserv'd her hate,
If I should thee beleeve; beleeve, (saith shee)
For why thy idle words are of no weight.
    Weigh it (shee replyes) I therefore will depart.
    To which, resounding Eccho answers ; part.

20.

Then from the Woods with wounded heart he goes,
Filling with legions of fresh thoughts his minde.
He quarrels with himselfe because his woes
Spring from himselfe, yet can no medicine finde :
    Hee weepes to quench the fires that burn in him,
    But teares doe fall to th'earth, flames are within.

21.

No morning banisht darkenesse, nor blacke night
By her alternate course expuls'd the day,
Which in *Philetus* by a constant rite
At *Cupids* Altars did not weepe and pray;
    And yet had reaped nought for all his paine
    But Care and Sorrow, that was all his gaine.

ABRAHAM COWLEY

22.

But now at last the pitying God, o'recome
By's constant votes and teares, fixt in her heart
A golden shaft, and she is now become
A suppliant to Love that with like Dart
    Hee'd wound *Philetus*, and doth now implore
    With teares, ayde from that power she scorn'd before.

23.

Little she thinkes she kept *Philetus* heart
In her schortcht breast, because her owne she gave
To him. Since either suffers equall smart,
And alike measure in their torments have :
    His Soule, his griefe, his fires, now hers are growne :
    Her heart, her minde, her love is his alone.

24.

Whilst thoughts 'gainst thoughts rise up in mutinie,
Shee took a Lute (being farre from any eares)
And tun'd this Song, posing that harmony
Which Poets wit attributes to the Sphears :
    Whose ravishing Notes, if when her Love was slaine
    She had sung ; from *Styx* t'had cald him backe againe.

The Song.

1.

TO whom shall I my Sorrowes show ?
   Not to Love, for he is blinde :
And my Philetus *doth not know*
   The inward sorrow of my minde.
And all the senceless walls which are
   Now round about me, cannot heare.

2.

For if they could, they sure would weepe,
   And with my griefes relent :
Unlesse their willing teares they keepe,
   Till I from th'earth am sent.
Then I beleeve they'l all deplore
My fate, since I them taught before.

CONSTANTIA AND PHILETUS

3.

I willingly would weepe my store,
  If the' floud would land thy Love,
My deare PHILETUS *on the shoare*
  Of my heart; but shouldst thou prove
Afeard of flames, know the fires are
But bonefires for thy comming there.

25.

Then teares in envie of her speech did flow
From her faire eyes, as if it seem'd that there
Her burning flame had melted hills of snow,
And so dissol'vd them into many a teare ;
    Which *Nilus* like, did quickly over-flow,
    And caused soone new serpent griefes to grow.

26.

Heere stay my *Muse*, for if I should recite,
Her mournefull Language, I should make you weepe
Like her a floud, and so not see to write,
Such lines as I and th'age requires to keepe
    Mee from sterne death, or with victorious rime,
    Revenge their Masters death, and conquer time.

27.

By this time, chance and his owne industry
Had helpt *Philetus* forward, that he grew
Acquainted with her Brother, so that he,
Might by this meanes, his bright *Constantia* view:
    And as time serv'd shew her his miserie :
    And this was the first Act in's Tragedie.

28.

Thus to himselfe sooth'd by his flattering state,
He said; *How shall I thanke thee for this gaine,*
O Cupid, *or reward my helping Fate,*
Which sweetens all my sorrowes, all my paine ;
    What Husband-man would any sweet refuse,
    To reape at last such fruit, his labours use?

ABRAHAM COWLEY

29.

But waighing straight his doubtfull state aright,
Seeing his griefes linkt like an endlesse chaine
To following woes, he could despaire delight,
Quench his hot flames, and empty love disdaine.
    But *Cupid* when his heart was set on fire,
    Had burnt his wings, and could not then retyre.

30.

The wounded youth, and kinde *Philocrates*
(So was her Brother call'd) grew soone so deare,
So true, and constant, in their Amities,
And in that league so strictly joyned were;
    That Death it selfe could not their friendship sever.
    But as they liv'd in love, they dyde together.

31.

If one be melancholy, th'other's sad;
If one be sicke, the other he is ill,
And if *Philetus* any sorrow had,
Philocrates was partner in it still:
    Pylades soule and mad *Orestes* was
    In these, if wee beleeve *Pythagoras*.

32.

Oft in the Woods *Philetus* walkes, and there
Exclaimes against his fate, fate too unkind.
With speaking teares his griefes he doth declare,
And with sad sighes teacheth the angrie *Wind*,
    To sigh, and though it nere so cruell were,
    It roar'd to heare *Philetus* tell his care.

33.

The Christall Brookes which gently runne betweene
The shadowing Trees, and as they through them passe
Water the Earth, and keepe the Medowes greene,
Giving a colour to the verdant Grasse:
    Hearing *Philetus* tell his wofull state,
    In shew of griefe runne murmuring at his Fate.

34.

Philomel answeres him againe and shewes
In her best language, her sad Historie,
And in a mournfull sweetnesse tels her woes,
Denying to be pos'd in miserie :
  Constantia he, she *Tereus, Tereus* cryes,
  With him both griefe, and griefes expression vies.

35.

Philocrates must needes his sadnesse know,
Willing in ills, aswell as joyes to share,
Nor will on them the name of friends bestow,
Who in sport, not in sorrowes partners are.
  Who leaves to guide the Ship when stormes arise,
  Is guilty both of sinne, and cowardise.

36.

But when his noble Friend perceiv'd that he
Yeelded to tyrant Passion more and more,
Desirous to partake his malady,
He watches him in hope to cure his sore
  By counsell, and recall the poysonous Dart,
  When it alas was fixed in his heart.

37.

When in the Woods, places best fit for care,
Hee to himselfe did his past griefes recite,
The 'obsequious friend straight followes him, and there
Doth hide himselfe from sad *Philetus* sight.
  Who thus exclaimes; for a swolne heart would breake,
  If it for vent of sorrow might not speake.

38.

Oh! I am lost, not in this Desart Wood,
But in loves pathlesse Labyrinth, there I
My health, each joy and pleasure counted good
Have lost, and which is more, my liberty,
  And now am forc't to let him sacrifice
  My heart, for rash beleeving of my eyes.

39.

Long have I stayed, but yet have no reliefe,
Long have I lov'd, yet have no favour showne,
Because she knowes not of my killing griefe,
And I have feard, to make my sorrowes knowne.
For why alas, if shee should once but dart
At me disdaine, 'twould kill my subject heart.

40.

But how should shee, ere I impart my Love,
Reward my ardent flame with like desire?
But when I speake, if shee should angry prove,
Laugh at my flowing teares, and scorne my fire?
Why, he who hath all sorrowes borne before,
Needeth not feare to be opprest with more.

41.

Philocrates no longer can forbeare,
But running to his lov'd Friend; *Oh* (said he)
My deare Philetus *be thy selfe, and sweare*
To rule that Passion which now masters Thee,
And all thy faculties; but if't may not be,
Give to thy Love but eyes that it may see.

42.

Amazement strikes him dumbe, what shall he doe?
Should he reveale his Love, he feares twould prove,
A hindrance; which should he deny to show,
It might perhaps his deare friends anger move:
These doubts like *Scylla* and *Charibdis* stand,
Whilst *Cupid* a blind Pilot doth command.

43.

At last resolv'd; how shall I seeke, said hee,
To excuse my selfe, dearest *Philocrates*;
That I from thee have hid this secrecie?
Yet censure not, give me first leave to ease
My case with words, my griefe you should have known
Ere this, if that my heart had beene my owne.

CONSTANTIA AND PHILETUS

44.

I am all Love, my heart was burnt with fire
From two bright Sunnes which doe all light disclose;
First kindling in my breast the flame desire,
But like the rare Arabian *Bird, there rose*
    From my hearts ashes never quenched Love,
    Which now this torment in my soule doth move.

45.

Oh! let not then my Passion cause your hate,
Nor let my choise offend you, or detayne
Your ancient Friendship; 'tis alas too late
To call my firme affection backe againe:
    No Physicke *can recure my weakn'd state,*
    The wound is growne too great, too desperate.

46.

But *Counsell sayd* his Friend, a remedy
Which never fayles the Patient, may at least
If not quite heale your mindes infirmity,
Asswage your torment, and procure some rest.
    But there is no Physitian can apply
    A medicine, ere he know the Malady.

47.

Then heare me, said *Philetus*; but why? Stay,
I will not toyle thee with my history,
For to remember Sorrowes past away,
Is to renew an old Calamity.
    Hee who acquainteth others with his mone,
    Addes to his friends griefe, but not cures his owne.

48.

But said *Philocrates*, 'tis best in woe,
To have a faithfull partner of their care;
That burthen may be undergone by two,
Which is perhaps too great for one to beare.
    I should mistrust your love to hide from me
    Your thoughts, and taxe you of *Inconstancy.*

C. II.   B   17

49.

What shall he doe? or with what language frame
Excuse? He must resolve not to deny,
But open his close thoughts, and inward flame,
With that, as prologue to his Tragedy.
    Hee sigh'd, as if they'd coole his torments ire,
    When they alas, did blow the raging fire.

50.

When yeeres first styl'd me Twenty, I began
To sport with catching snares that love had set,
Like birds that flutter 'bout the gyn, till tane,
Or the poore Fly caught in *Arachnes* net:
    Even so I sported with her Beauties light,
    Till I at last grew blind with too much sight.

51.

First it came stealing on me, whil'st I thought,
'Twas easie to expulse it, but as fire,
Though but a sparke, soone into flames is brought,
So mine grew great, and quickly mounted higher;
    Which so have scorcht my love-strucke soule, that I
    Still live in torment, though each minute dye.

52.

Who is it, said *Philocrates*, can move
With charming eyes such deep affection?
I may perhaps assist you in your love,
Two can effect more than your selfe alone.
    My counsell this thy error may reclaime,
    Or my salt teares quench thy annoying flame.

53.

Nay said *Philetus*, oft my eyes doe flow
Like *Nilus*, when it scornes th'opposed shore:
Yet all the watery plenty I bestow,
Is to my flame an oyle, which feedes it more.
    So fame reports of the *Dodonean* spring,
    That lights a torch the which is put therein.

54.

But being you desire to know her, she
Is call'd (with that his eyes let fall a shower
As if they faine would drowne the memory
Of his life keepers name,) *Constantia*; more
 Griefe would not let him utter; *Teares the best*
 Expressers of true sorrow, spoke the rest.

55.

To which his noble friend did thus reply:
And was this all? What ere your griefe would ease
Though a farre greater taske, beleev't for thee
It should be soone done by *Philocrates*;
 Thinke all you wish perform'd, but see, the day
 Tyr'd with its heate is hasting now away.

56.

Home from the silent Woods, night bids them goe,
But sad *Philetus* can no comfort finde,
What in the day he feares of future woe,
At night in dreames, like truth, affrights his mind.
 Why do'st thou vex him, Love? Hadst eyes (I say)
 Thou wouldst thy selfe have lov'd *Constantia*.

57.

Philocrates pittying his dolefull mone,
And wounded with the Sorrowes of his friend,
Brings him to fayre *Constantia* ; where alone
Hee might impart his love, and eyther end
 His fruitlesse hopes, cropt by her coy disdaine,
 Or *by her liking, his wish't Joyes attaine.*

58.

Fairest (quoth he) *whom the bright Heavens doe cover,*
Doe not these teares, these speaking teares, despise,
And dolorous sighes, of a submissive Lover,
Thus strucke to th'earth by your all dazeling Eyes.
 And doe not you contemne that ardent flame,
 Which from your selfe, Your owne faire Beauty came.

ABRAHAM COWLEY

59.

Trust me, I long have hid my love, but now
Am forc't to show't, such is my inward smart,
And you alone (sweet faire) the meanes do know
To heale the wound of my consuming heart.
Then since it onely in your power doth lie
To kill, or save, Oh helpe! or else I dye.

60.

His gently cruell Love, did thus reply ;
I for your paine am grieved, and would doe
Without impeachme[n]t to my Chastity
And honour, any thing might pleasure you.
But if beyond those limits you demand,
I must not answer, (Sir) nor understand.

61.

Beleeve me vertuous maiden, my desire
Is chast and pious, as thy Virgin thought,
No flash of lust, 'tis no dishonest fire
Which goes as soone as it was quickly brought :
But as thy beauty pure, which let not bee
Eclipsed by disdaine, and cruelty.

62.

Oh ! how shall I reply (quoth shee) thou'ast won
My soule, and therefore take thy victory :
Thy eyes and speaches have my heart o'recome,
And if I should deny thee love, then I
Should bee a Tyrant to my selfe ; that fire
Which is kept close, burnes with the greatest ire.

63.

Yet doe not count my yeelding, lightnesse in mee,
Impute it rather to my ardent love,
Thy pleasing carriage long agoe did win me,
And pleading beauty did my liking move.
Thy eyes which draw like loadstones with their might
The hardest hearts, won mine to leave me quite.

64.

Oh ! I am rapt above the reach, said hee,
Of thought, my soule already feeles the blisse
Of heaven, when (sweet) my thoughts once tax but thee
With any crime, may I lose all happinesse
  Is wisht for : both your favour here, and dead,
  May the just Gods [pour] vengeance on my head.

65.

Whilst he was speaking this (behold their fate)
Constantia's father entred in the roome,
When glad *Philetus* ignorant of his state,
Kisses her cheekes, more red then setting Sun,
  Or else, the morne, blushing through clouds of water,
  To see ascending *Sol* congratulate her.

66.

Just as the guilty prisoner fearefull stands
Reading his fatall *Theta* in the browes
Of him, who both his life and death commands,
Ere from his mouth he the sad sentence knowes,
  Such was his state to see her father come,
  Nor wisht for, nor expected to the roome.

67.

The inrag'd old man bids him no more to dare
Such bold intrudence in that house, nor be
At any time with his lov'd daughter there
Till he had given him such authority,
  But to depart, since she her love did shew him
  Was living death, with lingring torments to him.

68.

This being knowne to kind *Philocrates,*
He cheares his friend, bidding him banish feare,
And by some letter his griev'd minde appease,
And shew her that which to her friendly eare,
  Tyme gave no leave to tell, and thus his quill
  Declares to her, the absent lovers will.

ABRAHAM COWLEY

THE LETTER.
PHILETUS TO CONSTANTIA.

I Trust (deare Soule) my absence cannot move
   You to forget, or doubt my ardent love;
For were there any meanes to see you, I
Would runne through Death, and all the miserie
Fate could inflict, that so the world might say,
In Life and Death I lov'd Constantia.
Then let not (dearest Sweet) our absence sever
Our loves, let them join'd closely still together
Give warmth to one another, till there rise
From all our labours, and our industries
The long expected fruits; have patience (Sweet)
There's no man whom the Summer pleasures greet
Before he tast the Winter, none can say,
Ere night was gone, he saw the rising Day.
    So when we once have wasted Sorrowes night,
    The sunne of Comfort then shall give us light.

69.

PHILETUS.

This when Constantia read, shee thought her state
Most happy by Philetus Constancie,
And perfect Love: she thankes her flattering Fate,
Kisses the paper, till with kissing she
    The welcome Characters doth dull and stayne,
    Then thus with inke and teares writes backe againe.

CONSTANTIA TO PHILETUS.

YOur absence (Sir) though it be long, yet I
   Neither forget, nor doubt your Constancie.
Nor need you feare, that I should yeeld unto
Another, what to your true Love is due.
My heart is yours, it is not in my claime,
Nor have I power to giv't away againe.
There's nought but death can part our soules, no time
Or angry Friends, shall make my Love decline:
    But for the harvest of our hopes I'le stay,
    U[n]lesse Death cut it, ere't be ripe, away.

CONSTANTIA.

70.

Oh ! how this Letter did exalt his pride !
More proud was he of this, then *Phaeton* ;
When *Phœbus* flaming Chariot he did guide,
Before he knew the danger was to come.
      Or else then *Jason*, when from *Colchos* hee
      Returned, with the *Fleeces* victory.

71.

But ere the Autumne which faire *Ceres* crown'd,
Had paid the sweating Plow-mans greediest prayer ;
And by the Fall disrob'd the gawdy ground
Of all her Summer ornaments, they were
      By kind *Philocrates* together brought,
      Where they this means t'enjoy their freedome wrought.

72.

Sweet Mistresse, said *Philetus*, since the time
Propitious to our votes, now gives us leave
To enjoy our loves, let us not deare resigne
His long'd for favour, nor our selves bereave
      Of what we wisht for, opportunitie ;
      That may too soon the wings of Love out-flie.

73.

For when your Father, as his custome is,
For pleasure, doth pursue the timerous Hare ;
If you'l resort but thither, I'le not misse
To be in those Woods ready for you, where
      We may depart in safety, and no more
      With Dreames of pleasure onely, heale our sore.

74.

This both the Lovers soon agreed upon,
But ere they parted, he desires that she
Would blesse his greedy hearing, with a *Song*
From her harmonious voyce, she doth agree
      To his request, and doth this Ditty sing,
      Whose ravishing *Notes* new fires to's old doe bring.

The Song.

1.

Time flye with greater speed away,
    Adde feathers to thy wings,
    Till thy hast in flying brings
That wisht for, and expected Day.

2.

Comforts sunne, we then shall see,
Though at first it darkned bee,
With dangers, yet those Clouds being gone,
Our Day will put his lustre on.

3.

Then though Deaths sad night doe come,
    And we in silence sleepe,
    'Lasting Day agen will greet
Our ravisht Soules, and then there's none

4.

Can part us more, no Death, nor Friends,
Being dead, their power o're us ends.
Thus there's nothing can dissever,
Hearts which Love hath joyn'd together.

75.

Feare of being seen, *Philetus* homeward drove,
But ere they part she willingly doth give
As faithfull pledges of her constant love
Many a kisse, and then each other leave
    In griefe, though rapt with joy that they have found
    A way to heale the torment of their wound.

76.

But ere the Sun through many dayes had run,
Constantia's charming beauty had o'recome
Guiscardo's heart, and's scorn'd affection won,
Her eyes, they conquered all they shone upon,
    Shot through his eyes such hot desire,
      As nothing but her love could quench the fire.

77.

In roofes which Gold and *Parian* stone adorn,
Proud as their Landlords minde, he did abound,
In fields so fertile for their yeerly corne,
As might contend with scorcht *Calabria's* ground;
    But in his soule where should be the best store
      Of surest riches, he was base and poore.

78.

Him was *Constantia* urg'd continually
By her friends to love, sometimes they did intreat
With gentle speeches, and mild courtesie,
Which when they see despis'd by her, they threat,
    But love too deep was seated in her heart,
      To be worn out with thought of any smart.

79.

Her father shortly went unto the Wood
To hunt, his friend *Guiscardo* being there,
With others who by friendship and by blood
Unto *Constantia's* aged Father were
    Allyed neere, there likewise were with these,
      His beautious Daughter, and *Philocrates*.

80.

Being entred in the pathlesse woods, whilst they
Pursue their game, *Philetus* which was late
Hid in a thicket, carries straight away
His Love, and hastens his owne hastie fate.
    Which came too soone upon him, and his Sunne
      Eclipsed was, before it fully shone.

25

81.

For when *Constantia's* missed, in a maze,
Each takes a severall course, and by curst fate
Guiscardo runs, with a love-carried pace
Towards them, who little knew their sorrowfull state:
    So hee like bold *Icarus* soaring hye
    To Honours, fell to th'depth of misery.

82.

For when *Guiscardo* sees his Rivall there,
Swelling with envious rage, hee comes behind
Phileus, who such fortune did not feare,
And with his flaming sword a way doth find
    To his heart, who ere that death possest him quite,
    In these few words gaspt out his flying sprite.

83.

O see Constantia, *my short race is runne,*
See how my blood the thirsty ground doth dye,
But live thou happier then thy love hath done,
And when I'm dead, thinke sometime upon me.
    More my short time permits me not to tell,
    For now death ceizeth me, *oh my deare farewell.*

84.

As soon as he had spoke these words, life fled
From's wounded body, whil'st *Constantia* shee
Kisses his cheekes which lose their lively red,
And become pale, and wan, and now each eye
    Which was so bright, is like, when life was done
    A fallen starre, or an eclipsed Sunne.

85.

Thither *Philocrates* by's fate being drove
To accompany *Philetus* Tragedy,
Seeing his friend was dead, and's sorrowfull love
Sate weeping o're his bleeding body, I
    Will now revenge thy death (best friend) said he,
    Or in thy murther beare thee company.

CONSTANTIA AND PHILETUS

86.

I am by *Jove* sent to revenge this fate,
Nay, stay *Guiscardo*, thinke not heaven in jest,
'Tis vaine to hope flight can secure thy state.
Then thrusting's sword into the Villaines brest :
    Here, said *Philocrates*, thy life I send
    A sacrifice, t'appease my slaughter'd friend.

87.

But he falls : here take a reward said he
For this thy victory, with that he flung
His killing Rapier at his enemy,
Which hit his head, and in his brain-pan hung.
    With that he falls, but lifting up his eyes,
    Farewell *Constantia*, that word said, he dyes.

88.

What shall she doe ? she to her brother runnes
And's cold, and livelesse body doth imbrace,
She calls to him, he cannot heare her moanes :
And with her kisses warmes his clammy face.
    My deare Philocrates, *shee weeping cryes,*
    Speake to thy Sister : but no voyce replyes.

89.

Then running to her Love, with many a teare,
Thus her minds fervent passion she express't,
O stay (blest Soule) stay but a little here,
And we will both hast to a lasting rest.
    Then to *Elisiums* Mansions both together
    Wee'l journey, and be marryed there for ever.

90.

But when she saw they both were dead, quoth she,
Oh my *Philetus*, for thy sake will I
Make up a full and perfect Tragedy,
Since 'twas for me (Deare Love) that thou didst dye;
    Ile follow thee, and not thy losse deplore,
    These eyes that saw thee kill'd, shall see no more.

91.

It shall not sure be said that thou didst dye,
And thy *Constantia* live since thou wast slaine :
No, no, deare Soule, I will not stay from thee,
But constant be in act, as well as Name.
    Then piercing her sad brest, *I come,* she cryes,
    And Death for ever clos'd her weeping eyes.

92.

Her Soule being fled to its eternall rest,
Her Father comes, who seeing this, he falls
To th'earth, with griefe too great to be exprest :
Whose dolefull words my tyred *Muse* me calls
    T' o'repasse, which I most gadly doe, for feare
    That I should toyle too much, the *Readers eare.*

FINIS.

THE
TRAGICALL
HISTORY OF
PIRAMUS
AND
THISBE.

The third Edition.

Enlarged by the Author.

——fit surculus Arbor.

LONDON.

Printed by *E. P.* for HENRY SEILE,
and are to bee sold at his shop at the signe of
[the] Tygers-head in Fleet-street between
the Bridge and the Conduit.

1637.

To the Right Worshipfull,

my very loving Master, Master
Lambert Osbolston, chiefe School-
master of *Westminster-*
Schoole.

Sir,

MY *childish Muse is in her Spring, and yet*
    Can onely shew some budding of her Wit.
One frowne upon her Workè (learn'd Sir) from you,
Like some unkinder storme shot from your brow,
Would turn her Spring to withering Autumn's time,
And make her Blossomes perish, ere their Prime.
But if you smile, if in your gracious Eye
Shee an auspicious Alpha can descrie:
How soone will they grow Fruit? How will they flourish,
That had such beames their infancie to nourish?
  Which being sprung to ripenesse, expect then
  The best, and first fruits of her gratefull Pen.

Your most dutifull Scholler,

ABRA. COWLEY.

30

THE
TRAGICALL
HISTORIE
OF
PYRAMUS *and* THISBE.

1.

WHere *Babylons* high Walls erected were
   By mighty *Ninus* wife ; two houses joyn'd.
One *Thisbe* liv'd in, *Pyramus* the faire
In th'other : Earth nere boasted such a paire.
   The very sencelesse walls themselves combin'd,
   And grew in one ; just like their Masters mind.

2.

Thisbe all other women did excell,
The Queene of *Love*, lesse lovely was than she :
And *Pyramus* more sweet than tongue can tell,
Nature grew proud in framing them so well.
   But *Venus* envying they so faire should be,
   Bids her sonne CUPID shew his crueltie.

3.

The all-subduing God his Bow doth bend,
And doth prepare his most remorselesse Dart,
Which he unseene unto their hearts did send,
And so was Love the cause of Beauties end.
   But could he see, he had not wrought their smart :
   For pittie sure would have o'recome his heart.

4.

Like as a Bird which in a Net is tane,
By strugling more entangles in the ginne;
So they who in Loves Labyrinth remaine,
With striving never can a freedome gaine.
  The way to enter's broad; but being in,
  No art, no labour, can an *exit* win.

5.

These Lovers, though their Parents did reprove
Their fires, and watch'd their deeds with jealousie,
Though in these stormes no comfort could remove
The various doubts, and feares that coole hot love:
  Though he nor hers, nor she his face could see,
  Yet this did not abolish Loves Decree.

6.

For age had crack'd the wall which did them part,
This the unanimate couple soone did spie,
And here their inward sorrowes did impart,
Unlading the sad burthen of their heart.
  Though Love be blinde, this shewes he can descry
  A way to lessen his owne misery.

7.

Oft to the friendly Crannie they resort,
And feede themselves with the cœlestiall ayre
Of odoriferous breath; no other sport
They could enjoy, yet thinke the time but short:
  And wish that it againe renewed were,
  To sucke each others breath for ever there.

8.

Sometimes they did exclaime against their fate,
And sometimes they accus'd imperiall *Jove*;
Sometimes repent their flames: but all too late;
The Arrow could not be recall'd: their state
  Ordained was by *Jupiter* above,
  And *Cupid* had appointed they should love.

PYRAMUS AND THISBE

9.

They curst the wall which did their kisses part,
And to the stones their dolorous words they sent,
As if they saw the sorrow of their heart,
And by their teares could understand their smart :
    But it was hard, and knew not what they meant,
    Nor with their sighs (alas) would it relent.

10.

This in effect they said; *Curs'd wall, O why*
Wilt thou our bodies sever, whose true love
Breakes thorow all thy flintie crueltie :
For both our soules so closely joyned lye,
    That nought but angry Death can them remove,
    And though he part them, yet they'l meet above.

11.

Abortive teares from their faire eyes straight flow'd,
And damm'd the lovely splendour of their [si]ght,
Which seem'd like *Titan*, whilst some watry Cloud
O'respreads his face, and his bright beames doth shrowd.
    Till *Vesper* chas'd away the conquered light,
    And forceth them (though loth) to bid *Good-night*.

12.

But ere *Aurora*, Usher to the Day,
Began with welcome lustre to appeare,
The Lovers rise, and at that crannie they
Thus to each other, their thoughts open lay,
    With many a Sigh, many a speaking Teare,
    Whose griefe the pitying Morning blusht to heare.

13.

Deare Love (quoth PYRAMUS) *how long shall wee*
Like fairest Flowers, not gathered in their prime,
Waste precious youth, and let advantage flee,
Till wee bewaile (at last) our crueltie
    Upon our selves, for Beautie though it shine
    Like day, will quickly finde an Evening time.

C. II.   c

ABRAHAM COWLEY

14.

Therefore (sweet THISBE) let us meet this night
At Ninus Tombe, without the Citie wall,
Under the Mulberry-Tree, with Berries white
Abounding, there t'enjoy our wisht delight.
    For mounting Love stopt in his course, doth fall,
    And long'd for, yet untasted Joy, kills all.

15.

What though our cruell parents angry bee?
What though our friends (alas) are too unkinde?
Time now propitious, may anon deny,
And soone hold backe, fit opportunity.
    Who lets slip Fortune, her shall never finde.
    Occasion once pass'd by, is balde behinde.

16.

Shee soone agreed to that which hee requir'd,
For little Wooing needs, where both consent;
What hee so long had pleaded, shee desir'd:
Which Venus seeing, with blinde Chance conspir'd,
    And many a charming accent to her sent,
    That shee (at last) would frustrate their intent.

17.

Thus Beautie is by Beauties meanes undone,
Striving to close these eyes that make her bright;
Just like the Moone, which seekes t'eclipse the Sun,
Whence all her splendour, all her beames doe come:
    So shee, who fetcheth lustre from their sight,
    Doth purpose to destroy their glorious light.

18.

Unto the Mulberry-tree, sweet Thisbe came;
Where having rested long, at last shee gan
Against her Pyramus for to exclaime,
Whil'st various thoughts turmoile her troubled braine:
    And imitating thus the Silver Swan,
    A little while before her Death shee sang.

PYRAMUS AND THISBE

The Song.

1.

COme Love, why stayest thou ?   The night
     Will vanish ere wee taste delight :
The Moone obscures her selfe from sight,
Thou absent, whose eyes give her light.

2.

Come quickly, Deare, be briefe as Time,
Or wee by Morne shall be o'retane,
Loves Joy's thine owne as well as mine,
Spend not therefore the time in vaine.

19.

Here doubtfull thoughts broke off her pleasant *Song*,
Against her love for staying shee gan crie ;
Her *Pyramus* shee thought did tarry long,
And that his absence did her too much wrong.
     Then betwixt longing hope, and jealousie,
     Shee feares, yet's loth, to tax his loyaltie.

20.

Sometimes shee thinkes, that hee hath her forsaken ;
Sometimes, that danger hath befallen to him ;
Shee feares that hee another love hath taken :
Which being but imagin'd, soone doth waken
     Numberlesse thoughts, which on her heart doe fling
     Feares, that her future fate too truely sing.

21.

Whil'st shee thus musing sate, ranne from the Wood
An angry Lyon, to the cristall Springs
Neere to that place ; who comming from his food,
His chaps were all besmear'd with crimson bloud :
     Swifter then thought, sweet *Thisbe* straight begins
     To flye from him, feare gave her Swallowes wings.

ABRAHAM COWLEY

22.

As shee avoids the Lion, her desire
Bids her to stay, lest *Pyramus* should come,
And be devour'd by the sterne Lions ire,
So shee for ever burne in unquencht fire:
 But feare expells all reasons, shee doth runne
 Into a darksome Cave, ne'r seene by Sunne.

23.

With haste shee let her looser Mantle fall:
Which when th'enraged Lion did espie,
With bloudy teeth, he tore't in pieces small,
Whil'st *Thisbe* ran and lookt not backe at all.
 For could the sencelesse beast her face descrie,
 It had not done her such an injurie.

24.

The night halfe wasted, *Pyramus* did come;
Who seeing printed in the subtill sand
The Lions paw, and by the fountaine some
Of *Thisbes* garment, sorrow strucke him dumbe:
 Just like a Marble Statue did he stand,
 Cut by some skilfull Gravers cunning hand.

25.

Recovering breath, 'gainst Fate he gan t'exclaime,
Washing with teares the torne and bloudy weed:
I may, said he, my selfe for her death blame;
Therefore my bloud shall wash away that shame:
 Since shee is dead, whose Beautie doth exceed
 All that fraile man can either heare or reade.

26.

This speaking, hee his sharpe Sword drew, and said;
Receive thou my red bloud, as a due debt
Unto thy constant Love, to which 'tis paid:
I straight will meete thee in the pleasant shade
 Of coole Elysium; *where wee being met,*
 Shall taste the Joyes, that here wee could not yet.

PYRAMUS AND THISBE

27.

Then thorow his brest thrusting his Sword, Life hies
From him, and hee makes haste to seeke his faire.
And as upon the crimsond ground hee lies,
His bloud spirt'd up upon the Mulberries:
  With which th'unspotted berries stained were,
  And ever since with Red they coloured are.

28.

At last, came *Thisbe* from the Den, for feare
Of disappointing *Pyramus*, being shee
Was bound by promise, for to meete him there:
But when shee saw the Berries changed were
  From white to blacke, shee knew not certainely
  It was the place where they agreed to be.

29.

With what delight from the darke Cave shee came,
Thinking to tell how shee escap'd the Beast;
But when shee saw her *Pyramus* lie slaine,
In what perplexitie shee did remaine!
  Shee teares her Golden haire, and beates her brest,
  All signes of raging sorrow shee exprest.

30.

Shee cries 'gainst mighty *Jove*, and then doth take
His bleeding body from the moistned ground.
Shee kisses his pale face, till shee doth make
It red with kissing, and then seekes to wake
  His parting soule with mournfull words, and's wound
  Washeth with teares, which her sweet speech confound.

31.

But afterwards recovering breath, quoth shee,
(Alas) what chance hath parted thee and I?
O tell what evill hath befallen to thee,
That of thy Death I may a Partner bee:
  Tell *Thisbe*, what hath caus'd this Tragedie.
  He hearing *Thisbe's* name, lift up his eye,

32.

And on his Love he rais'd his dying head:
Where striving long for breath, at last, said hee;
O Thisbe, *I am hasting to the dead,*
And cannot heale that Wound my feare hath bred:
  Farewell, sweet Thisbe, *wee must parted bee,*
  For angry Death will force me goe from Thee.

33.

Life did from him, hee from his Mistris part,
Leaving his *Love* to languish here in woe.
What shall shee doe? How shall shee ease her heart?
Or with what language speake her inward smart?
  Usurping passion reason doth o'reflow,
  Shee sweares that with her *Pyramus* shee'l goe.

34.

Then takes the Sword wherewith her Love was slaine,
With *Pyramus* his crimson blood warme still;
And said, *Oh stay (blest Soule) that so wee twaine*
May goe together, where wee shall remaine
  In endlesse Joyes, and never feare the ill
  Of grudging Friends: Then she her selfe did kill.

35.

To tell what griefe their Parents did sustaine,
Were more than my rude Quill can overcome.
Many a teare they spent, but all in vaine,
For weeping calls not backe the Dead againe.
  They both were layed in one Grave, life done,
  And these few words were writ upon the Tombe.

PYRAMUS AND THISBE

Epitaph.

1.

UNderneath this Marble Stone,
    Lye two Beauties joyn'd in one.

2.

Two whose loves Death could not sever,
For both liv'd, both dy'd together.

3.

Two whose Soules, being too divine
 For earth, in their owne Spheare now shine.

4.

Who have left their Loves to Fame,
And their earth to earth againe.

FINIS.

ABRAHAM COWLEY

An Elegie on the Death of the Right Honourable, *Dudley* Lord *Carleton*, Viscount *Dorchester*, late Principall Secretary of State.

THe infernall Sisters, did a Counsell call
  Of all the fiends, to the black Stygian *Hall;*
The dire Tartarean *Monsters, hating light,*
Begot *by dismall* Erebus, *and Night.*
Wheresoe're dispers'd abroad, hearing the Fame
Of their accursed meeting, thither came
Revenge, *whose greedy mind no Blood can fill,*
And Envie, *never satisfied with ill.*
Thither blind Boldnesse, *and impatient* Rage,
Resorted, *with Death's neighbour envious* Age,
And Messengers diseases, wheresoe're
Then wandring, at the Senate present were:
Whom to oppresse the Earth, the Furies sent
To spare the Guilty, vex the innocent.
The Councell thus dissolv'd, an angry fever,
Whose quenchlesse thirst, by blood was sated never:
Envying the Riches, Honour, Greatnesse, Love,
And Vertue (Loadstone, which all these did move)
Of Noble CARLETON, *him she tooke away,*
And like a greedy Vulture seis'd her prey:
Weep with me each who either reades or heares,
And know his losse, deserves his Countries teares:
The Muses *lost a Patron by his Fate,*
Vertue *a Husband, and a Prop the* State,
Sol's *Chorus weepes, and to adorne his Herse*
Calliope *would sing a Tragick Verse.*
  And had there been before no Spring of theirs,
  They would have made a Helicon *with teares.*

ABRA. COWLEY.

AN ELEGIE

An *Elegie* on the death of my loving Friend
and Cousen, Master *Richard Clerke*, late of
Lincolns Inne, Gent.

IT was decreed by stedfast Destinie,
  (*The world from* Chaos *turn'd*) *that all should die.*
Hee who durst fearelesse passe blacke Acheron
And dangers of the infernall Region,
Leading Hells triple Porter captivate,
Was overcome himselfe, by conquering Fate.
The Roman Tullie's *pleasing Eloquence,*
Which in the Eares did locke up every Sence
Of the rapt hearer, his mellifluous breath
Could not at all charme unremorselesse Death,
Nor Solon *so by* Greece *admir'd, could save*
Himselfe with all his Wisdome, from the Grave.
Sterne Fate brought Maro *to his Funerall flame,*
And would have ended in that fire his Fame;
Burning those lofty Lines, which now shall be
Times conquerers, and out-last Eternity.
Even so lov'd Clerk *from death no scape could find,*
Though arm'd with great Alcides *valiant mind.*
He was adorn'd in yeeres though farre more young,
With learned Cicero's, *or a sweeter* Tongue.
And could dead Virgil *heare his lofty straine,*
He would condemne his owne to fire againe.
His youth a Solons *wisdome did presage,*
Had envious Time *but given him* Solons *age.*
Who would not therefore now, if Learnings friend,
Bewaile his fatall and untimely end:
Who hath such hard, such unrelenting Eyes,
As would not weep when so much Vertue dyes?
The God of Poets *doth in darknesse shrowd*
His glorious face, and weepes behind a Cloud.
The dolefull Muses *thinking now to write*
Sad Elegies, *their teares confound their sight:*
  But him to Elysiums *lasting Joyes they bring,*
  Where winged Angels his sad Requiems *sing.*

A. C.

41

A DREAME

OF

ELYSIUM.

PHœbus expuls'd by the a[pp]roaching Night
   Blush'd, and for shame clos'd in his bashfull light;
Whilst I with leaden *Morpheus* overcome,
The *Muse*, whom I adore, enter'd the roome.
Her hayre with looser curiositie,
Did on her comely backe dishevel'd lye.
Her Eyes with such attractive beauty shone,
As might have wak'd sleeping *Endymion*.
She bid me rise, and promis'd I should see
Those Fields, those Mansions of Felicity,
Wee mortalls so admire at: Speaking thus,
She lifts me up upon wing'd *Pegasus*.
On whom I rid: knowing where ever she
Did goe, that place must needs a *Tempe* be.
  No sooner was my flying Courser come
To the blest dwellings of *Elysium*:
When straight a thousand unknowne joyes resort,
And hemm'd me round: Chast loves innocuous sport.
A thousand sweets, bought with no following Gall,
Joyes, not like ours, short, but perpetuall.
How many objects charme my wandring eye,
And bid my soule gaze there eternally?
Here in full streames, *Bacchus* thy liquor flowes,
Nor knowes to ebbe: here *Jove* broad Tree bestowes
Distilling hony, heere doth *Nectar* passe
With copious current through the verdant Grasse.
Here *Hyacinth*, his fate writ in his lookes,
And thou *Narcissus* loving still the Brookes,

42

A DREAME OF ELYSIUM

Once lovely boyes; and *Acis* now a Flower,
Are nourisht, with that rarer herbe, whose power
Created thee, Warres potent God, here growes
The spotlesse Lillie, and the blushing Rose.
And all those divers ornaments abound,
That variously may paint the gawdy ground.
No Willow, sorrowes Garland, there hath roome,
Nor Cypresse, sad attendant of a Tombe.
None but *Apollo's* Tree, and th'Ivie Twine
Imbracing the stout Oake, the fruitfull Vine,
And Trees with golden Apples loaded downe,
On whose faire toppes sweet *Philomel* alone,
Unmindfull of her former miserie,
Tunes with her voyce a ravishing Harmonie.
Whilst all the murmuring Brookes that glide along,
Make up a burthen to her pleasing Song.
No *Scritchowle*, sad companion of the Night,
Or hideous Raven with prodigious flight
Presaging future ill. Nor, *Progne*, thee
Yet spotted with young *Itis* Tragedie,
Those Sacred Bowers receive. There's nothing there,
That is not pure, immaculate, and rare.
Turning my greedy sight another way,
Under a row of storme-contemning Bay,
I saw the *Thracian* Singer with his lyre
Teach the deafe stones to heare him, and admire.
Him the whole Poets *Chorus* compass'd round,
All whom the Oake, all whom the Lawrell crown'd.
There banish'd *Ovid* had a lasting home,
Better than thou couldst give ingratefull *Rome*;
And *Lucan* (spight of *Nero*) in each veine
Had every drop of his spilt bloud againe :
Homer, *Sol's* first borne, was not poore or blinde,
But saw as well in body as in minde.
Tullie, grave *Cato*, *Solon*, and the rest
Of *Greece's* admir'd Wisemen, here possest
A large reward for their past deeds, and gaine
A life, as everlasting as their Fame.
    By these, the valiant *Heroes* take their place,
All who sterne Death and perils did imbrace

For *Vertues* cause.   Great *Alexander* there
Laughing at the Earth's small Empire, did weare
A Nobler Crowne, than the whole world could give.
There did *Horatius Cocles*, *Sceva*, live,
And valiant *Decius*, who now freely cease
From Warre, and purchase an eternall peace.
 Next them, beneath a Mirtle Bowre, where Doves,
And gall-lesse Pidgeons build their nests, all Loves
Faithfull perseverers, with amorous kisses,
And soft imbraces, taste their greediest wishes.
Leander with his beauteous *Hero* playes,
Nor are they parted with dividing Seas.
Porcia injoyes her *Brutus*, Death no more
Can now divorce their Wedding, as before.
Thisbe her *Pyramus* kiss'd, his *Thisbe* hee
Embrac'd, each blest with th'others company.
And every couple alwayes dancing, sing
Eternall Ditties to *Elysiums* King.
But see how soone these pleasures fade away,
How neere to Evening is delights short Day?
For th'watching Bird, true *Nuncius* of the Light
Straight crowd: and all these vanisht from my sight.
My very *Muse* her selfe forsooke mee too.
Me griefe and wonder wak'd: What should I doe?
Oh! let me follow thee (said I) and goe
From life, that I may Dreame for ever so.
With that my flying *Muse* I thought to claspe
Within my armes, but did a shadow graspe.
  Thus chiefest Joyes glide with the swiftest streame,
  And all our greatest pleasure's but a Dreame.

A. C.

FINIS.

SYLVA,

OR,

DIVERS COPIES

OF VERSES,

Made upon sundry occasions
by *A. C.*

LONDON.

Printed by *E. P.* for HENRY SEILE
and are to bee sold at his shop at the signe of
the Tygers-head in Fleet-street betweene
the Bridge and the Conduit.

1637.

ABRAHAM COWLEY

On his Majesties returne out of SCOTLAND.

Great *Charles*: there stop you Trumpeters of Fame,
  (For he who speakes his Titles, his great Name
Must have a breathing time,) *Our King:* stay there,
Tel't by degrees, let the inquisitive eare
Be held in doubt, and ere you say, *I: come*,
Let every heart prepare a spatious roome
For ample joyes: then *Iö* sing as loud
As thunder shot from the divided cloud.
  Let *Cygnus* plucke from the *Arabian* waves
The ruby of the rocke, the pearle that paves
Great *Neptunes* Court, let every sparrow beare
From the three Sisters weeping barke a teare.
Let spotted *Lynces* their sharpe tallons fil
With chrystall fetch'd from the *Promethean* hill.
Let *Cythereas* birds fresh wreathes compose,
Knitting the pale fac't Lillie with the Rose.
Let the selfe-gotten Phœnix rob his nest,
Spoile his owne funerall pile, and all his best
Of Myrrhe, of Frankincense, of *Cassia* bring,
To strew the way for our returned King.
  Let every post a *Panegyricke* weare,
Each wall, each pillar gratulations beare:
And yet let no man invocate a Muse;
The very matter will it selfe infuse
A sacred fury. Let the merry Bells
(For unknowne joyes worke unknowne miracles)
Ring without helpe of *Sexton*, and presage
A new-made holy-day for future age.
  And if the Ancients us'd to dedicate
A golden Temple to propitious fate,
At the returne of any Noble men,
Of Heroes, or of Emperours, wee must then
Raise up a double *Trophee*, for their fame
Was but the shadow of our *CHARLES* his name.
Who is there where all vertues mingled flow?
Where no defects, no imperfections grow?

SYLVA

Whose head is alwayes crown'd with victory,
Snatch'd from *Bellonas* hand, him luxury
In peace debilitates, whose tongue can win,
Tullies owne Garland, to him pride creeps in.
On whom (like *Atlas* shoulders) the propt state
(As he were *Primum Mobile* of fate)
Solely, relies, him blind ambition moves,
His tyranny the bridled subject proves.
But all those vertues which they all possest
Divided, are collected in thy brest,
Great *Charles*; Let *Cæsar* boast P[ha]rsalias fight,
Honorius praise the *Parthians* unfeyn'd flight.
Let *Alexander* call himself *Joves* peere,
And place his Image next the Thunderer,
Yet whilst our *Charles* with equall ballance reignes
'Twixt Mercy and *Astrea*, and maintaines
A noble peace, 'tis he, 'tis onely he
Who is most neere, most like the Deitie.

A Song on the same.

Hence clouded lookes, hence briny teares
  Hence eye, that sorrows livery weares.
What though a while Apollo *please*
To visit the Antipodes?
Yet he returnes, and with his light
Expels, what he hath caus'd, the night.
What though the spring vanish away,
And with it the earths forme decay?
Yet at's new birth it will restore
What it's departure tooke before.
What though we mist our absent King
Erewhile? Great Charles *is come agin,*
And, with his presence makes us know,
The gratitude to Heaven wee owe.
So doth a cruell storme impart
And teach us Palinurus *art.*
So from salt flouds, wept by our eyes,
A joyfull Venus *doth arise.*

ABRAHAM COWLEY

A Vote.

1.

LEst the misconstring world should chance to say,
    I durst not but in secret murmurs pray,
        To whisper in *Joves* eare,
How much I wish that funerall,
Or gape at such a great ones fall,
        This let all ages heare,
And future times in my soules picture see
What I abhorre, what I desire to bee.

2.

I would not be a Puritan, though he
Can preach two houres, and yet his Sermon be
        But halfe a quarter long,
Though from his old mechanicke trade
By vision hee's a Pastor made,
        His faith was growne so strong.
Nay though he thinke to gaine salvation,
By calling th'Pope the Whore of Babylon.

3.

I would not be a School-master, though he
His Rods no lesse than *Fasces* deemes to be,
        Though he in many a place,
Turnes *Lilly* oftner than his gownes,
Till at the last hee make the Nownes,
        Fight with the Verbes apace.
Nay though he can in a Poeticke heat,
Figures, borne since, out of poore *Virgill* beat.

4.

I would not be Justice of Peace, though he
Can with equality divide the Fee,
        And stakes with his Clarke draw.
Nay though he sit upon the place
Of Judgement with a learned face
        Intricate as the Law.
And whilst he mulcts enormities demurely,
Breaks *Priscians* head with sentences securely.

SYLVA

5.

I would not be a Courtier, though he
Makes his whole life the truest Comedy:
      Although he be a man
In whom the Taylors forming Art,
And nimble Barber claime more part
      Than Nature her selfe can.
Though, as he uses men, 'tis his intent
To put off death too, with a Complement.

6.

From Lawyers tongues, though they can spin with ease
The shortest cause into a Paraphrase,
      From Usurers conscience
(For swallowing up young Heyres so fast
Without all doubt, they'l choakt at last)
      Make me all innocence
Good Heaven; and from thy eyes, ô Justice keepe,
For though they be not blind, they're oft asleepe.

7.

From Singing-mens Religion; who are
Always at Church just like the Crowes, 'cause there
      They build themselves a nest.
From too much Poetry, which shines
With gold in nothing but its lines,
      Free, ô you powers, my brest.
And from Astronomy within the skies
Finds fish, and bulls, yet doth but Tantalize.

8.

From your Court-Madams beauty, which doth carry
At morning May, at night a January.
      From the grave City brow
(For though it want an R, it has
The letter of *Pythagoras*)
      Keepe me ô Fortune now,
And chines of beefe innumerable send me,
Or from the stomacke of the Guard defend me.

9.

This onely grant me : that my meanes may lye
Too low for envie, for contempt too high.
      Some honour I would have,
Not from great deeds, but good alone,
Th'ignote are better than ill knowne
      R[u]mor can ope the grave.
Acquaintance I would hug, but when't depends
Not from the number, but the choyse of friends.

10.

Bookes should, not businesse, entertaine the light,
And sleepe, as undisturb'd as death the night.
      My house a cottage more
Then palace, and should fitting be
For all my use, no luxurie.
      My garden painted ore
With natures hand, not arts and pleasures yield,
Horace might envie in his *Sabine* field.

11.

Thus would I double my lifes fading space,
For he that runs it well, twice runs his race.
      And in this true delight,
These unbought sports, and happy state,
I would nor feare, nor wish my fate,
      But boldly say each night,
To morrow let my Sunne his beames display,
Or in clouds hide them ; *I have liv'd to day.*

A Poeticall Revenge.

W *Estminster-Hall* a friend and I agreed
     To meet in ; hee (some busines 'twas did breed
His absence) came not there ; I up did goe,
To the next Court for though I could not know
Much what they meant, yet I might see and heare
(As most spectators doe at Theater)
Things very strange ; Fortune did seeme to grace
My comming there, and helpt me to a place.

SYLVA

But being newly setled at the sport,
A semi-gentleman of th'Innes of Court,
In a Sattin suite, redeem'd but yesterday;
One who is ravisht with a Cock-pit Play,
Who prayes God to deliver him from no evill
Besides a Taylors bill, and feares no Devill
Besides a Serjeant, thrust me from my seat:
At which I gan to quarrell, till a neat
Man in a ruffe (whom therefore I did take
For Barrister) open'd his mouth and spake;
Boy, get you gone, this is no Schoole: Oh no;
For if it were, all you gown'd-men would goe
Up for false Latin: they grew straight to be
Incenst, I fear'd they would have brought on me
An Action of Trespas, till th'young man
Aforesaid, in the Sattin suit, began
To strike me: doubtlesse there had beene a fray,
Had not I providently skipp'd away,
Without replying; for to scould is ill,
Where every tongue's the clapper of a Mill,
And can out-sound *Homers Gradivus*; so
Away got I: but ere I farre did goe,
I flung (the Darts of wounding *Poetrie*)
These two or three sharpe curses backe: May hee
Be by his Father in his Study tooke
At *Shakespeares* Playes, in stead of my L. *Cooke.*
May hee (though all his Writings grow as soone
As *Butters* out of estimation)
Get him a Poets name, and so ne'r come
Into a Sergeants, or dead Judges roome.
May hee (for 'tis sinne in a Lawyer)
True Latin use to speake, even at the Barre.
May hee become some poore Physicians prey,
Who keepes men with that conscience in delay
As he his Clyents doth, till his health bee
As farre fetch'd as a Greeke Nownes pedigree.
Nay, for all that, may the disease be gone
Never but in the long Vacation.
May Neighbours use all Quarrels to decide;
But if for Law any to *London* ride,

D 2

51

Of all those Clyents may no one be his,
Unlesse he come in *Forma Pauperis.*
  Grant this you Gods, that favour *Poetry,*
That so at last these ceaselesse tongues may be
Brought into reformation, and not dare
To quarrell with a thredbare Black ; but spare
  Them who beare Scholars names, lest some one take
  Spleene, and another *Ignoramus* make.

To the Duchesse of Buckingham.

IF I should say, that in your face were seene
  Natures best Picture of the *Cyprian* Queene ;
If I should sweare under *Minerva's* Name,
Poets (who Prophets are) fore-told your fame,
The future age would thinke it flatterie,
But to the present which can witnesse be,
'Twould seeme beneath your high deserts, as farre,
As you above the rest of Women are.
  When *Mannors* name with *Villiers* joyn'd I see,
How doe I reverence your Nobilitie !
But when the vertues of your Stock I view,
(Envi'd in your dead Lord, admir'd in you)
I halfe adore them : for what woman can
Besides your selfe (nay I might say what man)
Both Sexe, and Birth, and Fate, and yeeres excell
In minde, in fame, in worth, in living well ?
  Oh, how had this begot Idolatrie,
If you had liv'd in the Worlds infancie,
When mans too much Religion, made the best
Or Deities, or Semi-gods at least ?
But wee, forbidden this by pietie,
Or, if wee were not, by your modestie,
Will make our hearts an Altar, and there pray
Not to, but for you, nor that *England* may
Enjoy your equall, when you once are gone,
But what's more possible, t'enjoy you long.

SYLVA

To his very much honoured Godfather,
Master A. B.

I Love (for that upon the wings of Fame
  Shall perhaps mock Death or times Darts) my *Name.*
I love it more, because 'twas given by you;
I love it most, because 'twas your name too.
  For if I chance to slip, a conscious shame
  Plucks me, and bids me not defile your name.

I'm glad that Citie t'whom I ow'd before,
(But ah me! Fate hath crost that willing Score)
A Father, gave me a Godfather too,
And I'm more glad, because it gave me you;
  Whom I may rightly thinke, and terme to be
  Of the whole Citie an Epitomie.

I thanke my carefull Fate, which found out one
(When Nature had not licenced my tongue
Farther then cryes) who should my office doe;
I thanke her more, because shee found out you:
  In whose each looke, I may a sentence see;
  In whose each deed, a teaching Homily.

How shall I pay this debt to you? My Fate
Denyes me *Indian* Pearle or *Persian* Plate.
Which though it did not, to requite you thus,
Were to send Apples to *Alcinoüs,*
And sell the cunning'st way: No, when I can
In every Leafe, in every Verse write Man,
When my Quill relisheth a Schoole no more,
When my pen-feather'd Muse hath learnt to soare,
And gotten wings as well as feet; looke then
For equall thankes from my unwearied Pen:
  Till future ages say; 'twas you did give
  A name to me, and I made yours to live.

53

ABRAHAM COWLEY

An Elegie on the Death of
Mʳⁱˢ *Anne Whitfield.*

SHee's dead, and like the houre that stole her hence,
  With as much quietnesse and innocence.
And 'tis as difficult a taske to winne
Her travelling soule backe to its former Inne,
As force that houre, fled without tract away,
To turne, and stop the current of the day.
  What, shall we weepe for this? and cloath our eye
With sorrow, the Graves mourning Liverie?
Or shall we sigh? and with that pious winde
Drive faster on what we alreadie finde
Too swift for us, her soule? No; shee who dy'de
Like the sicke Sunne, when Night entombes his pride;
Or Trees in Autumne, when unseene decay
And slow consumption steales the leaves away,
Without one murmur, shewes that she did see
Death as a good, not as a miserie.
  And so she went to undiscovered Fields,
From whence no path hope of returning yeelds
To any Traveller, and it must be
Our solace now to court her memorie.
Wee'l tell how love was dandled in her eye,
Yet curb'd with a beseeming gravitie.
And how (beleeve it you that heare or reade)
Beautie and Chastitie met and agreed
In her, although a Courtier: Wee will tell
How farre her noble spirit did excell
Hers, nay our Sexe: wee will repeat her Name,
And force the Letters to an Anagram.
Whitfield wee'l cry, and amorous windes shall be
Ready to snatch that words sweet harmonie
Ere 'tis spoke out: Thus wee must dull griefes sting,
And cheat the sorrow that her losse would bring:
Thus in our hearts wee'l bury her, and there
Wee'l write, Here lyes *Whitfield* the chast, and faire.
  Art may no doubt a statelier Tombe invent,
    But not like this, a living Monument.

An Elegie on the Death of *John Little-ton* Esquire, Sonne and Heire to Sir *Thomas Littleton*, who was drowned leaping into the water to save his younger Brother.

ANd must these waters smile againe? and play
    About the shore, as they did yesterday?
Will the Sun court them still? and shall they show
No conscious wrinckle furrowed on their brow,
That to the thirsty Travellor may say,
I am accurst, goe turne some other way?
   It is unjust; black floud, thy guilt is more,
Sprung from his losse, then all thy watry store
Can give thee teares to mourne for: Birds shall bee
And Beasts henceforth afraid to drinke of thee.
   What have I said? my pious rage hath beene
Too hot, and acts whilst it accuseth sinne.
Thou'rt innocent I know, still cleare, and bright,
Fit whence so pure a seule should take it's flight.
How is my angry zeale confin'd? for hee
Must quarrell with his love and pietie,
That would revenge his death. Oh I shall sinne,
And wish anon he had lesse vertuous beene.
For when his Brother (teares for him I'de spill,
But they're all challeng'd by the greater ill)
Strugled for life with the rude waves, he too
Leapt in, and when hope no faint beame could show,
His charitie shone most; thou shalt, said hee,
Live with me, Brother, or Ile dye with thee;
And so he did: Had he beene thine, ô Rome,
Thou wouldst have call'd this death a Martyrdome,
And Saynted him; my conscience give me leave,
Ile doe so too: if fate will us bereave
Of him we honour'd living, there must be
A kinde of reverence to his memorie,

55

ABRAHAM COWLEY

After his death: and where more just then here,
Where life and end were both so singuler?
Of which th'one griefe, the other imitation
Of all men vindicates, both admiration.
He that had onely talkt with him, might finde
A little Academie in his minde;
Where Wisedome, Master was, and Fellowes all
Which we can good, which we can vertuous call.
Reason and Holy Feare the Proctors were,
To apprehend those words, those thoughts that erre.
His learning had out-run the rest of heyres,
Stolne Beard from time, and leapt to twentie yeares.
And as the Sunne, though in full glorie bright,
Shines upon all men with impartiall light,
And a good morrow to the begger brings
With as full rayes as to the mightiest Kings:
So he, although his worth just state might claime,
And give to pride an honourable name,
With curtesie to all, cloath'd vertue so,
That 'twas not higher then his thoughts were low.
In's body too, no Critique eye could finde
The smallest blemish, to belye his minde;
He was all purenesse, and his outward part
The looking-glasse and picture of his heart.
When waters swallow'd mankinde, and did cheat
The hungry Worme of its expected meat;
When gemmes, pluckt from the shore by ruder hands,
Return'd againe unto their native sands;
'Mongst all those spoyles, there was not any prey
Could equall what this Brooke hath stolne away.
  Weepe then, sad Floud; and though thou'rt innocent,
Weepe because fate made thee her instrument:
And when long griefe hath drunke up all thy store,
Come to our eyes, and we will lend thee more.

SYLVA

A translation of Verses upon the B. Virgin,
written in Latine by the right
Worshipfull D^r. A.

Ave Maria.

ONce thou rejoycedst, and rejoyce for ever,
    Whose time of joy shall be expired never:
Who in her wombe the *Hive of Comfort* beares,
Let her drinke *Comforts Honey* with her eares.
You brought the word of joy, which did impart
An Haile to all, let us *An Haile* redart.
From you *God save* into the World there came;
Our *Eccho Haile* is but an empty name.

Gratia Plena.

How loaded Hives are with their Honie fill'd,
From diverse Flowres by *Chimicke* Bees distill'd:
How full the *Collet* with his Jewell is,
Which, that it cannot take, by love doth kisse:
How full the *Moone* is with her Brothers ray,
When shee drinks up with thirsty orbe the day,
How full of *Grace* the *Graces* dances are,
So full doth *Mary* of *Gods* light appeare.
It is no wonder if with *Graces* she
Be full, who was full with the *Deitie*.

Dominus tecum.

The fall of mankind under deaths extent
The quire of blessed *Angels* did lament,
And wisht a reparation to see
By him, who manhood joyn'd with *Deitie*.
How gratefull should Mans safety then appeare
T'himselfe, whose safety can the *Angels* cheare?

57

ABRAHAM COWLEY

Benedicta tu in mulieribus.

Death came, and troopes of sad diseases led
To th'earth, by womans hand solicited.
Life came so too, and troopes of Graces led
To th'earth, by womans *faith* solicited.
As our lifes spring came from thy blessed wombe,
So from our mouthes springs of thy praise shall come.
Who did lifes blessing give, 'tis fit that she
Above all women should thrice blessed be.

Et benedictus fructus ventris tui.

With mouth divine the Father doth protest,
Hee a good word sent from his stored brest,
'Twas *Christ*: which *Mary* without carnall thought,
From the unfathom'd depth of goodnesse brought,
The word of blessing a just cause affoords,
To be oft blessed with redoubled words.

Spiritus Sanctus superveniet in te.

As when soft West winds strooke the Garden Rose,
A showre of sweeter ayre salutes the Nose.
The breath gives sparing kisses, nor with powre
Unlocks the Virgin bosome of the Flowre.
So th'*Holy Spirit* upon *Mary* blow'd,
And from her sacred Box whole rivers flow'd.
Yet loos'd not thine eternall chastity,
Thy Roses folds doe still entangled lye.
Beleeve *Christ* borne from an unbruised wombe,
So from unbruised Barke the Odors come.

Et virtus altissimi obumbrabit tibi.

God his great Sonne begot ere time begunne,
Mary in time brought forth her little Sonne.
Of double substance, one, life hee began,
God without *Mother*, without *Father* Man.
Great is this birth, and 'tis a stranger deed,
That *shee* no *man*, then *God* no wife should need.

SYLVA

A shade delighted the Child-bearing Maid,
And *God* himselfe became to her a shade.
O strange descent! who is lights Author, hee
Will to his creature thus a shadow bee.
As unseene light did from the Father flow,
So did seene light from *Virgin Marie* grow.
When *Moses* sought *God* in a shade to see,
The Fathers shade was, *Christ* the *Deitie*.
Let's seeke for day we darknesse, whil'st our sight
In light findes darknesse, and in darknesse light.

ODE I.

On the praise of Poetry.

'TIs not a *Pyramide* of Marble stone,
    Though high as our ambition,
'Tis not a Tombe cut out in Brasse, which can
    Give life to th'ashes of a man,
But Verses onely; they shall fresh appeare,
    Whil'st there are men to reade, or heare.
When Time shall make the lasting Brasse decay,
    And eate the *Pyramide* away,
Turning that Monument wherein men trust
    Their names, to what it keepes, poore dust:
Then shall the *Epitaph* remaine, and be
    New graven in Eternitie.
Poets by death are conquered, but the *wit*
    Of *Poets* triumph over it.
What cannot Verse? When *Thracian Orpheus* tooke
    His Lyre, and gently on it strooke,
The learned stones came dancing all along,
    And kept time to the charming song.
With artificiall pace the Warlike *Pine*,
    Th'*Elme*, and his Wife the *Ivy twine*,
With all the better trees, which erst had stood
    Unmov'd, forsooke their native Wood.

ABRAHAM COWLEY

The *Lawrell* to the *Poets* hand did bow,
    Craving the honour of his brow :
And every loving arme embrac'd, and made
    With their officious leaves a shade.
The beasts too strove his auditors to be,
    Forgetting their old Tyrannie.
The fearefull *Hart* next to the *Lion* came,
    And *Wolfe* was *Sheppeard* to the *Lambe*.
Nightingales, harmlesse *Syrens* of the ayre,
    And *Muses* of the place, were there.
Who when their little windpipes they had found
    Unequall to so strange a sound,
O'recome by art and griefe they did expire,
    And fell upon the conquering Lyre.
Happy, ô happy they, whose Tombe might be,
    Mausolus envied by thee !

ODE II.

*That a pleasant Poverty is to be preferred
before discontented Riches.*

1.

WHy ô doth gaudy *Tagus* ravish thee,
    Though *Neptunes* Treasure-house it be?
    Why doth *Pactolus* thee bewitch,
Infected yet with *Midas* glorious Itch?

2.

Their dull and sleepie streames are not at all
    Like other Flouds, *Poeticall*,
    They have no dance, no wanton sport,
No gentle murmur, the lov'd shore to court.

3.

No Fish inhabite the adulterate Floud,
    Nor can it feed the neighbouring Wood,
    No Flower or Herbe is neere it found,
But a perpetuall Winter serves the ground.

SYLVA

4.

Give me a River which doth scorne to shew
    An added beauty, whose cleere brow
    May be my looking-glasse, to see
What my face is, and what my mind should be.

5.

Here waves call waves, and glide along in ranke,
    And prattle to the smiling banke.
    Here sad *King fishers* tell their tales,
And fish enrich the Brooke with silver scales.

6.

Dasyes the first borne of the teeming Spring,
    On each side their embrodery bring,
    Here *Lillies* wash, and grow more white,
And *Daffadills* to see themselves delight.

7.

Here a fresh Arbor gives her amorous shade,
    Which *Nature*, the best *Gard'ner* made.
    Here I would set, and sing rude layes,
Such as the *Nimphs* and *me my selfe* should please.

8.

Thus I would waste, thus end my carelesse dayes,
    And *Robin-red-brests* whom men praise
    For pious birds, should when I dye,
Make both my *Monument* and *Elegie*.

ODE III.

To his Mistris.

[1.]

TYrian dye why doe you weare
    You whose cheekes best scarlet are?
      Why doe you fondly pin
      Pure linnens ore your skin,
    Your skin that's whiter farre,
Casting a duskie cloud before a Starre?

2.

Why beares your necke a golden chayne?
Did Nature make your haire in vaine,
    Of Gold most pure and fine?
    With gemmes why doe you shine?
    They, neighbours to your eyes,
Shew but like *Phosphor*, when the *Sunne* doth rise.

3.

I would have all my *Mistris* parts,
Owe more to *Nature* then to *Arts*,
    I would not woe the dresse,
    Or one whose nights give lesse
    Contentment, then the day.
Shee's faire, whose beauty onely makes her gay.

4.

For 'tis not buildings make a Court
Or pompe, but 'tis the Kings resort:
    If *Jupiter* downe powre
    Himselfe, and in a showre
    Hide such bright *Majestie*
Lesse then a *golden one* it cannot be.

ODE IV.

On the uncertainty of Fortune.   A Translation.

1.

Leave off unfit complaints, and cleere
    From sighs your brest, and from black clouds your brow,
When the Sunne shines not with his wonted cheere,
And Fortune throwes an adverse cast for you.
    That Sea which vext with *Notus* is,
The merry *Eastwinds* will to morrow kisse.

62

SYLVA

2.

The Sunne to day rides drousily,
To morrow 'twill put on a looke more faire,
Laughter and groaning doe alternately
Returne, and teares sports neerest neighbours are.
 'Tis by the *Gods* appointed so
That good fate should with mingled dangers flow.

3.

Who drave his Oxen yesterday,
Doth now over the Noblest *Romanes* reigne.
And on the *Gabii*, and the *Cures* lay
The yoake which from his *Oxen* he had tane.
 Whom *Hesperus* saw poore and low,
The mornings eye beholds him greatest now.

4.

If Fortune knit amongst her play
But seriousnesse; he shall againe goe home
To his old Country Farme of yesterday,
To scoffing people no meane jest become.
 And with the *crowned Axe*, which he
Had rul'd the World, goe backe and prune some Tree.
 Nay if he want the fuell cold requires,
 With his owne *Fasces* he shall make him *fires*.

ODE V.

In commendation of the time we live under the
Reign of our gracious K. Charles.

[1.]

CUrst be that wretch (Deaths Factor sure) who brought
 Dire Swords into the peacefull world, and taught
 Smiths, who before could onely make
 The Spade, the Plowshare, and the Rake;
  Arts, in most cruell wise
  Mans life t'epitomize.

ABRAHAM COWLEY

2.

Then men (fond men alas) rid post to th'grave,
And cut those threads, which yet the *Fates* would save.
  Then *Charon* sweated at his trade,
  And had a bigger *Ferry* made,
    Then, then the silver hayre,
    Frequent before, grew rare.

3.

Then *Revenge* married to *Ambition*,
Begat blacke *Warre*, then *Avarice* crept on.
  Then limits to each field were strain'd,
  And *Terminus* a *Godhead* gain'd.
    To men before was found,
    Besides the Sea, no bound.

4.

In what Playne or what River hath not beene
Warres story, writ in blood (sad story) seene?
  This truth too well our *England* knowes,
  'Twas civill slaughter dy'd her *Rose*:
    Nay then her *Lillie* too,
    With bloods losse paler grew.

5.

Such griefes, nay worse than these, we now should feele,
Did not just *Charles* silence the rage of steele;
  He to our Land blest peace doth bring,
  All Neighbour Countries envying.
    Happy who did remaine
    Unborne till *Charles* his reigne!

6.

Where dreaming *Chimicks* is you[r] paine and cost?
How is your oyle, how is your labour lost?
  Our *Charles*, blest *Alchymist* (though strange,
  Beleeve it future times) did change
    The *Iron* age of old,
    Into an age of *Gold*.

64

ODE VI.

Upon the shortnesse of Mans life.

MArke that swift Arrow how it cuts the ayre,
  How it out-runnes thy hunting eye,
  Use all perswasions now, and try
If thou canst call it backe, or stay it there.
  That way it went, but thou shalt find
  No tract of 't left behind.
Foole 'tis thy life, and the fond *Archer*, thou,
  Of all the time thou'st shot away
  Ile bid thee fetch but yesterday,
And it shall be too hard a taske to doe.
  Besides repentance, what canst find
  That it hath left behind?
Our life is carried with too strong a tyde,
  A doubtfull *Cloud* our substance beares,
  And is the *Horse* of all our yeares.
Each day doth on a winged *whirle-wind* ride.
  Wee and our *Glasse* run out, and must
  Both render up our dust.
But his past life who without griefe can see,
  Who never thinkes his end too neere,
  But sayes to *Fame*, thou art mine *Heire*.
That man extends lifes naturall brevity,
  This is, this is the onely way
  T' out-live *Nestor* in a day.

ABRAHAM COWLEY

An Answer to an Invitation to Cambridge.

1.

N*Ichols*, my better selfe, forbeare,
    For if thou telst what *Cambridge* pleasures are,
        The *Schoole-boyes* sinne will light on me,
I shall in mind at least a *Truant* be.
    Tell me not how you feed your minde
    With dainties of *Philosophy*,
    In *Ovids Nut* I shall not finde,
    The taste once pleased me.
O tell me not of *Logicks* diverse cheare,
I shall begin to loath our *Crambe* here.

2.

    Tell me not how the waves appeare
Of *Cam*, or how it cuts the *learned shiere*,
        I shall contemne the troubled *Thames*,
On her chiefe *Holiday*, even when her streames,
    Are with rich folly guilded, when
    The *quondam Dungboat* is made gay,
    Just like the bravery of the men,
    And graces with fresh paint that day:
When th' *Citie* shines with *Flagges* and *Pageants* there,
And Sattin Doublets, seen not twice a yeere.

3.

    Why doe I stay then? I would meet
Thee there, but *plummets* hang upon my feet:
        'Tis my chiefe wish to live with thee,
But not till I deserve thy company:
    Till then wee'l scorne to let that toy,
    Some forty miles, divide our hearts:
    Write to me, and I shall enjoy,
    Friendship, and *wit*, thy better parts.
Though envious *Fortune* larger hindrance brings,
Wee'l easely see each other, *Love hath wings*.

FINIS.

LOVES RIDDLE.

A PASTORALL COMÆDIE;

Written,

At the time of his being
Kings Scholler in *West-minster* Schoole,
by *A. Cowley.*

LONDON,

Printed by *John Dawson*, for *Henry Seile*, and are to be sold at the Tygres head in Fleet-street over against St. *Dunstans*-Church. 1638.

To the truly Worthy, and Noble, Sir KENELME DIGBIE Knight.

THis latter Age, the Lees of Time, hath knowne,
  Few, that have made both Pallas arts their owne.
But you, Great Sir, two Lawrels weare, and are
Victorious in Peace, as well as War.
Learning by right of Conquest is your owne,
And every liberall Art your Captive growne.
As if neglected Science (for it now
Wants some defenders) fled for help to you.
Whom I must follow, and let this for mee
An earnest of my future service bee.
Which I should feare to send you, did I know
Your judgement onely, not your Candor too.
For t'was a Worke, stolne (though you'le justly call
This Play, as fond as those) from Cat, or Ball.
Had it beene written since, I should, I feare,
Scarse have abstain'd from a Philosopher.
Which by Tradition here is thought to bee,
A necessarie Part in Comedie.
Nor need I tell you this; each line of it
Betray's the Time and Place wherein t'was writ.
And I could wish, that I might safely say
To th'Reader, that t'was done but th'other day.
Yet 'tis not stuff'd with names of Gods, hard words,
Such as the Metamorphosis affords.
Nor has't a part for Robinson, whom they
At schoole, account essentiall to a Play.
The stile is low, such as you'le easily take
For what a Swaine might speake, and a Boy make.
Take it, as early fruits, which rare appeare
Though not halfe ripe, but worst of all the yeare.
And if it please your tast, my Muse will say,
The Birch which crown'd her then, is growne a Bay.

Yours in all observance,

A. COWLEY.

69

The Scæne Sicily.

The Actors names.

Demophil
Spodaia } two old folke of a Noble family.

Florellus
Callidora } their Children.

Philistus
Aphron } two Gent. both in love with *Callidora.*

Clariana, sister to *Philistus.*

Melarnus
Truga } a crabbed old Shepheard.
Hylace } his Wife.
} their Daughter.

Ægon—an ancient Countrey man.

Bellula—his supposed Daughter.

Palæmon—a young Swaine in love with *Hylace.*

Alupis—a merry Shepheard.

Clariana's Mayd.

Actus I. Scæna I.

Enter Callidora *disguised in mans apparell.*

M Adde feet, yee have beene traytours to your Master :
Where have you lead me ? sure my truant mind
Hath taught my body thus to wander too ;
Faintnesse and feare surprize me ; Yee just gods,
If yee have brought me to this place to scourge
The folly of my love, (I might say madnesse)
Dispatch me quickly ; send some pittying men
Or cruell beast to find me ; let me bee
Fed by the one, or let mee feed the other.
Why are these trees so brave ? why doe they weare
Such greene and fresh apparell ? how they smile !
How their proud toppes play with the courting wind !
Can they behold me pine and languish here,
And yet not sympathize at all in mourning ?
Doe they upbraid my sorrowes ? can it bee
That these thick branches never seene before
But by the Sunne, should learne so much of man ?
The trees in Courtiers gardens, which are conscious
Of their guilt Masters statelinesse and pride,
Themselves would pitty me ; yet these—Who's there ?

Enter Alupis *singing.*

1.

Rise up thou mournfull Swaine,
For 'tis but a folly
To be melancholy
And get thee thy pipe againe.

2.

Come sing away the day,
For 'tis but a folly
To be melancholly,
Let's live here whilst wee may.

71

    Cal. I marry Sir, this fellow hath some fire in him,
Me thinkes a sad and drowsie shepheard is
A prodigie in Nature, for the woods
Should bee as farre from sorrow, as they are
From sorrowes causes, riches and the like.
Haile to you swaine, I am a Gentleman
Driven here by ignorance of the way, and would
Confesse my selfe bound to you for a curtesie,
If you would please to helpe me to some lodging
Where I may rest my selfe.
    Alu. *For 'tis but a folly*, &c.
    Cal. Well; if the rest bee like this fellow here;
Then I have travel'd fairely now; for certainly
This is a land of fooles; some Colonie
Of elder brothers have beene planted here,
And begot this faire generation.
Prithee, good Shepheard, tell mee where thou dwelst?
    Alu. *For 'tis but a folly*, &c.
    Call. Why art thou madde?
    Alu. What if I bee?
I hope 'tis no discredit for me Sir?
For in this age who is not? I'le prove it to you,
Your Citizen hee's madde to trust the Gentleman
Both with his wares and wife. Your Courtier
Hee's madde to spend his time in studying postures,
Cringes and fashions, and new complements;
Your Lawyer hee's madde to sell away
His tongue for money, and his Client madder
To buy it of him, since 'tis of no use
But to undoe men, and the Latine tongue;
Your Schollers they are madde to breake their braines,
Out-watch the Moone, and looke more pale then shee,
That so when all the Arts call him their Master,
Hee may perhaps get some small Vicaridge,
Or be the Usher of a Schoole; but there's
A thing in blacke called Poet, who is ten
Degrees in madnesse above these; his meanes
Is what the gentle Fates please to allow him
By the death or mariage of some mighty Lord,
Which hee must solemnize with a new song.

LOVES RIDDLE

Cal. This fellowes wit amazeth me ; but friend,
What doe you thinke of lovers ?
   Alu. Worst of all ;
Is't not a pretty folly to stand thus,
And sigh, and fold the armes, and cry my *Cœlia*,
My soule, my life, my *Cælia*, then to wring
Ones state for presents, and ones brayne for Sonnets ?
O ! 'tis beyond the name of Phrenzie.
   Cal. What so Satyricke Shephea[r]ds ? I beleeve
You did not learne these flashes in the Woods ;
How is it possible that you should get
Such neere acquaintance with the Citie manners,
And yet live here in such a silent place,
Where one would thinke the very name of City
Could hardly Enter.
   Alu. Why, I'le tell you Sir :
My father dyed, (you force me to remember
A griefe that deserves teares) and left me young,
And (if a Shepheard may be said so) rich,
I in an itching wantonnesse to see
What other Swaines so wondred at, the Citie,
Streight sold my rurall portion (for the wealth
Of Shepheards is their flockes) and thither went,
Where whil'st my money lasted I was welcome,
And liv'd in credit, but when that was gone,
And the last piece sigh'd in my empty pocket,
I was contemn'd, then I began to feele
How dearely I had bought experience,
And without any thing besides repentance
To load me, return'd back, and here I live
To laugh at all those follyes which I saw.

Song.

The merry waves dance up and downe, and play,
   Sport is granted to the Sea.
Birds are the queristers of th'empty ayre,
   Sport is never wanting there.
The ground doth smile at the Springs flowry birth,
   Sport is granted to the earth.

The fire it's cheering flame on high doth reare,
Sport is never wanting there.
If all the elements, the Earth, the Sea,
Ayre, and fire, so merry bee;
Why is mans mirth so seldome, and so small,
Who is compounded of them all?

Cal. You may rejoyce; but sighes befit me better.
Alu. Now on my conscience thou hast lost a Mistris;
If it be so, thanke God, and love no more;
Or else perhaps she'has burnt your whining letter,
Or kist another Gentleman in your sight,
Or else denyed you her glove, or laught at you,
Causes indeed, which deserve speciall mourning,
And now you come to talke with your God *Cupid*
In private here, and call the Woods to witnesse,
And all the streames which murmure when they heare
The injuries they suffer; I am sorry
I have been a hindrance to your meditations,
Farewell Sir.
Cal. Nay, good Shepheard, you mistake mee.
Alu. Faith, I am very chary of my health,
I would be loath to be infected Sir.
Cal. Thou needest not feare; I have no disease at all
Besides a troubled mind.
Alu. Why that's the worst, the worst of all.
Cal. And therefore it doth challenge
Your piety the more, you should the rather,
Strive to be my Physitian.
Alu. The good Gods forbid it; I turne Physitian?
My Parents brought me up more piously,
Then that I should play booty with a sicknesse,
Turne a consumption to mens purses, and
Purge them, worse then their bodyes, and set up
An Apothecaries shop in private chambers,
Live by revenew of close-stooles and urinals,
Deferre off sick mens health from day to day
As if they went to law with their disease,
No, I was borne for better ends, then to send away
His Majesties subjects to hell so fast,

74

LOVES RIDDLE

As if I were to share the stakes with *Charon*.

Cal. Your wit erres much:
For as the soule is nobler then the body,
So it's corruption askes a better medicine
Then is applyed to Gouts, Catarrs, or Agues,
And that is counsell.

Alu. So then: I should bee
Your soules Physitian; why, I could talke out
An houre or so, but then I want a cushion
To thump my precepts into; but tell me 'pray,
What name beares your disease?

Cal. A feaver, shepheard, but so farre above
An outward one, that the vicissitudes
Of that may seeme but warmth, and coolenesse only;
This, flame, and frost.

Alu. So; I understand you,
You are a lover, which is by translation
A foole, or a beast, for I'le define you; you're
Partly *Chamæleon*, partly *Salamander*,
You're fed by th'ayre, and live i'the fire.

Cal. Why did you never love? have you no softnesse,
Nought of your mother in you? if that Sun
Which scorched me, should cast one beame upon you,
T'would quickly melt the ice about your heart,
And lend your eyes fresh streames.

Alu. Faith, I thinke not;
I have seen all your beautyes of the Court,
And yet was never ravisht, never made
A dolefull Sonnet unto angry *Cupid*,
Either to warme her heart, or else coole mine,
And no face yet could ever wound me so,
But that I quickly found a remedie.

Cal. That were an art worth learning, and you need not
Be niggard of your knowledge; See the Sunne
Though it have given this many thousand yeares
Light to the world, yet is as bigge and bright
As e're it was, and hath not lost one beame
Of his first glory; then let charity
Perswade you to instruct me, I shall bee
A very thankfull scholler.

Alu. I shall: for 'tis both easily taught and learn'd,
> *Come sing away the day,* &c.
Mirth is the only physick.
Cal. It is a way which I have much desired
To cheate my sorrow with; and for that purpose
Would faine turne shepheard, and in rural sports
Weare my lifes remnant out; I would forget
All things, my very name if it were possible.
Alu. Pray let me learne it first.
Cal. 'Tis *Callidorus.*
Alu. Thanke you; if you your selfe chance to forget it
Come but to me I'le doe you the same curtesie,
In the meane while make me your servant Sir,
I will instruct you in things necessary
For the creation of a Shepheard, and
Wee two will laugh at all the world securely,
And fling jests 'gainst the businesses of state
Without endangering our eares.

> *Come, come away,*
> > *For 'tis but a folly*
> > *To be melancholy,*
> *Let's live here whil'st we may.*   *Exeunt.*

Enter *Palæmon, Melarnus, Truga, Ægon*
Bellula, Hylace

Pa. I see I am undone.
Mel. Come no matter for that, you love my Daughter?
By *Pan*; but come, no matter for that; you my *Hilace*?
Tru. Nay good Duck, doe not vexe your selfe; what
though he loves her? you know she will not have him.
Mel. Come, no matter for that; I will vex my selfe, and
vex him too, shall such an idle fellow as he strive to entice
away honest mens children? let him goe feed his flocks; but
alas! he has none to trouble him; ha ha, ha, yet hee would
marry my daughter.
Pa. Thou art a malicious doting man,
And one who cannot boast of any thing
But that shee calls thee father, though I cannot

76

LOVES RIDDLE

Number so large a flock of sheepe as thou,
Nor send so many cheeses to the City,
Yet in my mind I am an Emperour
If but compar'd with thee.

    Tru. Of what place I pray?
'Tis of some new discovered Countrey, is't not?

    Pa. Prithee good *Wintor* if thou wilt be talking,
Keepe thy breath in a little, for it smells
Worse then a Goat; yet thou must talke,
For thou hast nothing left thee of a woman
But lust, and tongue.

    Hyl. Shepheard, here's none so taken with your wit
But you might spare it; if you be so lavish,
You'le have none left another time to make
The song of the forsaken Lover with.

    Pa. I'me dumbe, my lips are seal'd, seal'd up for ever
May my rash tongue forget to be interpreter,
And organ of my senses, if you say,
It hath offended you.

    Hyl. Troth if you make
But that condition, I shall agree to't quickly:

    Mel. By *Pan* well said Girle; what a foole was I
To suspect thee of loving him? but come
'Tis no matter for that; when e're thou art maried
I'le adde ten sheepe more to thy portion,
For putting this one jest upon him.

    Ægon. Nay now I must needs tell you that your anger
Is grounded with no reason to maintaine it,
If you intend your daughter shall not marry him,
Say so, but play not with his passion,
For 'tis inhumane wit which jeeres the wretched.

    Mel. Come 'tis no matter for that; what I doe, I
        doe;
I shall not need your counsell.

    Tru. I hope my husband and I have enough wisdome
To governe our owne child; if we want any
'Twill be to little purpose, I dare say,
To come to borrow some of you.

    Æg. 'Tis very likely pritty Mistris *Maukin*,
You with a face lookes like a winter apple

77

ABRAHAM COWLEY

When 'tis shrunke up together and halfe rotten,
I'de see you hang'd up for a thing to skare
The crowes away before Ile spend my breath
To teach you any.

   Hyl. Alas good shepheard!
What doe you imagine that I should love you for?

   Pal. For all my services, the vertuous zeale
And constancie with which I ever woed you,
Though I were blacker then a starlesse night,
Or consciences where guilt and horror dwell,
Although splay-legd, crooked, deform'd in all parts,
And but the Chao's only of a man;
Yet if I love and honor you, humanitie
Would teach you not to hate, or laugh at me.

   Hy. Pray spare your fine perswasions, and set speeches,
And rather tell them to those stones and trees,
'Twill be to as good purpose quite, as when
You spend them upon me.

   Pa. Give me my finall answer, that I may
Bee either blest for ever, or die quickly;
Delay's a cruell rack, and kils by piece-meales.

   Hy. Then here 'tis, you're an asse,
(Take that for your incivilitie to my mother)
And I will never love you.

   Pal. You're a woman;
A cruell and fond woman, and my passion
Shall trouble you no more, but when I'me dead
My angry Ghost shall vex you worse then now
Your pride doth mee, Farewell.

     Enter Aphron *madde, meeting* Palæmon *going out.*

   Aph. Nay stay Sir, have you found her?

   Pa. How now? whats the matter?

   Aph. For I will have her out of you, or else
I'le cut thee into atomes, til the wind
Play with the threeds of thy torne body. Looke her
Or I will do't.

   Pal. Whom; or where?

   Aph. I'le tell thee honest fellow; thou shalt goe

LOVES RIDDLE

From me as an Embassador to the Sunne,
(For men call him the eye of heaven, from which
Nothing lyes hid) and tell him—doe you marke me—tell him
From me—that if he send not word where shee is gone,
—I will—nay by the Gods I will.

Æg.   Alas poore Gentleman !
Sure he hath lost some Mistris ; beautious women
Are the chiefe plagues to men.

Tru.   Nay, not so shepheard, when did I plague any ?

Ægon.   How farre is he beyond the name of slave,
That makes his love his Mistris ?

Aph.   Mistris ? who's that ? her Ghost ? 'tis shee ;
It was her voyce ; were all the flouds, the rivers,
And seas that with their crooked armes embrace
The earth betwixt us, I'de wade through and meet her,
Were all the Alpes heap'd on each others head,
Were *Pelion* joyn'd to *Ossa*, and they both
Throwne on *Olympus* top, they should not make
So high a wall, but I would scal't and find her.

Bel.   Unhappy man.

Aph.   'Tis empty ayre : I was too rude, too saucy.
And she hath left me ; if shee be alive
What darknesse shall be thicke enough to hide her ?
If dead, I'le seeke the place which Poets call *Elizium*,
Where all the soules of good and vertuous mortalls
Enjoy deserved pleasures after death.
What should I feare ? if there be an *Erynnis*
'Tis in this brest, if a *Tisiphone*
'Tis here, here in this braine are all her serpents ;
My griefe and fury armes me.

Pal.   By your leave Sir.

Aph.   Now by the Gods, that man that stops my journey
Had better have provokt a hungry Lionesse
Rob'd of her Whelpes, or set his naked brest
Against the Thunder.   *Exit Aphron.*

Tru.   'Tis well hee's gone,
I never could endure to see these madde men.

Mel.   Come no matter for that   *Enter* Alupis
For now he's gone, here comes another.   *and* Callidorus
But it's no matter for that neither.

79

ABRAHAM COWLEY

How now? who has hee brought with him?

Al.   Hayle to yee Shepheards, and yee beautious Nymphs,
I must present this stranger to your knowledge,
When you're acquainted well, you'le thanke me for't.

Cal.   Blest Masters of these Woods, hayle to you al[l],
'Tis my desire to be your neighbour here;
And feed my flocks (such as they are) neere yours,
This Shepheard tels me, that your gentle nature
Will be most willing to accept my friendship;
Which if yee doe, may all the Sylvan Deityes
Bee still propitious to you, may your flocks
Yearely increase above your hopes or wishes;
May none of your young lambes become a prey
To the rude Wolfe, but play about securely;
May dearths be ever exil'd from these woods,
May your fruits prosper, and your mountaine strawberyes
Grow in abundance, may no Lovers be
Despis'd, and pine away their yeares of spring:
But the young men and maides be strucken both
With equall sympathy.

Pa.   That were a golden time; the Gods forbid
Mortalls to bee so happy.

Ægon.   I thanke you; and we wish no lesse to you:
You are most welcome hither.

Tru.   'Tis a handsome man,
I'le be acquainted with him; we most heartily
Accept your company.

Mel.   Come no matter for that; we have enough
Already who can beare us company,
But no matter for that neither; wee shall have
Shortly no roome left us to feed our flockes
By one another.

Alup.   What alwayes grumbling?
Your father and your mother scoulded sure
Whil'st you were getting; well, if I begin
I'le so abuse thee, and that publiquely.

Mel.   A rott upon you; you must still be humoured,
But come, no matter for that; you're welcome then.

Al.   What, beauties, are you silent?
Take notice of him, (pray) your speaking is

80

LOVES RIDDLE

Worth more then all the rest.

Bell. You're very welcome.

Cal. Thanke you fayre Nymph, this is indeed a welcome.

Bell. I never saw, beauty and affability (Salutes her.
So well conjoyn'd before; if I stay long
I shall be quite undone.

Alu. Nay come, put on too.

Hyl. You are most kindly welcome.

Cal. You blesse mee too much;
The honour of your lip is entertainment
Princes might wish for.

Hyl. Blesse me how hee lookes!
And how he talkes; his kisse was honey too,
His lips as red and sweet as early cherryes,
Softer then Bevers skins.

Bel. Blesse me how I envy her!
Would I had had that kisse too!

Hyl. How his eye shines! what a bright flame it shootes!

Bel. How red his cheekes are! so our garden apples
Looke on that side where the hot Sun salutes them.

Hyl. How well his haires become him!
Just like that starre which ushers on the day.

Bell. How faire he is! fairer then whitest blossomes.

Trug. They two have got a kisse;
Why should I lose it for want of speaking?
You're welcome shepheard.

Alu. Come on: *For 'tis but a folly*, &c.

Tru. Doe you heare, you are welcome.

Alu. Oh! here's another must have a kisse:

Tru. Goe you're a paltry knave, I, that you are,
To wrong an ho[n]est woman thus.

Alu. Why hee shall kisse thee, never feare it, alas!
I did but jest, he'le do't for all this,
Nay, because I will be a Patron to thee
I'le speake to him.

Tru. You're a slandering knave,
And you shall know't, that you shall.

Al. Nay, if you scould so lowd
Others shall know it too; He must stop your mouth,
Or you'le talke on this three houres; *Callidorus*

C. II. F

81

If you can patiently endure a stinke,
Or have frequented ere the City Beare-garden,
Prithee salute this fourescore yeares, and free me,
She sayes you're welcome too.
   Cal. I cry you mercy Shepheardesse,
By *Pan* I did not see you.
   Tru. If my husband and *Alupis* were not here
I'de rather pay him back his kisse againe,
Then be beholding to him.
   Al. What, thou hast don't?
Well if thou dost not dye upon't, hereafter,
Thy body will agree even with the worst
And stinking'st ayre in *Europe.*
   Cal. Nay, be not angry Shepheardesse, you know
He doth but jest as 'tis his custome.
   Tru. I know it is his custome ; he was always
Wont to abuse me, like a knave as he is,
But I'le endure't no more.
   Al. Prithee good *Callidorus* if her breath
Be not too bad, goe stop her mouth againe,
She'le scould till night else.
   Tru. Yes marry will I, that I will, you rascall you,
I'le teach you to lay your frumps upon me ;
You delight in it, doe you ?
   Al. Prithee be quiet, leave but talking to me
And I will never jeere thee any more,
We two will be so peaceable hereafter.
   Tru. Well upon that condition.
   Al. So, I'me deliver'd, why how now Ladds ?
What have you lost your tongues ? Ile have them cry'd,
Palæmon, Ægon, Callidorus, what ?
Are you all dumbe ? I pray continue so,
And i'le be merry with my selfe.

Song.

   'Tis better to dance then sing,
   The cause is if you will know it,
   That I to my selfe shall bring
      A Poverty
      Voluntary
   If once I grow but a Poet.

LOVES RIDDLE

Ægon. And yet me thinkes you sing,

Al. O yes, because here's none doe dance,
And both are better farre then to be sad.

Ægon. Come then let's have a round.

Al. A match; *Palæmon* whither goe you?

Pa. The Gods forbid that I should mock my selfe,
Cheate my owne mind, I dance and weepe at once?
You may: Farewell.   *Exit.*

Al. 'Tis such a whining foole; come, come, *Melarnus.*

Mel. I have no mind to dance; but come no matter for
that, rather then breake the squares.—

Cal. By your leave, fayre one.

Hil. Would I were in her place.

Al. Come *Hilace,* thee and I wench I warrant thee,
You and your wife together. God blesse you; so—
        For 'tis but a folly, &c.   *Dance.*

Tru. So there's enough, I'me halfe a weary,

Mel. Come no matter for that,
I have not danc't so much this yeare.

Al. So farewell, you'le come along with me?

Cal. Yes, farewell gentle Swaines.

Tru. Farewell good Shepheard,

Bel. Your best wishes follow you.

Hyl. *Pan* alwayes guide you.

Mel. It's no matter for that, come away.   *Exeunt.*

Finis Actus primi.

Actus II. Scæna I.

Emo. Nay, shee is lost for ever, and her name
Which us'd to be so comfortable, now
Is poyson to our thoughts, and to augment
Our misery paints forth our former happinesse,
O *Callidora*, O my *Callidora!*
I shall ne're see thee more.
  Spo. If cursed *Aphron*
Hath caryed her away, and tryumphs now
In the destruction of our hoary age
'Twere better shee were dead;
  Dem. 'Twere better we were all dead; the enjoying
Of tedious life is a worse punishment
Then losing of my Daughter; Oh! my friends,
Why have I lived so long?
  Cla. Good Sir be comforted : Brother speake to them.
  Spo. Would I had dyed, when first I brought thee forth
My Girle, my best Girle, then I should have slept
In quiet, and not wept now.
  Phi. I am halfe a statue
Freeze me up quite yee Gods, and let me be
My owne sad monument.
  Cla. Alas! you doe but hurt your selves with weeping;
Consider pray, it may be she'le come back.
  Dem. Oh! never, never, 'tis impossible
As to call back sixteene, and with vaine Rhetoricke
Perswade my lifes fresh Aprill to returne,
Shee's dead, or else farre worse, kept up by *Aphron*
Whom if I could but see, me thinkes new bloud
Would creepe into my veines, and my faint sinewes
Renew themselves, I doubt not but to find
Strength enough yet to be reveng'd of *Aphron*.
  Sp. Would I were with thee, Girle, where ere thou art.

LOVES RIDDLE

Cla. For shame good Brother, see if you can comfort them,
Me thinkes you should say something.
   Phi. Doe you thinke
My griefes so light? or was the interest
So small which I had in her? I a comforter?
Alas! she was my wife, for we were married
In our affection, in our vowes; and nothing
Stopt the enjoying of each other, but
The thinne partition of some ceremonies.
I lost my hopes, my expectations,
My joyes, nay more, I lost my selfe with her;
You have a son, yet left behind, whose memorie
May sweeten all this gall.
   Spo. I, we had one,
But fate's so cruell to us, and such dangers
Attend a travelling man, that 'twere presumption
To say we have him; we have sent for him
To blot out the remembrance of his sister:
But whether we shall ever see him here,
The Gods can only tell, we barely hope.
   Dem. This newes, alas!
Will be but a sad welcome to him.
   Phi. Why doe I play thus with my misery?
'Tis vaine to thinke I can live here without her,
Ile seeke her where e're she is; patience in this
Would be a vice, and men might justly say
My love was but a flash of winged lightning,
And not a Vestall flame, which alwayes shines.
His woing is a complement, not passion,
Who can if fortune snatch away his Mistris,
Spend some few teares, then take another choyce,
Mine is not so; Oh *Callidora!*
   Cla. Fye Brother, you're a man,
And should not be shaken with every wind,
If it were possible to call her back
With mourning, mourning were a piety,
But since it cannot, you must give me leave
To call it folly:
   Phi. So it is;
And I will therefore shape some other course,

This dolefull place shall never see me more,
Vnlesse it see her too in my embraces,
You sister may retyre unto my Farme,
Adjoyning to the woods;
And my estate I leave for you to manage,
If I find her, expect me there, if not
Doe you live happier then your Brother hath:
   Cla. Alas! how can I if you leave me? but
I hope your resolutions may be altered.
   Ph. Never, farewell: good *Demophil,*
Farewell *Spodaia,* temper your laments;
If I returne we shall againe be happy.
   Spo. You shall not want my prayers.
   Dem. The Gods that pitty Lovers (if there bee any)
      attend upon you.
   Cla. Will you needs goe?
   Ph. I knit delayes; 'twere time I were now ready,
And I shall sinne if I seeme dull or slow
In any thing which touches *Callidora.*
   Dem. Oh! that name wounds me; we'le beare you company
A little way, and *Clariana* looke
To see us often at your Countrey Farme,
Wee'le sigh, and grieve together.   *Exeunt.*

       Enter Alupis *and* Palæmon.

   Alu. *Come, come away,* &c.
Now where are all your sonnets? your rare fancies?
Could the fine morning musick which you wak'd
Your Mistris with, prevaile no more then this?
Why in the Citie now your very Fidlers
Good morrow to your worship, will get something,
Hath she denyed thee quite?
   Pa. Shee hath undone me; I have plow'd the Sea,
And begot storming billowes.
   Al. Can no perswasions move her?
   Pa. No more then thy least breath can stirre an oake,
Which hath this many yeares scorn'd the fierce warres
Of all the winds.
   Al. 'Tis a good hearing; then

LOVES RIDDLE

She'le cost you no more payres of Turtle Doves,
Nor garlands knit with amorous conceits,
I doe perceive some ragges of the Court fashions
Visibly creeping now into the woods,
The more hee shewes his love, the more shee slights him,
Yet will take any gift of him, as willingly
As Countrey Justices the Hens and Geese
Of their offending neighbours; this is right;
Now if I lov'd this wench I would so handle her,
I'de teach her what the difference were betwixt
One who had seene the Court and Citie tricks,
And a meere shepheard.
    Pa.   Lions are tam'd, and become slaves to men,
And Tygres oft forget the cruelty
They suckt from their fierce mothers; but, a woman
Ah me! a woman!—
    Al.   Yet if I saw such wonders in her face
As you doe, I should never doubt to win her.
    Pa.   How pray? if gifts would doe it, she hath had
The daintiest Lambes, the hope of all my flock,
I let my apples hang for her to gather,
The painfull Bee did never load my hives,
With honey which she tasted not.
    Al.   You mistake me Friend; I meane not so.
    Pa.   How then? if Poetry would do't, what shade
Hath not beene Auditor of my amorous pipe?
What bankes are not acquainted with her prayses?
Which I have sung in verses, and the sheepheards
Say they are good ones, nay they call me Poet,
Although I am not easie to beleeve them.
    Al.   No, no, no; that's not the way.
    Pa.   Why how?
If shew of griefe had Rhetorick enough
To move her, I dare sweare she had beene mine
Long before this, what day did ere peepe forth
In which I wept not dulier then the morning?
Which of the winds hath not my sighes encreas'd
At sundry times? how often have I cryed
Hylace, Hylace, till the docile woods
Have answered *Hylace*; and every valley

ABRAHAM COWLEY

As if it were my Rivall, sounded *Hylace*.

   Al. I, and you were a most rare foole for doing so,
Why 'twas that poyson'd all; Had I a Mistris
I'de almost beat her, by this light, I would,
For they are much about your Spaniels nature,
But whilst you cry deare *Hylace*, ô *Hylace!*
Pitty the tortures of my burning heart,
She'le alwayes mince it, like a Citizens wife,
At the first asking; though her tickled bloud
Leapes at the very mention; therefore now
Leave off your whining tricks, and take my counsell.
First then be merry; *For 'tis but a folly*, &c.

   Pal. 'Tis a hard lesson for my mind to learne,
But I would force my selfe, if that would helpe me!

   Al. Why thou shalt see it will; next I would have thee
To laugh at her, and mocke her pittifully;
Study for jeeres against next time you see her,
I'le goe along with you, and helpe to abuse her,
Till we have made her cry, worse then e're you did;
When we have us'd her thus a little while,
Shee'le be as tame and gentle.—

   Pa. But alas!
This will provoke her more.

   Al. Ile warrant thee: besides, what if it should?
She hath refus'd you utterly already,
And cannot hurt you worse; come, come, be rul'd;
And follow me, we'le put it straight in practize.
      For 'tis but a folly, &c.

   Pa. A match; Ile try alwayes; she can but scorne me,
There is this good in depth of misery
That men may attempt any thing, they know
The worst before hand.   *Exeunt.*

      Enter Callidorus.

How happy is that man, who in these woods
With secure silence weares away his time!
Who is acquainted better with himselfe
Then others; who so great a stranger is
To Citie follyes, that he knowes them not.

88

LOVES RIDDLE

He sits all day upon some mossie hill
His rurall throne, arm'd with his crooke, his scepter,
A flowry garland is his country crowne ;
The gentle lambes and sheepe his loyall subjects,
Which every yeare pay him their fleecy tribute ;
Thus in an humble statelinesse and majestie
He tunes his pipe, the woods best melody,
And is at once, what many Monarches are not,
Both King and Poet. I could gladly wish
To spend the rest of my unprofitable,
And needlesse dayes in their innocuous sports,
But then my father, mother, and my brother
Recurse unto my thoughts, and straight plucke downe
The resolution I had built before ;
Love names *Philistus* to me, and o'th' sudden
The woods seeme base, and all their harmlesse pleasures
The daughters of necessity, not vertue.
Thus with my selfe I wage a warre, and am
To my owne rest a traytor ; I would faine
Goe home, but still the thought of *Aphron* frights me.
How now ? who's here ? ô 'tis faire *Hylace*
The grumbling shepheards daughter.   *Enter* Hylace.
Brightest of all those starres that paint the woods,
And grace these shady habitations,
You're welcome, how shall I requite the benefit
Which you bestow upon so poore a stranger
With your faire presence ?
     Hyl. If it be any curtesie, 'tis one
Which I would gladly doe you, I have brought
A rurall present, some of our owne apples,
My father and my mother are so hard,
They watch'd the tree, or else they had beene more,
Such as they are, if they can please your tast,
My wish is crown'd.
     Cal. O you're too kind,
And teach that duty to me which I ought
To have perform'd ; I would I could returne
The halfe of your deserts ! but I am poore
In every thing but thankes.
     Hy. Your acceptation only is reward

Too great for me.

Cal.   How they blush?
A man may well imagine they were yours,
They beare so great a shew of modesty.

Hyl.   O you mock my boldnesse
To thrust into ycur company ; but truly
I meant no hurt in't ; my intents were vertuous.

Cal.   The Gods forbid that I should nurse a thought
So wicked, thou art innocent I know,
And pure as *Venus* Doves, or mountaine snow
Which no foot hath defil'd, thy soule is whiter
(if there be any possibilitie of't)
Then that cleere skin which cloathes thy dainty body.

Hy.   Nay my good will deserves not to be jeer'd,
You know I am a rude and countrey wench.

Cal.   Farre be it from my thoughts, I sweare I honour
And love those maiden vertues which adorne you.

Hy.   I would you did, as well as I doe you,
But the just Gods intend not me so happy,
And I must be contented— I'me undone.   *Ent.* Bellula
Here's *Bellula* ; what is she growne my rivall?

Bell.   Blesse me! whom see I? *Hylace?* some cloud
Or friendly mist involve me.

Hy.   Nay *Bellula* ; I see you well enough.

Cal.   Why doth the day start backe? are you so cruell
To shew us first the light, and having struck
Wonder into us snatch it from our sight?
If Spring crown'd with the glories of the earth
Appeare upon the heavenly Ram, and streight
Creepe back againe into a grey-hayr'd frost,
Men will accuse its forwardnesse.

Hy.   Pray heaven
Hee be not taken with her ; shee's somewhat faire ;
He did not speake so long a speech to mee
I'me sure of't, though I brought him apples.

Bell.   I did mistake my way ; Pray pardon me.

Hyl.   I would you had else.

Cal.   I must thanke fortune then which lead you hither,
But you can stay a little while and blesse us?

Bel.   Yes (and Love knowes how willingly) alas!

LOVES RIDDLE

I shall quite spoyle my garland ere I give it him,
With hiding it from *Hylace*, Pray *Pan*
Shee hath not stolne his heart already from him,
And cheated my intentions.
    Hy. I would faine be going, but if I should leave her,
It may be I shall give her opportunity
To winne him from me, for I know she loveth him,
And hath perhaps a better tongue then I,
Although I should bee loth to yeeld to her
In beauty or complexion.
    Bell. Let me speake
In private with you; I am bold to bring
A garland to you, 'tis of the best flowers
Which I could gather, I was picking them
All yesterday.
    Cal. How you oblige me to you!
I thanke you sweetest, How they flourish still!
Sure they grow better, since your hand hath nipt them.
    Bell. They will doe, when your brow hath honour'd them,
Then they may well grow proud, and shine more freshly.
    Cal. What perfumes dwell in them?
They owe these odours to your breath.
    Hy. Defend me yee good Gods, I thinke he kisses her,
How long they have beene talking? now perhaps
Shee's woing him; perhaps he forgets me
And will consent, I'le put him in remembrance;
You have not tasted of the apples yet,
And they were good ones truly.
    Cal. I will doe presently best *Hilace*.
    Hy. That's some thing yet, would he would speake so
        alwayes.
    Cal. I would not change them for those glorious apples
Which give such fame to the *Hesperian* gardens.
    Bell. She hath out-gone me in her present now,
But I have got a Beechen cup at home
Curiously graven with the spreading leaves,
And gladsome burthen of a fruitful vine,
Which *Damon*, the best Artist of these woods
Made and bestow'd upon me, I'le bring that to morrow
And give it him, and then I'le warrant her

She will not goe beyond me.

Hy. What have you got a chaplet? ôh!
This is I see of *Bellula's* composing.

Bell. Why *Hylace*? you cannot make a better,
What flowers 'pray doth it want?

Cal. Poore scules I pitty them, and the more,
Because I have not beene my selfe a stranger
To these love passions, but I wonder
What they can find in me worth their affection,
Truly I would faine satisfie them both,
But can doe neither; 'tis fates crime, not mine.

B[e]ll. W[h]ither goe you shepheard?

Hyl. You will not leave us will you?

Cal. Indeed I ought not,
You have bought me both with your courtesies
And should divide me.

Hy. Shee came last to you.

Bell. She hath another love,
And kills *Palæmen* with her cruelty,
How can shee expect mercy from another;

[*Cal.*] In what a Labarinth doth Love draw mortalls
And then blindfolds them! what a mist it throwes
Upon their senses! if he be a God
As sure he is (his power could not be so great else)
He knowes the impossibilitie which Nature
Hath set betwixt us, yet entangles us,
And laughs to see us struggle. D'yee both love me?

Bell. I doe I'me sure.

Hyl. And I as much as she.

Cal. I pitty both of you, for you have sow'd
Upon unthankfull sand, whose dry'd up wombe
Nature denyes to blesse with fruitfulnesse,
You are both fayre, and more then common graces
Inhabite in you both, *Bellula's* eyes
Shine like the lampe of Heaven, and so doth *Hylaces*,
Hylaces cheekes are deeper dy'd in scarlet
Then the chast mornings blushes, so are *Bellula's*,
And I protest I love you both. Yet cannot,
Yet must not enjoy either.

Bell. You speake riddles.

LOVES RIDDLE

Cal. Which times commentarie
Must only explaine to you; and till then
Farewell good *Bellula*, farewell good *Hylace*,
I thanke you both.   *Exit.*
    Hyl. Alas! my hopes are strangled.   *Exit.*
    Bell. I will not yet despaire: He may grow milder,
He bade me farewell first; and lookt upon me
With a more stedfast eye, then upon her
When he departed hence: 'twas a good signe;
At least I will imagine it to be so,
Hope is the truest friend, and seldome leaves one.   *Exit.*

Enter Truga.

I doubt not but this will move him,
For they're good apples, but my teeth are gone,
I cannot bite them; but for all that though
Ile warrant you I can love a young Fellow
As well as any of them all: I that I can,
And kisse him too as sweetly. Oh! here's the mad-man.

Enter Aphron.

    Ap. *Hercules, Hercules,* ho *Hercules,* where are you?
Lend me thy club and skin, and when I ha' done,
Ile fling them to thee againe, why *Hercules?*
Pox on you, are you drunke? can you not answer?
Ile travell then without them, and doe wonders.
    Tru. I quake all over, worse then any fitt
Of the palsie which I have had this forty yeares
Could make me doe.
    Ap. So I ha' found the plot out,
First I'le climbe up, on Porter *Atlas* shoulders,
And then craule into Heaven, and I'me sure
I cannot chuse but find her there.
    Tru. What will become of me if he should see me?
Truly he's a good proper Gentleman,
If he were not mad, I would not be so 'fraid of him.
    Ap. What have I caught thee fayrest of all women?
Where hast thou hid thy selfe so long from *Aphron?*
Aphron who hath beene dead till this blest minute?

ABRAHAM COWLEY

Tru. Ha, ha, ha, whom doth he take me for!
Ap. Thy skin is whiter then the snowy feathers
Of *Leda's* Swannes.
Tru. Law you there now,—
I thought I was not so unhandsome, as they'd make me.
Ap. Thy haires are brighter then the Moones,
Then when she spreads her beames and fills her orbe.
Trug. Beshrew their heart that call this Gentleman mad,
He hath his senses Ile warrant him, about him,
As well as any fellow of them all.
Apu. Thy teeth are like two Arches made of Ivory,
Of purest Ivory.
Tru. I for those few I have,
I thinke they're white enough.
Ap. Thou art as fresh as May is, and thy look
Is picture of the Spring.
Tru. Nay, I am but some fourscore yeares and tenne
And beare my age well; yet *Alupis* sayes
I looke like January, but I'le teach the knave
Another tune I'le warrant him.
Ap. Thy lips are cheryes, let me tast them sweet?
Tru. You have begd so handsomly.
Ap. Ha! yee good Gods defend me! 'tis a Witch, a Hag.
Trug. What am I?
Ap. A witch, one that did take the shape
Of my best Mistris, but thou couldst not long
Belye her purenesse.
Tru. Now he's starke mad againe upon the sudden;
He had some sense even now.
Ap. Thou lookst as if thou wert some wicked woman
Frighted out of the grave; defend me, how
Her eyes doe sinke into their ugly holes,
As if they were afraid to see the light.
Tru. I will not be abus'd thus, that I will not.
My haire was bright even now, and my lookes fresh:
Am I so quickly changed?
Ap. Her breath infects the ayre, and sowes a pestilence
Where e're it comes; what hath she there?
I! these are apples made up with the stings
Of Scorpions, and the bloud of Basiliskes;

Which being swallowed up, a thousand paines
Eate on the heart, and gnaw the entrailes out.
  Tru. Thou lyest; I, that thou do'st,
For these are honest apples, that they are;
I'me sure I gathered them my selfe.
  Ap. From the Stygian tree; Give them me quickly, or
      I will—
  Tru. What will you doe? pray take them.
  Ap. Get thee gone quickly, from me, for I know thee;
Thou art *Tisiphone.*
  Tru. 'Tis false; for I know no such woman.
I'me glad I am got from him, would I had
My apples too, but 'tis no matter though,
I'le have a better gift for *Callidorus*
To morrow.
  Ap. The fiend is vanisht from me,
And hath left these behind for me to tast of,
But I will be too cunning; Thus I'le scatter them,
Now I have spoyl'd her plot; Unhappy hee
Who finds them.   *Exit.*

            Finis Actus secundi.

Actus III. Scæna I.

Enter Florellus.

THe Sun five times hath gone his yearly progresse,
    Since last I saw my Sister, and returning
Bigge with desire to view my native *Sicilie*,
I found my aged parents sadly mourning
The funerall (for to them it seemes no lesse)
Of their departed Daughter ; what a welcome
This was to me, all in whose hearts a veine
Of marble growes not, easily may conceive
Without the dumbe perswasions of my teares.
Yet as if that were nothing, and it were
A kind of happinesse in misery
If't come without an army to attend it,
As I pass'd through these woods I saw a woman
Whom her attyre call'd Shepheardesse, but face
Some disguis'd Angell, or a Silvan Goddesse ;
It struck such adoration (for I durst not
Harbour the love of so divine a beauty)
That ever since I could not teach my thoughts
Another object ; In this happy place
(Happy her presence made it) she appear'd,
And breath'd fresh honours on the smiling trees,
Which owe more of their gallantry to her
Then to the musky kisses of the West wind.
Ha ! sure 'tis she ; Thus doth the Sunne breake forth
From the blacke curtaine of an envious cloud.

Enter Alupis, Bellula, Hylace.

Al. *For 'tis but a folly,* &c.
Hyl. Wee did not send for you ; pray leave us.
Alu. No, by this light, not till I see you cry ;
When you have shed some penitentiall teares

96

LOVES RIDDLE

For wronging of *Palæmon*, there may be
A truce concluded betwixt you and me.
   Bell. This is uncivill
To thrust into our company; doe you thinke
That we admire your wit? pray goe to them
That doe, we would be private.
   Al. To what purpose?
You'd aske how many shepheards she hath strooken,
Which is the properest man? which kisses sweetest?
Which brings her the best presents? And then tell
What a fine man wooes you, how redde his lips are?
How bright his eyes are? and what dainty sonnets
He hath composed in honor of your beauty?
And then at last, with what rare tricks you foole him?
These are your learn'd discourses; but were all
Men of my temperance, and wisdome too,
You should wooe us, I, and wooe hardly too
Before you got us.
   Flo. Oh prophanenesse!
Can hee so rudely speake to that blest virgin,
And not be strucken dumbe?
   Al. Nay, you have both a mind to me; I know it,
But I will marry neither; I come hither
Not to gaze on you, or extoll your beauty;
I come to vex you.
   Flo. Ruder yet? I cannot,
I will not suffer this; madde fellow, is there
No other Nymph in all these spacious woods,
To fling thy wilde, and saucie laughter at,
But her, whom thy great Deity even *Pan*
Himselfe would honor, doe not dare to utter
The smallest accent if not cloath'd with reverence,
Nay, doe not looke upon her but with eyes
As humble and submissive as thou wouldst
Upon the brow of Majesty, when it frownes,
I speake but that which duty binds us all to,
Thou shalt not thinke upon her, no not thinke,
Without as much respect and honor to her
As holy men in superstitious zeale
Give to the Images they worship.

Bell. Oh! this is the Gentleman courted me th'other day.

Al. Why? have you got a Pattent to restraine me?
Or doe you thinke your glorious sute can fright me?
'Twould doe you much more credit at the Theater,
To rise betwixt the Acts, and looke about
The boxes, and then cry, God save you Madame,
Or beare you out in quarreling at an Ordinary,
And make your oathes become you; have you shown
Your gay apparell every where in towne,
That you can afford us the sight oft, or
Hath that Grand Divell whose eclipped sergeant,
Frighted you out of the City?

Flo. Your loose jests
When they are shot at me, I scorne to take
Any revenge upon them, but neglect,
For then 'tis rashnesse only, but as soone
As you begin to violate her name,
Nature and conscience too bids me be angry,
For then 'tis wickednesse.

Al. Well, if it be so,
I hope you can forgive the sinne that's past
Without the dolefull sight of trickling teares,
For I have eyes of pumice; I'me content
To let her rest in quiet, but you have given me
Free leave t'abuse you, on the condition
You will revenge it only with neglect,
For then 'tis rashnesse only.

Flo. What are you biting?
Where did you pick these fragments up of wit.

Al. Where I pay'd deare enough a conscience for them,
They should be more then fragments by their price,
I bought them sir, even from the very Merchants,
I scorn'd to deale with your poore City pedlers, that sell
By retayle: But let that passe; *For 'tis but a folly:*

Flo. Then you have seene the City.

Al. I and felt it too, I thanke the Divell; I'me sure
It suckt up in three yeares the whole estate
My father left, though he were counted rich,
A pox of forlorne Captaines, pittifull things,
Whom you mistake for souldiers, only by

LOVES RIDDLE

Their sounding oathes, and a buffe jerkin, and
Some Histories which they have learn'd by roate,
Of battailes fought in *Persia*, or *Polonia*,
Where they themselves were of the conquering side,
Although God knowes one of the City Captaines,
Arm'd with broad scarfe, feather, and scarlet breeches,
When he instructs the youth on Holy dayes,
And is made sicke with fearfull noyse of Guns,
Would pose them in the art Military ; these
Were my first Leeches.

    Flo. So, no wonder then you spent so fast.

    Al. Pish, these were nothing :
I grew to keepe your Poets company
Those are the soakers, they refin'd me first
Of those grosse humors that are bred by money
And made me streight a wit, as now you see,
For 'tis but a folly.

    Flo. But hast thou none to fling thy salt upon
But these bright virgins ?

    Al. Yes now you are here ;
You are as good a theame as I could wish.

    Hy. 'Tis best for me to goe, whilst they are talking,
For if I steale not from *Alupis* sight,
He'le follow me all day to vex me.   *Exit.*

    Al. What are you vanishing coy Mistris *Hylace* ?
Nay, I'le be with you streight, but first I'le fetch
Palæmon, now if he can play his part
And leave off whining, wee'le have princely sport,
Well, I may live in time to have the women
Scratch out my eyes, or else scould me to death,
I shall deserve it richly : Farewell Sir :
I have employment with the Damsell gone
And cannot now intend you.   *Exit.*

    Flo. They're both gone,
Direct me now good love, and teach my tongue
Th'inchantments that thou woo'dst thy *Psyche* with.

    Bell. Farewell Sir.

    Flo. Oh ! be not so cruell,
Let me enjoy my selfe a little while,
Which without you I cannot.

Bell. Pray let me goe,
To tend my sheepe, there's none that lookes to them,
And if my father misse me, he'le so chide.

    Flo. Alas! thou needest not feare, for th'Wolfe himselfe
Though hunger whet the fury of its nature,
Would learne to spare thy pretty flocks, and be
As carefull as the shepheards dog to guard them,
Nay if he should not, *Pan* would present be,
And keepe thy tender lambes in safety for thee,
For though he be a God he would not blush
To be thy servant.

    Bell. Oh! you're courtly Sir.
But your fine words will not defend my sheepe,
Or stop them if they wander; Let me goe.

    Flo. Are you so fearefull of your cattels losse?
Yet so neglectfull of my perishing,
(For without you how can I choose but perish?)
Though I my selfe were most contemptible,
Yet for this reason only, that I love
And honour you, I deserve more then they doe.

    Bell. What would you doe, that thus you urge my stay?

    Flo. Nothing I sweare that should offend a Saint,
Nothing which can call up thy maiden bloud
To lend thy face a blush, nothing which chaste
And vertuous sisters can deny their Brothers,
I doe confesse I love you, but the fire
In which *Jove* courted his ambitious Mistris,
Or that by holy men on Altars kindled,
Is not so pure as mine is; I would only
Gaze thus upon thee; feed my hungry eyes
Sometimes with those bright tresses, which the wind
Farre happier then I, playes up and downe in,
And sometimes with thy cheekes, those rosy twins;
Then gently touch thy hand, and often kist it,
Till thou thy selfe shouldst checke my modesty
And yeeld thy lips, but further, though thou should'st
Like other maids with weake resistance aske it,
(Which I am sure thou wilt not) I'de not offer
Till lawfull *Hymen* joyne us both, and give
A licence unto my desires.

LOVES RIDDLE

Bell. Which I
Need not bestow much language to oppose,
Fortune and nature have forbidden it,
When they made me a rude and homely wench
You (if your clothes and cariage be not lyers,)
By state and birth a Gentleman.
   Flo. I hope
I may without suspition of a boaster
Say that I am so, else my love were impudence
For doe you thinke wise Nature did intend
You for a Shepheardesse, when she bestow'd
Such paines in your creation? would she fetch
The perfumes of *Arabia* for your breath?
Or ransack *Pestum* of her choycest roses
T'adorne your cheekes? would she bereave the rock
Of corall for your lips? and catch two starres
As they were falling, which she form'd your eyes of?
Would she her selfe turne work-woman and spinne
Threeds of the finest gold to be your tresses?
Or rob the Great to make one Microcosme?
And having finisht quite the beauteous wonder,
Hide it from publique view and admiration!
No; she would set it on some Pyramide,
To be the spectacle of many eyes:
And it doth grieve me that my niggard fortune
Rays'd me not up to higher eminency,
Not that I am ambitious of such honors
But that through them I might be made more worthy
To enjoy you.
   Bell. You are for ought I see
Too great already; I will either live
An undefiled virgin as I am
Or if I marry, not belye my birth,
But joyne my selfe to some plaine vertuous shepheard
(For *Callidorus* is so, and I will ⎱ Aside.
   be either his or no bodyes.)⎰
   Flo. Pray heare me.
   Bell. Alas! I have Sir, and doe therefore now
Prepare to answer, if this passion
Bee love, my fortune bids me to deny you;

If lust, my honesty commands to scorne you,
Farewell.

Flo. O stay a little! but two words: she's gone,
Gone like the glorious Sun, which being sette
Night creepes behind and covers all; some way
I must seeke out to win her, or what's easier
(And the blind man himselfe without a guide
May find) some way to dye; would I had beene
Borne a poore shepheard in these shady woods.
Nature is cruell in her benefits
And when she gives us honey, mingles gall.
She said that if she married, the woods
Should find a husband for her. I will wooe her
In Sylvan habit, then perhaps she'le love me—
But yet I will not, that's in vaine; I will too,
It cannot hurt to try.   *Exit.*

Enter Alupis, Palæmon, *after them* Hylace.

Al. Nay come, she's just behind us, are you ready?
When she scoulds, bee you lowdest, if she cry
Then laugh abundantly, thus we will vex her
Into a good conceit of you.

Pal. I'le warrant you; you have instructed me enough,
Shee comes.

Hyl. Is't possible that *Bellula*—

Pal. Fayre creature—

Hyl. Sure thou wert borne to trouble me, who sent for thee?

Pa. Whom all the Nymphs (though women use to be
As you know, envious of anothers beauty)
Confesse the pride and glory of these woods.

Hyl. When did you make this speech? 'tis a most neat one
Goe, get you gone, looke to your rotting cattell,
You'le never keepe a wife, who are not able
To keepe your sheepe.

Al. Good! she abuses him
Now 'tis a miracle he doth not cry.

Pal. Thou whom the starres might envy 'cause they are
Outshone by thee on earth.

Hyl. Pray get you gon,

Or hold your prating tongue, for whatsoever
Thou sayest, I will not heare a syllable,
Much lesse answer thee.

   Pa. No ; I'le try that streight
I have a present here—
Which if you'le give me leave, I shall presume
To dedicate to your service.

   Hy. You're so cunning,
And have such pretty wayes to entice me with,
Come let me see it.

   Pa. Oh ! have you found a tongue ?
I thought I had not beene worth an answer ?

   Hy. How now ; what tricks are these ?
Give it me quickly, or—

   Pa. Pray get you gon, or hold your prating tongue ;
For whatsoever thou sayest I will not heare
A syllable, much lesse answer thee.

   Al. Good boy 'faith : now let me come.

   Hy. This is some plot I see, would I were gone,
I had as lief see the wolfe as this *Alupis.*

   Al. Here's a fine Ring, I faith, a very pretty one,
Doe your teeth water at it Damsell ? ha ?
Why we will sell our sheepe, and oxen, girle,
Hang them scurvy beasts, to buy you pretty knacks,
That you might laugh at us, and call us fooles
And jeere us too, as farre as your wit reaches,
Bid us be gone, and when we have talkt two houres,
Deny to answer us ; Nay you must stay   *She offers*
And heare a little more.   *to be gone.*

   Hy. Must I ? are you
The master of my businesse ? I will not.

   Al. Faith but you shall ; heare therefore and be patient.
I'le have thee made a Lady, yes a Lady,
For when thou'st got a chaine about thy necke
And comely bobes to dandle in thine eares ;
When thou'st perfum'd thy haire, that if thy breath
Should be corrupted, it might scape unknowne,
And then bestow'd two houres in curling it,
Uncovering thy breast hithe[r], thine armes hither,
And had thy *Fucus* curiously lay'd on ;

Thou'dst be the finest proud thing, Ile warrant thee
Thou would'st outdoe them all. So, now goe thee to her
And let me breathe a little ; *For 'tis but a folly*, &c.

   Hy. Oh ! is't your turne to speake againe ? no doubt
But we shall have a good oration then,
For they call you the learned shepheard ; well
This is your love I see.

   Pa. Ha, ha, ha,
What should I love a stone ? or wooe a picture ?
Alas ! I must be gone, for whatsoe're
I say, you will not heare a syllable
Much lesse answer ; goe, you thinke you are,
So singularly handsome, when alas,
Galla, Menalca's daughter, *Eellula,*
Or *Amaryllis* overcome you quite.

   Hy. This is a scurvy fellow ; Ile fit him for't,
No doubt they are ; I wonder that your wisdome
Will trouble me so long with your vaine suite,
Why doe you not wooe them ?

   Pa. Perhaps I doe ;
I'le not tell you, because you'le envy them,
And alwayes be dispraising of their beauties.

   Hy. It shall appeare I will not, for I'le sooner
Embrace a Scorpion, then thee, base man.

   Pa. Ha, ha, ha.
Alupis do'st thou heare her ? she'le cry presently,
Doe not despaire yet girle, by your good carriage
You may recall me still ; some few entreatyes
Mingled with teares may get a kisse perhaps.

   Hy. I would not kisse thee for the wealth of *Sicily*
Thou wicked perjur'd Fellow.

   Pal. *Alupis,* eh !
We have incenst her too much ! how she lookes ?
Prithee *Alupis* helpe me to intreate,
You know we did but jest, deare *Hylace,*
Alupis, prithee speake, best, beauteous *Hylace,*
I did but doe't to try you, pray forgive me,
Upon my knees I begge it.

   Al. Here's a pretious foole.

   Hyl. Do'st thou still mock me ? hast thou found more wayes ?

LOVES RIDDLE

Thou need'st not vex thy wit to move my hate,
Sooner the Sunne and starres shall shine together,
Sooner the Wolfe make peace with tender lambes
Then I with thee; thou'rt a disease to me
And wound'st my eyes.   *Exit.*

   Pal. Eternall night involve me! if there be
A punishment, (but sure there is not any)
Greater then what her anger hath inflicted,
May that fall on me too? how have I fool'd
Away my hopes? how have I beene my selfe
To my owne selfe a theefe?

   Al. I told you this,
That if she should but frowne, you must needs fall
To your old tricks againe.

   Pa. Is this your art?
A lovers curse upon it; Oh! *Alupis*
Thou hast done worse then murthered me: for which
May all thy flocks pine and decay like me,
May thy curst wit hurt all; but most its Master,
May'st thou (for I can wish no greater ill)
Love one like me, and be, like me, contemn'd.
Thou 'ast all the darts my tongue can fling at thee,
But I will be reveng'd some other way
Before I dye, which cannot now be long.

   Alu. Poore Shepheard, I begin to pitty him.
I'le see if I can comfort him; *Palæmon,*—

   Pal. Nay, doe not follow me, griefe, passion
And troubled thoughts are my companions,
Those I had rather entertaine then thee,
If you choose this way let me goe the other,
And in both parts distracted error, thee
May revenge quickly meet, may death meet me.   *Exit.*

   Alu. Well, I say *Pan* defend me from a lover
Of all tame mad-men certainly they're the worst,
I would not meet with two such creatures more
For any good, they without doubt would put me,
If it be possible into a fit of sadnesse,
Though it *Be but a folly*, &c.
Well; I must find some plot yet to salve this
Because I have engaged my wit in the businesse,

And 'twould be a great sca[n]dall to the Citie
If I who have spent my meanes there, should not be
Able to cheate these shepheards. How now, how now,
Have we more distressed lovers here? *Enter* Aphron.

Aph. No, I'me a madde man.

Al. I gave a shrewd ghesse at it at first sight
I thought thee little better.

Aph. Better? why?
Can there be any better then a mad-man?
I tell thee, I came here to be a mad-man,
Nay, doe not disswade me from't, I would bee
A very Madman.

Al. A good resolution!
'Tis as gentile a course as you can take,
I have knowne great ones have not beene asham'd of't,
But what cause pray drove you into this humour?

Aph. Why a Mistris,
And such a beauteous one—do'st thou see no body?
She sits upon a throne amongst the starres
And outshines them, looke up and bee amazed
Such was her beauty here,—sure there doe lye
A thousand vapours in thy sleepy eyes,
Do'st thou not see her yet? nor yet, nor yet?

Alu. No in good troth.

Aph. Thou'rt dull and ignorant,
Not skill'd at all in deepe Astrology.
Let me instruct thee?

Alu. Prithee doe, for thou
Art in an admirable case to teach now.

Ap. I'le shew thee first all the cœlestiall signes,
And to begin, looke on that horned head.

Al. Whose is't? *Jupiters?*

Ap. No, 'tis the Ramme!
Next that, the spacious Bull fils up the place.

Al. The Bull? 'tis well, the fellowes of the Guard
Intend not to come thither; if they did
The Gods might chance to lose their beefe.

Ap. And then,
Yonder's the signe of *Gemini*, do'st see it?

Alu. Yes, yes, I see one of the zealous sisters

LOVES RIDDLE

Mingled in friendship with a holy Brother
To beget Reformations.

Ap. And there sits *Capricorne*.

Al. A Welchman is't not?

Ap. There *Cancer* creepes along with gouty pace,
As if his feet were sleepy, there, Doe you marke it?

Al. I, I, Alderman-like a walking after dinner,
His paunch orechargd with capon and with white broth.

Ap. But now, now, now, now, gaze eternally
Hadst thou as many eyes as the blacke night
They would be all too little; seest thou *Virgo?*

Al. No by my troth, there are so few on earth,
I should be loth to sweare there's more in heaven,
Then onely one.

Ap. That was my Mistris once, but is of late
Translated to the height of deserv'd glory,
And addes new ornaments to the wondring heavens.
Why doe I stay behind then, a meere nothing
Without her presence to give life and being?
If there be any hill whose lofty top
Nature hath made contiguous with heaven,
Though it be steepe, rugged as *Neptunes* brow,
Though arm'd with cold, with hunger, and diseases,
And all the other souldiers of misery,
Yet I would climbe it up, that I might come
Next place to thee, and there be made a starre.

Al. I prithee doe, for amongst all the beasts
That helpe to make up the cœlestiall signes
There's a Calfe wanting yet.

Ap. But stay—

Al. Nay, I have learn'd enough Astrology.

Ap. Hunger and faintnesse have already seaz'd me,
'Tis a long journey thither, I shall want
Provision; canst thou helpe me, gentle shepheard?
And when I am come thither I will snatch
The Crowne of *Ariadne*, and fling't downe
To thee for a reward.

Al. No doubt you will;
But you shall need no victuals, when you have ended
Your toylesome journey, kill the Ram you talke of,
And feed your selfe with most celestiall mutton.

Ap. Thou'rt in the right, if they deny me that
I'le pluck the Beare downe from the Artique Pole,
And drowne it in those waters it avoids,
And dares not touch; I'le tugge the *Hyades*
And make them to sinke downe in spight of Nature;
I'le meet with *Charles* his Wayne, and overturne it
And breake the wheeles of't, till *Böotes* start
For feare, and grow more slow then e're he was.

Al. By this good light he'le snuffe the Moone anon,
Here's words indeed would fright a Conjurer
'Tis pitty that these huge Giganticke speeches
Are not upon the stage, they would doe rarely
For none would understand them, I could wish
Some Poet here now, with his table-booke.

Ap. I'le cuffe with *Pollux*, and out-ride thee, *Castor*,
When the fierce Lyon roares I'le plucke his heart out
And be call'd *Cordelion*; I'le grapple with the Scorpion,
Take his sting out and fling him to the earth.

Al. To me good Sir,
It may perhaps rayse me a great estate
With shewing it up and downe for pence apiece.

Ap. *Alcides* freed the earth from savadge monsters,
And I will free the heavens and bee call'd
Don Hercules Alcido de secundo.

Al. A brave Castilian name.

Ap. 'Tis a hard taske,
But if that fellow did so much by strength,
I may well do't arm'd both with love and fury.

Alup. Of which thou hast enough.

Aph. Farewell thou ratte.
The Cedar bids the shrub adiew.

Al. Farewell
Don Hercules Alcido de secundo.
If thou scar'st any, 'twill be by that name.
This is a wonderfull rare fellow, and
I like his humor mightily—who's here?

Enter Truga.

The Chronicle of a hundred yeares agoe!
How many crowes hath she outliv'd? sure death
Hath quite forgot her; by this *Memento mori*

LOVES RIDDLE

I must invent some trick to helpe *Palæmon*.

Tru. I am going againe to *Callidorus*,
But I have got a better present now,
My owne ring made of good Ebony,
Which a yong handsome shepheard bestow'd on me
Some fourescore years agoe, then they all lov'd me,
I was a handsome Lasse, I wosse in those dayes.

Al. I so thou wert I'le warrant; here's good signe of 't
Now Ile begin the worke, Reverend *Truga*,
Whose very Autumne shewes how glorious
The spring-time of your youth was—

Tru. Are you come
To put your mocks upon me?

Al. I doe confesse indeed my former speeches
Have beene too rude and saucy; I have flung
Madde jests too wildly at you; but considering
The reverence which is due to age, and vertue,
I have repented, will you see my teares?
And beleeve them? Oh for an onyon now!
Or I shall laugh alowd; ha, ha, ha!   *Aside.*

Tru. Alas good soule I doe forgive you truly;
I would not have you weepe for me, indeed
I ever thought you would repent at last.

Al. You might well,
But the right valewing of your worth and vertue
Hath turn'd the folly of my former scorne
Into a wiser reverence, pardon me
If I say love.

Tru. I, I, with all my heart,
But doe you speake sincerely?

Al. Oh! it grieves me
That you should doubt it, what I spoke before
Were lyes, the off-spring of a foolish rashnesse,
I see some sparks still of your former beauty,
Which spight of time still flourish.

Tru. Why, I am not
So old as you imagined, I am yet
But fourescore yeares. Am I a January now?
How doe you thinke? I alwayes did beleeve
You'd be of another opinion one day;
I know you did but jest.

Al. Oh no, oh no, (I see it takes) *Aside.*
How you bely your age—for—let me see—
A man would take you—let me see—for—
Some forty yeares or thereabouts (I meane foure hundred)
Not a jot more I sweare. *Aside.*
    Tru. Oh no! you flatter me,
But I looke something fresh indeed this morning.
I should please *Callidorus* mightily,
But I'le not goe perhaps; this fellow is
As handsome quite as he, and I perceive
He loves me hugely, I protest I will not Aside.
Have him grow madde, which he may chance to doe
If I should scorne him.
    Al. I have something here
Which I would faine reveale to you, but dare not
Without your licence.
    Tru. Doe in *Pans* name, doe; now, now.
    Al. The comely gravity which adornes your age,
And makes you still seeme lovely, hath so strucken me—
    Tru. Alas good soule! I must seeme coy at first,
But not too long, for feare I should quite lose him.
    Al. That I shall perish utterly, unlesse
Your gentle nature helpe me.
    Tru. Alas good Shepheard!
And in troth I faine would helpe you
But I am past those vanities of love.
    Al. Oh no!
Wise nature which preserv'd your life till now
Doth it because you should enjoy these pleasures
Which doe belong to life, if you deny me,
I am undone.
    Tru. Well you should not win me
But that I am loath to be held the cause
Of any young mans ruine, doe not thinke it
My want of chastity, but my good nature
Which would see no one hurt.
    Al. Ah pretty soule! Aside.
How supple 'tis like wax before the Sun!
Now cannot I chuse but kisse her, there's the plague of 't,
Let's then joyne our hearts, and seale them with a kisse.
    Tru. Well, let us then:

LOVES RIDDLE

'Twere incivility to be your debtor,
I'le give you back againe your kisse, sweetheart,
And come in th'afternoone, I'le see you ;
My husband will be gone to sell some kine,
And *Hylace* tending the sheepe, till then
Farewell good Duck   *(Offers to goe.)*
But doe you heare, because you shall remember   *(Turnes*
To come I'le give thee here this Ebon ring   *back.)*
But doe not weare it, lest my husband chance
To see't : Farewell Duck.
    Al.   Lest her husband chance
To see't ; she cannot deny this, here's enough ;
My Scœne of love is done then ; is she gone ?
I'le call her back ; ho *Truga* ; *Truga* hô :
    Tru.   Why doe you call me Duck ?
    Al.   Only to aske one foolish question of thee :
Ha'n't you a husband ?
    Tru.   Yes, you know I have.
    Al.   And doe you love him ?
    Tru.   Why doe you aske ? I doe.
    Al.   Yet you can be content to make him cuckold ?
    Tru.   Rather then to see you perish in your flames.
    Al.   Why art thou now two hundred yeares of age,
Yet hast no more discretion but to thinke
That I could love thee ? ha, ha, were't mine
I'de sell thee to some gardiner, thou wouldst serve
To scare away the theeves as well as crowes.
    Tru.   Oh, you're dispos'd to jest I see, Farewell.
    Al.   Nay, I'me in very earnest ; I love you ?
Why thy face is a vizard.
    Trug.   Leave off these tricks, I shall be angry else,
And take away the favours I bestow'd.
    Al.   'Tis knowne that thou hast eyes by the holes only,
Which are crept farther in, then thy nose out,
And that's almost a yard ; thy quarreling teeth
Of such a colour are, that they themselves
Scare one another, and doe stand at distance.
Thy skin hangs loose as if it fear'd the bones
(For flesh thou hast not) and is growne so black
That a wilde Centaure would not meddle with thee.
To conclude, Nature made thee when she was

Only dispos'd to jest, and length of time
Hath made thee more ridiculous.
    Tru. Base villaine, is this your love?
Give me my ring againe?
    Al. No, no; soft there:
I intend to bestow it on your husband;
He'le keepe it better farre then you have done.
    Trug. What shall I doe? *Alupis*, good *Alupis*,
Stay but a little while, pray doe but heare me.
    Al. No, I'le come to you in the afternoone
Your husband will be selling of some kine
And *Hylace* tending the sheepe.
    Tru. Pray heare me, command me anything
And be but silent of this, good *Alupis*;
Hugh, Hugh, Hugh.
    Al. Yes, yes, I will be silent,
I'le only blow a trumpet on yon hill,
Till all the countrey swaines are flockt about me,
Then shew the ring, and tell the passages
'Twixt you and me.
    Trug. Alas! I am undone.
    Al. Well now 'tis ripe; I have had sport enough
Since I behold your penitentiall teares
I'le propose this to you, if you can get
Your Daughter to be married to *Palæmon*
This day, for I'le allow no longer time;
To morrow I'le restore your ring, and sweare
Never to mention what is past betwixt us,
If not—you know what followes—take your choyse.
    Tru. I'le doe my best endevour.
    Al. Goe make hast then,
You know your time's but short, and use it well:
Now if this faile the Divel's in all wit.   *Exit Truga.*
I'le goe and thrust it forward, if it take,
        I'le sing away the day,
        For 'tis but a folly
        To be melancholly,
    Let's live here whilst wee may.   *Exit.*

Finis Actus Tertii.

Actus IIII.   Scæna I.

Enter *Callidorus*, *Bellula*, *Florellus*.

Cal. Pray follow me no more, me thinks that modesty
    Which is so lively painted in your face
Should prompt your maiden heart with feares and blushes
To trust your selfe in so much privatnesse
With one you know not.
    Bel. I should love those feares
And call them hopes, could I perswade my selfe,
There were so much heate in you as to cause them;
Prithee leave me; if thou dost hope successe
To thine owne love, why interrupt'st thou mine?
    Flo. If love cause you
To follow him, how can you angry bee?
Because love forces me without resistance
To doe the same to you?
    Bell. Love should not grow
So subtill as to play with arguments.
    Flo. Love should not be an enemy to reason.
    Cal. To love is of it selfe a kind of Folly,
But to love one who cannot render back
Equall desire, is nothing else but madnesse.
    Bell. Tell him so; 'tis a lesson he should learne.
    Flo. Not to love is of 't selfe a kind of hardnesse,
But not to love him who hath alwayes woo'd you
With chast desires, is nothing lesse then tyranny.
    Bell. Tell him so; 'tis a lesson he should learne.
    Call. Why doe you follow him that flyes from you?
    Flo. Why doe you fly from him that followes you?
    Bell. Why doe you follow? Why doe you fly from me?
    Call. The Fates command me that I must not love you.
    Flo. The Fates command me that I needs must love you.

ABRAHAM COWLEY

Bell. The Fates impose the like command on me,
That you I must, that you I cannot love.
    Flo. Unhappy man! when I begin to cloath
My love with words, and court her with perswasions,
She stands unmov'd, and doth not cleare her brow
Of the least wrinkle which sate there before;
So when the waters with an amorous noyse
Leape up and downe, and in a wanton dance
Kisse the dull rocke, that scornes their fond embraces,
And darts them back; till they with terror scattered,
Drop downe againe in teares.
    Bell. Unhappy woman!
When I begin to shew him all my passion,
He flyes from me, and will not cleare his brow
Of any cloud which covered it before;
So when the ravishing Nightingale hath tun'd
Her mournfull notes, and silenc'd all the birds,
Yet the deafe wind flirts by, and in disdaine
With a rude whistle leaves her.
    Cal. We are all three
Unhappy; borne to be the proud example
Of Loves great God-head, not his God-like goodnesse.
Let us not call upon our selves those miseries
Which love hath not, and those it hath beare bravely,
Our desires yet are like some hidden text,
Where one word seemes to contradict another,
They are Loves nonsense, wrapt up in thicke clouds
Till Fate be pleas'd to write a Commentary,
Which doubtlesse 'twill; till then [let] us endure,
And sound a parlee to our passions.
    Bell. We may joyne hands though, may we not?
    Flo. We may, and lips too may we not?
    Bell. We may; come let's sit downe and talke.
    Cal. And looke upon each other.
    Flo. Then kisse againe.
    Bell. Then looke.
    Cal. Then talke againe,
What are we like? the hand of Mother Nature
Would be quite pos'd to make our simile.
    Flo. We are the Trigon in Loves Hemisphere.

LOVES RIDDLE

Bel. We are three strings on *Venus* dainty'st Lute,
Where all three hinder one anothers musick,
Yet all three joyne and make one harmony.
Call. We are three flowers of *Venus* dainty garden,
Where all three hinder one anothers odor,
Yet all three joyne, and make one nosegay up.
Flo. Come let us kisse againe.
Bell. And looke.
Call. And talke.
Flo. Nay rather sing, your lips are Natures organs,
And made for nought lesse sweet then harmony.
Call. Pray doe.
Bell. Though I forfeit
My little skill in singing to your wit,
Yet I will do't, since you command.

Song.

It is a punishment to love,
And not to love a punishment doth prove;
But of all paines there's no such paine,
As 'tis to love, and not be lov'd againe.

Till sixteene parents we obey,
After sixteene, men steale our hearts away:
How wretched are we women growne,
Whose wills, whose minds, whose hearts are ne're our owne!

Call. Thanke you.
Flo. For ever be the tales of *Orpheus* silent,
Had the same age seene thee, that very Poet,
Who drew all to him by his harmony,
Thou would'st have drawne to thee.
Cal. Come shall we rise?
Bell. If it please you, I will.
Call. I cannot chuse
But pitty these two Lovers, and am taken
Much with the serious trifles of their passion.
Let's goe and see, if we can breake this net
In which we all are caught; if any man
Aske who we are, we'le say we are Loves riddle.   *Exeunt.*

ABRAHAM COWLEY

Enter Ægon, Palæmon, Alupis.

Pa. Thou art my better Genius, honest *Ægon*,
Al. And what am I?
Pa. My selfe, my soule, my friend,
Let me hugge thee *Alupis*, and thee *Ægon*,
Thee for inventing it, thee for putting it
In act; But doe you thinke the plot will hold?
Alu. Hold? why I'le warrant thee it shall hold,
Till we have ty'd you both in wedlock fast,
Then let the bonds of Matrimonie hold you
If 'twill, if that will not neither, I can tell you
What will I'me sure; A Halter.
      Then sing, &c.—
Ægon. Come, shall we knock?
Al. I doe; *For 'tis*, &c.—
Ægon. Ho *Truga*; who's within there?
Al. You, *Winter*, Ho, you that the grave expected
Some hundred yeares agoe, you that intend
To live till you turne *Skeleton*, and make
All men aweary of you but Physitians,
Pox on you, will you come.

Enter Truga.

Tru. I come, I come, who's there? who's there?
Al. Oh, in good time,
Are you crawl'd here at last? what are you ready
To give your Daughter up? the time makes hast
Looke here, doe you know this ring?
Tru. Harke aside I pray,
You have not told these, have you?
Al. No good Duck,
Only I told them that your mind was altered,
And that you lik'd *Palæmon*, so we three
Came here to plot the meanes.
Tru. So, so, you're welcome
Will you goe in and talke about it?   *Exeunt.*

LOVES RIDDLE

Enter Hylace.

Hyl. I wonder why my mother should invite,
Alupis and *Palæmon* into th' house:
Shee is not of my mind, nay, not the mind
Which she her selfe was of, but yesterday,
Besides as soone as they came in, she bid me
To get me gone, and leave them there in private,
By your good favour Mother, I must be
For this time disobedient; here Ile hearken.

Enter Truga, Palæmon, Ægon, Alupis.

Ægon. Come Ile tell you,
You know your husband hath refused *Palæmon*
Because his meanes were not unequall only
To his desires, but to your Daughters portion,
To salve this grand exception of *Melarnus*
I'le promise that *Palæmon* shall be made
My heire.
   Tru. Alas he knowes you have a Daughter!
   Æg. It is reported she is falne in love
With the new shepheard, for which cause I'le seeme
To be incenst most sharply, and forsweare
E're to acknowledge her for child of mine.
   Tru. 'Tis very well;
It grieves me truly that *Palæmon* should—
   Al. Perish in his owne flames; is't not so *Truga*?
I know you're gentle; and your peevish Daughter
Had not her cruelty from you, good soule.
   Pa. Why doe we stay? Each minute that we lose to
            you is only
A minute, but to me a day at least,
Why are we not now seeking of *Melarnus*?
Why is he not yet found? alas, that's nothing,
Me thinkes he should have given consent e're this;
Why are not I and beauteous *Hylace*
Married together?
   Hyl. Soft good hasty Lover,
I shall quite breake the neck of your large hopes,
Or I'me mistaken much.

Æg.   Come let's be gone

Truga, Farewell.   Be silent and assistant.

Al.   Or else you know what I have ; goe, no more.

Tru.   I'le warrant you : I am not to be taught
At this age, I thanke *Pan*, in such a businesse.
Farewell all.   *Exeunt.*

Al.   *Come sing*, &c.

Hy.   I know not whether griefe or else amazement
Seazeth me most, to see my aged Mother
Grow so unnaturall ; I faine would weepe,
But when I thinke with what an unfear'd blow
I shall quite dash their cunning, I can hardly
Bridle in laughter, Fate helps the innocent,
Although my Mother's false, the Gods are true.   *Exit.*

Enter Clariana *and her Maid.*

Cla.   Did you command the servants to withdraw ?

M.   I did forsooth.

Cla.   And have you shut the doores ?

M.   Yes.

Cl.   Is there none can over-heare our talke ?

M.   Your curious enquiry much amazeth me,
And I could wish you would excuse my boldnesse
If I should aske the reason.

Cl.   Thou knowest well
That thou hast found me always liker to
Thy Kinswoman then Mistris, that thy brest
Has beene the Cabinet of all my secrets,
This I tell thee, not as an exprobration,
But because I must require thy faith
And counsell here.   And therefore prithee sweare—

M.   Sweare ? to doe what ?

Cl.   To be more silent then the dead of night,
And to thy power to helpe me.

M.   Would my power
To assist you were as ready as my will,
And for my tongue that Mistris I'le condemne
Unto perpetuall silence, ere it shall
Betray the smallest word that you commit to't.
By all—

118

LOVES RIDDLE

Cl. Nay doe not sweare, I will not wrong thy vertue
To bind it with an oath, Ile tell thee all;
Doth not my face seeme paler then 'twas wont?
Doth not my eye looke as it borrowed flame
From my fond heart; could not my frequent weepings,
My sudden sighes, and abrupt speeches tell thee
What I am growne?
   M. You are the same you were,
Or else my eyes are lyars.
   Cl. No, I'me a wretched Lover; could'st thou not
Read that out of my blushes? fie upon thee;
Thou art a novice in Loves schoole I see;
Trust me I envy at thy ignorance,
That canst not find out *Cupids* characters
In a lost Mayd, sure thou didst never know him.
   M. Would you durst trust me with his name,
Sure he had charmes about him that might tempt
Chast Votaries, or move a Scythian rock
When he shot fire into your chaster breast.
   Cl. I am asham'd to tell thee, prithee ghesse him.
   M. Why 'tis impossible.
   Cl. Thou saw'st the gentleman whom I this morning
Brought in to be my guest.
   M. Yes, but am ignorant, who, or from whence he is.
   Cl. Thou shalt know all;
The freshnesse of the morning did invite me
To walke abroad, there I began to thinke
How I had lost my Brother, that one thought
Like circles in the water begat many,
Those and the pleasant verdure of the fields
Made me forget the way, and did entice me
Farther than either feare or modesty
Else would have suffred me, beneath an oake
Which spread a flourishing Canopy round about,
And was it selfe alone almost a wood,
I found a Gentleman distracted strangely,
Crying alowd for either food, or sleepe,
And knocking his white hands against the ground,
Making that groane like me, when I beheld it,
Pitty, and feare, both proper to us women,

Drave my feet backe farre swifter then they went,
When I came home, I tooke two servants with me
And fetch'd the gentleman, hither I brought him,
And with such cheare as then the house afforded,
Replenished him, he was much mended suddenly,
Is now asleepe, and when he wakes I hope
Will find his senses perfect.
   M. You did shew
In this, what never was a stranger to you,
Much piety; but wander from your subject;
You have not yet discovered, who it is
Deserves your love.
   Cl. Fy, Fy, how dull thou art,
Thou dost not use in other things to be so;
Why I love him; His name I cannot tell thee;
For 'tis my great unhappinesse to bee
Still ignorant of that my selfe. He comes,
Looke, this is hee, but doe not grow my rivall If thou canst [c]huse.
   M. You need not, fear't forsooth.   *Enter Aphron.*
   Cl. Leave me alone with him; withdraw.
   M. I doe.   *Exit* Maid.
   Ap. Where am I now? under the Northerne Pole
Where a perpetuall winter bincs the ground
And glazeth up the flouds? or where the Sun
With neighbouring rayes bakes the divided earth,
And drinkes the rivers up? or doe I sleepe?
Is't not some foolish dreame deludes my fancy?
Who am I? I begin to question that.
Was not my countrey *Sicily?* my name
Call'd *Aphron,* wretched *Aphron?*
   Cla. Yee good Gods
Forbid; is this that man who was the cause
Of all the griefe for *Callidora's* losse?
Is this the man that I so oft have curst?
Now I could almost hate him, and me thinkes
He is not quite so handsome as he was;
And yet alas he is, though by his meanes
My Brother is gone from me, and heaven knowes
If I shall see him more, Foole as I am,
I cannot chuse but love him.

LOVES RIDDLE

Ap.   Cheate me not good eyes,
What woman, or what Angel doe I see?
Oh stay, and let me worship e're thou goest,
Whether thou beest a Goddesse which thy beauty
Commands me to beleeve, or else some mortall
Which I the rather am induc'd to thinke,
Because I know the Gods all hate me so,
They would not looke upon me.
  Cl.   Spare these titles
I am a wretched woman, who for pitty
(Alas that I should pitty! t'had bin better   (*Aside*)
That I had beene remorslesse) brought you hither,
Where with some food and rest, thanks to the Gods
Your senses are recovered.
  Ap.   My good Angell!
I doe remember now that I was madde
For want of meat and sleepe, thrice did the Sun
Cheere all the world but me, thrice did the night
With silent and bewitching darknesse give
A resting time to every thing but *Aphron.*
The fish, the beasts, the birds, the smallest creatures
And the most despicable snor'd securely.
The aguish head of every tree by *Æolus*
Was rockt asleepe, and shooke as if it nodded.
The crooked mountaines seem'd to bow and slumber,
The very rivers ceas'd their daily murmur,
Nothing did watch, but the pale Moone, and I
Paler then shee; Griefe wedded to this toyle
What else could it beget but franticknesse?
But now me thinkes, I am my owne, my braine
Swimmes not as it was wont; O brightest Virgin
Shew me some way by which I may be gratefull,
And if I do't not, let an eternall Phrenzie
Immediatly seize on me.
  Cl.   Alas! 'twas only
My love, and if you will reward me for't,
Pay that I lent you, I'le require no interest;
The Principall's enough.
  Ap.   You speake in mists.
  Cl.   You're loth perhaps to understand.

Ap. If you intend that I should love and honour you,
I doe by all the Gods.

Cl. But I am covetous in my demands,
I am not satisfied with wind-like promises
Which only touch the lips ; I aske your heart
Your whole heart for me, in exchange of mine,
Which so I gave to you.

Ap. Ha ! you amaze me.
Oh ! you have spoken something worse then lightning,
That blasts the inward parts, leaves, the outward whole,
My gratitude commands me to obey you,
But I am borne a man, and have those passions
Fighting within me, which I must obey.
Whilst *Callidora* lives, although she bee
As cruell, as thy breast is soft and gentle ;
'Tis sinne for me to thinke of any other.

Cl. You cannot love me then ?

Ap. I doe I sweare,
Above my selfe I doe : my selfe ? what said I ?
Alas ! that's nothing ; above anything
But heaven and *Callidora*.

Cl. Fare you well then,
I would not doe that wrong to one I love,
To urge him farther then his power and will ;
Farewell, remember me when you are gone,
And happy in the love of *Callidora*.   *Exit.*

Ap. When I doe not, may I forget my selfe,
Would I were madde againe ; then I might rave
With priviledge, I should not know the griefes
That hurried me about, 'twere better farre
To lose the senses, then be tortured by them.
Where is she gone ? I did not aske her name,
Foole that I was, alas poore Gentlewoman !
Can any one love me ? yee cruell Gods,
Is't not enough that I my selfe am miserable,
Must I make others so too ? Ile goe in
And comfort her ; alas ! how can I though ?
Ile grieve with her, that is in ills a comfort.   *Exit.*

LOVES RIDDLE

Enter Alupis, Melarnus, Truga, Palæmon, Ægon.

Pa. Before when you denyed your Daughter to me
'Twas Fortunes fault, not mine, but since good Fate
Or rather *Ægon*, better farre then Fate
Hath raysd me up to what you aym'd at, riches,
I see not with what countenance you can
Coyne any second argument against me.
  Mel. Come, no matter for that:
Yes, I could wish you were lesse eloquent,
You have a vice call'd Poesie which much
Displeaseth me, but no matter for that neither.
  Al. Alas! hee'le leave that straight
When he has got but money; he that swims
In *Tagus*, never will goe back to *Helicon*.
Besides, when he hath maried *Hylace*
Whom should he wooe, to praise her comely feature,
Her skin like falling snow, her eyes like starres,
Her cheekes like roses (which are common places
Of all your lovers praises) ôh! those vanities,
Things quite as light, and foolish as a Mistris,
Are by a Mistris first begot, and left
When they leave her.
  Pa. Why doe you thinke that Poesie
An art which even the Gods—
  Al. Pox on your arts,
Let him thinke what he will; what's that to us?
  Ægon. Well, I would gladly have an answer of you,
Since I have made *Palæmon* here my sonne,
If you conceive your Daughter is so good,
Wee will not presse you, but seeke out some other
Who may perhaps please me and him as well.
  Pa. Which is impossi'—
  Al. Rot on your possibles—
Thy mouth like a crackt fiddle never sounds
But out of tune; Come, put on *Truga*
You'le never speake unlesse I shew the ring.
  Tru. Yes, yes, I doe, I doe; Doe yee heare sweet heart?
Are you madde to fling away a fortune
That's thrust upon you, you know *Ægon*'s rich.

Mel. Come, no matter for that,
That's thrust upon me? I would faine see any man
Thrust ought upon me; but's no matter for that,
I will doe that which I intend to doe,
And 'tis no matter for that neither, that's thrust upon me?
   Pa. Come, what say you *Melarnus?*
   Mel. What say I? 'tis no matter what I say,
I'le speake to *Ægon*, if I speake to any,
And not to you; but no matter for that;
Harke you, will you leave all the meanes you have
To this *Palæmon?*
   Tru. I Duck, he sayes he will.
   Mel. Pish, 'tis no matter for that, Ile heare him say so.
   Æg. I will, and here doe openly protest,
That since my *Bellula* (mine that was once)
Thinkes her selfe wiser then her father is,
And will be govern'd rather by her passions,
Then by the square that I prescribe to her,
That I will never count her as my Daughter.
   Al. Well acted by God *Pax*, see but what 'tis
To have me for a tutor in these rogueries.
   Mel. But tell me now, good neighbour, what estate
Doe you intend to give him?
   Æg. That estate
Which Fortune and my care hath given to me,
The money which I have, and that's not much,
The sheepe, and Goats.
   Mel. And not the oxen too?
   Æg. Yes; every thing.
   Mel. The Horses too?
   Æg. I tell you, every thing.
   Al. By *Pan* hee'le make him promise him particularly
Each thing above the valew of a Beanes-straw.
You'le leave him the pailes too, to milke the Kine in,
And harnesse for the horses, will you not?
   Mel. I, I, what else; but 'tis no matter for that,
I know *Palæmon's* an ingenious man,
And love him therefore; But's no matter for that neither.
   Æg. Well, since we are both agreed, why do we stay here?
I know *Palæmon* longs t'imbrace his *Hylace.*

LOVES RIDDLE

Mel. I, I, 'tis no matter for that, within this houre
Wee will be ready, *Ægon*, pray be you so,
Farewell my son in Law that shall be,
But's no matter for that : Farewell all :
Come *Truga.*   *Exeunt Melarnus and Truga.*
  Æg. Come on then, let's not stay too long in trifling,
Palæmon goe, and prepare your selfe against the time.
I'le goe acquaint my *Bellula* with your plot,
Lest this unwelcome newes should too much grieve her,
Before she know my meaning.
  A. Doe, doe ; and I'le goe study
Some new-found wayes to vex the foole *M[ela]rnus.*
              For 'tis but a folly,
              To be melancholy, &c.

              Enter Florellus.

Whilst *Callidorus* lives, I cannot love thee.
These were her parting words ; Ile kill him then ;
Why doe I doubt it Foole ? such wounds as these
Require no gentler med'cine ; me thinkes Love
Frownes at me now, and sayes I am too dull,
Too slow in his command : and yet I will not,
These hands are virgins yet, unstain'd with villany,
Shall I begin to teach them ?—me thinkes Piety
Frownes at me now, and sayes, I am too weake
Against my passions. Pietie !—
'Twas feare begot that Bugbeare ; for thee *Bellula*
I durst be wicked, though I saw *Joves* hand
Arm'd with a naked thunderbolt : Farewell,
(If thou beest any thing, and not a shadow
To fright boyes and old women) Farewell conscience,
Goe and be strong in other petty things
To Lovers come, when Lovers may make use of thee,
Not else : and yet,—what shall I doe or say ?
I see the better way, and know 'tis better,
Yet still this devious error drawes me backward.
So when contrary winds rush out and meet,
And wrastle on the Sea with equall fury
The waves swell into mountaines, and are driven

Now back, now forward, doubtfull of the two
Which Captaine to obey.

Enter Alupis.

Al. Ha, ha, Ile have such excellent sport
    For 'tis but a folly, &c.
Flo. Why here's a fellow now makes sport of every thing,
See one mans fate how it excels another,
Hee can sit, and passe away the day in jollity,
My musick is my sighes, whilst teares keepe time.
Al. Who's here? a most rare posture!
How the good soule folds in his armes! he dreames
Sure that he hugges his Mistris now, for that
Is his disease without all doubt, so, good,
With what judicious garbe hee plucks his hat
Over his eyes; so, so, good! better yet;
He cryes; by this good light, he cryes; the man
Is carefull, and intends to water his sheepe
With his owne teares; ha, ha, ha, ha.
Flo. Dost thou see any thing that deserves thy laughter,
Fond swaine?
Al. I see nothing in good troth but you.
Flo. To jeere those who are Fates May-game
Is a redoubled fault; for 'tis both sinne,
And folly too; our life is so uncertaine
Thou canst not promise that thy mirth shall last
To morrow, and not meet with any rubbe,
Then thou mayst act that part, to day thou laugh'st at.
Al. I act a part? it must be in a Comedy then,
I abhorre Tragedyes: besides, I never
Practiz'd this posture; Hey ho! woe, alas!
Why doe I live? my musick is my sighes
Whilst teares keepe time.
Flo. You take too great a licence to your wit;
Wit, did I say? I meane, that which you thinke so.
And it deserves my pitty, more then anger.
Else you should find, that blowes are heavier farre
Then the most studied jests you can throw at me.
Al. Faith it will be but labour lost to beat mee,

LOVES RIDDLE

All will not teach me how to act this part;
Woe's me! alas! I'me a dull rogue, and so
Shall never learne it.
   Flo. You're unmannerly
To talke thus sawcily with one you know not,
Nay, hardly ever saw before, be gone
And leave me as you found me, my worst thoughts
Are better company then thou.
   Al. Enjoy them then,
Here's no body desires to rob you of them.
I would have left your company without bidding,
'Tis not so pleasant, I remember well,
When I had spent all my money, I stood thus
And therefore hate the posture ever since.
D'yee heare? I'me going to a wedding now;
If you 'ave a mind to dance, come along with me,
Bring your hard-hearted Mistris with you too,
Perhaps I may perswade her, and tell her
Your Musick's sighes, and that your teares keepe time.
Will you not goe? Farewell then, good Tragicall actor.
Now have at thee *Melarnus*; *For 'tis but a folly*, &c.   *Exit.*
   Flo. Thou art a Prophet, Shepheard; She is hard
As rocks which suffer the continuall siege
Of Sea and wind against them; but I will
Win her or lose (which I should gladly doe)
My selfe: my selfe? why so I have already:
Ho! who hath found *Florellus?* he is lost,
Lost to himselfe, and to his parents likewise,
(Who having miss'd me, doe by this time search
Each corner for to find me) ôh! *Florellus*,
Thou must be wicked, or for ever wretched,
Hard is the Physick, harder the disease.

Finis Actus Quarti.

Actus V. Scæna I.

Enter *Alupis, Palæmon, Ægon.*

Pa. The Gods convert these omens into good:
    And mocke my feares; thrice in the very threshold,
Without its Masters leave my foot stood still,
Thrice in the way it stumbled.
    Al. Thrice, and thrice
You were a foole then for observing it.
Why these are follyes the young yeares of *Truga*
Did hardly know; are they not vanisht yet?
    Pa. Blame not my feare: that's *Cupids* Usher alwayes;
Though *Hylace* were now in my embraces,
I should halfe doubt it.
    Al. If you chanc'd to stumble.
    Æg. Let him enjoy his madnesse, the same liberty
Hee'le grant to you, when you're a Lover too.
    Al. I, when I am, he may; yet if I were one
I should not be dismay'd because the threshold—
    Pa. Alas! that was not all, as I came by
The oake to *Faunus* sacred, where the shepheards
Exercise rurall sports on Festivalls,
On that trees toppe an inauspicious Crow
Foretold some ill to happen.
    Æg. And because Crowes
Foretell wet weather, you interpret it
The raine of your owne eyes; but leave these tricks
And let me advise you.

Melarnus *speaking to* Hylace *within his dore.*

Mel. Well come, no matter for that; I doe beleeve thee;
    Girle
And would they have such sport with vexing me!
But's no matter for that; Ile vex them for't,

128

I know your fiery lover will be here strait,
But I shall coole him ; but come, no matter for that !
Goe get you in, for I doe see them comming.

    Æg.   Here comes *Melarnus.*

    Pa.   Hee lookes cheerefully, I hope all's well ?

    Æg.   *Melarnus,* opportunely : we were a comming
Just now unto you.

    Mel.   Yes, very likely ; would you have spoken with me ?

    Æg.   Spoken with you ?
Why, are you madde ? have you forgot your promise ?

    Mel.   My promise ? oh ! 'tis true, I said indeed
I would goe with you to day to sell some kine,
Stay but a little, Ile be ready streight.

    Pa.   I am amaz'd ; Good *Ægon* speake to him.

    Al.   By this good light,
I see no likelyhood of any mariage,
Except betwixt the Kine and oxen. Harke you hither ;
A rotte upon your beasts ; is *Hylace* ready ?

    Mel.   It's no matter for that ! who's there ? *Alupis?*
Give me thy hand 'faith, thou'rt a merry fellow,
I have not seene thee here these many dayes,
But now I thinke on't, it's no matter for that neither.

    Al.   Thy memory's fled away sure with thy wit.
Was not I here lesse then an houre agoe
With *Ægon,* when you made the match ?

    Mel.   Oh ! then you'le goe along with us,
Faith doe ; for you will make us very merry.

    Al.   I shall, if you thus make a foole of me.

    Mel.   Oh no ! you'le make you sport with vexing me,
But mum ; no matter for that neither : there
I bob'd him privatly, I thinke.   *Aside.*

    Æg.   Come, what's the businesse ?

    Al.   The businesse ? why hee's madde, beyond the cure
Of all the herbes grow in *Anticyra.*

    Æg.   You see we have not fayl'd our word *Melarnus,*
I and my sonne are come.

    Mel.   Your son ! goodlack !
I thought, I sweare, you had no other child
Besides your Daughter *Bellula.*

    Ægon.   Nay, then

I see you are dispos'd to make us fooles,—
Did not I tell you that 'twas my intent
To adopt *Palæmon* for my son and heire?

    Al. Did not you examine
Whether he would leave him all, lest that he should
Adopt some other heire to the cheese-presses,
The milking-pailes, and creame-boules? did you not?

    Mel. In troth 'tis well; but where is *Bellula?*

    Ægon. Nay; prithee leave these tricks, and tell me
What you intend, is *Hylace* ready?

    Mel. Ready? what else? shee's to be married presently:
To a young shepheard, but's no matter for that.

    Pa. That's I, hence feares;
Attend upon the infancie of love,
She's now mine owne.

    Al. Why I; did not the crow on the oake foretell you this?

    Mel. *Hylace*, *Hylace*, come forth,
Here's some are come to dance at your wedding,
And they're welcome.   (*Enter Hylace.*)

    Pa. The light appeares, just like the rising Sun,
When o're yon hill it peepes, and with a draught
Of morning dew salutes the day, how fast
The night of all my sorrow flyes away,
Quite banisht with her sight!

    Hy. Did you call for me?

    Mel. Is *Damætas* come? Fy, how slow he is
At such a time? but it's no matter for that;
Well get you in, and prepare to welcome him.

    Pa. Will you be gone so quickly, ôh! bright *Hylace*
That blessed houre by me so often begg'd,
By you so oft deny'd, is now approaching.

    Mel. What, how now? what doe you kisse her? (*Exit*
If *Damætas* were here, he would grow jealous,   *Hylace.*)
But 'tis a parting kisse, and so in manners
She cannot deny it you; but it's no matter for that.

    Al. How?

    Mel. What doe you wonder at?
Why doe you thinke as soone as they are maried,
Damætas such a foole, to let his wife
Be kist by every body?

LOVES RIDDLE

Pa. How now? *Damætas?*
Why what hath he to doe with her?
   Mel. Ha, ha!
What hath the husband then to doe with's wife?
Good: 'tis no matter for that though; he knowes what.
   Æg. You meane *Palæmon* sure, ha, doe you not?
   Mel. 'Tis no matter for that, what I meane, I meane;
Well, rest ye merry gentlemen, I must in,
And see my Daughters wedding, if you please
To dance with us; *Damætas* sure will thanke yee;
Pray bring your son and heire *Palæmon* with you,
Bellula's cast away, ha, ha, ha!
And the poore foole *Melarnus* must be cheated,
But it's no matter for that; how now *Alupis?*
I thought you would have had most excellent sport
With abusing poore *Melarnus?* that same coxcombe,
For hee's a foole; but it's no matter for that,
Ægon hath cheated him, *Palæmon* is
Maried to *Hylace*, and one *Alupis*
Doth nothing else but vex him, ha, ha, ha!
But it's no matter for that; farewell gentles,
Or if yee'le come and dance, yee shall be welcome,
Will you *Palæmon?* 'tis your Mistris wedding.
I am a foole, a coxcombe, gull'd on every side,
No matter for that though; what I have done, I have done!
Ha, ha, ha!   *Exit.*
   Æg. How now? what are you both dumbe? both thunder-
       strooke?
This was your plot *Alupis.*
   Al. I'le begin.
May his sheepe rotte, and he for want of food
Be forc't to eat them then; may every man
Abuse him, and yet he not have the wit
To abuse any man, may he never speake
More sence then he did now; and may he never
Bee ridde of his old wife *Truga*, may his sonne
In Law be a more famous Cuckold made
Then any one I knew when I liv'd in the City.
   Pa. Foole as thou art, the Sun shall lose his course,
And brightnesse too, ere *Hylace* her chastity.

ABRAHAM COWLEY

Oh no ! yee Gods, may she be happy alwayes,
Happy in the embraces of *Damætas*;
And that shall be some comfort to my Ghost
When I am dead ; and dead I shall be shortly.

Al. May a disease seize upon all his Cattle,
And a farre worse on him ; till he at last
Bee carried to some Hospitall i'the City,
And there kill'd by a Chirurgion for experience.
And when hee's gone, Ile wish this good thing for him,
May the earth lye gently on him.——that the dogges
May teare him up the easier.

Æg. A curse upon thee !
And upon me for trusting thy fond counsels !
Was this your cunning trick ? why thou hast wounded
My conscience and my reputation too,
With what face can I looke on the other Swaines ?
Or who will ever trust me, who have broke
My faith thus openly ?

Pa. A curse upon thee,
This is the second time that thy perswasions
Made me not only foole, but wicked too ;
I should have dyed in quiet else, and knowne
No other wound, but that of her denyall ;
Go now, and bragge how thou hast us'd *Palæmon*,
But yet me thinkes you might have chose some other
For subject of your mirth, not me.

Æg. Nor me.

Al. And yet if this had prospered (as I wonder
Who it should be, betray'd us, since we three
And *Truga* only knew it, whom, if she
Betray'd us, I—) if this, I say, had prospered,
You would have hugg'd me for inventing it,
And him for putting it in act ; foolish men
That doe not marke the thing but the event !
Your judgements hang on Fortune, not on reason.

Æg. Dost thou upbraid us too ?

Pa. First make us wretched,
And then laugh at us ? beleeve, *Alupis*,
Thou shalt not long have cause to boast thy villany.

Al. My villany ? doe what yee can : you're fooles,

And there's an end; Ile talke with you no more,
I had as good speake reason to the wind
As you, that can but hisse at it.
    Æg. Wee will doe more; *Palæmon*, come away,
He hath wrong'd both; and both shall satisfie.
    Al. Which he will never doe; nay, goe and plod,
Your two wise braines will invent certainely
Politique ginnes to catch me in.   *Exeunt.*
And now have at thee *Truga*, if I find
That thou art guiltie; mum,—I have a ring.—
Palæmon, Ægon, Hylace, Melarnus
Are all against me; no great matter: hang care,
        For 'tis but a folly, &c.   *Exit.*

Enter Bellula.

This way my *Callidorus* went, what chance
Hath snatch'd him from my sight? how shall I find him?
How shall I find my selfe, now I have lost him?
With yee my feet and eyes I will not make
The smallest truce, till yee have sought him out.   *Exit.*

Enter Callidorus *and* Florellus.

Come, now your businesse.
    Flo. 'Tis a fatall one,
Which will almost as much shame me to speake,
Much more to act, as 'twill fright you to heare it.
    Cal. Fright me? it must be then some wickednesse,
I am accustom'd so to misery,
That cannot do't.
    Flo. Oh! 'Tis a sinne young man,
A sinne which every one shall wond[e]r at,
None not condemne, if ever it be knowne:
Me thinkes my bloud shrinkes back into my veines,
And my affrighted hayres are turn'd to bristles.
Doe not my eyes creepe backe into their cells;
As if they seem'd to wish for thicker darknesse,
Then either night or death to cover them?
Doth not my face looke black and horrid too?
As black and horrid as my thoughts? ha! tell me.

Cal.   I am a novice in all villanyes,
If your intents be such, dismisse me, pray,
My nature is more easie to discover
Then helpe you ; so, Farewell.
   Flo.   Yet stay a little longer ; you must stay :
You are an actor in this Tragedy.
   Cal.   What would you doe ?
   Flo.   Alas ! I would doe nothing ; but I must—
   Cal.   What must you doe ?
   Flo.   I must.—Love thou hast got the victory—
Kill thee.
   Cal.   Who ? me ? you doe but jest,
I should believe you, if I could tell how
To frame a cause, or thinke on any injury
Worth such a large revenge, which I have done you.
   Flo.   Oh no ! there's all the wickednesse, they may seeme
To find excuse for their abhorred fact ;
That kill when wrongs, and anger urgeth them ;
Because thou art so good, so affable.
So full of graces, both of mind and body,
Therefore I kill thee, wilt thou know it plainely,
Because whilst thou art living, *Bellula*
Protested she would never be anothers,
Therefore I kill thee.
   Call.   Had I beene your rivall
You might have had some cause ; cause did I say ?
You might have had pretence for such a villany :
He who unjustly kills is twice a murtherer.
   Flo.   He whom love bids to kill is not a murtherer.
   Cal.   Call not that love that's ill, 'tis only fury.
   Flo.   Fury in ills is halfe excusable :
Therefore prepare thy selfe ; if any sinne
(Though I beleeve thy hot and flourishing youth
As innocent as other mens nativities)
Hath flung a spot upon they purer conscience
Wash it in some few teares.
   Call.   Are you resolv'd to be so cruell ?
   Flo.   I must, or be as cruell to my selfe.
   Call.   As sick men doe their beds, so have I yet
Injoy'd my selfe, with little rest, much trouble :

LOVES RIDDLE

I have beene made the Ball of Love and Fortune,
And am almost worne out with often playing.
And therefore I would enter taine my death
As some good friend whose comming I expected ;
Were it not that my parents—
   Flo. Here ; see, I doe not come   (*Drawes two swords*
Like a foule murtherer to intrap you falsly, *from under his*
Take your own choyse, and then defend your selfe. *garment*
   Cal. 'Tis nobly done ; and since it must be so, *and offers*
Although my strength and courage call me woman *one to*
I will not dye like sheepe without resistance,   *Call.*)
If innocence be guard sufficient,
I'me sure he cannot hurt me.
   Flo. Are you ready ? the fatall Cuckow on yon spreading
       tree
Hath sounded out your dying knell already.
   Cal. I am.
   Flo. 'Tis well, and I could wish thy hand
Were strong enough ; 'tis thou deservest the victory,
Nay, were not th'hope of *Bellula* ingraven
In all my thoughts, I would my selfe play booty
Against my selfe ; But *Bellula*—come on.   *Fight.*

Enter Philistus.

This is the wood adjoyning to the Farme,
Where I gave order unto *Clariana*
My sister, to remaine till my returne ;
Here 'tis in vaine to seeke her, yet who knowes ?
Though it be in vaine Ile seeke ; to him that doth
Propose no journeys end, no path's amisse.
Why how now ? what doe you meane ? for shame part
       Shepheards,
I thought you honest shepheards, had not had *Sees them*
So much of Court, and Citie follies in you.   *fighting.*
   Flo. 'Tis *Philistus* ; I hope he will not know me,
Now I begin to see how black and horrid
My attempt was ; how much unlike *Florellus*,
Thankes to the juster Deityes for declining
From both the danger, and from me the sin.

Phi. 'Twould be a wrong to charity to dismisse yee
Before I see you friends, give me your weapons.
    Cal. 'Tis he; why doe I doubt? most willingly,
And my selfe too, best man; now kill me shepheard—
    Phi. What doe you meane?   *(Swounds)*
Rise, prithee rise; sure you have wounded him.

Enter Bellula.

Deceive me not good eyes; what doe I see?
My *Callidorus* dead? 'Tis impossible!
Who is it that lyes slaine there? are you dumbe?
Who is't I pray?
    Flo. Faire Mistris—
    Bel. Pish, faire Mistris,—
I aske who 'tis; if it be *Callidorus*—
    Phi. Was his name *Callidorus?* it is strange.
    Bel. You are a villaine, and you too a villaine,
Wake *Callidorus*, wake, it is thy *Bellula*
That calls thee, wake, it is thy *Bellula*;
Why Gentlemen? why shepheard? fye for shame,
Have you no charity? ô my *Callidorus*!
Speake but one word—
    Cal. 'Tis not well done to trouble me,
Why doe you envy me this little rest?
    Bel. No; I will follow thee.   *(Swounds.)*
    Flo. O helpe, helpe quickly,
What doe you meane? your *Callidorus* lives.
    Bel. *Callidorus*!
    Flo. And will be well immediatly, take courage,
Looke up a little: wretched as I am,
I am the cause of all this ill.
    Phi. What shall we doe? I have a sister dwells
Close by this place, let's hast to bring them thither.
But lets be sudden.
    Flo. As wing'd lightning is.
Come *Bellula* in spite of Fortune now
I doe embrace thee.
    Phi. I did protest without my *Callidora*
Ne're to returne, but pitty hath o'recome.

136

LOVES RIDDLE

Bel. Where am I?

Flo. Where I could alwayes wish thee: in those armes
Which would enfold thee with more subtill knots,
Then amorous Ivy, whilst it hugges the oake.

Cal. Where doe ye beare me? is *Philistus* well?

Phi. How should he know my name? 'tis to me a riddle.
Nay Shepheard find another time to court in,
Make hast now with your burthen.

Flo. With what ease should I goe alwaies were I burthened
(thus! Exeunt

Enter Aphron.

She told me she was sister to *Philistus,*
Who having mist the beauteous *Callidora,*
Hath undertooke a long, and hopelesse journey
To find her out; then *Callidora*'s fled,
Without her parents knowledge, and who knowes
When shee'le returne, or if she doe, what then?
Lambes will make peace, and joyne themselves with wolves
Ere she with me, worse then a wolfe to her:
Besides, how durst I undertake to court her?
How dare I looke upon her after this?
Foole as I am, I will forget her quite,
And *Clariana* shall hence-forth—but yet
How faire she was! what then? so's *Clariana*;
What graces did she dart on all beholders?
Shee did; but so does *Clariana* too,
Shee was as pure and white as *Parian* marble,
What then? Shee was as hard too; *Clariana*
Is pure and white as *Ericina*'s Doves,
And is as soft, as gallesse too as they,
Her pitty sav'd my life, and did restore
My wandring senses, if I should not love her,
I were farre madder now, then when she found me,
I will goe in and render up myselfe,
For her most faithfull servant.
Wonderfull!   Exit.   Enter againe.
Shee has lockt me in, and keepes me here her prisoner:
In these two chambers; what can she intend?

137

No matter, she intends no hurt I'me sure,
I'le patiently expect her comming to me.   *Exit.*

    Enter Demophil, Spodaia, Clariana, Florellus,
       Callidora, Bellula, Philistus.

  Dem. My Daughter found againe, and son returnd !
Ha, ha ! me thinkes it makes me young againe.
My Daughter and my Son meet here together !
Philistus with them too ! that we should come
To grieve with *Clariana,* and find her here.
Nay, when we thought we had lost *Florellus* too
To find them both, me thinkes it makes me young againe.
  Spo. I thought I never should have seene thee more
My *Callidora* ; come wench, now let's heare,
The story of your flight and life in the woods.
  Phi. Doe happy Mistris for the recordation,
Of forepast ils, makes us the sweetlier rellish
Our present good.
  Cal. Of *Aphrons* love to me, and my antipathy
Towards him, there's none here ignorant, you know too
How guarded with his love, or rather fury,
And some few men he broke into our house
With resolution to make me the prey
Of his wild lust.
  Sp. I, there's a villaine now ; oh ! that I had him here.
  Cla. Oh ! say not so :
The crymes which Lovers for their Mistris act
Beare both the weight and stampe of piety.
  Dem. Come girle ; goe on, goe on. His wild lust——
  Cla. What sudden feare shooke me, you may imagine,
What should I doe ? you both were out of towne,
And most of the servants at that time gone with you.
I on the sudden found a corner out,
And hid my selfe, till they wearied with searching,
Quitted the house, but fearing lest they should
Attempt the same againe ere your returne,
I tooke with me money and other necessaries ;
And in a sute my Brother left behind
Disguis'd my selfe, thus to the woods I went,

LOVES RIDDLE

Where meeting with an honest merry Swaine,
I by his helpe was furnisht, and made Shepheard.
    Sp. Nay, I must needs say for her, she was alwayes
A witty wench.
    Dem. Pish, pish : And made a Shepheard—
    Cal. It hapned that this gentle Shephea[r]desse,
(I can attribute it to nought in me
Deserv'd so much) began to love me.
    Phi. Why so did all besides Ile warrant you,
Nor can I blame them, though they were my rivall.
    Cal. Another Shepheard with as much desire
Wooed her in vaine, as she in vaine wooed me,
Who seeing that no hope was left for him,
Whilst I enjoy'd this life t'enjoy his *Bellula*,
(For by that name she's knowne) sought to take me
Out of the way as a partition
Betwixt his love and him, whilst in the fields
Wee two were strugling, (him his strength defending,
And me my innocence.)
    Flo. I am asham'd to looke upon their faces.
What shall I say? my guilt's above excuse.
    Cal. *Philistus* ; as if the Gods had all agreed
To make him mine, just at the nick came in
And parted us, with sudden joy I sounded,
Which *Bellula* perceiving (for even then
Shee came to seeke me) sudden griefe did force
The same effect from her, which joy from me.
Hither they brought us both, in this amazement,
Where being straight recover'd to our selves,
I found you here, and you your dutifull Daughter.
    Spo. The Gods be thankt. *Dem.* Goe on.
    Cal. Nay, you have all Sir.
    Dem. Where's that Shepheard? *Flo.* Here. *Dem.* Here,
        where?
    Flo. Here, your unhappy sonne's the man ; for her
I put on *Sylvan* weeds, for her faire sake
I would have stayn'd my innocent hands in bloud,
Forgive me all, 'twas not a sin of malice,
'Twas not begot by lust, but sacred love ;
The cause must be the excuse for the effect.

ABRAHAM COWLEY

Dem. You should have us'd some other meanes, *Florellus.*
Cal. Alas! 'twas the Gods will Sir, without that
I had beene undiscovered yet ; *Philistus*
Wandred too farre, my Brother yet a Shepheard,
You groaning for our losse, upon this wheele
All our felicity is turn'd.
 Sp. Alas! you have forgot the power of love, sweet-heart.
 Dem. Be patient Son, and temper your desire,
You shall not want a wife that will perhaps
Please you as well, I'me sure befit you better.
 Flo. They marry not, but sell themselves t'a wife,
Whom the large dowry tempts, and take more pleasure
To hugge the wealthy bagges then her that brought them.
Let them whom nature bestowes nothing on
Seeke to patch up their want by parents plenty ;
The beautifull, the chast, the vertuous,
Her selfe alone is portion to her selfe.

Enter Ægon.

By your leave ; I come to seeke a Daughter.
O ! are you there, 'tis well.
 Flo. This is her Father,
I doe conjure you Father, by the love
Which parents beare their children, to make up
The match betwixt us now, or if you will not
Send for your friends, prepare a coffin for me
And let a grave be dig'd, I wil be happy,
Or else not know my misery to morrow ;
 Spo. You doe not thinke what ill may happen husband,
Come, let him have her, you have meanes enough
For him, the wench is faire, and if her face
Be not a flatterer, of a noble mind,
Although not stocke.
 Æg. I doe not like this stragling, come along,
By your leave Gentlemen, I hope you will
Pardon my bold intrusion.
 Cl. You're very welcome.
What are you going *Bellula* ? pray stay,
Though Nature contradicts our love, I hope
That I may have your friendship.

Æg.   *Bellula!*
Bel.   My father calls; farewell; your name, and memory
In spite of Fate, I'le love, farewell.
Flo.   Would you be gone, and not bestow one word
Upon your faithfull servant? doe not all
My griefes and troubles for your sake sustaynd,
Deserve, Farewell *Florellus? Bel.* Fare you well then.
Flo.   Alas! how can I, Sweet, unlesse you stay,
Or I goe with you? you were pleas'd ere while
To say you honoured me with the next place
To *Callidorus* in your heart, then now
I should be first: doe you repent your sentence?
Or can that tongue sound lesse then Oracle?
Bel.   Perhaps I am of that opinion still,
But must obey my Father.
Æg.   Why *Bellula?* would you have ought with her Sir?
Flo.   Yes, I would have her selfe; if constancy
And love be meritorious, I deserve her.
Why Father, Mother, Sister, Gentlemen,
Will you plead for me?
Dem.   Since't must be so, I'le beare it patiently,
Shepheard you see how much our son is taken
With your faire Daughter, therefore if you thinke
Him fitting for her husband speake, and let it
Be made a match immediatly, we shall
Expect no other dowrie then her vertue.
Æg.   Which only I can promise; for her fortune
Is beneath you so farre, that I could almost
Suspect your words, but that you seeme more noble.
How now, what say you Girle?
Bel.   I only doe depend upon your will.
Æg.   And Ile not be an enemy to thy good fortune.
Take her Sir, and the Gods blesse you.
Flo.   With greater joy then I would take a Crowne.
Al.   The Gods blesse you.
Flo.   They have don't already.
Æg.   Lest you should thinke when time, and oft enjoying
Hath dul'd the point, and edge of your affection
That you have wrong'd your selfe and family,
By marying one whose very name, a Shepheardesse,

141

Might fling some spot upon your birth, I'le tell you,
She is not mine, nor borne in these rude woods.

    Flo. How! you speake misty wonders.

    Æg. I speake truths Sir,
Some fifteene yeares agoe, as I was walking
I found a Nurse wounded, and groning out
Her latest spirit, and by her a faire child,
And, which her very dressing might declare,
Of wealthy parents, as soone as I came to them
I as'kd her who had us'd her so inhumanly:
She answered Turkish Pirats; and withall
Desired me to looke unto the child,
For 'tis, said she, a Noblemans of *Sicily*,
His name she would have spoke, but death permitted not.
Her as I could, I caused to be buried,
But brought home the little Girle with me,
Where by my wives perswasions wee agreed,
Because the Gods had blest us with no issue,
To nourish as our owne, and call it *Bellula*
Whom now you see, your wife, your Daughter.

    Spo. Is't possible? *Flo.* Her manners shew'd her noble.

    Æg. I call the Gods to witnesse, this is true.
And for the farther testimony of it,
I have yet kept at home the furniture,
And the rich mantle which she then was wrapt in,
Which now perhaps may serve to some good use
Thereby to know her parents.

    Dem. Sure this is *Aphrons* sister then, for just
About the time he mentions, I remember,
The governour of *Pachinus*, then his Father
Told me that certaine Pirats of *Argier*
Had broke into his house, and stolne from thence
With other things his Daughter, and her Nurse,
Who being after taken, and executed,
Their last confession was, that they indeed
Wounded the Nurse, but she fled with the child,
Whilst they were busie searching for more prey.
Whom since her father, neither saw, nor heard of.

    Cla. Then now I'me sure Sir, you would gladly pardon
The rash attempt of *Aphron*, for your Daughter,

Since fortune hath joyn'd, both of you by kindred.

   Dem. Most willingly: *Spo.* I, I, alas! 'twas love.

   Flo. Where should wee find him out?

   Cla. Ile save that labour.   *Exit Clariana.*

   Cal. Where's *Hylace* pray shepheard? and the rest
Of my good Silvan friends? me thinkes I would,
Faine take my leave of them.

   Æg. I'le fetch them hither.
They're not farre off, and if you please to helpe
The match betwixt *Hylace* and *Palæmon*,
'Twould be a good deed, Ile goe fetch them.   *Exit.*

Enter Aphron, Clariana.

   Ap. Ha! whether have you led me *Clariana?*
Some steepy mountaine bury me alive,
Or rock intombe me in its stony intrayles,
Whom doe I see?

   Cla. Why doe you stare my *Aphron?*
They have forgiven all.

   Dem. Come, *Aphron*, welcome,
We have forgot the wrong you did my Daughter,
The name of love hath cover'd all; this is
A joyfull day, and sacred to great Hymen
'Twere sin not to be friends with all men now.

   Sp. Methinks, I have much adoe to forgive the rascall.
                                       (Aside.)

   Ap. I know not what to say; doe you all pardon me?
I have done wrong to yee all, yea, to all those
That have a share in vertue. Can yee pardon me?

   All. Most willingly.

   Aph. Doe you say so faire Virgin?
You I have injur'd most: with love,
With saucy love, which I henceforth recall,
And will looke on you with an adoration,
Not with desire hereafter; tell me, pray,
Doth any man yet call you his?

   Cal. Yes; *Philistus.*

   Ap. I congratulate it Sir.
The Gods make yee both happy: foole, as I am,

You are at the height already of felicity,
To which there's nothing can be added now,
But perpetuity ; you shall not find me
Your rivall any more, though I confesse
I honor her, and will for ever doe so.
Clariana, I am so much unworthy
Of thy love.   That—
   Cl.   Goe no farther Sir, 'tis I should say so
Of my owne selfe.
   Phi.   How Sister? are you two so neere upon a match?
   Ap.   In our hearts Sir,
Wee are already joyn'd, it may be though
You will be loth to have unhappy *Aphron*,
Stile you his Brother?
   Phi.   No Sir, if you both
Agree, to me it shall not be unwelcome.
Why here's a day indeed ; sure *Hymen* now
Meanes to spend all his torches.
   Dem.   'Tis my Son Sir,
New come from travaile, and your Brother now.
   Ap.   I understand not.   *Dem.*   Had you not a sister?
   Ap.   I had Sir ; but where now she is none knowes,
Besides the Gods.
   Dem.   Is't not about some fifteene yeares agoe
Since that the Nurse scap't with her from the hands
Of Turkish Pyrats that beset the house?
   Ap.   It is Sir.
   Dem.   Your sister lives then, and is maried
Now to *Florellus* ; this is she, you shall be
Enform'd of all the circumstances anon.
   Ap.   'Tis impossible.
I shall be made too happy on the sudden.
My Sister found, and *Clariana* mine !
Come not too thick good joyes you will oppresse me.

     Enter Melarnus, Truga, Ægon, Hylace, Palæmon.

   Cal.   Shepheards you're welcome all ; though I have lost
Your good society, I hope I shall not
Your friendship, and best wishes.

LOVES RIDDLE

Ægon. Nay, here's wonders;
Now *Callidorus* is found out a woman,
Bellula not my Daughter, and is maried
To yonder Gentleman, for which I intend
To doe in earnest what before I jested,
To adopt *Palæmon* for my heire.
  Mel. Ha, ha, ha!
Come it's no matter for that; doe you thinke
To cheate me once againe with your fine tricks?
No matter for that neither. Ha, ha, ha!
Alas! shee's maried to *Dametas.*
  Æg. Nay, that was your plot *Melarnus,*
I met with him, and he denyes it to me.
  Hy. Henceforth I must not love, but honor you—to
                                    (*Callidora.*

  Æg. By all the Gods I will.
  Tru. He will, he will; Duck.
  Mel. Of every thing?
  Æg. Of every thing; I call
These gentlemen to witnesse here, that since
I have no child to care for; I will make
Palæmon heire to those small meanes the Gods,
Have blest me with, if he doe marry *Hylace.*
  Mel. Come it's no matter for that, I scarce beleeve you.
  Dem. Wee'le be his suretyes.
  Mel. *Hylace*
What thinke you of *Palæmon?* can you love him?
H'as our consents, but it's no matter for that,
If he doe please you, speake, or now, or never.
  Hyl. Why doe I doubt fond Girle? shee's now a woman.
  Mel. No matter for that, what you doe, doe quickly.
  Hyl. My duty binds me not to be averse
To what likes you—
  Mel. Why take her then *Palæmon*; she's yours for ever.
  Pa. With farre more joy
Then I would doe the wealth of both the *Indyes,*
Thou art above a father to me, *Ægon.*
W'are freed from misery with sense of joy,
Wee are not borne so; oh! my *Hylace,*
It is my comfort now that thou wert hard,

ABRAHAM COWLEY

And cruell till this day, delights are sweetest
When poysoned with the trouble to attaine them.

Enter Alupis.

    For 'tis but a folly, &c.
By your leave, I come to seeke a woman,
That hath outlived the memorie of her youth,
With skin as black as her teeth, if she have any,
With a face would fright the Constable and his watch
Out of their wits (and that's easily done you'le say) if they
        should meet her at midnight.
O! are you there? I thought I smelt you somewhere;
Come hither my she Nestor, pretty *Truga,*
Come hither, my sweet Duck.
    Tru. Why? are you not asham'd to abuse me thus,
Before this company?
    Al. I have something more;
I come to shew the ring before them all;
How durst you thus betray us to *Melarnus?*
    Tru. 'Tis false, 'twas *Hylace* that over-heard you;
Shee told me so; but they are maried now.
    Al. What doe you thinke to flam me? why ho! here's
        newes.
    Pa. *Alupis* art thou there? forgive my anger,
I am the happiest man alive, *Alupis,*
Hylace is mine, here are more wonders too,
Thou shalt know all anon.
    Tru. *Alupis,* give me. *Al.* Well, rather then be troubled.
    Æg. *Alupis* welcome, now w'are friends I hope?
Give me your hand. *Mel.* And me.
    Al. With all my heart,
I'me glad to see yee have learn'd more wit at last.
    Cal. This is the Shepheard, Father, to whose care
I owe for many favours in the woods,
You're welcome heartily; here's every body
Payr'd of a sudden; when shall's see you maried?
    Al. Me? when there are no ropes to hang my selfe,
No rocks to breake my neck downe; I abhorre
To live in a perpetuall Belfary;

146

LOVES RIDDLE

I never could abide to have a Master,
Much lesse a Mistris, and I will not marry,
Because, *I'le sing away the day,*
   For 'tis but a folly to be melancholly,
   Ile be merry whilst I may.
 Phi. You're welcome all, and I desire you all
To be my guests to day ; a Wedding dinner,
Such as the sudden can afford, wee'le have,
Come will yee walke in Gentlemen?
 Dem. Yes, yes,
What crosses have yee borne before yee joyn'd !
What seas past through before yee touch't the port !
Thus Lovers doe, ere they are crown'd by Fates
With Palme, the tree their patience imitates.

FINIS.

Epilogue

Spoken by *Alupis*.

THe Author bid me tell you—'faith, I have
  Forgot what 'twas; and I'me a very slave
If I know what to say; but only this,
Bee merry, that my counsell elwayes is.
Let no grave man knit up his brow, and say,
'Tis foolish : why? 'twas a Boy made the Play.
Nor any yet of those that sit behind,
Because he goes in Plush, be of his mind.
Let none his Time, or his spent money grieve,
Bee merry; Give me your hands, and I'le believe.
Or if you will not, I'le goe in, and see,
If I can turne the Authors mind, with mee
    To sing away the day.
        For 'tis but a folly
        To bee melancholy
    Since that can't mend the Play.

A
SATYRE.

THE
PURITAN
AND THE
PAPIST.

By a Scholler in Oxford.

[*design*]

Printed in the Yeare M.DC.XLIII.

A Satyre.

THE *PURITAN*
AND
THE *PAPIST*.

SO two rude *waves*, by stormes together throwne,
   Roare at each other, fight, and then grow *one*.
Religion is a *Circle*; men contend,
And runne the round in dispute without end.
Now in a *Circle* who goe contrary,
Must at the last *meet* of necessity.
The *Roman* to advance the *Catholicke cause*
Allowes a *Lie*, and calls it *Pia Fraus*.
The *Puritan* approves and does the same,
Dislikes nought in it but the *Latin name*.
He flowes with these devises, and dares *ly*
In very *deed*, in *truth*, and *verity*.
He whines, and sighes out *Lies*, with so much ruth,
As if he griev'd, 'cause he could ne're speake truth.
Lies have possest the *Presse* so, as their due,
'Twill scarcely, 'I feare, henceforth print *Bibles* true.
Lies for their next strong Fort ha'th' *Pulpit* chose,
There throng out at the *Preachers mouth*, and *nose*.
And how e're grosse, are certaine to beguile
The poore *Booke-turners* of the *midale Isle*.
Nay to th' *Almighty's* selfe they have beene bold
To *ly*, and their blasphemous *Minister* told
They might say false to *God*, for if they were
Beaten, he knew't not, for he was not there.
But *God*, who their great *thankefulnesse* did see,
Rewards them straight with another *Victorie*,
Just such another at *Brainceford*; and san's doubt
Will *weary* er't be long their *gratitude* out.

THE PURITAN AND THE PAPIST

Not all the *Legends* of the *Saints* of old,
Not vast *Baronius*, nor sly *Surius* hold
Such plenty of apparent *Lies*, as are
In your one *Author*, *Jo. Browne Cleric. Par.*
Besides what your small *Poets* have said, or writ,
Brookes, *Strode*, and the *Baron* of the *Saw-pit* :
With many a *Mentall Reservation*,
You'le maintaine *Liberty*, *Reserv'd* [your owne.]
For th' publique good the summes rais'd you'le disburse ;
Reserv'd, [The greater part for your owne purse.]
You'le root the *Cavaliers* out, every man ;
Faith, let it be *reserv'd* here ; [*If yee can.*]
You'le make our gracious CHARLES, a *glorious King* ;
Reserv'd [in *Heaven*,] for thither ye would bring
His *Royall Head* ; the onely secure roome
For *glorious Kings*, whither *you'le* never come.
To keepe the estates o'th' Subjects you pretend ;
Reserv'd [in your owne *Trunkes* ;] you will defend
The *Church* of *England*, 'tis your *Protestation* ;
But that's *New-England*, by'a small *Reservation*.
    Power of dispensing *Oaths* the *Papists* claime ;
Case hath got leave *o'* *God*, to doe the same.
For you doe hate all *swearing* so, that when
You have sworne an *Oath*, ye *breake it* streight agen.
A Curse upon you ! which hurts most these Nations,
Cavaliers swearing, or your *Protestations?*
Nay, though *Oaths* by you be so much abhorr'd,
Ye allow *God damne me* in the *Puritan Lord*.
    They keepe the *Bible* from *Lay-men*, but ye
Avoid this, for ye have no *Laytie*.
They in a forraigne, and unknowne *tongue* pray,
You in an unknowne *sence* your prayers say :
So that this difference 'twixt ye does ensue,
Fooles understand not *them*, nor *Wise* men *you*.
    They an unprofitable zeale have got,
Of invocating *Saints* that heare them not.
'Twere well you did so ; nought may more be fear'd
In your fond prayers, then that they should be heard.
To them your *Non-sence* well enough might passe,
They'd ne're see that i'th' *Divine Looking-glasse* :

Nay, whether you'de worship *Saints* is not yet knowne,
For ye'have as yet of your *Religion* none.
    They by *good-workes* thinke to be *justified*,
You into the same errour deeper slide ;
You thinke by *workes* too *justified* to be,
And those *ill workes*, *Lies*, *Treason*, *Perjurie*.
But oh your *faith* is mighty, that hath beene,
As true *faith* ought to be, of things *unseene*.
At *Worc'ster*, *Brainceford*, and *Edge hill*, we see,
Onely by *faith* you'have gotten *victory*.
Such is your *faith*, and some such *unseene* way
The *publique faith* at last your *debts* will pay.
    They hold *free-will* (that nought their soules may bind)
As the great *Priviledge* of all *mankind*.
You're here more *moderate*, for 'tis your intent,
To make't a *Priv'ledge* but of *Parliament*.
They forbid *Priests* to marry ; you worse doe,
Their *Marriage* you allow, yet punish too :
For you'de make *Priests* so poore, that upon all
Who *marry*, *scorne* and *beggery* must fall.
    They a bold power o're sacred *Scriptures* take,
Blot out some Clauses, and some new ones make.
Your great *Lord Jesuite Brookes* publiquely said,
(*Brookes* whom too *little learning* hath made *mad*)
That to correct the *Creed* ye should doe well,
And blot out *Christs descending into Hell*.
Repent wild man, or you'le ne're change, I feare,
The *sentence* of your *owne descending there*.
    Yet modestly they use the *Creed*, for they
Would take the *Lords prayer Root and Branch* away.
And wisely said a *Levit* of our nation,
The *Lords Prayer* was a *Popish Innovation*.
Take heed, you'le grant ere long it should be said,
An't be but to desire your *daily Bread*.
    They keepe the *people ignorant*, and you
Keepe both the *People*, and yourselves so too.
They *blind obedience* and *blind duty* teach ;
You *blind Rebellion* and *blind faction* preach.
Nor can I blame you much, that yee advance
That which can onely save yee, *Ignorance* ;

THE PURITAN AND THE PAPIST

Though Heaven be praysed, t'has oft beene proved well
Your *Ignorance* is not *Invincible.*
Nay such bold lies to *God* him selfe yee vaunt,
As if you'd faine keepe *him* too *ignorant.*
   Limbus and *Purgatory* they beleive
For lesser *sinners,* that is, I conceive,
Malignants onely ; you this Tricke does please,
For the same Cause ye'have made new *Limbuses,*
Where we may ly imprison'd long ere we
A *day* of *Judgement* in your Courts shall see.
But *Pym* can, like the *Pope* with this dispence ;
And for a *Bribe* deliver *Soules* from thence.
   Their *Councels* claime *Infallibility,*
Such must your *Conventicle-synod* be ;
And Teachers from all Parts of th' Earth yee call,
To mak't a *Councell Oecumenicall.*
   They sev'rall times appoint from meats t'abstaine ;
You now for th' *Irish* warres a *Fast* ordaine ;
And that that Kingdome might be sure to *fast*
Yee take a Course to *sterve* them all at last.
Nay though yee keepe no *Eves, Fridayes,* nor *Lent,*
Not to dresse meate on *Sundayes* you're Content ;
Then you repeat, repeat, and pray, and pray ;
Your *Teeth* keepe *Sabboth,* and *Tongues working day.*
   They preserve *Reliques* ; you have few or none,
Unlesse the *Clout* sent to *John Pym* be one.
And *Hollises* rich *Widow,* Shee who carryed
A *Relique* in her *wombe* before she married.
   They in succeeding *Peter* take a Pride ;
So doe you ; for your Master ye'have denyed.
But cheifely *Peters Priviledge* yee choose,
At your own wills to *bind* and to *unloose.*
He was a *Fisherman* ; you may be so too,
When nothing but your *ships* are left to you.
He went to *Rome,* to *Rome* you *Backward ride,*
(Though both your goings are by some denyed.)
Nor i'st a Contradiction, if we say,
You goe to *Rome* the *quite Contrary way* ;
He dy'd o'the *Crosse* ; that death's unsuall now ;
The *Gallowes* is most like't, and that's for you.

ABRAHAM COWLEY

They musicke love i'th *Church* ; it offends your *sence*,
And therefore yee have *sung* it out from thence,
Which shewes, if right your mind be understood,
You hate it not as *Musicke*, but as *Good*.
Your madnesse makes you *sing*, as much as they
Dance, who are bit with a *Tarantula*.
But do not to your selves (alas) appeare
The most *Religious Traitors* that ere were,
Because your *Troopes singing* of *Psalmes* do goe ;
Ther's many a *Traytor* has marcht *Holbourn* so.
Nor was't your wit this holy project bore ;
Tweed and the *Tyne* has seene those *Trickes* before.
 They of strange *Miracles* and wonders tell,
You are your selves a kind of *Miracle* ;
Even such a miracle as in writ divine
We read o'th *Devills* hurrying downe the *Swine*.
They have made *Images* to *speake*, 'tis said,
You a dull *Image* have your *Speaker* made ;
And that your bounty in *offerings* might abound,
Y'have to that *Idoll* giv'n six thousand pound.
They *drive out* Devills, they say ; here yee begin
To differ, I confesse ; you *let them in*.
 They maintaine *Transubstantiation* ;
You by a *Contrary Philosophers stone*,
To *Transubstantiate* Mettalls, have the skill ;
And turne the Kingdomes *Gold* to *I'ron* and *Steele*.
I'th' *Sacrament* yee agree not, but 'tis noted,
Bread must be *Flesh*, *Wine Blood*, if ere't be *voted*.
 They make the *Pope* their *Head*, you'exalt for him
Primate and *Metropolitane*, Master *Pym* ;
Nay, *White*, who sits in the *Infallible Chaire*,
And most *Infallibly* speakes *Non-sence* there :
Nay *Cromwell*, *Pury*, *Whistler*, Sir *John Wray*,
He who does say, and say, and say, and say.
Nay *Lowry*, who does new *Church-Gover'ment* wish,
And *Prophesies*, like *Jonas*, midst the *Fish*.
Who can such various businesse wisely sway,
And handle *Herrings*, and *Bishops* in one day.
Nay all your *Preachers*, Women, Boyes, or Men,
From *Master Calamy*, to *Mistresse Ven*,

154

THE PURITAN AND THE PAPIST

Are perfect *Popes* in their owne *Parish* growne;
For to outdoe the story of *Pope Jone*:
Your *Women* preach too, and are like to bee
The *Whores* of *Babylon*, as much as *Shee*.

 They *depose Kings* by force; by force you'de doe it,
But first use faire meanes to *perswade* them to it.
They dare *kill Kings*; now 'twixt ye here's the strife,
That you dare *shoot* at *Kings*, to *save* their *life*.
And what's the difference, 'pray, whether he fall
By the *Popes Bull* or your *Oxe Generall?*
Three Kingdomes thus ye strive to make your owne;
And, like the *Pope*, usurpe a *Triple Crowne*.

 Such is your *Faith*, such your *Religion*;
Let's view your *manners* now, and then I ha' done.
Your *Covetousnesse* let gasping *Ireland* tell,
Where first the *Irish Lands*, and next ye *sell*
The *English Bloud*; and raise *Rebellion* here,
With that which should suppresse, and quench it there.
What mighty summes have ye squeez'd out o'th' *City?*
Enough to make 'em *poore*, and *something witty*.
Excise, Loanes, Contributions, Pole-moneys,
Bribes, Plunder, and such *Parliament Priviledges,*
Are words which you'le ne're learne in holy Writ,
'Till the *Spirit* and your *Synod* ha's mended it.
Where's all the *Twentieth* part now, which hath beene
Paid you by some, to forfeit the *Nineteene?*
Where's all the *Goods distrain'd*, and *Plunders* past?
For you're growne wretched, *pilfering* knaves at last;
Descend to *Brasse* and *Pewter*; till of late,
Like *Midas*, all ye *toucht*, must needs be *Plate*.

 By what vast hopes is your *Ambition* fed?
'Tis writ in *bloud*, and may be plainly read.
You must have *Places*, and the Kingdome sway;
The *King* must be a *Ward* to your *Lord Say*.
Your innocent *Speaker* to the *Rolles* must rise,
Six thousand pound hath made him *proud* and *wise*.
Kimbolton for his Fathers place doth call;
Would be *like* him; would he were, *face* and all.
Isaack would alwayes be *Lord Mayor*, and so
May alwayes be, as much as he is now.

For the *Five Members*, they so richly thrive,
They'le but continue alwayes *Members Five*.
Onely *Pym* doth his *naturall right* enforce,
By the *Mothers* side he's *Master* of the *Horse*.
Most shall have *Places* by these popular tricks,
The rest must be content with *Bishopricks*.
    For 'tis 'gainst *Superstition* your intent,
First to root out that *great Church Ornament*,
Money and *Lands* ; your swords, alas, are drawne,
Against the *Bishop*, not his *Cap*, or *Lawne*.
    O let not such loud *Sacriledge* begin,
Tempted by *Henries* rich successefull sinne.
Henry the *Monster* King of all that age ;
Wilde in his *Lust*, and wilder in his *Rage*.
Expect not you his Fate, though *Hotham* thrives
In imitating *Henries* tricke for *Wives*,
Nor fewer *Churches* hopes then *Wives* to see
Buried, and then their *Lands* his owne to bee.
    Ye boundlesse *Tyr[a]nts*, how doe you outvy
Th' *Athenian Thirty*, *Romes Decemviri?*
In Rage, Injustice, Cruelty as farre
Above those men, as you in *number* are.
What *Mysteries* of *Iniquity* doe we see ?
New *Prisons* made to defend *Libertie* ;
Where without cause, some are undone, some dy,
Like men *bewitcht*, they know not *how*, nor *why*.
Our *Goods* forc'd from us for *Propriety*'s sake ;
And all the *Reall Non-sence* which ye make.
Ship-money was unjustly ta'ne, ye say ;
Unjustlier farre you take the *Ships* away.
The *High-Commission* you calld Tyrannie,
Ye did ; Good God ! what is the *High-Committee* ?
Ye said that *gifts* and *bribes Preferments* bought,
By *Money* and *Bloud* too, they now are sought.
To the *Kings will* the *Lawes* men strove to draw ;
The *Subjects will* is now become the *Law*.
'Twas fear'd a *New Religion* would begin ;
All new Religions now are entred in.
The King *Delinquents* to protect did strive ;
What Clubs, Pikes, Halberts, Lighters, sav'd the Five ?

THE PURITAN AND THE PAPIST

You thinke the *Parliament*, like *your State* of *Grace*,
What ever sinnes men doe, they keepe their place.
Invasions then were fear'd against the *State*,
And *Strode* swore that last yeare would be *'Eighty-Eight*.
You bring in Forraine aid to your designes ;
First those great *Forraine Forces* of *Divines*,
With which Ships from *America* were fraught ;
Rather may *stinking Tobacco* still be brought
From thence, I say ; next ye the *Scots* invite,
Which ye terme *Brotherly Assistants* right ;
For with them you intend *England* to share :
They, who, alas, but *younger Brothers* are,
Must have the *Monies* for their *Portion* ;
The *Houses* and the *Lands* will be your *owne*.
We thanke ye for the *wounds* which we endure,
Whil'st *scratches* and slight pricks ye seeke to *cure*.
We thanke ye for *true reall feares* at last,
Which free us from so ma[n]y *false ones* past.
We thanke ye for the *Bloud* which *fats* our *Coast*,
(That fatall debt paid to great *Straffords* Ghost.)
We thanke ye for the ills receiv'd, and all
Which by your *diligence* in good time we shall.
We thanke ye, and our *gratitude's* as great
As *yours*, when you thank'd *God* for being *beat*.

A. C.

FINIS.

THE
GUARDIAN;

A

COMEDIE.

Acted before

Prince CHARLS
His *HIGHNESS*

At Trinity-Colledg in *Cambridge*,
upon the twelfth of *March*, 1641.

Written by
ABRAHAM COWLEY.

LONDON,
Printed for *JOHN HOLDEN* at the
Anchor in the New-Exchange,
1650.

The Actors Names.

Captain Blade *the Guardian.*
O[l]d Truman, *a teasty old man.*
Young Truman *his Son, in love with* Lucia.
Col Cutter *a sharking Souldier*⎫
Dogrel *a sharking Poëtaster*⎭ *Lodgers at the Widows house.*
Puny *a young Gallant, a pretender to wit.*

Lucia *Neece and Ward to Captain* Blade, *in love with young*
    Truman.
Aurelia *daughter to* Blade.
Widow, [an] *old Puritan, Landlady to Colonel* Cutter *and* Dogrel.
Tabytha *her Daughter.*

Jaylors, Servants, *and* Fidlers.

The Scene London.

160

The
PROLOGUE.

WHo says the Times do Learning disallow?
  ['T]is false; 'twas never honour'd so as now
When you appear, great Prince, our night is done:
You are our Morning-star, and shall b'our Sun.
But our Scene's London now, and by the rout
We perish if the Roundheads be about:
For now no ornament the head must wear,
No Bays, no Mitre, not so much as Hair.
How can a Play pass safely, when we know,
Cheapside-Cross falls for making but a show?
Our onely hope is this, that it may be
A Play may pass too, made ex tempore.
Though other Arts poor and neglected grow,
They'll admit Poetry, which was always so.
Besides, the Muses of late times have bin
Sanctifi'd by the Verse of Master Prin.
  But we contemn the fury of these days,
And scorn as much their Censure as their Praise.
Our Muse, blest Prince, does onely on you relie;
Would gladly live, yet not refuse to die.
Accept our hastie zeal; a thing that's play'd
Ere 'tis a Play, and acted ere 'tis made.
Our Ignorance, but our Duty too, we show:
I would all ignorant people would do so.
At other times, expect our Wit and Art;
This Comedy is acted by the Heart.

The Guardian.

Act. 1. Scæn. 1.

Widow, *Tabytha*, Colonel *Cutter*, *Dogrel*.

Cutter. PRithee widow be not incens'd, we'll shew our selves
like yong Lords shortly; and you know, I Hope,
they use to pay their debts.

Wid. I, you talk of great matters, I wis, but I'm sure
I could never see a groat yet of your money.

Dog. Alas, we carry no silver about us,
    That were mechanical and base;
      Gold we about us bring:
    Gold, thou art mighty in each place,
      Of Metals Prince and King.

Why I tell you my pockets have not been guilty of any small
money in my remembrance.

Wid. I know not, but all things are grown dear of late;
our Beef costs three shillings a stone, and the price of corn is
rais'd too.

Taby. Nay, mother, coals are rais'd too, they say. These
things you think cost nothing.

Dog. Nay, *Tabytha*, Mistress *Tabytha!* ifaithlaw now I'll
make a Psalm for you, and be but peaceable.

    Contain thy tongue, and keep it in
      Within thy mouths large prison.
    Both jars, and also many a sin
      From out the mouth has risen.

I'm onely for Odes, by the Muses, and the quickest for them,
I think, in the Christian world, take in Turks, Infidels, Jews
and all.

THE GUARDIAN

Cutt. Have but a little patience, widow; well—I'll say this for thee, thou art the honestest Landlady upon the face of the earth, which makes me desire to live in your house; and you shall not lose by't: do but mark the end.

Wid. I stand not so much upon that; but I use to ha' Lawyers in my house, such civil compleat gentlemen in their Sattin doublets (I warrant you) and broad ruffs, as passes; and Courtiers, all to be lac'd and slasht, and fine fellows as you shall see in a summers day; they would not say Why do ye this? to a woman: and then Knights.

Tab. I, and Gentlemen too, mother.

Wid. But you, forsooth, come in drunk every night, and fall a swearing as if you would rend the house in two, and then mumble and tumble my daughters cloathes, she says.

Tab. I, and would have——

Cutt. What would we have done?

Tab. Nay no good, I warrant you.

Wid. And then you drink up a kilderkin of small beer next morning.

Dog. All this shall be corrected and amended, Landlady: yes faith, *Cutter*, thou must repent, thou hast been to blame sometimes.

Wid. Besides, you are always so full of your fripperies, and are always a grinning and sneering at every thing: I was wont to have sober boorders in my house, and not such hee-hee-heeing fellows.

Tab. Nay, they mock'd and fleer'd at us as we sung the Psalm the last Sunday-night.

Cutt. That was that mungrel Rhymer; by this light, he envies his brother Poet honest *John Sternhold*, because he cannot reach his heights.

Wid. O the father! the Colonel's as full of waggery as an egge's full of meat: I warrant, M. *Dogrel*, what you get by him you may e'en put i' your eye, and ne'er see the worse for't.

Cutt. Well, and how dost ifaith now, honest Landlady? when shall we walk again into Moor-fields, and rejoyce at the Queens Cake-house?

Dog. I'll bespeak Cakes and Ale o'th' purpose there; and thou shalt eat stew'd Prunes, little *Tabytha*, till thy smock drop

again. A word i' you[r] ear, Landlady: Can you accommodate
us with two shillings?

> To morrow ere the rosie finger'd morn
> Starts from *Tithonus* bed, as Authors write;
> Ere *Phœbus* cry Gee-hoe unto his team,
> We will restore again, and thank you for your pain.

Cutt. I'll tell you a secret, Landlady: Captain *Blade* and
I shall be call'd shortly to the Court; the King has taken
notice of our deserts: I say no more: though yet thou
scorn'st me, *Tabytha*, I'll make thee a Lady one day. Will
you lend, widow? Great affairs bid me make haste.

Wid. I care not much if I trust you for once: Come in
and take it.

Dog. Then Mistress let me lead you thus,
And as we go let's buss.

Tab. Buss me no bussings. O lord, how you tumble my
gorget! *Exeunt.*

Act. 1. Scæn. 2.

Captain Blade, solus.

I could now be as melancholy as an old scabbie Mastiff, or
the Lions in the Tower: 'twere a good humour to repent.
Well, Captain, something must be done, unless a man could
get true gems by drinking, or, like a mouse in a cheese, enlarge
his house-room by eating. Four hundred pound a yeer
cashier'd? Four hundred, by this light, Captain. All my
comfort is, that now the usurer's damn'd; and now that nig-
gardly threescore and ten wither'd chap-faln Puritanical thing,
his wife, refuses to marry me: I would see her burnt for an old
witch before I'd take her for a wife, if she had not Agues,
Squinancies, Gouts, Cramps, Palsies, Apoplexies, and two dozen
of diseases more then S. *Thomas* Hospital; and if she live
long with all these, I'm sure she'll kill me quickly. But let her
be damn'd with her husband: Bring some drink, boy; I'm
foxt, by this light, with drinking nothing yet.

THE GUARDIAN

Act. 1. Scæn. 3.

Blade, Cutter, Dogrel.

Blade. What are ye come? Bring us a Tun then, and that so big, that that of Heidelberg may seem but like a barrel of pickl'd Oysters to't. Welcome Snapsack, welcome little vermin of *Parnassus:* how is't, my Laureate Rhymer? dost thou sing *Fortune my foe* still with thy brother Poet?

Dog. Ye Muses nine assist my verse,
  That dwell by *Helicon* along;
  Captain *Blades* praise I will rehearse,
    With lyre and with song.

Bla. Why this right Ballad, and they hobble like the fellow with the wooden leg that sings them. And how dost, man o' blood?

Cutt. As well as a man of worth can do in these days, where deserts are so little regarded: if Wars come once, who but *Cutter?* who else but Colonel *Cutter?* God save you, Colonel *Cutter,* cry the Lords; the Ladies they smile upon Colonel *Cutter,* and call Colonel *Cutter* a proper Gentleman: every man strives who shall invite Colonel *Cutter* to dinner: not a Cuckoldly creditor dares pluck me by the cloak, and say, Sir, you forgot your promise, I'm in a strait for moneys, my occasions force me, or the like.

Bla. Cheer up, my *Hercules* upon a signe, I have a plot for ye, which if it thrive, thou shalt no more lie sunning in a bowling-alley, nor go on special holidays to the three-peny Ordinary, and then cry It pleases my humor better then to dine at my Lord Maiors.

Cutt. Would we had some drink here to stop your mouth.

Bla. No more be sick two or three days while thy boots are vamping: no more outswear whores in a reckoning, and leave the house in an anger.

Cut. Ha' you done?

Bla. Nor sup at Taverns with Radishes: nor for a meals meat o'erthrow the King of Spain of the Hollanders when you please: nor when you go to bed produce ten several Tavern snuffs to make one pipe of Tobacco.

Cut. 'Slid would I had one here.

Bla. Nor change your name and lodging as often as a whore; for as yet, if you had liv'd like a Tartar in a cart, (as you must die, I fear, in one) your home could not have been more uncertain. Your last Gests were these: From a Watermans house at the Banks side, (marry you stay'd there but a small while, because the fellow was jealous of his wife) passing o'er like great King *Xerxes* in a Sculler, you arriv'd at a Chandlers house in Thames-street, and there took up your lodging. The day before you should have paid, you walkt abroad, and were seen no more: for ever after the smell of the place offended you. Next, you appear'd at an Ale-house i'th' Covent-Garden, like a Duck that dives at one end of the pond, but rises unexpectedly at the other. But that place (though there was Beer and Tobacco there) by no means pleas'd you; for there dwelt so many cheaters thereabouts, that you could not live by one another; they spoil'd your trade quite. Then from a Shoo-makers, (as you entitl'd him; marry some authors call him a Cobler) to a Basket-makers; from thence to the Counter: from thence, after much benevolence, to a Barbers; changing more lodgings then *Pythagoras* his soul did. At length, upon confidence of those new breeches, and the scouring of that everlasting Buff, you ventur'd upon the widows, that famous house for boorders, and are by this time hoysing up your sails, I'm sure; the next fair winde y'are gone.

Cut. I wonder, Captain, among so many rascally houses, how I happen'd to miss yours. 'Tis true, I have not lien leaguer always at one place: Souldiers must remove their tents: *Alexander* the Great did it an hundred times.

Bla. Now to the words of comfort—drink first—then Lordings listen all.

Dog. We do, both great and small.

O my conscience this cup of wine has done my genius good.

Bla. When first my brother departed—

Dog. 'Twas poorly spoken, by this day.

Bla. He committed his daughter and estate to my care; which if she either di'd, or married without my consent, he bequeath'd all to me. Being five yeers gone, he died.

THE GUARDIAN

Dog. How frail is humane life! Well sung the divine Poet
> *Like to the damask rose you see,*
> *Or like the blossom on the tree,*
> *Or like,* &c.

Cutt. Sirrah, Trundle, either hear out peaceably, or I shall
cut your ears off. Proceed, Captain.

Bla. I falling into ill company, yours, or some other such
idle fellows, began to be misled, could drink and swear, nay, at
last, whore sometimes too; which courses having now at last
made me like *Job* in every thing but patience; your Landlady
(for to her husband my estate was morgag'd) I have sought all
means to marry.

Dog. That *Niobe!* that *Hecuba!*

Bla. Pish! I could have lien with either of the two, so't
had been before *Hecuba* was turn'd into a bitch, or t'other into
a stone: for though I hate her worse then small beer.

Cutt. Or pal'd wine.

Dog. Or proverbs and Latine sentences in discourse.

Cutt. Or a Sermon of two hours long.

Bla. Or *Dogrels* verses, or what you will else; yet she has
money, blades; she would be a Guiana or Peru to me, and we
should drink four or five yeers securely, like Dutchmen at a
Wedding. But hang her, let her die and go to hell, 'tis onely
that can warm her: she scorns me now my money's gone.

Dog. Thus Pride doth still with Beauty dwell,
And like the Baltick ocean swell.

Bla. Why the Baltick, *Dogrel?*

Dog. Why the Baltick? This tis not to have read the
Poets.

Bla. Now if my neece should marry, *præsto*, the means
are gone; and I must, like some Gentleman without fear or
regard of the gallows, betake my self to the high-way, or else
cheat like one of you, and tremble at the sight of a pillory.
Therefore—(prick up your ears, for your good angel speaks)
upon conditions of share, I marry her to one of you.

Both. I but how, Captain? how?

Bla. Why either she shall have one of you, or no body;
for if she marry without my consent, the money's mine own:
and she'll be hang'd first i'th' Friers rope, ere she turn Nun.

Cutt. I'll be a Franciscan, if she do.

ABRAHAM COWLEY

Bla. Not a Carthusian, I warrant thee, to abstain from flesh. Thou mightst well have taken holy Orders, if it were not for chastity and obedience: their other vow of never carrying money about thee, thou hast observed from thy youth up.

Dog. I'll have her, by *Mercury*; I have two or three Love-odes ready made; they can't chuse but win her. *Cutter*, adore me, *Cutter*, thou shalt have wine thy fill, though thou couldst out-drink *Xerxes* his army.

Cutt. You get her? what with that Ember week-face of thine? that Rasor of thy nose, those ears that prick up like a Puritanical button-makers of *Amsterdam?* thou lookst as if thou never hadst been fed since thou suck'dst thy mothers milk: thy cheeks begin to fall into thy mothers mouth, that thou mightst eat 'em. Why thou very lath with a thing cut like a face atop, and a slit at the bottom! I am a man, and can do her service; here's metal, boy.

Dog. 'Tis i' your face then.

Cutt. I can fight her quarrels, boy, and beget on her new *Achilleses.*

Dog. Yes—thou art a very *Achilles*—in the swiftness of thy feet: but thou art a worser coward then any of the Train'd Bands: I'll have a school-boy with a cat-stick take away thy Mistress from thee. Besides, what parts hast thou? hast thou scholarship enough to make a Brewers clerk? Canst thou read the Bible? I'm sure thou hast not. Canst thou write more then thine own name? and that in such vile characters, that most men take them for Arabian pot-hooks; and some think thou dost but set thy mark when thou writest thy name. I'm vers'd, *Cutter* in the whole Encyclopædie, a word that's Greek to you. I am a Wit, and can make Greek verses *ex tempore.*

Bla. Nay not so; for if you came to your verses, *Dogrel*, I'm sure you ha' done with wit. He that best pleases her, take her a Gods name, and allow the tother a pension: What think you, gallants?

Cutt. Agreed; thou shalt have three pound and a cloak.

Dog. Away, you puff, you kickshaw, you quaking custard.

Cutt. Prethee be patient, thou shalt have lace to't too.

Bla. Pox take you both; drink and be friends.

Dog. Here's to you, *Cutter*. I'm something cholerick, and given to jeering: but what, man? words are but winde.

THE GUARDIAN

Bla. I'll call her in. Why boy within th[er]e, call my neece quickly hither.

Dog. I'm undone; I ha' left my Ode at home: undone, by *Mercury*, unless my memory help me.

Cutt. Thus and thus will I accoast her: I'm the man; *Dogrels* clothes will cast him.

Act. 1.   Scæn. 4.

Blade, Cutter, Dogrel, Lucia.

Bla. When she has seen you both, one void the room, and so wooe by turns.

Dogrel. I'll go out first, and meditate upon my Ode.

Bla. Welcome, dear neece; I sent for you to entertain these Gentlemen my friends: and heark you, neece, make much of them; they are men of worth and credit at the Court, though they go so plain; that's their humour onely: And heark you, neece, they both love you; you cannot chuse amiss. I ha' some business——Your servant, Gentlemen.

Luc. Not chuse amiss? indeed I must do, Uncle, if I should chuse again. Y'are welcom, Gentlemen.

Cutt. I thank you, fairest Lady: I am a Souldier, Lady, and cannot complement; but I ha' travell'd over all the world, Germany, Morocco, Swethland, Persia, France, Hungary, Caleput, Peru.

Dog. 'Slid, how he shuffles all the Countries together like lots in a hat!

Cut. Yet I never saw before so fair a Lady. I cannot complement i' faith.

Luc. Y'have taken a long journey, Sir, 'twere best To rest your self a little: Will you sit? Will you, Sir, take a seat too?

Dog. 'Slife I can't say my Ode now. I'll wait upon you presently.   *Exit.*

Cutt. Fair Lady—(This 'tis to converse with none but whores: I know not what to say to her.) You are the onely mistress of my thoughts. My service to you, Lady.   *Drinks to her.*

169

Luc. To me, Sir, do you speak, or to the wine?

Cutt. To you, by *Mars.* Can you love me, Beauty? I'm sure your uncle prefers no man under the cope—

Luc. Soft, Sir, d'ye use to take in Towns so soon?
My uncle gave an equal commendation
To both of you.

Cutt. What? to that mole-catcher i'th' old Serge? he brought him in for humour, to make you sport. I'll tell you what he is.

Luc. Pray do, Sir.

Cutt. The very embleme of poverty and poor poetry: the feet are worse patcht of his Rhymes, then of his Stockings: if one line forget it self, and run out beyond his elbow, while the next keeps at home (like him) and dares not shew his head; he calls that an Ode. Your uncle and I maintain him onely for sport. I'll tell you how I found him; marry walking in Moor-fields cross arm'd: he could not pluck his hat over his eyes, there were so many holes in it: he had not so much linen about him as would make a cuff for a Bartlemew-fayr-baby. Marry the worst I like in him is, he will needs sometimes, in way of gratitude, present me with a paper of Verses. Here comes the vermin.

Act. 1. Scæn. 5.

Cutter, Dogrel, Lucia.

I'll leave him alone with you, that you may have the better sport: he'll not shew half his tricks before me. I think I ha' spoil'd his markets. Now will I stand behinde the hangings, and hear how she abuses him. I know by her eye she loves me. *Cutter*, thou'rt blest.   *Exit.*

Dog. Fairer, O fairer then the Lilly,
Then Primerose fair, or Daffa[d]ily;
Less red then thy cheeks the Rose is,
When the Spring it doth disclose his
Leaves; thy eyes put down the star-light;
When they shine, we see afar—light.
O these eyes do wound my heart
With pretty little *Cupids* dart;

THE GUARDIAN

Wounded I am with deadly smart;
The pain raigns in every part.
Thy beauty and thy great desart
Draw me as horses draw a Cart.
O that I had Rhetoricks art—impart—fart—mart—start.
To move thee; for I would not start
Till I—
　　Luc. Take heed, Sir, you'll be out of breath anon.
Y'ha' done enough for any honest Poet.
　　Dog. Fairest nymph, I swear to thee,
The later part was made *ex tempore!*
Not a bit of prose goes down with me.
　　Luc. (I must know't.)
May I be so bold as to enquire of you
Your friends name that was here; he seems to be
A man of worth and quality.　　　　*Cut.* That's I.
　　Dog. Quality? yes?　　　　　*Cut.* That's I again.
If whoring, drinking, cheating, poverty and cowardice be
qualities, he's one of the best qualified men in the Christian
world.　　　　　　　　　　*Cut.* O the devil!
　　Luc. He's a great traveller.
　　Dog. In suburbs and by-lanes; he never heard a gun but
in Moor-fields or Finsbury at a mustering, and quak'd then as
if they had been the Spaniards: I'll undertake a Pot-gun shall
dismay him.
　　Cutt. A plague upon him—
　　Dog. Those breeches he wears, and his hat, I gave him:
till then, he went like a Paper-mill all in rags, and like some
old statue in a ruin'd Abbey. About a month ago, you might
ha' seen him peep out at a grate, and cry, *Kinde merciful Gentle-
men, for the Lords sake, poor prisoners undone by suretiship*, and
the like.
　　Cut. Contain thy self, great spirit; keep in a while.
　　Dog. We call him Colonel in an humour onely. The
furniture of his chamber (for now, at mine and some other
Gentlemens charges, he has got one) is half a chair, and an
earthen chamber-pot, the bottom of an inkhorn for a candle-
stick, and a dozen of little gally-pots with salve in 'um; for he
has more diseases—
　　Cut. I can endure no longer.　　　　　*Enters.*

Dogrel, thou lyest; there's my glove; meet me an hour hence.

   Dog. And there's mine. I'll put a good face on't; he dares not fight, I'm sure.

   Cut. Two hours hence
Expect the Saracens head; I'll do't, by heavens.
Though hills were set on hills, and seas met seas, to guard thee,
I'd reach thy head, thy head, proud *Dogrel*.   *Exit.*

   Luc. Nay, y'are both even: just such an ex'lent character
He did bestow on you. Why thou vile wretch
Go to the stews, the gaole, seek there a wife;
Thou'lt finde none there but such as will scorn thee.
Was thy opinion of my birth or fortune,
My chastity or beauty (which I willingly
Confess to be but small) so poor and lowe,
That thou couldst think thy self a match for me?
I'll sooner marry with my grave; for thou
Art worser dirt then that. See me no more.   *Exit.*

   Dog. Scorn'd by a mistress? with a friend to fight?
Hence, lighter Odes; I'll biting Satyrs write.   *Exit.*

Act. 1. Scæn. 6.

Truman filius, Lucia.

   Tru. I must be gone, my *Lucia*; I must leave
My self, and thee, more then my self, behinde me.
Thus parts the greedy usurer from his bags,
With an heart heavier then those: he fixes
His covetous eye upon the charming metal,
As if he meant to throng those many pleasures
Which several times would yeeld, into one minute.
With as much joy he kisses his lov'd Idol,
As I do thee, to whom all gold compar'd,
Seems but like Pebbles to the Diamond:
And then he sighs, my *Lucia*.

   Luc. And weeps too, if, like us, he bid farewel.
Why should your father be so cruel?

Tru.   He's old and angry, *Lucia*, very angry,
And either has forgot his youthful days,
Or else I'll swear he did not love my mother
With half that noble heat that I do thee:
For when he heard your uncles resolutions,
Doubting your portion if we two should marry,
He forc'd me to an oath so strange, which though
I then durst swear, I scarce dare now repeat;
An oath ne'er more to see nor hear thee, *Lucia*,
After the envious shortness of this hour,
Without his leave.
   Luc.   You will forget me quite then.
   Tru.   Forget thee, *Lucia?* 'tis not death it self
Has so much Lethe in't: I shall not chuse
In the long sleep o'th' grave, but dream of thee,
If it be true that souls which leave hid treasures
(Being buried far less peaceable then their gold)
Walk up and down, and in their urns want rest,
How will my ghost then wander, which has left
Such precious wealth behinde it? Sure it will
Desire to see thee, and I fear will fright thee.
I would say more, but I shall weep anon.   *Exit.*
   Luc.   So quickly gone! he might have staid, me thinks,
A little longer, and I ow'd that happiness
To the misfortune of his future absence.
Why did he swear to's father? I'm a fool,
And know not what to say.

Act 1.   Scæn. 7.

Truman filius, *Lucia.*

   Tru.   Stay, *Lucia*, prithee stay; I had forgot
The business which I came for.
   Luc.   I owe much
To your forgetfulness, my *Truman :* if
It be such always, though you forget me,
I'll pardon you.   What was your business, pray?
   Tru.   To kiss your hand, my dearest.

ABRAHAM COWLEY

Luc. Was that all?
I'm glad to see your grief so small and light,
That it can finde leasure to complement:
'Tis not like mine, believe me.
    Tru. Was not that business, *Lucia?*
In my opinion now, th'affairs of Kings,
The honourable troubles of a Counsellor,
Are frivolous and light, compar'd to this.
May I not kiss your lips too, dearest *Lucia?*
I have an inward dropsie; and my remedy
Enflames my thirst: 'tis that best Nectar onely
Which has the power to quench it.
    Luc. If there be Nectar there,
It was your lip that brought it thither first;
And you may well be bold to claim your own.
Shall we sit down and talk a little while?
They will allow us sure a parting-time.
    Tru. And that I would not change, not this poor minute
In which I see, and hear, and touch thee, *Lucia,*
For th'age of Angels, unless thy lov'd presence
Make a heav'n there for me too.
What shall I do to bring the days t'an end?
Sure they'll be tedious when I want thy company.
    Luc. I'll pray for the success of our chaste loves,
And drop down tears for beads.
    Tru. I'll read o'er the large volume of the creatures;
And where I finde one full of grace and beauty,
I'll gaze and think on that; for that's thy picture.
    Luc. Whatever kinde of Needle-work I make,
Thy name I'll intermingle, till at last,
Without my mindes conjunction and consent,
The needle and my hand shall both agree
To draw thy name out.
    Tru. I will gather flowers,
Turn wanton in the truness of my love,
And make a posie too, where *Lucia*
Shall be mysteriously writ in flow'rs:
They shall be fair and sweet, such as may paint
And speak thee to my senses.
    Within. Mistress *Lucia, Lucia.*
    Luc. I am call'd: farewel.

THE GUARDIAN

Act. 1. Scæn. 8.

Truman filius, *Lucia*, *Aurelia*.

Aur. My father, cousin, would speak with you.
Luc. I'll wait upon him.   *Exit.*
Aur. Will you be gone so soon, Sir?
Tru. I must offend your father else.
Aur. You would have stay'd longer with her, I'm sure.
Tru. It may be so. Your servant, Lady.   *Exit.*
Aur. Contemn'd by all? while my proud cousin walks
With more eyes on her then the moon: but I,
Like some small petty star without a name,
Cast unregarded beams.
It must not be; I snatch of all those glories
Which beauty or feign'd vertue crown her with,
Till her short light confess her but a Comet.
I love thee, *Truman*; but since 'tis my fate
To love so ill, I'll try how I can hate.

Finis Actus primi.

Act. 2. Scæn. 1.

Cutter, Dogrel.

Cut. Come on, *Dogrel*, now will I cut your throat.
Dog. You'll be hang'd first.
Cut. No, by this light.
Dog. You'll be hang'd after then.
Cut. I'll slice thee into steaks.
Dog. I believe indeed thou art so hungry, thou couldst feed like a *Cannibal.*
Cut. No, thou'lt be a dish for the devil; he'll dress thee at his own fire. You call'd me Coward: hadst thou as many lives as are in *Plutarch*, I'd make an end of 'um. (I must daunt him, for fear he should fight with me.) I will not leave

175

so much blood in thee as will wet my nail: and for thy flesh,
I'll mangle it in such manner, that the Crowes shall not know
whether it were a mans body or no.

Dog. (He was once a Coward, and I never heard yet of his
reformation)
Hear thou altitonant *Jove*, and Muses three.
(Muses? a plague upon 'um, I meant Furies.)
Hear, thou altitonant *Jove*, and Furies three.

Cut. Nay then
Leap from the leathern dungeon of my sheath,
Thou *Durindana* brave.
(Will nothing do?) Come on, miscreant. *They draw.*

Dog. Do, do, strike if thou dar'st.

Cut. Coward, I'll give thee the advantage of the first push.

Dog. I scorn to take any thing of thee, I.

Cut. Thou hadst better eat up thy mothers soul, then
touch me.

Dog. If thou wilt not strike first, take thy life.

Cut. I had rather die then give the first blowe, since thou
hast said it.

Dog. I see this quarrel, *Cutter*, will come to a quart of
wine: shall's go?

Cut. How rash is anger! had not reason check'd me,
I should have kill'd my Poet for a woman,
A very woman. Let's sheath, *Dogrel*—

Act. 2.   Scæn. 2.

Cutter, Dogrel, Puny.

Here's company; 'slid I'll fight then.

Pun. How now, Paynims? fighting like two sea-fishes in
a map? slaying and killing like horse-leaches? Why my little
gallimaufry, what Arms and Arts?

Dog. *Tam Marti, quam Mercurio*, I. 'Slife, outbrav'd by
a fellow that has no more valour in him then a womans Tailor?

Cutt. By my fathers Soul, I'll kill him an he were an
Army.

176

Pun. Hold! stop! this Colonels spirit's all flame.

Dog. 'Tis the flame of a flap-dragon then, for 'twill hurt no body.

Cutt. Mr. *Puny*, you do me wrong.

Pun. What do ye mean bufles?

Cutt. 'Slife, an you hinder me *Puny*—

Pun. Pox take you, kill one another and be hanged then, doe, stab, why don't ye?

Cutt. At your command Mr. *Puny*? I'll be forc'd by no man; put up *Dogrel*, wee'll fight for no mans pleasure but our own.

Dog. Agreed, I'll not make another sport by murthering any man though he were a Tinker.

Pun. Why now you speak like righteous Homuncles, ye ha' both great spirits, as big as Indian-whales, for wit and valour a couple of Phœnixes.

Cut. 'Tis my fault *Puny*; I'm the resolutest man if I be but a little heated. Pox take't, I'm a fool for't.

Dog. Give me thy hand.

Cutt. I did not think thou hadst been so valiant, i'faith: I should have killed my self, if I had hurt thee in my fury.

Dog. So should I by this hand.

Pun. This is rare! up and down like a game at chess.

Dog. Why a game at chess more then any other?

Pun. A game at chess? why-pox thou'rt a kinde of Poet I confess, but for wit you shall pardon me—ther's as much in *Tom Coriats* shooes. But prithee, why did you two Pythagorians fall out?

Dog. A trifle, onely a Mistris.

Cutt. A pox take her, I woo'd her in an humor onely, I had rather marry a wench of ginger-bread, they're both of a Complexion.

Dog. And then her mouth's as wide as a Crocodiles, her kisses devour a man.

Cutt. Her eyes are like the eyes of a needle, and her nose pointed like that; I wonder her face is no cleaner, for those two perpetually water it: As for her lower parts, blessed are they that live in ignorance.

Pun. What an Heliogabalus make you of this wench? would I could see this Barbara Pyramidum.

Dog. Hang her, she looks like a gentlewoman upon the top of a ballad.

Cutt. Shavers, who i'the divels name would you guess to be my Mistris?

Pun. Some wench at a red lattice.

Dog. Some beast that stincks worse then Thames-street.

Pun. And looks like a shoulder of mutton stufft with parsly.

Cutt. 'Faith guess who.

Pun. 'Tis impossible among so many whores.

Cutt. 'Faith *Tabitha*, none but gentle Mistris *Tabitha*.

Dog. We shall have him turn Brownist now, and read Comments upon the Revelations.

Cutt. Thou hast hit it *Dogrel*: I'le put my self into a rare garbe; Buffe, thou must off, truly Buffe thou must.

Pun. 'Slid a good humour; I could find in my heart to change religion too.

Dog. Pox! no body will change with me, I'm sure. But canst thou put off swearing with Buffe? canst thou abstain in the middle of long grace from crying a plague upon him, the meats cold? canst thou repeat scripture enough to make a Puritan? I'me sure for understanding thou'lt be like enough to any of 'um.

Cutt. Let me alone, I'le deal with no oath above gods fatlikins, or by my truly: exclaim upon the sickness of drinking healths, and call the Players rogues, sing psalms, hear lectures; and if I chance to preach my self, woe be to the act, the object, the use, and application.

Pun. Thou art an everlasting stinker Colonel, 'tis a most potent humour, ther's mustard in't, t bits i'the nose.

Cutt. *Dogrel*, take heed of swearing before *Tabitha*.

Dog. If I look not as grave as a Judge upon the bench, let me be hanged for't.

Pun. Come away Physitians; 'slid I'le be of some Religion ere't be long too.

Act 2.   Scæn. 3.

Truman pater, *Truman* filius.

Tru. p.   You hear me—

Tru. f.   Sir—

Tru. p.   Sir me no sirs: I say you shall marry Mistris *Tabitha*.

Tru. f.   I hope sir—

Tru. p.   I, when I bid you do any thing, then you are a hoping; well, what do you hope sir?

Tru. f.   That you'ld be pleas'd—

Tru. p.   No, I will not be pleas'd till I see your manners mended: marry gap, you'le be teaching your father.

Tru. f.   I am—

Tru. p.   Go to, you're a foolish boy, and know not what's good for your self: you are? what are you, pray? we shall ha' you crow over your father.

Tru. f.   I shall observe—

Tru. p.   You will not sure? will you observe me? 'tis very well if my son come to observe me i'my old days, you will observe me? will ye?

Tru. f.   I mean sir—

Tru. p.   You shall mean what I please, if you be mine: I must be bound to your meaning?

Tru. f.   It may be—

Tru. p.   You'll teach me what may be, will you? do not I know what may be? 'tis fine, 'tis very fine: now i'your wisdom, now what may be?

Tru. f.   That Captain *Blade*—

Tru. p.   That what? what can he do? I'll see his nose cheese before you shall marry his neece. Captain *Blade*'s a swaggering companion; let 'um swagger, and see what he gets by his swaggering; I would have swaggered with him for his ears when I was a young man. And though I ha' done swaggering—well—I shall meet with Captain *Blade*, I hold him a tester on't—

Tru. f.   (Would he were gone.)   I shall obey—

Tru. p. Obey me no obeyings, but do what I command you. I'll to the Widow, and talk about her portion: stay! I had almost forgot to tel you, oh—Mistris *Tabitha*'s a vertuous maid, a very religious wench; I'll go speak concerning her portion.

Tru. f. It may be sir—

Tru. p. You'll never leave this trick, you'll be at your may-bees; take heed boy, this humour will undoe thee—she cannot have less then three thousand pounds: well—I'll go see—and d'ee hear? she goes plain, and is a good huswife; which of your spruce mincing squincing dames can make bone-lace like her? o tis a notable, apt, quick, witty girle—I'll goe to her mother about the portion. *Exit.*

Tru. f. About this time her letter promis'd me a meeting here: destiny it self will sooner break its word then she. Dear Mistris, there's none here besides your vassal. She's ready—

Act. 2.   Scæn. 4.

Truman filius, *Lucia* veil'd.

Ha! why this covering?
This is mistery darker then the veile
That clouds thy glorious face; unless t'encrease
My desire first, and then my joy to see thee,
Thou cast this subtler night before thy beauty.
And now like one scorched with some raging feaver,
Upon whose flames nor dew nor sleep hath faln,
I could begin to quarrel with the darkness,
And blame the slothful rising of the morn;
But with more gladness entertain't, then they,
Whose icy dwellings the cold Bare orelooks,
When after half the yeers continued night,
And the most tedious night of all but death;
A sudden light shot from their horizon,
Brings the long wisht-for day, which with such glory
Leaps from the East, as doth thy mateless beauty.
When thus the mist departs—   *Offers to pull*
Why shrinkst thou back?   *away the*
I prithee let me see thee, *Lucia.*   *veil.*

I'd rather some good power would strike me blinde,
Then lose the cause for which I love mine eyes:
At least speak to me: well may I call it night,
When silence too has joyn'd it self to darkness.
And did I not swear I would not—
Thy witty goodness can save others too
From sinning: I had quite forgot my oath:
Yet sure an oath forc'd from a lovers tongue
Is not recorded in heav'ns dreadful book,
But scatter'd loosely by that breath that made it.
However thy blest Letter makes me patient:
Thou giv'st all vertues: I can love thee thus.
And though thy skin were such, that it might seem
A black veil cast by nature o'er thy body,
Yet I would love thee, *Lucia*: every night,
Which is the harvest-time of all our hopes,
Will make thee as th'art now; and dost thou think
I shall not love thee most then?
We trifle here: I'll follow thee, O heaven;
Prosper the wise invention which it hath taught thee.

                                                    Exeunt.

Act. 2. Scæn. 5.

Captain *Blade, Servant.*

Bla. Is he carried to prison? that damn'd Urinal-monger,
that stinking Clyster-pipe-rogue! that ignorant Sattin cap! He
has not so much physick as would cure the tooth-ach. A slave
that poisons Gentlemen, to keep his hand in ure. Must a slave
come up stairs, mount the bank for money, and not be dis-
honoured down? He look'd as patiently then, as any Fidler
need to do. Give me some small beer, and the godly book;
I must not go to hell; there are too many Physitians there.
I was never in a worse disposition to die, in my life: my guts
begin to squeak already. Nothing vexes me now, but that
I shall stand pictur'd in a Ballad, with *Beware the physitian*, or
some such sentence, coming out of my mouth. I shall be sung
in Smithfield: not a blinde Ale-house, but *the life and miserable*

death of captain Blade shall be pasted up in: there shall I be brought confessing my sins at the later end, and giving good counsel. (You will be jumbling still.) Ten to one but *Dogrel* makes an Epitaph; there's another mischief. Here, take the book again; I'll not trouble my brain now I'm a dying.

Serv. Here's the widow, Sir, and her daughter, come to see you; and they have brought M. *Knockdown* to comfort you.

Bla. How? everlasting *Knockdown*? 'Slid, will they trouble a man when he's a dying? Sirrah, blockhead, let in *Knockdown*, and I'll send thee to heaven before me. I ha' but an hour to live, my Physitian says, and that's too little for him to preach in.

Serv. Shall I let the widow come in?

Blade. That's a she-*Knockdown* too. Well, let her come in; I must bear all torments patiently now. But, rogue, take heed of *Joseph Knockdown*: thou shalt not live with ears, if *Joseph Knockdown* enter. A plague upon all Physitians.

Act. 2.   Scæn. 6.

Capt. *Blade*, *Widow*, *Tabytha*.

Wid. How do you? how is't, Sir?

Bla. Cut off i'the flower o' my age, widow.

Wid. Not so, Sir, you are old, neighbour, God he knows.

Bla. I' the very flower, i'faith. That damn'd quacksalver.

Tab. He look'd like a rogue; a man might know him for a rogue, by his very eyes. Take comfort, Sir; ye know we must all die sooner or later. Our life is compared to a flower; and a flower is subject to uncertainty, as M. *Knockdown* observes.

Bla. O the torture of such a tongue! Would I were dead already.

Wid. Alas, good man! his tongue, I warrant ye, is hot: look how he raves, daughter! I have heard, indeed, that many rave when they are poison'd. Think o' your sins, Sir.

Bla. I prithee molest me not; there's none of 'um worth thinking of. I'm hotter then a dozen of Fevers: give me a cup of Sack there: Shall I die thirsty?

Wid. By no means, M. *Blade.* Fellow, take heed what ye give him : he must ha' none ; it breeds inflammations.

Bla. I'll never repent without a cup of Sack. Do, do, chuse whether you'll ha'me sav'd or no.

Wid. For his souls sake then, I'll drink to him in a cup of Sack. *Drinks.*

Bla. To my good journey, widow. Sirrah, fill me a brim-mer. Here, *Tabytha.* *Drinks.*

Act. 2. Scæn. 7.

Blade, Widow, Tabytha, Aurelia, Cutter, Dogrel.

Aur. Stand to 't now.

Dog. I'll warrant you I'll stand like a knight o'the post : I'll forswear with the devil. As for *Cutter,* he has don't fourty times before a Judge already.

Aur. My dearest father, though we cannot call
The sentence of fate back that's past upon you,
Yet heav'n has mixt some mercy with its anger,
And shewn us the curst plotters of your ruine.

Bla. How now, varlets? ye see I'm going to heaven, and ye must follow ; but the Captain must be sav'd before the Colonel. Who art thou? a godly Weaver?

Cut. I am not he that I was of old : what hath passed, is gone and vanisheth ; but what is now, remaineth.

Wid. No I'll besworn is he not ; never was Christian creature so alter'd, as they say.

Tab. He said a prayer last night so zealously, that all the house heard him, did they not? Brother M. *Cutter.*

Cut. Sister, I did pour out my self last night. Captain, y'are abus'd.

Bla. A small abuse ; nothing but onely poison'd.

Dog. Yes 'faith, we saw the Physitian, Mistress *Lucia* and *Truman* consulting all together : the Physitian pluck'd a box out, shew'd it them ; they seem'd to approve : an oath of secresie we heard them take, but suspected nothing, by this hand. We honest men do seldom suspect others.

Bla. Is this true, Colonel?

Cut. Should I say it is not true, I should not tell the truth if I should say so.

Bla. You swear 'tis true?

Cut. Before an Elder I shall swear.

Bla. *Aurelia*, send for 'um immediately, as if I meant to see 'um contracted; and bid the servants be ready to carry 'um away. I'll see 'um clapt up close before I die.

Aur. I go, Sir.   *Exit.*

Act. 2.   Scæn. 8.

Blade, Widow, Tabytha, Cutter, Dogrel, Lucia.

Luc. Dearest Uncle,
I come to beg one boon of you, the last
Which you can grant me, or I need to wish.

Bla. Speak, gentle Neece.

Luc. That since the love 'twixt *Truman* and my self
Hath been so fixt, and (as our fortunes) equal,
You will be pleas'd to seal with your last breath
The confirmation of our loves, our Contract:
And when your soul shall meet in heav'n my fathers,
As foon as he has bid you welcome thither,
He'll thank you for our marriage.

Bla. Oh by all means: where's gentle M. *Truman?* He's sorry for my death, good man, I warrant ye. Weep not for me, dear Neece, I know it greives you. Where's loving Mr. *Truman?*

Luc. Without Sir, waiting on your will, as on the voice of his good fate.

Bla. Pray call him in.   *Exit Luc.*
Sirrah, fetch two or three more of my knaves in.

Dog. Oh the dissembling of these women; they're like a folded picture, that every diversity of light represents diversly.

Bla. Hang all women beside you and your daughter, widow: I could almost like *Mahomets* religion, for turning all the sex out of Heaven.

184

THE GUARDIAN

Act. 2.   Scæn. 9.

*Blade, Cutter, Dogrel, Widow, Tabitha, Truman filius,
Lucia veil'd.*

Tru.   'Tis as we wisht, dear Lady; O this blest hour!

Bla.   Away with 'um immediately, let 'um be sent to prison straight.

Tru.   What means this rudeness? I understand not this incivility.

Cutt.   Ungratious children, ye have poysoned a most vertuous Souldier here.

Tru.   I poysoned? what d'ye mean?

Bla.   Away with 'um I say, they shall finde another place to answer for't.   *Exeunt Servants, with Truman and Lucia.*

Wid.   Hei ho! what pitty 'tis.

Cutt.   Captain, prithee away with these two impertinences; since you must dye, let's have a parting cup for shame.

Bla.   But thou art turn'd Apostate.

Cutt.   I did but fain all this; I'm as very a Rogue as ever I was.

Bla.   Thou speakst righteously, we will not make a dry far-wel on't.   Widow, I have some business with these two; shall I desire privacy a little while?

Wid.   Fare ye well. Mr. *Cutter*, you can speak comfortably to him: I'll see you again anon.   Oh the wickedness of these worldlings? Come *Tabitha*.   *Exeunt Widow and Tabitha.*

Bla.   The Doctor says, I shall dye without pain; therefore my sparks of Asia, let's be merry for a while.   Boy, fetch some wine and an hour-glass.

Cutt.   An hour-glass! what emblem shall we have? bring a sithe too; and this same lean, greedy, hungry Poet, shall act Time here.   *Enter boy with wine, and an hour glass.*

Bla.   Well said my little Pawn.   So, thus I'll husband my time.   According to my Emperick's computation I am to live an hour; half which I do allot to drink with you, a quarter to settle some business; and the rest, to good meditations and repentance.   How like ye this my gallants?

Cutt. Most Logically divided; never Scholer divided mess better *The boy fils wine.*

Bla. How it sparkles! Never be drunk again? My *Homer* junior, have at thee; this will string up thy Muse: rejoyce young frog of *Hellicon.* *Drinks.*

Dog. No, rather let me weep, drop briny tears,
Till I like *Niobe*—

Cutt. There's a piece of her sticks in his throat still, drink it down *Dogrel.*

Bla. Do, for when I am once gone, ye must e'en like *Mahumetans*, count wine a thing forbidden.

Cutt. Let's drink, let's drink, whilst life we have:
You'll finde but cold drinking, cold drinking in the grave.

Dog. A catch i'faith.
Boy go down,
And fill's the tother quart;
That we may drink the Captains health,
Before that we do part.

Cutt. Why dost thou frown, thou arrant Clown &c.

Bla. Ha hei boy's! another catch i'faith.
And all our men were very very merry.
And all our men were drinking,

Cutt. One man o' mine,
Dog. Two men o' mine,
Bla. Three men o' mine,
Cutt. And a man o' mine,
Om. As we went by the way, were
Drunk, Drunk, Damnable Drunk;
And all our men were very very merry &c.

Bla. Hei brave boys! now, *Cutter*, thou art a pretious Puritan.

Cutt. And thou a puissant Captain. Some wou'd ha' pin'd, and kept a quarter, and howl'd at their death, and ha' been more froward and troublesome then a Citizens wife when she takes Physick. This is true valour.

Dog. Sure he has dy'd before, he's so expert at it.

THE GUARDIAN

Act 2. Scæn. 10.

To these, old *Truman*.

Bla. What says old Priam to *Achilles* great?

Tru. 'Tis well, I'm glad to see you in you[r] Priams; but for all your Priams, and your Killisses, what ha' you done with my Son?

Bla. Thrice was thy *Hector* drawn about the walls.

Cutt. *Xanthus* and *Simois*, with his purple gore.

Dog. Alas, and welladay! we are stain'd all o're.

Om. Ha, ha, ha.

Tru. 'Tis very well, excellent well, all's well that ends well; I say—I shall finde Law I hope. My Son *Dick* in prison, and old *Dick* laughed at here by Raggamuffins: 'Tis very excellent well; I thank you gentlemen, I thank you heartily.

Bla. 'Tis not so much worth i'faith Sir; what do you mean Sir? pray spare your courtesie, nay, I pray be covered Sir.

Tru. It may be so, 'tis very likely Sir, an there be Law in Westminster—

Cutt. —And what dost thou mean, old man?

Dog. —And what dost thou mean, old man?

Cutt. —If thou mean'st to live long, plump, lusty, and strong;

Dog. —Then take of the cup and the Can.

Om. Ha, ha, ha.

Tru. Well, I'm made a laughing stock, it seems.

Bla. And good Sir—

Tru. Yes, I am made the laughing stock; I shall take some other course, I hold you a groat. Rest ye merry Gentlemen, I pray be merry, very very merry.

Dog. Nay, you shall stay and drink first.

Tru. Shall I, *Jacksauce*?   *Strikes off*
Pray Sir, be you covered too.   *his hat.*

Bla. Come old *Jethro*, here's a cup of wine will stir thy brains again, they're mouldy now.

Tru. I, you'd poyson me, wou'd you? 'tis very well if a man may be suffered to poyson whom he pleases.

Breakes the glass.

Bla. No, your good Son has got the art of poysoning.

Tru. My Son? Thou liest. My Son?

Bla. If ye be raging Lyon-mad, d'ye see that door? Be gone to your Son, and take some juice of Opium: Thou wants sleep, *Jethro.*

Truman offers to go out, and turns back again.

Tru. There's Law, Captain.

Bla. There is so; wou'd you'd go fetch it.

Tru. Nay, there's none it seems.

Bla. True, there shall be no Law, so you'll be gone.

Tru. There shall be no Law, say you? I desire no more, 'tis very exceeding dainty. There shall be no Law; I desire no more, 'tis a kinde of petty Treason: You'll remember, Sir, that there shall be no Law: That's enough, I pray remember Sir: and so farewell. There shall be no Law. *Exit.*

Bla. This worm-eaten old fellow has spoil'd our sport. And what says my hour-glass now? Time was i'faith.

Cutt. How do you feel your self?

Bla. As hot as Hell. Come wee'l take our last farewel within; and farwel here all drinking. God send me a good journey, I say.

Dog. Then briny tears come trickling down apace, For loss of him——

Cutt. And what?

Dog. Nay, ye put me out. *Exeunt.*

Finis Actus Secundi.

Act. 3. Scæn. 1.

Dogrel, Aurelia.

Dog. Not poysoned you say?

Au. No, he's as well as we.

Dog. It may be he has more lives then one, or used himself to poyson; as we now, that are Scholars, and Poets read, of one *Mithidrates.*

Au. He was never sick.

Dog. Yes, very hot.

Au. I, as a painted fire, his fancy made him so; I smell a plot in't. *Lucia*, you say, urged him then for *Truman*. 'Twas a meer plot, I doubt, to put him in fear of death.

Dog. I shall be taken for a kind of Rogue then, for bearing false witness.

Au. You shall not be mistaken, Sir, at all.

Dog. Pillory'd, and whipt, with my godly brother *Cutter*.

Au. Abus'd by the Prentices as you walk in the streets, and have rotten apples flung at you.

Dog. Have a hundred blustring oaths o' mine no more beleeved, then when I swear to my Creditors, I'll pay all.

Au. Be abandon'd by all men above a Tapster; and not dare to looke a gentleman i'the face; unless perhaps you sneak into a Play-house, at the fifth Act.

Dog. If ever I have to do with women again, but i'the way of all flesh, may I dye an *Eunuch*. I'll never lye or swear hereafter, but for my self. Were not you the vertuous gentlewoman, with the brown paper-face, that perswaded me to it?

Au. The very same, Sir; and I ha' just such another exploit here to imploy thee in: therefore be secret, close as a cokle, my good Rymer.

Dog. To imploy me in!

Au. Nay, you must do't i'faith; I ha' sworn first, *Dogrel*.

Dog. By this good light, I will do nothing at thy intreaty: not if thou shouldst intreat me to lye with thee. Must Poet *Dogrel?*

Au. I, must, if he intend e're to drink Sack again; or to make more use of his little-pocket, then to carry Tavern-bills in't; must do't, unless he intend to die without a shirt, and be buried without a winding-sheet.

Dog. I like thy wit yet wench, what is't?

Au. I would marry *Puny*; he's rich you know, and a bravery, and a wit.

Dog. He says himself he is so; but few are of his faith.

Au. He dances too, and courteth the Ladies.

Dog. Yes, in more postures then a dozen of Bowlers.

Au. But he's rich, *Dogrel*, and will be wise enough; when I have got 'um knighted, then I shall be a Lady, *Dogrel*; have a dozen of French-Taylors, Doctors, Jewellers, Perfumers, Tyre-women, to sit in consultation every morning, how I shall be drest up to play at Gleek, or dance, or see a Comedy, or go to the Exchange i'the afternoon; send every day my Gentleman, to know how such a Lady slept, and dream'd; or whether her dog be yet in perfect health: Then have the young smelling braveries; all adore me, and cut their arms, if I be pleased to be angry: Then keep my close and open Coaches, my yellow sattin Pages, Monkies, and women, or (as they call 'um) creatures.

Dog. Be then a politick, Lady; keep none but ugly ones, you'll ne'er be handsome else. But suppose all this, what's this to *Dogrel*?

Au. *Dogrel* shall be maintain'd by me, he shall ha' fine new Serge; and every day more wine then's drunk at a Coronation.

Dog. This qualifies. And when the good Knight's dicing, or at bowls, or gathering notes in private out o' Romances; might not *Dogrel* have a bit?

Au. Yes, like enough your Poetry might tempt some of my under-women to't. But are you prepar'd to cheat, in your own behalf, and mine?

Dog. I, but how must this be done?

Au. Why thus briefly. First read this Letter.

Dog. (*reads*) Dearest *Truman*,

We have long desired to be contracted together, that nothing might be wanting to our Loves, but Ceremony: To night about nine a clock, I shall finde opportunity to meet you at the garden door, and let you in; silence, and the help of veiles, will save the violating of your oath. Farewel.

Yours, *Luc. Blade.*

I'faith, was this her writing?

Au. No, but the hand's as like hers as the left is to the right. This you shall shew to *Puny*; and tell him that you found or stole it from *Truman*: I need not I suppose instruct you, to polish over a lye; he knows their love, and cannot suspect any thing; perswade him to make use of the occasion, and come himself.

Dog. And you'll meet him vail'd.

Au. Hast thou found it out? thou hast shrew'd reaches *Dogrel.*

190

THE GUARDIAN

Dog. I'll do't. Thou shalt be blest. I'll do't i'faith.

Au. About it then; I'll leave you: and fail not, *Dogrel*; remember wine and serge. But first, I have another way t' undoe thee, *Lucia*: And that I'll try too.   *Exit.*

Dog. Go thy ways girl for one, and that's for *Puny* I hope; I see thou'lt ne'er turn Semstress, nor teach girls; thou'dst be a rare wife for me, I should beget on thee *Donnes*, and *Johnsons*: but thou art too witty. We men that are witty, know how to rule our selves, can cheat with a safe conscience; 'tis charity to help thee, *Aurelia*, and I will do't, and merit.

                                                    Exit.

Act. 3. Scæn. 2.

Truman filius, *Solus.*

Tru. Our minds are like the Sea, and every Passion
Like some fierce Tempest stricken from the North,
Disturbs the Peaceful calmness of our thoughts:
Custom of anger drives us from our selves,
The *Adrian* Gulf a milder fury hurries;
Those Waves touch Heaven, but these arise to Hell.
Sometimes the winged whirle-wind of blind Avarice
Shoots it self forth, and sweeps up all before it.
Now we with greedy hope, knock at the Sphears,
Anon the deadly hand of cold dispair
Throws us beneath the grave: and midst these dangers
The flame of Love appears in stead of lightning;
And with sad glory frights the night it self.
Oh! 'tis a subtil fire! and kills, but wounds not.
Good God! What more then man can safely pass
The Billows, Rocks, and Monsters of this Ocean,
Unless some pow'r Divine, become his Pilot?
For then the windes would scatter, the waves shrink,
And th'outworn storm suffer it self a shipwrack.

191

ABRAHAM COWLEY

Act 3. Scæn. 3.

Aurelia, Taylor, Truman filius.

Au. Thanks good Taylor; now I'll onely beg that I may
buy your secrecy: Fare thee well, Friend.   *at the door.*
Tru. Ha! I did but speak just now of Heav'nly pow'rs,
And my good Angel enters! welcome
Lucia; I can scarce say so here, yet welcome heartily:
You see how ill our honest Plot succeeds;
I see we must out-weary fortunes anger,
And I have arm'd my self for't—ha!
          She gives him a note, and imbraces him. He reads.
I have with much ado gotten to you, and can stay with you
to night. (Ha!) Why should we defer our joys longer, since
we are married in heart? The opportunity, and impatience of
such delays, forc'd me to desire that which else my modesty
would not suffer me—(Modesty?)—Your desires—to your bed—
long wisht-for—(why this is strange) hum—hum—hum—
                              Yours, *Lucia*.
No, no, thou art not *Lucia*. If thou dost
(As thou saist) love me, do not use that name. *She embraces,*
Some devil has chang'd thee—   *and goes to kiss him.*
This is worse stil—with much ado—to night—joys longer—
opportunity—   *Reads: then walks*
                         about the room; goes to the
                         Candle, and burns the Letter.
May all remembrance of thee perish with thee,
Unhappie paper, made of guilty linen,
The menstruous reliques of some lustful woman:
The very ashes here will not be innocent,
But flie about, and hurt some chaste mens eyes,
As they do mine.   *Weeps.*
Oh thou that once wert *Lucia!* thy soul
Was softer then, and purer then swans feathers,
Then thine own skin: Two whitest things, that paper,
And thine own self, thou didst at once defile.

192

But now th'art blacker then the skin that covers thee:
And that same gloomy shade not so much hides
Thy Bodies colour, as it shews thy Mindes.   *She kneels.*
Kneel not to me, fond woman, but to heav'n;
And prithee weep: tears will wash cleaner Ethiops—
Wouldst thou have had me been mine own adult'rer?
Before my Marriage too? Wouldst thou ha' giv'n me
An earnest of the horns I was to wear?
Is Marriage onely a Parenthesis
Betwixt a maid and wife? Will they remain
Entire without it? Go, pray go back,
And leave me too, since thou hast left thy self:
When peace is made with heav'n, 'tis made with me.
          Exit Aurelia.
What are these women made of? Sure we men
Are of some better mold. Their vows and oaths
Are like the poisonous Spiders subtil net,
As dangerous to entrap, and broke as soon.
Their love, their faith, their selves enslav'd to passion.
Nothing's at their command, except their tears,
And we frail men, whom such heat-drops entice.
Hereafter I will set my self at liberty,
And live more free then is the air I breathe in:
And when I sigh, henceforth, it shall not be
For love of one, but pity of all the Sex.   *Exit.*

Act. 3.   Scæn. 4.

Dogrel, Puny.

Pun. But how shall I represent this Anthropophagus?

Dog. Onely speak softly, lest she chance to know your voice.

Pun. I warrant you I'll whisper like wet wood in a Justices chimney at Christmas.

Dog. But of all things, take heed of too much wit; that's always dangerous, but especially now. *Truman*, you know, is an honest harmless fellow, and is contented to speak sense.

Pun. I, hang him; there's clotted cream in his head in stead of brains; and no more o' that then will compleatly serve to fill the eye of a needle. But I shall ne'er abstain from these fine things, hyperboles and similitudes: my nature stands a tiptoe: *Truman* has got the cramp; his genius is like some gouty Alderman's that sits in a chair. An' I were in *Phalaris*'s Bull, I think I should be witty.

Dog. Nay, I know't; a man may as well keep a prentice from Moor-fields on a holiday, as you from your Muses, and C[o]nundrums; they're meat and drink to you.

Pun. No, my good bag-pipe, they're meat and drink to you, that feed by 'um.

Dog. I see you're ashamed of the Muses, and I hope they're even with you. But so much for this: you'll finde wine, I hope, when I have found you the wench.

Pun. Though thou wouldst drink cups bigger then Pauls-steeple, or the great bell at Westminster, thou shouldst have 'um. How long dost thou think has this night worn her mourning-gown, and lookt like a funeral?

Dog. Indeed, she has many torches. Why sure, 'tis just about the Critical time which she appointed. You know your business: First break a piece of Gold; profess before Heav'n and Angels, you take her for your wife; then give her half of it: and after that, somewhat as you understand me.

Pun. Will she be malleable, d'ye think? Shall I stamp *Puny* on her?

Dog. There's a Metaphor indeed! It seems 'tis the fashion; you take your wife for Gold. Hark! the door opens, use your fortune well. *Exit.*

Pun. Now, if my Alcocadin be right, I'm sure, I am made.
She opens the door, and lets him in.

Act. 3. Scæn. 5.

Captain *Blade, Servant.*

Bla. Pox upon 'um, they put me into a horrible fear; but I am glad I am so happily cheated, for all that. Well, I must devise some horrible lye, to justifie my fears; some trick must be thought upon to gull *Truman*. How now? What news from *Tripoly*.

Serv. Sad news, my Lord; here's an Army at the door, to speak with you.

Bla. Who are they? Creditors? a Merchant, a Mercer, a Scrivener, a Taylor, a Butcher, Six Cookes, a dozen of Vintners, and the rest? Ha? Tell 'um I am sick, taking Physick, or else abroad; hang 'um Rogues, come like quotidian Agues on a man.

Serv. No, Sir, 'tis old Mr. *Truman*, the Widow, and her daughter, and Mr. *Dogrel*, and I know not who; there's a stock of 'um.

Bla. They are those I wisht for, let 'um in.   *Exit Serv.*
Now, Signior *Blade*, If ever thou wouldst see the golden age of yore, this is the time.

Act. 3.   Scæn. 6.

Blade, *Truman* Pater, *Widow*, *Dogrel*.

Tru. O Sir, my Son has poyson'd you, I see; there's no Law yet, is there?

Bla. Mr. *Truman*—

Tru. True me no more then I true you. Come, Captain *Blade*, I know what you are, and so shall others too.

Bla. You'll hear me, Sir, I hope—

Tru. And so shall you hear me, Sir; I can be heard, I would you should know, in as good a place as this is; and before as good as you are, Captain *Blade*.

Bla. First leave your raging, Sir: for though you should roar like *Tamerlin* at the Bull, 'twould do no good with me.

Tru. I *Tamerlin*? I scorn him, as much as you do, for your ears. I'll have an action of slander against you, Captain; you shall not miscal me at your pleasure: remember you call'd me *Jethro* once before.

Wid. O the Father! little did I think, I wuss, to see you ever with these eyes again.

Bla. Pray, Sir, hear me; The wrong I did you, when you were last here, came from distraction onely, and not my will;

and therefore deserves pardon. The business, if you please, I'll relate truly to you; and by what special providence I escap'd the danger.   *they whisper.*

Tru. Well, Sir, I'm not angry; but I'll not be call'd *Tamerlin* by any man.

Bla. Upon my faith, Sir, it was an Antidote; I vomited up more then any whale could have done; things of more colours then twenty Rhetoricians were ever able to invent.

Tru. I shall teach my son—

Bla. No, good Sir, I forgive him with all my heart: but for my Neece—You remember, Sir, the Will my brother left; you were witness to it. For this her disobedience, the means are faln to me. Now if you please to marry M. *Richard* to my daughter, *Lucia*'s portion shall all be hers.

Tru. Thank you good Captain *Blade*; I thank you for your love heartily: pray send for 'um; he shall do't presently. I thank you heartily for your love, good Captain: he shall do't, he shall do't.   *Calls his servant,*
                                              and sends for 'um.

(What good luck was this, that I spoke not to the widow for her daughter!) How do you, widow? you're melancholy me-thinks; you're melancholy i'faith, that you are.

Wid. Well, I praise God, Sir, in better health then I deserve, vile wretch. I'm glad to see our neighbour so recovered.

Tru. I, good man, he has had a dangerous time of it, that he has, a very dangerous time: his neece is a naughty wench, a scurvie girl, to repay him thus for all his care and trouble: he has been a father to her, Widow, that he has; to my knowledge he has: Her father was an honest man, I'm sure on't.

Wid. Was he? I, as ever trod upon Gods ground, peace be with him; I, and as loving a neighbour too—

Tru. We have drunk our half pintes of Muscadel together many a morning, that we have.

Wid. My husband too was all in all with him. Hei-ho! I shall never forget how merry we were when we went with him to Mortlake in the Easter-holy-days: and we carried a shoulder of Mutton with us, and a fat Pig, and he carried his bottle of wine down with him: I warrant you [he] lov'd a cup of wine as well as his brother; in a fair sort, I mean.

Tru. Ah widow! those days are gone: we shall never see

196

those days again. I was a merry grig too then, and would ha'
danc'd and cut capers: ha—who but I? I was as merry as the
maids.

Wid. My daughter *Tabytha* was just four yeer old then,
come *Lamas*-tide.

Dog. Captain, I thought thou hadst been at *Erebus* by this
time: but 'tis no matter; 'tis but an Epitaph lost: hang't, 'twas
made *ex tempore*, and so let it pass.

Bla. Hadst thou made one i'faith?

Dog. Yes, by this light.

Bla. I'm glad I did not die then. O here they come. She's
a good handsome wench; 'tis pity to cozen her. But who can
help it? Every one for himself, and God for us all.

Act. 3. Scæn. 7.

Blade, *Widow*, *Truman* pater, *Dogrel*, *Truman* filius, *Lucia*.

Bla. Welcome, kinde Neece; you see I live still: there
were Antidotes as well as Poisons.

Wid. He has been a loving Uncle to you, Mistress *Lucia*:
he might have deserv'd better at your hands: you might had
Master *Truman*, I warrant you, had you but held up your
finger to him: he would not ha' seen you perish, Mistris *Lucia*;
I may say I know him so far. Speak, Mistris *Lucia*, speak for
your self, good chuck; your Uncle will forgive you: we'll all
speak for you: He shall forgive you, that he shall: he knows
we have all our faults.

Dog. I understand the language of her silence; it's strong
and good. You bound your son, Sir, to an oath never to see
nor hear her without your commission: 'tis that troubles her
conscience; she has a tender one.

Tru. p. I bound 'um? Well, I absolve 'um then; what's
that to you, Sir? I'll binde 'um again, if 't be my pleasure so:
if not, a fig for you; that's all I care. I love to speak my
minde; you must pardon me; I ha' spoke to as good as you i'
my days.

Dog. D'ye speak thus always? I'll ha' you in a Play if
you do.

ABRAHAM COWLEY

Tru. p. I'm glad you are so religious, Sir; did I bind you too to silence? Go too, Sir; I told you what your may-bees would bring you to, you'll always be wiser then your father: Nay, you may speak, and your Minion too, if she pleases.

Lucia, pulls off her vail.

Luc. Does any man here accuse me of any thing?

Bla. We, and your conscience do.

Luc. My Conscience? 'tis as pure as Sythian Christal,
From any spot; I can see through't at pleasure.
Whatever crime you mean, (for yet I know not)
Would it were written in my face.

Bla. Thou'dst be blacker then a Moor if 'twere. Did not you consent with that damn'd Physitian to give me poyson?

Luc. There was none given you, I call God to witness:
If such a thought had slipt into my dream,
The horror would have wak'd me, and I fear'd
Ever to sleep again. No; what we did, Sir,
Was but to fright you with a painted danger;
That the just terror of your own destruction
Might call to your remembrance my dead father:
For sure, Sir, you forgot him when you thought
To match his onely child with one of these
Fellowes that live *extempore*; whose fortunes
Are patch'd up like their wit by several patrons.
Should I have married thus, (but I would sooner
Endure the shameful end which they deserve)
Your conscious Ghost would start to meet my fathers,
And look more pale then death it self hath made it.

Dog. Let her alone, she'll call names and fling stones about anon.

Wid. Alas poor soul! you may see she's not her own woman.

Tru. p. What a poor excuse she made! a very idle simple excuse; have you never a better for us?

Tru. f. No, she says true.

Tru. p. You wo'nt bite off my nose? will ye, Sir? pray do not bite off my nose, I pray, Sir, do not?

208

Act. 3.   Scæn. 8.

Blade, Widow, Truman pater, *Dogrel.*
Truman filius, *Lucia, Puny.*

Pun. What a bevy o' men's here! ha! My little Load-
stone, art thou here, my little Diamond? I'll speak to your
Uncle now; we'll have a Parson cry I *Nicholas* presently.

Luc. You'r rude, Sir: what do you mean?

Pun. I, so you said i'the garden, when I began to gather,
you know what fruit: Come put on your vail, you'll blush else;
and look like the picture of a red-rose i'the hangings. Captain,
Salve, 'tis done.

Bla. Done! What?

Pun. I have her, i'faith.

Bla. God give you joy, Sir.

Pun. Nay, she's my own.

Bla. I am very glad of 't.

Pun. I scal'd the walls, entered the Town, and left a garison
there, I hope.

Bla. I congratulate your Victory, Mr. *Puny.*

Pun. You shall goe to my wedding, with me and this fair
Chorus. I'm as nimble as a Lybian Rabbit: Come, you must
go, though you be as lame as a criple, that begs at Westminster,
or a Crow in a gutter without her right leg. What d'ye wonder
at? I tell you, she's my *Penelope* now.

Bla. May I be so bold, Sir, as to ask, who 'tis you mean?

Pun. 'Slid, canst thou not see my meaning? are your brains
in a litter? I'm contracted to your Neece, and have got upon
her—Nay, never blush, we're as good as married, my dear Agat.

Bla. Have you then lien with her?

Truman fil. Ha! No figures nor similitudes, good Mr.
Puny; be as open and naked with me, as you were with her.

Pun. As plain as a Scholars mourning-cloak. I ha' don't
i'faith, but d'ye see? We broke this gold between us first,
and will be married to day. Who's that? *Truman,* ha, ha;
he looks like the Globe of the World, now: look how he
scratcheth his poul.

Bla. God give you joy, Sir : but she has not a farthing portion.

Pun. How, Captain ?

Bla. Not so much as will buy ribbands : all's mine own : a lawful prize, i'faith.

Tru. fil. Oh monster of her sex !

Luc. Wilt thou, vile man—I cannot speak to him—Witness all these—   *Weeps.*

Bla. So 'tis all forfeited to me. Will you try how your sons affection stands towards *Aurelia?*

Tru. p. Come, *Dick*, the Captain has forgiven you : never think of *Lucia*; she's not worth your thinking on ; a scurvie girl : ne'er think o'her ; thou shalt marry fair *Aurelia* : there's a wench, a wench worth gold i'faith.

Tru. f. I can't marry.

Tru. p. What can't you do, Sir ?

Tru. f. I can't marry.

Tru. p. Do you know who 'tis you speak to, Sir ? you don't sure : Who am I, pray ? you can't, when I bid you. Surely you know not who 'tis you speak to : you shall do't, or I'll know why you shall not.

Tru. f. I wo'n't marry.

Tru. p. Get you out o' my sight : come within my doors no more ; not within my doors, Sir.

Bla. Take heed, M. *Truman*, what you do.

Tru. f. I wo'n't marry.

Luc. Pray hear me all—

Bla. Come, M. *Truman*, let's talk of these things within : come, Gentlemen.

Wid. Ha-ho ! I'll ne'er trust a wart o' the right cheek and a twinkling eye again whilst I breathe, for Mistress *Lucia's* sake. A man would think, that sees her, that butter would not ha' melted in her mouth. Take heed, *Tabytha* ; the still Sow eats up all the draff, I see.

Tru. p. I'll never acknowledge him for my son again : I tell you, Captain he's always thus ; he's always with his may-be's and his wo'nots : I can't abide these wo'nots, not abide 'um.

Pun. I'll follow him about the portion ; he sha' not think to make an Asdrubal of me.

Dog. Now my plot works.

                        Exeunt omnes præter Tru. fil. & Lucia.

Aɕt. 3. Scæn. 9.

Truman fil. *Lucia weeping.*

Tru. How precious were those tears, if they were true ones!
How much more worth then all the Oceans Jewels!
But they are onely false and empty bubbles;
Fair to the sight, but hollow as her heart:
There's nothing, nothing in 'um: he that weighs 'um,
Shall finde 'um lighter then a mad mans dreams,
Or womens resolutions.

Luc. I never did that fellow any wrong.
Why should he pay so dearly for the loss
Of my poor honour, as to sell his soul for't?

Tru. O she confesses, now, sh'has lost her honour.

Luc. They triumph in the ruine of us women,
And wooe our beauties onely, or our dowries;
Which when they miss of, they resolve to take
Revenge of their unworthiness on us;
Stealing away all that makes rich our dowry,
And beauty fair, our Name. But 'tis no matter,
Since heaven and *Truman* know my chastity.
Ha! he's here still! How do you, Sir?

Tru. Well, well.

Luc. You look ill.

Tru. No, no, no.

Luc. Indeed you do: [you] are not well, I'm sure.

Tru. I am. Will you be gone?

Luc. How, Sir! You do not know me, sure.

Tru. I would I never had.

Luc. What do you mean?

Tru. To see thy face no more.

Luc. You said you could not live without the sight on't.

Tru. It was a good one then.

Luc. Has one day spoil'd it?

Tru. O yes, more then an hundred yeers of time,
Made as much more by a continual sorrow,
Could e'er ha' done.

Luc. I do not think my glass will say so.

Tru. That's
As false as you, perhaps; but 'tis not half
So brittle. Dares your husband trust me alone
With you so long?
    Luc. My husband?
    Tru. I cry you mercy;
The man you sin withal. You scorn to use
Pretences.
    Luc. Yes, I do, Sir:
For she that scorns th' offence, needs no excuse
Have you so little confidence in that
Which you have seem'd to praise so oft, my Vertues?
Or did you flatter onely? Sure you did not:
For I remember I have heard you swear
You spoke your thoughts. Are Oathes but complements?
'Tis done unkindly, very unkindly, *Truman*;
And were 't not your self, I should be angry.
Had a bright Angel come to me, and said
That you were false, I should have sworn 't had ly'd,
And thought that rather false then you. Nothing
Could ever move th' opinion of thy constancy
But thine own self; and thee I must believe.
    Tru. And I'll believe my self in what I saw.
I know thou canst speak prettily; but thy words
Are not what Nature meant 'um, thy mindes picture.
The Bee has left his honey in thy tongue,
But in thy heart his sting.
    Luc. O do not say so:
My heart is honest still, unless thou spoildst it
When it receiv'd thee in. 'T had but three corners,
And thou hadst two, at least. Would thou couldst see
How little room I've left my self there in it.
    Tru. Yes, for 'tis crouded up with many guests;
So many guests, that they excluded me:
And now I freeze without; but never more,
Never will enter: 'twas a Palace once,
But now 'tis turn'd a Dungeon.
    Luc. Will you leave me?
I will not call you fickle nor unconstant;
But sure you are [to] blame: you will not find

THE GUARDIAN

A woman that will love you half so well.

   Tru. I do not mean to try.

   Luc. Yes, prithee do.

But when y'have talk'd, and lov'd, and vow'd, and sworn
A little while, take heed of using her
As you do me. No, may your love to her
Be such as mine to you; it can't be better,
What e'er you think; I'm sure it cannot, *Truman.*
May she be worthier of your bed then I,
And bring forth many little selves to you:
And when the happie course of divers yeers
Makes you seem old to all besides your wife,
May you in the fair glass of your blest issue,
See your own youth again. But I would have 'um
True in their loves, and kill no innocent maids.
For me it is no matter: when I'm dead,
My busie soul shall flutter still about you;
'Twill not be else in heaven: it shall watch
Over your sleeps, and drive away all dreams
That flie not with a soft and downy wing.
If any dangers threaten, it shall becken,
And call your spirit away till they be past;
And be more diligent then your Guardian-Angel.
Onely sometimes, when your best leasure serves,
(For I'd not trouble you more dead then living)
Bestow one thought on *Lucia,* and then sigh,
And (if you will) drop down a tear or two.
But that's a task I'll not enjoyn you to:
And if you do't, spend not too many on me;
One will suffice: then onely say, That maid
Deserv'd more of me. And again t'your business.
For my wrongd vertue and forsaken truth,
I ask no more. So, dear *False-man,* farewel.   *Exit.*

   Tru. Farewel? That word has charms and poisons in't;
It makes my frighted soul start back and tremble.
'Tis but an aery word. D'ye hear me, *Lucia?*

   Luc. (within) Who calls?

   Tru. Farewel, *Lucia,* farewel; that's all: farewel.
Repent, and meet me in heav'n—
Why did rash Nature quarrel with her self,

In making one so excellently bad?
She is more fair then *May*'s new painted blossoms,
But falser then the smiles of faithless *April*:
And this I know, and yet me thinks I love her.
O she has kill'd my Reason: I have lost
That and my self for ever.   *Exit.*

Finis Actus tertii.

Act. 4.   Scæn. 1.

Lucia sola.

Every thing now has left me; tears themselves,
The riches of my very grief, forsake me:
Sorrow, me thinks, shews nakedly without 'um.
My sighs are spent too; and my wearied lungs
Deny me fresh supplies: and I appear
Like some dull melancholy *April*-even,
When after many a showre the heav'ns still lowre,
As if they threatned more; and the fled Sun
Leaves nothing but a doubtful blush behinde him.
And I could wish my eternal night were coming,
Did I but know who 'tis that makes me wish it:
Else, when my soul is ready for her flight,
And knows not who it is she must forgive,
A thousand light suspicions will call
Her charity several ways; and I may chance
To doubt thee, *Truman*. But thou art abus'd:
I know not why; but sure thou couldst not do it.
I fear thee, cousin. When we were both girls,
Thou wouldst accuse me falsely to my Mistress,
And laugh to see my tears. I fear thee, cousin;
But I'll not judge too rashly: for I would not
Have any innocent wrong'd as I have been.
But I'm resolv'd to try her. She's now seeking
(Hoping that all my fortunes now are hers)
For a new maid t'attend her. That maid I'll be.

THE GUARDIAN

Cloathes I have got already; and my face
Grief has disguis'd: that and my voice some art
Will quickly alter. I have left a Note
Upon my chamber-window, which will keep 'um
From all suspicion of my staying here.

Act. 4. Scæn. 2.

Cutter, Dogrel, Puny, Lucia.

Cut. Hei! the Sisters are ravisht, and we have holy kisses
enough. I shall be as great among 'um as—Who's there?
What, your Spouse, *Puny?*
Dog. She looks like *Niobe* on the mountains top.
Cut. That *Niobe, Dogrel,* you have us'd worse then *Phœbus*
did. Not a dog looks melancholy, but he's compar'd to *Niobe*.
He beat a villanous Tapster t'other day, to make him look like
Niobe.
Pun. Why 'faith that's pretty odde, like one o' mine.
Luc. O, Sir, had you the vertuous impudence to slander a
poor maid thus?
Pun. Poor enough now indeed. I will not marry thee:
thy portion was a condition of the Contract. I'll sooner marry
a woman that sells Orenges with a face like Belinsgate.
Luc. I scorn thee—I contracted to thee?
Pun. Wert not? Answer.
Luc. No, by heaven.
Pun. Bear witness, Gentlemen; these words are *Carduus
benedictus* to me.
Cut. And what will you do now, fair Gammer *Lucia,* you
that contemn'd the Colonel? Will you knit for your living?
Dog. Or else weed gardens for six pence a day and bread.
Luc. This is unheard-of rudeness.
Pun. Nay let me ha' mine too; I ha' got a pat one for her.
Or else turn Apple-woman, live in a stall, and sell pippins for
eight a peny.
Dog. Or hither in triumph 'twixt two panniers ride,
And sell the bouls of wheat and butter in Cheapside.
The last is a little too long: but I imitate *Spencer.*

Cut. What think ye, Gentlemen? she'll make a pretty Landress.

Pun. A Landress? hang her, she looks like a foul hand-kercher.

Luc. Pray let me go; I ha' business requires me.

Cut. What? you're to meet some Gentlemen? How is't? twelve pence a time, I warrant, in these cloathes.

Dog. Where do you set up? Nay, we are true strikers. What, is't in Covent-garden?

Cut. Or do you renew the decay'd credit of Turnbal-street?

Pun. Or honour the Mill-bank at Westminster.

Dog. Or flee to Wapping, and engross the Sailors.

Cut. Or Moor-fields, and sell cakes.

Luc. Are all barbarous here?

Dog. Nay tell's; we shall be customers.

Pun. Enough, enough; give her a clap o' the breech, and let her go.

Cut. Well, fare thee well, girl; we shall finde you at the Play-house i' the six-peny-room sometimes.

Dog. And d'ye hear, *Lucia*, Keep your self wholesome: your tub's a terrible thing.

Luc. Unworthy villains—But I'm born to wrongs,
And must endure 'um.   *Exit.*

Omn. Ha, ha, ha.

Cut. A pretty Scene i' faith. Now for the Captain; he'll entertain us like forraign Princes: we'll drink this half-yeer with him, before we eat or sleep.

Pun. I'll drink like *Gog-Magog* himself, or the Spanish Tinker on a holy-day.

Dog.   There will I whet my Lyrick Muse
        With Falern wine as I do use.
        Captain *Blade* cannot refuse
        To entertain us; he cannot chuse,
        When we bring him such good news,
        As that his neece is gone to the stews.

Cut. Leave your verses, *Dogrel*. I hate your verses, *Dogrel*, till I be drunk. 'Tis a glorious Captain.

Dog. As free as Free-town in Germany. Here comes *Jeronymo*.

THE GUARDIAN

Act. 4. Scæn. 3.

Cutter, Puny, Dogrel, Blade.

Bla. The story says my neece is run away. The story is
not bad. Now will I get the widow, turn off my old rascally
companions, and live like an Emperour.

Cut. He says he will live like an Emperour; ha, ha, ha,
brave Captain.

Pun. Invincible Captain *Priam*.

Omn. Hei brave Captain!

Bla. What do you mean, Gentlemen? Are ye broke loose
from Bedlam? Ha' you no other place to play your tricks in,
but at my door? If you come here as Mummers, much may
be done; haply you may have twelve-pence: or else depart;
depart, if you be wise.

Omn. Why how now, Captain!

Bla. If you be not gone immediately, I'll ha' my men
switch you further off—Here are saucy knaves indeed with all
my heart—   *Offers to go out.*

Cut. By this light the Captain's drunk without us.

Pun. Prethee, Captain, thou art as humorous as a bell-
rope. Dost thou know me, man? I'm M. *Puny*.

Blade. Y' are a fool, an addle egge: there's nothing else but
cobwebs i' your head: The height of all thy knowledge is to
find out the quarter day against thy rents come in, and thou
couldst not finde out that, if 'twere not marke'd i' the Almanack
with red letters. Yet you forsooth, because you see some
Gentlemen and Poets of late, a little extravagant sometimes in
their similitudes; because they make a pretty kinde of sound to
those that mark 'um not; make that your way of wit, and
never speak without comparisons. But never were comparisons
so odious as thine are. And these two Rabbit-suckers, for a
quart of wine extol thee, and cry good when thou speakest so.

Pun. The Captains raging mad like a Baker when his oven
is over heated.

Bla. And that was one of um—

Cut. Come leave your humors, hang you, confound you,
pox take you, Captain, we come to drink here.

Bla. Mine's no blind Ale-house, where you may roar and swagger with half a pipe of Tobacco in your mouth.

Cut. Do you know me, Captain?

Bla. I would I never had. Thou art one that sayest thou hast seen the wars, but thou liest basely; for if thou ever wast in a battle, [I'm] sure tho[u] winkest there. Thou art one that liv'st like a Raven by providence and rapine : one that if thou shouldst chance to go to bed sober, thou wouldst put it down in thy Almanack for an unlucky day; sleep is not death's image with thee, unless thou beest dead-drunk.

Dog. He dares not abuse me thus.

Cut. Is't even so, Captain? Has your money exalted you?

Bla. No, it has humbled me, and made me know my self and you, whom I shall study to forget hereafter.

Dog. Come, Captain, shall you and I drink hand to hand?

Bla. Oh, you're his Lansprizado, Sirrah, Trundle.

Dog. Let not thy wrath swell like the Adrian Sea.

Bla. Thou that troublest thy self to be a fool; I will so beat thee, Trundle, that thou shalt hobble like one of thy own Rhyms. Therefore, if ever thou shewest that Poetical face of thine within my doors again, I'e use thee worse then thou didst me, when thou mad'st an Ode in commendation of me.

Dog. Then break thine oaten reed—

Bla. Fare ye well Gentlemen. I shall see thee *Cutter* a brave Tapster shortly; it must be so i'faith, *Cutter*; thou must like *Bardolph* i'the play, the spiggot weild. *Dogrel* shall make and sell smal Pamphlets i'the play-house, or else Tobacco, or else snuffe Candles. As for *Puny*, his means will serve him to be cheated of these five or six yeers.

Cut. 'Tis very well the times are so alter'd.

Bla. Ye cannot want a living Gentlemen, as long as there are Whores, Bowling-allies, or Ordinaries; especially such able men as you are. There will be wars too shortly; never quake, *Cutter*; here's *Dogrel*, when his want has spun him out a little thinner, will serve you for a pike.

Cut. 'Tis very well: pray God your mirth last, Captain.

Bla. When you're grown old, and your fingers then only nimble with the palsie, I'll provide an Hospital for you—*Sedes ubi fata quietas*—Fare ye well, Gallants; and pray be merry: Fare ye well heartily.   *Exit.*

Cut. Poverty, the pox, an ill wife, and the Devil go with thee, Captain.

Pun. I vexed him, when I put that jest upon him, like a Baker when his oven's overheated.

Dog. If I don't compose a Satyre shall make him hang himself, may I never write verse more.

Cut. I would beat him like a Buck, but I shall be bound to the peace for't, and be affronted afterward by every one.

Dog. No, no, no—let me see—Besides my Satyre I have another way—let me see—His brother traffickt at Guiny.

Cut. Yes, but the Merchants there report him dead.

Dog. The more knaves they : he lives, and I am he.

Cut. How ? How, *Dogrel*, thou the Merchant man ?

Dog. By this light, I either am, or will be.

Cut. How, *Dogrel* ! Though thou be as thin and penetrable as a spirit, yet thou canst not assume dead bodies.

Pun. Prithee, *Dogrel*, hold thy peace; thou talkest like a hogs face.

Dog. Deride not, *Puny :* if I be not more like then any of your similitudes, I'll be hang'd for't.

Cut. Thy face, indeed, will do exceeding well to represent one risen from the grave.

Dog. By long conversation with the Captain, I know all the passages between him and his brother ; know what his humour, what his state and fortunes were, better then himself did when he lived.

Cut. I, but thou'lt ne'er act him. Why, man, he was a thing more strange then any monster in Africk where he travell'd.

Pun. What was he, prithee ?

Dog. I knew him well enough ; he had lost his memory, and therefore either writ down every thing, and took his business with him in a scroll, or else trusted it to his man *John*, whom he carried with him.

Cut. O I, that *John* and he went perpetually together, like the blinde man and his dog.

Pun. Or a Tinker and his trull. But d'ye hear, gallants, let me do apple-*John :* never was such a *John* as I'll be, not *John a Gaunt* himself, nor *John a Noak*.

Cut. But *Dogrel*, how wilt thou be made like that *Cinque-quater?*

Dog. Why we Poets can do any thing. First you may remember (unless you be like him) 'tis seven yeers since he went from hence; and time, you know, will alter men. I made an Ode upon that subject once: *Time, that dost eat, and makst no Lent*—

Cut. Pox take your Ode; go on i' your business, *Dogrel.*

Dog. Then I and my man *John* (as simply as he stands here) will swarthy over our faces as if the Countrey had made us so: for if you remember my verses, *In Africk they are black as coals*—

Cut. The devil's i' thy verses. Prithee on.

Dog. Besides, we'll be attir'd in some strange habit of those Countries: I know not how; but you shall see 't in *Speeds* Maps.

Cut. Why now I like thee, my little *Ovid*; go about thy Metamorphosis. I'm for *Tabytha*; she's taken, *Dogrel*, melted like virgins wax. I'll to her presently, and tell her that the vision appeared to me last, and warn'd me to carry her to S. *Ant'lins*; there will I have a Priest.

Dog. A Priest, *Cutter?*

Cut. A Minister, I mean; a holy, godly, zealous Minister: and she—You conceive me, *Dogrel*—

Dog. Well, let's be going then. *Puny*, take heed o' your wit when you act *John*: I shall beat my servant *John*, if he be witty.

Pun. That's the devil; I shall hardly abstain.

Cut. And *Dogrel*, you must make no verses, *Dogrel*: let that be the first thing your memory fails you in.

Pun. Well, I'll follow you in a pissing-while.

Dog. Do so, good *John*.   *Exit Dog. Cut.*

Pun. Now will I turn *John*, as round as a Wedding-ring: and if that plot be cut off by the nose—Ha? Here comes sententious Bias that walks gravely. I'll observe my young *Laconian*.

Act. 4. Scæn. 4.

Puny, Truman filius.

Tru. She's gone for ever. Peace be with thee, *Lucia*,
Where ever thou art.

Pun. Now he begins his Epithalamium.

Tru. If she be guilty,
Forgive her, heav'n; she'll repent. I'm sure:
For she is soft, and melting as the dew,
That kisses ev'ry morn the trembling roses;
And howsoe'er beauty and youth misled her,
She cannot be, I know, a stubborn sinner.

Pun. Did ever Basket-maker talk thus? to himself too,
like a Conjurer in a garden?

Tru. Ha! This is he, that wicked man,
That devil which betray'd her.

Pun. O, are you thereabouts?   *Offers to go out.*

Tru. Nay stay,
For wert thou arm'd with thunder and my anger,
Yet I would bring thee back. Tell me what charms,
(For I will rip thy heart up but I'll know it)
What witch-craft didst thou use t'entice her thus?
Never deny't. For hadst thou been more handsome
Then other mens, or thine own flattery
Could ever make thee: hast thou been as beautiful,
And couldst have spoke as well as she her self,
All this were nothing; she would look upon thee,
But lust no more then thine own Angel does.
No, thou didst use some cursed art to tempt her,
Some Philter—

Pun. Not I by all—what d'ye mean pray, Sir?

Tru. Why then you ravisht her, by Heav'n you ravisht her:
Alas, she's weak and tender, very tender,
And was not able to resist that strength
Which youth and furious lust did arm thee with.
'Twas basely done, above expression basely,
And I would presently revenge it fully,
But that my sword would take from the laws justice,
And from thy shame.

Pun. I ravish her? By this light I scorn't.
Tru. You did enjoy her body? Did you not?
Pun. I did so.
Tru. You did? I prithee do not say you did so;
This is to brag of the vile act th'ast done:
But I shall spoil your pride and shameful glory
Which your base sin affords you.
   Pun. You bid me tell you the truth, what would you
ha'me do?
   Tru. Do? I would have thee fix thy adulterous eye
Upon the ground, which thy cursed feet dishonour;
And blush more red then is the sin th'ast acted.
What would I have thee do? I'd have thee weep,
Shed as true tears as she does for thy fault,
And sigh away thy body into air.
What would I have thee do? I'd have thee kill thy self,
And sacrifice thy life to her wrong'd Soul.
Canst thou refuse to do all this for her,
For whom th'ast damn'd thy self?
   Pun. We were contracted first e'er I enjoyed her.
   Tru. Didst thou enjoy her then? How durst thou do it?
Why she was mine, I tell thee she was mine;
All the Seas wealth should not have bought her from me,
While she remain'd as spotless as my love:
And so she did remain till thy sin stain'd her.
I tell thee to that hour she was more innocent
Then thou, false man, wert in thy mothers womb.
Didst thou enjoy her? Either fetch back that word,
Say, nay I'll have thee swear thou didst not touch her,
Or by those joyes which thou hast rob'd me of,
I'll kill thee strait.
   Pun. 'S[ ]id I did not touch her. What would you ha' me
say? would I were *John* the Merchants man now.
   Tru. O Heav'ns! O most unheard of villany!
Th' hast done a crime so great, that there is hardly
Mercy enough in Heav'n to pardon thee.
Tell me, (for now I'll argue mildly with thee)
Why should you seek t' undo a harmless maid?
To rob her of her friends, her life perhaps,
I'm sure her fame, which is much dearer to her.

THE GUARDIAN

'Twas an inhuman act; an act so barbarous,
That Nations unciviliz'd would abhor it:
I dare say boldly she n[e]v'r injured you;
For she was gentle as the breath of Zephyrus:
And if she e'er did but begin a thought
Of wronging any man, she would have wept
Before she thought it out.

 Pun. I had rather be a pickl'd-Oister, then i'this case I am in now.

 Tru. Is *Lucia* abus'd? and I stand here
T'expostulate with words her injuries?
Draw, for I'll talk no more with thee.

 Pun. D'ye hear, Sir—by Heaven I lay with her, but we were contracted first—will you be pleas'd to hear me?

 Tru. No, be gone.

 Pun. Most willingly. Fare ye well heartily, Sir; I wish you a good night-cap.   *Exit.*

 Tru. The want of sleep and diet has distempered me,
If I stay thus I shall be quite distracted;
Me thinks a kinde of strangeness seizes me:
And yet if I go home I shall be forc'd
To marry with *Aurelia.* Is it possible
There should be women good, if *Lucia* be not?
They are not sure: She lookt as well as any,
And spoke as well too.

Act. 4.   Scæn. 5.

Truman pater, *Truman* filius, *Blade.*

 Tru. p. I tell you, Captain, he's a stubborn boy, a self-will'd hair-brain'd boy: he has his know-nots, and his wo'nots, and his may-be's, when I speak. I have told him of his manner a hundred times; nay I may say a thousand.

 Bla. Pray take my counsel for this once: though I be a souldier, yet I love not to do all things by force. Speak fairly to him.

 Tru. p. Speak fairly to my son? I'll see him buried, I'll see his eyes out first.

213

ABRAHAM COWLEY

Bla. I mean, desire him.

Tru. p. O, that's another matter. Well, for your perswasion, I'll do it: but if ever I speak fair to him—

Bla. I know his nature's such, that kindness will sooner win him—Look you, he's here i' faith, as melancholy as an owl i' the day-time.

Tru. p. O, are you there, Jacksauce—

Bla. Nay, remember what I told you.

Tru. p. 'Tis true indeed. How now, son *Dick*? you're melancholy still, I see.

Tru. f. It best becomes my fortune, Sir, now you have cast me off.

Tru. p. I cast thee off? marry God forbid, *Dick*. How dost do, *Dick*? Thou lookst ill, *Dick*, in troth thou dost: I must have thee merry.

Bla. I see all kindness is against this dotards nature, he does so over-act it.

Tru. p. Wilt thou have a Physitian, *Dick*? Thou art my onely son, *Dick*, and I must have a care of thee: thou shouldst ride abroad sometimes, *Dick*, and be merry. We'll ha' a wife too for thee, *Dick*, a good wife, ha—

Tru. fil. I thank you, Sir; but I know not—

Tru. p. I, now he's at his know-nots. I will make you leave those know-nots, boy—

Bla. Remember, M. *Truman*, what I told you.

Tru. p. 'Tis true indeed. Your father's old now, *Dick*, you see, and would fain see a grandchilde: tis out of love to you, *Dick*, that I perswade you to't; you may be a comfort, *Dick*, to your father now.

Tru. f. You may command me.

Tru. p. Well said, *Dick*, I see thou lovest me now, *Dick*; dost thou want any money, *Dick*? or cloathes? or horses? You should tell me what you want, you shall have any thing—here's the Captain, a hearty friend of yours—where's your Daughter, Captain? there's a wench, *Dick*! ha you seen her?

Tru. f. Yes, Sir.

Tru. p. And how do you like her, *Dick*? speak freely.

Tru. f. I know no cause why any should dislike her.

Tru. p. Why well said, *Dick*; keep thee o' that minde still, and God will bless thee.

Bla. Your father means, Mr. *Truman*, I suppose, how you like her for a wife.

Tru. p. I can tell my own meaning my self I hope, I'm old enough I'm sure.

Tru. f. You wrong her much, I never shall deserve her.
Alas, I am a man so weak in all things,
So lost both to the world and to my self;
That if I lov'd a woman heartily,
And woo'd her with all zealous passions,
And valu'd her love 'bove all things else but Heaven;
Yet, when I thought upon my own unworthiness,
I should my self perswade her not to marry me.

Bla. Well, Sir, if you esteem her worth your choise, she shall be yours.

Tru. p. Why what should ayle him, Captain? He esteem her? Must he, forsooth, or I be Master pray? Captain *Blade*, you make him too saucy with such talk; never tell me, Captain *Blade*, I say it makes him too saucy, I marry does it, it does i'faith; must he be his own Carver? Come no more words, I'll have you married presently: i'faith law, Captain, you make him too saucy, that you do, you do i'faith, Sir; I can't abide when sons must come to esteem, he esteem her with a vengeance?

Tru. f. I desire time onely to consider—

Tru. p. I, why I told you this; 'tis such a another wilful, hair-braind Coxcomb, he's always a considering. Captain *Blade*, I could never keep him from his considering; but I shall so consider you—go get you in, Sir, I'll have it done when I please; get you in, Sir, I'll keep you from considering hereafter.

Exeunt.

Act. 4. Scæn. 6.

Aurelia, Lucia disguis'd.

Aur. What did you say your name was?
Luc. *Jane*, forsooth.
Aur. Well said, *Jane*; and as I told you, *Jane*, you shall have six pound a yeer, *Jane*, for your wages; and then my cloathes will serve you with a little alteration: There's a gown

ABRAHAM COWLEY

of my Cosens within will almost fit you, you're much about her height, you shall ha' that too. I had a Cousin here was a foolish thing god wot, 'tis well I'm rid of her—and d'ye hear— you must be very secret and faithful to your Mistris; a waiting womans place, is a place requires secrecy.

Luc. I shall ill deserve your favour else.

Aur. Nay, I dare trust thee, *Jane*, thou lookst ingenuously: didst thou ever live at Court?

Luc. No forsooth.

Aur. O, you must learn the fashions of the Court: I'm already contracted to one Mr. *Puny*, though he little thinks of it; Take heed of speaking, *Jane*, you see I trust you. And when I'm married to him I'll live at Court: He's a simple thing God knows, but I'll have him knighted, and I like him the better for't: A wise woman you know will make the best use of a foolish husband. You know how to dress me, *Jane*, i'the Court fashion?

Luc. Yes forsooth.

Aur. And you can lay me on a Fucus hansomly?

Luc. I hope I shall quickly learn it.

Aur. And when you see a friend with me, or so, that I would be private with; you can stay i'the next room, and see that no body come in, to interrupt us?

Luc. I shall not be deficient in my duty.

Aur. Well said. And can you tell in private such a Gentleman that you heard me speak in commendation of him, and that I dreamt of him last night? that will be in your way, *Jane*, such men will be grateful. And say that I was longing t'other day, for such a jewel or such a toy?

Lucia makes a court'sy.

Luc. I hope you shall not finde me wanting in any service to you.

Aur. I beleeve thee, *Jane*. To morrow I'll teach thee more: I shall read to you every day a lesson, til I see you perfect in the science: 'tis requisite that you have a little of the Theory first. Go look out the pearle chain in the Cabinet within; and stay till I come to you. *Exit Jane.*

The wench I see is docile, and will learn, but alas she must have time; she has a little [too] much City breeding, I see, by Court'sies and forsooths.

216

Act. 4.   Scæn. 7.

Aurelia, Blade.

Bla. How now? all alone, *Aurelia*? you're eating soap and ashes here, I warrant you, without so much as saying grace for 'um.

Aur. I'd rather repent in ashes, Sir, then eat 'um.

Bla. What would you think if I should marry now this very day?

Aur. I should think, Sir, you'd repent to morrow for't.

Bla. And the widow too.

Aur. The widow? then you'll repent to night, Sir, I believe.

Bla. I woo'd her long ago, and now she sees there's an estate faln to me, faith she's content; and, to save charges, is willing to be married to day privately.

Aur. But I hope you are not so, Sir: why we shall have all the silenc'd Ministers humming and hawing thrice a week here; not a dish o' meat but will be longer a blessing then a rosting. I shall never hear my Virginals when I play upon 'um, for her daughter *Tabytha*'s singing of Psalms. The first pious deed will be, to banish *Shakespear* and *Ben. Johnson* out of the parlour, and to bring in their rooms *Mar-prelate*, and *Pryns* works. You'll ne'er endure 't, Sir. You were wont to have a Sermon once a quarter at a good time; you shall have ten a day now.

Bla. Let me alone to deal with 'um. If any of her eating talking tribe shew their ears here, I will so use her tribe, that they shall free the Pope, and call me Antichrist hereafter: and the widow, I'll warrant you, I'll convert: I'll carry her to Plays, in stead of Lectures: she shall see them, as well as the dancing o' the ropes, and the Puppet-play of Nineve. But this is not my business, girl: I have an husband too for you.

Aur. I could wish you would keep him, Sir, if you have him; I know not what to do with him my self.

Bla. Come, 'tis a man you'll like, I'm sure; I have heard you often commend him for his parts. 'Tis young M. *Truman*.

Aur. *Truman*, Sir? the melancholy cross-arm'd Gentleman that talks to trees and rivers as he goes by 'um? We should

sit all day together like pictures of man and wife, with our
faces towards one another, and never speak. I'll undertake,
upon our Marriage-night he'll onely sigh a little, cry *Cruel
Fate*, and then go sleep.

Bla. Never fear't. Come, thou shalt have him, girl: go
quickly and dress your self; we'll both be married on a day.
The humor is good, and it saves charges: there's the widows
humour too.

Aur. You'll give me leave Sir——

Bla. No, no, no; prithee go dress thy self: by heaven
it must be as I say: the fates have ordain'd it.

Aur. Be pleas'd to hear me, Sir.

Bla. I would not hear thee, though thou wert an angel.
I'm as resolute as he that writ the Resolves. Come away, and
adorn thy self.   *Exeunt.*

Act. 4.   Scæn. 8.

Cutter, *Dogrel*, and *Puny* disguis'd.

Pun. Me thinks I look now like a two-peny apple pye,
I know not how.

Dog. *John*, What's your name, *John?* I have forgot your
name, *John*.

Pun. Do you mean the name that was given me at the
Font?

Dog. Font? Font? I do not remember that Font. Let
me see my scroll.   *(Reads.)*
There's ne'er a such town in Africa as Font.
I do not remember Font.

Pun. Your memory, Sir, 's as short as an Ephemerides.

Dog. Did not I warn you, *John*, of such strange what-d'ye-
call-ums? Here's for that word. *(Strikes.)* I have forgot
what word 'twas: for the word I mean.

Pun. Pox take you, *Dogrel*, you strike too hard.

Cut. Thou'dst act well, I see: we'll ha' thee to Golden-
lane, and there thou shalt do a King, or else some God in thine
own cloathes.

THE GUARDIAN

Dog. When a dead man from Orcus I retract,
Well may you see that to the life I act.

Pun. Did not I warn you o' these what-d'ye-call-ums?
'Faith we'll be even, Master. *Strikes him.*

Cut. Very well, *John*; those be good Memorandums for
your Master.

Dog. I should be angry with thee for it, but that I ha' quite
forgot it.

Cut. Let's see your scroll. *(Reads)* Memorandum for my
house: I have a house in Fleetstreet, with a garden to't. My
daughter is call'd *Lucia*; a handsome fair maid with red cheeks,
black eyes, and brown hair, and a little dimple in her chin. My
brother's name (to whom I left the charge of my daughter) is
Blade. (A most excellent Note indeed.) What ha' we here?
Memorandums concerning my estate. What, they're all of this
stamp, are they not? Take heed, *Dogrel*, the Captain's a
shrewd fellow; he'll examine you more strictly then the Spanish
Inquisition can.

Dog. Pish, if he pose me in any thing, my memory's weak,
he knows; I h' forgot it quite.

Cut. And then your voice I fear; and then—

Dog. Pox take you, *Cutter*; a Casuist would not finde so
many scruples.

Pun. The devil's in't, I shall never do this part; I know
not how to speak and not be witty.

Cut. Well, look to't, gallants; if the Captain finde you out,
he'll abuse you most unmercifully—I'm now for *Tabytha*.

Pun. The Captain abuse me? By this day, I'll jeer with
him with my hands bound behinde me. Come away, Master.

Dog. I, *John*; but which way did we come?

Pun. Why this way, Master.

Dog. Then that way we must go. Is not this my house in
Fleet street, *John*? I thought you had said t'had been in Fleet
street.

Pun. Yes, so 'tis, Sir.

Dog. Truly I thought you said so. Come away, *John*.
Exeunt.

Finis Actus quarti.

Act. 5. Scæn. 1.

Cutter, Tabytha.

Cut. And the vision told me, sister *Tabytha*, that this same day, the twelfth of March, in the yeer of grace 1641, at this same holy place, by a holy man, we two, who are both holy vessels, should be joyned together in the holy band of Matrimony.

Tab. My mother will be angry, I'm affeard.

Cut. Your mother will rejoyce. I would not for a world that you should do it, but that we were commanded from above; yea, I may say commanded: for, to do things without a divine warrant, is like unto the building of a fire without a bottom cake.

Tab. I (God knows) that it is.

Cut. Very well, sister. Now when my eyes were opened in the morning. I awoke: for it was morning-tide, and my eyes were opened; and I looked into my pockets; for my breeches lay upon a joyn'd stool not far from the beds side: and in my pockets, even made with leather. I looked (I say) and found; What did I finde? marry a License written with ink and pen: Where did I finde it? in no other place, but even in a godly Catechism which I had wrapt and folded up long-ways, even in that very pocket.

Tab. I wou'd my mother knew it. But I'll not resist, God willing.

Cut. There is a godly Teacher within, that never was defiled with the Cap and Surplice, never wore that gambol call'd the Hood; even he shall joyn our hands. Shall we enter, sister?

Tab. Brother, I'll not resist.   *Exeunt.*

Act. 5. Scæn. 2.

Truman filius, Aurelia.

Tru. And must we marry then?
Aur. It appears so by the story.
Tru. Why will you marry me? What is there in me

THE GUARDIAN

That may deserve your liking? I shall be
The most ill-favour'd m[e]lancholy Bridegroom
That ever took a melting maid t'his bed:
The faculties of my Soul are all untun'd,
And every glory of my spreading youth
Is turn'd into a strange and sudden winter.
You cannot love me sure.
    Aur. No by my troth, Sir.
    Tru. No, nor I you. Why should we marry then?
'Twere a meer folly, were it not *Aurelia*?
    Aur. Nay, ask our Parents why. But, Sir, they say
'Tis the best marriage where like is joyned to like;
Now we two are a very even match;
For neither I love you, nor you love me;
And 'tis ten to one but we shall beget
Children that will love neither of us.
    Tru. Nay, by my Soul I love you, but alas,
Not in that way that husbands love their wives;
I cannot play, nor toy, nor kiss, nor do
I know not what: And yet I was a lover,
As true a lover—
    Aur. Alack a day, Sir.
    Tru. 'Twas then me-thought the greatest happiness
To sit and talk, and look upon my Mistris,
Or (if she was not by) to think upon her.
Then every morning next to my devotion,
And sometimes too (forgive me Heav'n) before it,
She slipt into my fancy, and I took it
As a good omen for the following day.
It was a pretty foolish kind of life,
An honest harmless vanity: But now
The fairest face moves me no more then Snow
Or Lillies when I see 'um and pass by.
And I as soon shall deeply fall in love
With the fresh scarlet of an Easterne cloud,
As the red lips and cheeks of any woman.
I do confess, *Aurelia*, thou art fair
And very lovely, and (I think) good natur'd.
    Aur. Faith, Sir, I would not willingly be a man, if they
be all like you.

ABRAHAM COWLEY

Tru. And prithee now, *Aurelia*, tell me truly,
Are any women constant in their vowes?
Can they continue a whole week? a month?
And never change their faith? O if they could,
They would be excellent things. Nay, ne'er dissemble:
Are not their lusts unruly, insolent,
And as commanding as their beauties are?
Are their tears true and solid when they weep?
  Aur. Sure, Mr. *Truman*, you ha'n't slept of late;
If we be married to night, what will
You do for sleep?
  Tru. Why? Do not married people use to sleep?
  Aur. Yes, yes. Alas good innocence!
  Tru. They have a scurvy time of't if they do not;
But we'll not be as other people are,
We'll finde out some new hansome way of love,
Some kind of way that few shall imitate,
But all admire. For 'tis a sordid thing
That lust should dare t'insinuate it self
Into the marriage-bed. We'll get no children,
The worst of men and women can do that.
Besides too, if our issue should be female,
They would all learn to flatter and dissemble,
They'd all deceive with promises and vowes
Some simple man, and then turn false and kill him.
Would they not do't *Aurelia*?
  Aur. Our sex is little beholding to you, Sir; I would your
mother were alive to hear you. But pray, Mr. *Truman*, what
shall we do when we are married?
  Tru. Why we'll live lovingly together:
Sometimes we'll sit and talk of excellent things,
And laugh at all the nonsense of the world:
Sometimes we'll walk together into the fields:
Sometimes we'll pray and read, and sometimes eat,
And sometimes sleep; and then at last we'll die,
And go to heav'n together. 'Twill be dainty.
  Aur. We may do this, me thinks, and never marry for
the business.
  Tru. 'Tis true, we might do so:
But since our parents are resolv'd upon't,

222

THE GUARDIAN

In such a trifle let 'um have their humour.
My father sent me here to complement,
And keep a prating here, and play the fool:
I cannot do 't. What should I do, *Aurelia*?
What do they use to say?
   Aur. Sure, Sir, you knew, when you were a suitor to my
cousin *Lucia*.
   Tru. I, but those days are past, and I have now
Forgot what manner of man a lover is:
I was one then, I'm sure cn't. O that *Lucia*,
That *Lucia* was so wonderful a creature—
There was a cheek, a lip, a nose, an eye!
Did you observe her eye, *Aurelia*?
   Aur. Yes, yes, Sir, you were wont to sit all day,
And look upon the pretty babies in it.
   Tru. It was as glorious as the eye of heav'n,
Like the souls eye, dispers'c through ev'ry thing.
And then her hands! her hands of liquid Ivory!
Did she but touch her Lute (the pleasing'st harmony
Then upon earth, when she her self was silent)
The subtil motion of her flying fingers
Taught Musick a new art, To take the sight
As well as th'ear.
   Aur. I, I, Sir, y'had best go look her out, and marry
her.
   Tru. Nay prithee be not angry, good *Aurelia*;
I do not say she is more fair then thou art:
Yet if I did—No, but I wil not say so:
Onely I strive to cherish the remembrance
Of one I lov'd so well. And, now I think on't,
I'll beg a favour of you: you'll laugh at me,
I know, when you have heard me: but I'll beg it:
Prithee be veil'd as *Lucia* was of late;
Cast such a silken cloud upon thy beauty
For this one day: I'd fain marry you so.
'Tis an odde foolish humour, I confess:
But love and grief may be allow'd sometimes
A little innocent folly.
   Aur. Well, I'll obey your humour; pray walk in there;
I'll onely dress my self, and wait upon you.

Tru. And we'll be married very privately.
None but our selves, it will be best, *Aurelia.*   *Exit.*

Aur. Why here's a husband for a wench of clouts! May
I never laugh again, if his company has not made me duller
then Ale and butter'd cakes wou'd ha' done. I marry him?
the old men must excuse me. I'l sooner chuse a fellow that
lies bed-rid, and can do nothing a-nights but cough. Well, if
I don't teach 'um what 'tis to force a wench that has wit, may
my husband beat me when I have one, and I sit still and cry.
I like this very well—It shall be so. *Jane,* come hither, *Jane.*

Act. 5.   Scæn. 3.

Aurelia, Lucia.

Aur. O *Jane*, that's well; little think you what good's
towards you; 'tis that you have wisht for, I dare say, these five
yeers; a good handsome husband   What think you of young
Truman?

Luc. I think every thing
That makes a man compleat, and his wife happie,
The richest glories of a minde and body,
And their not ill companion, Fortune too,
Are reconcil'd and married all in him:
And I commend the wisdom of your stars,
That joyn you two together.

Aur. Nay faith thou shalt e'en have him thy self for better
or worse. He's too hansome indeed, unless he could make
better use of his beauty; for by my troth, wench, I'm affraid
thou'lt finde thy pillow as good a bed-fellow.

Luc. I pray do not mock your servant.

Aur. Thou shalt see, *Jane* I do not; come in, wench,
and I'll tell thee all my plot.   *Exeunt.*

THE GUARDIAN

Act. 5. Scæn. 4.

Blade, Servant.

Bla. Well, Sir, is the Cook doing according to my directions?

Serv. Yes, Sir, he's very hard at his business i'the kitchin: h' has been a swearing and cursing at the scullions at least this hour, Sir.

Bla. 'Tis such an over-wasted Coxcomb; an other wedding dinner would make him a S. *Laurence*: bid him be sure the Venison be well season'd.

Serv. Troth, Sir, I dare not speak to him now, unless I put on the armor in the hall: he had like to have spitted me next to a goose, for saying that he look'd like an ox that was roasted whole at S. *Jame's* fayre.

Bla. You have invited all the guests to dinner you talk'd of?

Serv. Yes, Sir.

Bla. And the widdows round-headed kindred?

Serv. Yes, Sir.

Bla. They'l come i'their garded petticoats, will they not? You should have bid 'um eat no porrige at home, to seem more mannerly here at dinner. The widdow will be angry at their charges, but I'll please her at night. Go bid the Butler look to his plate, and not be drunk till he sees it all in again. Whose at the door there?

Act. 5. Scæn. 5.

Blade, Dogrel, and Puny disguis'd.

Serv. Faith, Sir, you know as well as I; some charitable beast come to be drest here. Shall I call the Cook, Sir?

Dog. Why this is my house here, *John*: ha! ha! little thought I to have seen my house in Fleet-street again. Where's my brother *Blade*?

Bla. They call me Captain *Blade*.

Dog. Is this he *John?* Let me see (*reads*) A proper burly man, with a whiteish beard, a quick eye, and a nose inclining to red, 'tis true. Save you good brother, you did not expect me here; did you brother? Stay let me see how many yeers ago is't since we went from home?

Pun. 'Tis now just seven, Sir.

Dog. Seven! me think's I was here but yesterday: How the what-d'ye-call-'um runs? What do ye call it?

Pun. Time, Sir.

Dog. I, I, Time. What was't I was saying? O, I was telling you brother, that I had quite forgot you: was I not telling him so *John?*

Bla. By my troth, Sir, we are both quits then; for I have forgot you too. Why, you were dead five yeers ago.

Dog. Was I so? I ha' quite forgot it. *John*, was I dead five yeers ago? My memory failes me very much of late.

Pun. We were worse then dead I'm sure; we were taken by a barbarous kind of Nation, and there made slaves these five yeers. *John* quoth he! I was poor *John* indeed: I'm sure they fed us three whole yeers with nothing but Acorns and water: we lookt like wicker-bottles.

Dog. How, Sirrah? Did your Master look like a wicked boat-man? (*strikes him*) Nay I remember what you said we lookt like. Did we look like what-d'ye-call-ums?

Bla. Where did they take you prisoners?

Dog. Nay ask *John*, he can tell you I warrant you. 'Twas in—tel him, *John*, where it was.

Pun. In Guiny, Sir.

Bla. By what Country-men were you taken?

Dog. Why they were call'd—I know not what they call'd 'um 'twas an odde kinde of name; but *John* can tell you.

Pun 'Slife, who I, Sir? d'ye think I can remember all things?

Dog 'Tis in my book here; I remember well the name of any Country under the Sun.

Pun. I know their names, Sir, well enough; but I onely tri'd my Masters memory. They're call'd Tartarians.

Dog. How say you? what were they?

Pun. Tartarians, Sir.

Dog. I, I, these were the men.

226

Bla. How, *John*! why all the world, man, lies between 'um : they live up i' the North.

Pun. The North?

Bla. I, the very North, *John*.

Pun. That's true indeed: but these were another nation of the Tartarians that liv'd by us.

Bla. Well, how escap'd you, *John*, at last?

Pun. Why 'faith, Sir, to tell you the truth, for I love not to tell a lye, the Kings daughter fell in love with me, and for my sake there set us free. My master has it all in his book; 'tis a fine story.

Bla. Strange! In what ship did you come back?

Dog. What ship? why 'twas call'd—a thing that swims— How d'ye call it?

Bla. What? the Mermaid?

Dog. No, no, no, let me see—

Bla. What? was't the Triton?

Dog. No, no—it swims, I tell you.

Bla. The Dolphin?

Dog. No, no—I have forgot what 'twas.

Bla. What say you, *John*?

Pun. (Pox take him.) I, Sir? O God, my Master, Sir, can tell as well as I.

Bla. He says he has forgot.

Pun. 'Tis his pleasure to say so, Sir : he may say what he pleases. (A plague upon him.) You can't conceive the misery we have past, Sir.

Bla. Well, brother, I'll make bold to ask one question more of you. Where did you leave your Will when you went away?

Pun. 'Slife, now he's pos'd again.

Dog. I'll tell you presently, brother; let me see. *(Reads.)* Memorandum for my Will: Left to my brother *Blade* the whole charge of my estate—hum—What did you ask me, brother?

Bla. In what place you left your Will?

Dog. I, that was it indeed; you're i' the right; 'twas the very thing you askt me; and yet see how quickly I forgot it. My memory's short, alas, God help me.

Bla. This is no answer to my question, yet.

Dog. 'Tis true indeed. What was your question, pray?

Bla. Where you left your Will.

Dog. Good lord! I had forgot you askt me this; I had forgot, i' faithlaw, that I had: you'll pardon my infirmity, I hope brother; for alas—alas—I ha' forgot what I was going to say to you; but I was a saying somthing, I am sure.

Pun. Did not you know us, *Will*? prithee tell's true.

Serv. No, by this light: why, you're grown as black as the chimney-stock.

Pun. That's the nature of the Country where we liv'd. O the stories that I shall tell you! And how does *Nell*, and little bonny *Bess*? are they as merry grigs as e'er they were?

Serv. No; *Bess*, poor wench is married to a Chandler; but she's true blue still, as right as my leg, I'll warrant you.

Dog. What is't, *John*? what was I going to say, *John*, to my brother?

Pun. I know not, Sir; was't not about your daughter?

Dog. I, I, my daughter—What d'ye call her?

Pun. *Lucia*, Sir.

Dog. 'Tis true indeed; my daughter *Lucia*, brother.

Bla. Pray walk into the parlour; I'll come to you presently, and tell you all.

Dog. Well, *John*, put me in minde o' my daughter *Lucia*. (A plague o' your Tartarians.)

Pun. (And o' your what-d'ye-call ums.)

Dog. ('Slife, Tartarians.)   *Exeunt Dog. Pun.*

Bla. If these be rogues, they are as impudent as Mountebanks and Juglers: and if I finde 'um to be rogues, (as I see nothing yet to the contrary) how I will exercise my rogues! The tyranny of a new Beadle over a beggar, shall be nothing to mine. Come hither, *Will*, what think you of these two fellows?

Serv. 'Faith, Sir, I know not: but if you think it be not my old Master, I'll beat 'um worse then the Tartarians did.

Bla. No, no, let's try 'um first. Thou wast wont to be a very precious knave, and a great acter too, a very *Roscius*. Didst not thou once act the Clown in *Musidorus*?

Serv. No, Sir; but I plaid the Bear there.

Bla. The Bear? why that's a good part; th'art an acter then, I'll warrant thee. The Bear's a well-pen'd part. And

228

you remember my brothers humour, don't you? They have almost hit it.

Serv. Yes, Sir, I know the shortness of my Masters memory; he would forget sometimes to pay me my wages till he was put in minde on't.

Bla. Well said. I'll dress thee within in his own chamber; and all the servants shall acknowledge you. But who shall do trusty *John?*

Serv. O, *Ralph* the Butler, Sir; he's an old actor, Sir, h'has plaid a King he says. I have heard him speak a Play *ex tempore* in the Buttry, Sir.

Bla. O *Ralph*, excellent *Ralph*, incomparable *Ralph*, *Ralph* against the world! Come away, *William*; I'll give you instructions within. It must be done in the twinkling of an eye.

Exeunt.

Act. 5.   Scæn. 6.

Cutter, Tabytha, Boy.

Cut. Now, Mistress *Tabytha Cutter*, let me kiss thee.

Tab. Pray God my mother be not angry.

Cut. Think not o' thy mother, Spouse; I tell thee, Spouse, thou shalt be a mother thy self, within these nine months.

> Come to my bed, my dear; my dear come to my bed:
> For the pleasant pain,
> And the loss with gain,
>   Is the loss of a maidenhead.

Tab. Is that a Psalm, brother husband, that you sing?

Cut. No, no, a short ejaculatory. Sirrah boy, are the things within that I spoke for?

Boy. Yes, Sir.

Cut. Go fetch 'um in.   *Exit Boy.*

Come, *Tabytha*, let's be merry: Canst thou sing a catch, wench? O well said, Boy!   *Enter boy with a hat and a feather, a broad band, a sword & a belt, & a periwig.*

Tab. What do you mean, brother husband? I hope you'll not turn roarer.

Cut. What? do these cloathes befit Queen *Tabytha*'s husband? this hat with a chimny-crown, and brims no broader then a moderate hat-band? Give me the Periwig, boy. What? shall Empress *Tabytha*'s husband go as if his head were scalded? or with the seam of a shirt for a band? Shall I walk without a sword, and not dare to quarrel i' the streets, and thrust men from the wall? Will the Fidlers be here presently, boy?

Boy. Yes, Sir.

Tab. Pish, I can't abide these doings. Are you mad? O lord! what will my mother say? There shall come no Fidlers here.

Cut. Be peaceable, gentle *Tabytha*; they will not bring the Organs with 'um. I say be peaceable; [t]he vision bid me do thus. Wilt thou resist the vision?

Tab. An' these be your visions—Little did I think 'twere—Is this your religion and praying? Which of all the Prophets wore such a map about his head, or such a sheet about his neck? What shall I do? I am undone.

Cut. What shalt thou do? Why, thou shalt dance, and sing, and drink, and laugh; thou shalt go with thy brests open, and thy hair braided; thou shalt put fine black stars upon thy face, and have great bobs for thy ears. Nay, if thou dost begin to look rustily, I'll have thee paint thy face like the whore of Babylon.

Tab. O that ever I was born to see this day!

Cut. What? dost thou weep, Queen *Dido*? Thou shalt have Sack to drive away thy sorrow. Come hither, boy, fetch me a quart of Canary. (*Exit boy.*) Thou shalt see I'll be a loving husband to thee. The vision, *Tabytha*, bid me give you drink: we must obey these visions. Sing, *Tabytha*: Cry on your wedding-day? 'tis ominous.

Come to my bed, my dear;
　　　Come to my bed:
For the pleasant pain—　　　　　*Enter boy with wine.*
O art thou come, boy—Well said, fill a brimmer; nay fuller yet, yet a little fuller. So. Here's to the Lady-Spouse; to our good sport to night.

Tab. Drink it your self, if you will; I'll not touch it.

Cut. By this hand, thou shalt pledge me, seeing the vision

THE GUARDIAN

said so. Drink, or I'll take a Coach and carry thee to a Play immediately.

Tab. I can't abide—   *(She drinks.)*

Cut. Why, this will clear thy heart, wench: Sack, and an husband, wench, are both comfortable things. Have at you again.

Tab. I'll pledge you no more, not I.

Cut. Here, take this glass, and take it off too, or else I'll swear an hundred oathes in a breathing-time. Here—

Tab. Well, you're the strangest man—

Cut. Why this is right now. Nay off with it. So. But the vision said that whatsoever we left of this same wine, would turn to poison straight. There, here's to you, *Tabytha*, once again: 'tis the visions will.

Tab. What? must I drink again, then? Well, I'll not resist. You're such another brother-husband.   *(Drinks.)* There's a whole one now—

> Come to my bed, my dear;
> Come to my bed—

How was't? Twas a pretty one.

Cut. O divine *Tabytha*! Here come the Fidlers too. Strike up, you rogues.

Tab. What? must we dance now? is not that the fashion? I could have danc'd the Coranto when I was a girl. The Coranto's a curious dance.

Cut. We'll dance out the disease of the Tarantula: but first we'll have a health to my pretty *Tabytha*.

Tab. I'll begin't my self. Here, Duck, here's to all that love us.

Cut. A health, you eternal scrapers, sound a health. Bravely done, *Tabytha*: what thinkst thou now o' thy mother?

Tab. A fig for my mother; I'll be a mother my self. Come, Duckling, shall we go home?

Cut. Go home? the Bride and the Bridegroom go? We'll dance home. Afore us, squeakers: that way, and be hang'd. So. O brave Queen *Tabytha*! excellent Empress *Tabytha*! On, you rogues.   *They go out dancing, with the musick before 'um.*

Act. 5. Scæn. 7.

Blade, Dogrel, Puny.

Dog. I must not be fob'd off thus about my daughter: I remember not your excuse; but *John* can tell well enough, I warrant you.

Bla. I have told you the plain truth: you'll not be angry, I hope.

Dog. I shall have cause to be angry, I fear: Did not I leave her to his charge, *John?* Brother, I tell you—

Bla. I must not answer, brother—

Dog. I know you put me out that I might forget what I said to you before: remember, *John:* I'll be as cunning as you're crafty: remember, *John.* How now? what's the matter?   *Enter servant.*

Serv. Ho, my old Master's come; he's lighted now at the door with his man *John:* he's asking for you; he longs to see you: my Master, my old Master.

Bla. This fellow's mad.

Serv. If you wo'n't believe me, go in and see, Sir: he's not so much alter'd, but you'll quickly know him. I knew him as soon as I saw him. Pray, Sir, go in.

Exeunt Blade and servant.

Bla. Why this is strange.

Pun. If this be true, what course shall we take, *Dogrel?* I begin to shake like a plum-tree-leaf.

Dog. We'll shift some way or other, I warrant you.

Pun. How, *Dogrel?* prithee how?

Dog. Let the worst come, we can be but whipt, or burnt in the hand, at the most.

Pun. Ho, our best way will be to hang our selves—'Slife, here's *John.*

Act. 5. Scæn. 8.

Dogrel, Puny, John, two or three servants.

1 Serv. Give me thy hand i'faith, boy: is't possible that thou shouldst be alive still?

2 Serv. Ha rogue! art thou come i'faith? I have a pottle o' Sack to welcome thee.

3 Serv. Why you'll not look upon your poor friends, *John.* Give my thy golls, *John.* How hast thou done this great while?

John. I thank you all heartily for your love; thank you with all my heart-law. What? my old bed-fellow *Robin?* how dost do? when shall we steal Apricocks again? d'ye remember, *Robin?*

2 Serv. A murrain take you; you'll never forget your roguery.

Pun. A murrain take you all: this was your plot, and be hang'd. Would I were *Puny* the Wit again.

Dog. Accursed Fate—

3 Serv. Come, *John,* let's go to the Buttry and be merry: *Ralph* longs to see you, I'm sure.

John. And how does *Ralph?* good honest *Ralph?* That *Ralp[h]'s* as honest a fellow, though I say 't my self; I love him with all my heart-law, that I do; and there's no love lost, I dare say for him.

2 Serv. Come, my masters, will you go in? I'll prevail with the Cook for a slice or two of Beef; and we'll have a cup of Stingo, the best in the cellar.

John. Well said, steel to the back still; that was your word, you know. My master's coming in: go, I'll follow you straight.

1 Serv. Make haste, good *John,* for I can't stay.

Exeunt Servants.

John. Here's a company of as honest fellows as a man would wish to live i' the house withal; all, no man excepted.

Dog. Would I were out of the house, as honest as they are. Here they come, *John.*

Pun. *John,* quoth he, with a pox.

ABRAHAM COWLEY

Act. 5. Scæn. 9.

Dogrel, Puny, John, Blade, William.

Bla. Me trinks you're not return'd, Sir,
But born to us anew, and I could wish
My tongue were not more niggardly then my heart
In giving you a welcom.

Will. Thank you good brother. Truly we ha' past
through many dangers; my man shall tell you all, I'm old
and crasy, and forget these things. (*Enter Widow.*

Bla. Pox on't, the Widow's come already; keep 'um here,
John, till I come back. O are you here sweet-heart?

Wid. Who have you yonder, I pray?

Bla. O, you should not ha' seen 'um yet, they are Maskers.

Wid. Not vagrant players, I hope?

Bla. No, no, they can onely tumble, and dance upon the
rope, you shall see 'um after dinner. Let's away sweet-heart,
the Parson stays for us, he has blown his fingers this hour.

(*Exeunt Blade and the Widow.*

Dog. I'm glad the Captain's gone, now will I sneak away,
like one that has stolen a silver-spoone.

Pun. I'll be your man and follow you.

Wil. Who are these *John?* By your leave, Sir; would
you speak with any here?

Dog. The Captain, Sir. But I'll take some other time to
wait on him, my occasions call me now.

Wil. Nay, pray, Sir, stay. Whom did you say you would
speak withall?

Dog. The Captain, Sir. But another time will serve. I
ha' some haste of business.

Will. Whom would he speak with, *John?* I forget still.

Joh. The Captain Sir.

Will. Captain? What Captain Sir?

Dog. Your brother I suppose he is.

Will. 'Tis true indeed, I had forgot that my brother was a
Captain. I cry you mercy, Sir, he'll be here presently. Are
you an English-man, Sir?

Dog. Yes, Sir.

234

Will.   Where were you born I pray?

Dog.   In London, Sir. I must leave you—

Will.   In London? y'are an English-man then I see, Sir.
Would you have spoke with me Sir?

Dog.   No, with your brother, but my business with him
requires not haste, and therefore—

Will.   You're not in haste you say; pray sit down then:
may I crave your name, Sir?

Dog.   My name's not worth your knowled[g]e, Sir; but my
mans name's *John.*

Pun.   (If I be *John* any more I'll be hang'd) No my name's
Timothy, Sir.

Will.   Mr. *John Timothy?* Very well, Sir. You seem to
Be a Travellor.

Dog.   We're newly come out of Affrick, and therefore have
some business that requires us.

Will.   Of Affrick? Law you there now. What Country
pray?

Dog.   *Prester John's* Country. Fare you well, Sir, now.

Will.   Marry God forbid. What come from *Prester John,*
and we not drink a cup of Sack together?

Dog.   (What shall I do?) Friend, shall I trouble you to
shew me where your house of office is?

Will.   You'll stay here Mr.—what's your name, pray?

Pun.   *Timothy,* Sir.

Will.   Gods me, 'tis true indeed Mr. *John Timothy.*

Pun.   I'll only make water, and come to you.

Joh.   The door, Sir, is lockt; the Captain has lockt us all in
here, if you'll be pleas'd to stay, Sir, till he comes—

Dog.   (I'd as live stay to meet the Devil, or a Sargeant.)

Pun.   (Would I were hid like maggot in a pescod; we shall
be abused I see, oh, oh, oh,)

Joh.   What makes you quake so, Sir?

Pun.   Nothing, onely I have an extream list to make water:
'Tis nothing else by this light.

Will.   My brother would not have you gone it seems.
Your names Mr. *John Timothy,* is it?

Dog.   No, that's my mans name.

Will.   O, your mans name; 'tis true, 'tis ve[r]y true indeed,
that's your man's name. You'll pardon me, Sir?

Joh. Pray, friend, do you know the great City call'd Aster-vadil, where my name-sake *Prester-John* keeps his Court?

Pun. Know't? I, very well; I have liv'd there a great while, I have cause to know't.

Joh. Ther's a brave Castle of three miles long.

Pun. I, and many stately building too.

Joh. The noble mens houses are all built of Marble.

Pun. They make indeed a glorious show. I ha' seen 'um.

Joh. It may be so. But to my knowledg, friend, there is no such City there.

Pun. It may be the names are alter'd since I was there. (Here's the Captain, I'll sneak behind the hangings.)

Act. 5.   Scæn. 10.

Dogrel, Puny, William, John, Blade, Widow.

Bla. I like this Person well, a' has made short work on't, he had appointed sure some mee[t]ng at an Ale-house. Welcome wife, welcome home now. But I ha' two brethren which you must know.

Wid. Marry, Heav'ns foresheild, Sir.

Bla. Brethren in God sweet-heart, no otherwise. Come hither Guiny brother; what say you?

Will. This Gentleman, Brother, has stay'd for you here; pray use him kindly, he's a Traveller: where did you say you travell'd, Sir?

Bla. O yes! How do you, brother?

Dog. I your brother? what d'ye mean?

Bla. Why, are not you my brother *Blade* that was taken captive by the Tartars? Ha!

Dog. You're merrily dispos'd. Sr: I your brother! I taken captive by the Tartars! Ha, ha, ha! I understand not your meaning, Sir.

Bla. What an impudent slave's this! Sirrah monster, didst not thou come with thy man *John?*

Dog. I, my man *John?* here's no such fellow here, you see: how you're mistaken, Sir! you mean some other man. This is the strangest humour.

236

Bla. Sirrah, dost thou see this ~~fist~~? dost thou see this foot?
I'll wear these out upon thee—

Dog. Hold, pray Sir, hold. I remember now indeed that I
was *Blade* the Merchant; but I had quite forgot it. You
must pardon me; my memory's very weak.

Bla. I like the humour. But I must know, Sir, who you
are, now you ha' left being my brother.

Dog. Who, I? don't you know me? I'm *Dogrel* the Poet,
and *Puny* was my man *John*. Lord that you should not know
me all this while! not know Poet *Dogrel!*

      Why I intended here this merry play,
      To solemnize your nuptial-day.

Wid. O thank you, M. *Dogrel*; Can you dance upon the
ropes, and tumble? Truely I never knew it before, not I.

Bla. Where's that fool, *Puny?* Is he slipt away?

Pun. (He was wise enough to do so, I'll warrant you.)

Bla. I will beat him so, that he shall not finde a similitude
for himself. As for you, *Dogrel*, because you came off pretty
handsomely, with the best at the last, like an Epigram, I may
chance to pardon you; but upon this condition, that you make
no Epithalamiums upon my marriage.

Well said, *Will*; bravely done, *Will*: i' faith
thou shalt ha' two laces more to thy Livery, for
doing this so well. I told thee, *Will*, what 'twas
to have acted the Bear in *Musidorus*. And *Ralph*
was a brave *John* too—

*He pulls
off his mens
disguises.*

Dog. How's this? I plainly see I'm an Ass then: 'twas
this damn'd *Puny*'s fearfulness spoil'd all.

Pun. (A pox o' this coward *Dogrel*: I thought they were
not the right ones.)

Bla. I see my Players had more wit then my Poet. Here's
something for you to drink. Go in now: this is your Cue of
Exit; and see all things there in a readiness.

Will. Nay, let the Master go first. Follow me, *John*.

                Exeunt Will. and Ralph.

Wid. What, husband? Ha' you giv'n 'um any thing?
Indeed, Love, you're too lavish.

Dog. 'Twas very wittily put off o' me, howsoever.

Act. 5.   Scæn. 11.

Blade, Widow, Dogrel, Puny, Cutter, and Tabytha,
with Fidlers before 'um.

Bla. How now ? what ha' we here ? another Puppet-play ?
Any thing now but brothers, and I'm for 'um. Who ? *Cutter?*
What's the matter, Poet ? Come, what device is this ? like one
o' yours ?

Cut. Stay at the door, ye sempiternal squeakers. Come,
Queen o' fame.

Tab. Lord, I'm so weary with dancing as passes. Yonder's
my mother. On mother ! what d'ye think I ha' been doing
to day ?

Wid. Why what, childe ?

Tab. Nay nothing: I have onely been married a little ; and
my husband and I ha' so danced it since !

Cut. Brave *Tabytha* still ! Never be angry, Widow ; you
know where Marriages are made. How now, Captain ? If I
turn Tapster now, 'twill be happie for you: for I shall be rich
enough to trust you, Captain.

Wid. 'Twas Gods will, I see, and therefore there's no
resisting. But what d'ye mean, son ? I hope you'll not turn
swaggerer ?

Cut. 'Tis for special reasons, gentle mother. Why how
now, *Dogrel?* M. *Blade* the Merchant looks as if he were
broke: he has turn'd away his servant too.

Tab. Who 's that ? M. *Dogrel* i' these Players clothes ?
Can M. *Dogrel* dance too, husband ?

Bla. Prithee, *Cutter,* what hath exalted *Tabytha* thus ?

Cut. What ? this good fortune she has got by me: You
know what a dull creature she was before ; her soul was in her
body, like butter in a hot cake ; now she's as full of Spirits as
Hell it self. My counsel and two cups o' Sack, have wrought
this miracle.

Act. 5. Scæn. 12.

To these, *Truman* Pater, *Truman* Filius, *Lucia* veil'd.

Tru. p.   Well said!   You are joyn'd then now, my blessing on you both; come in to your father *Blade*.   Nay, daughter *Aurelia*, off with your veil now.   Ha!   Whom ha' you married here?

Tru. f.   I know not, Sir.   She was *Aurelia* when we went to Church.

Bla.   This is my daughters maid.   Where's the wench? Ho!   *Aurelia*?

Act. 5. Scæn. 13.

To them, Aurelia.

Aur.   Here, Sir.

Bla.   Here, Sir?   Why do you make your husband lead your maid in thus?

Aur.   My husband, Sir?   what's that?

Bla.   Why, huswife is not Mr. *Truman* your husband?

Aur.   No, by my troth, Sir, I thank God.

Tru. p.   These are fine tricks; delicate, dainty tricks. Sirrah, how durst you Sirrah?—and for your minion—marry come up, marry a Chamber-maid?   Well, Captain, this was your plotting.   You said indeed you'd make a *tethron* o' me: y' ha' don't indeed; I thank you, Captain *Blade*, 'tis well.   Out o' my sight, Sir, with your minion there, I say out o' my sight. Ha!   am I fool'd thus?   I shall make some repent it, I hold a groate on't.

Bla.   D'ye hear, Mr. *Truman*—

Tru. p.   Yes, Sir, I do hear; and I will not hear if it please me, Sir; but some body shall hear o' this Captain.   But, Captain, you're deceived, this is not a lawful marriage.

Luc.   Pray, hear me all; for I shall tell those things That will appease your wrath, and move your wonder. I've married *Truman*, and I will enjoy him,

And he will love me, I am sure he will;
For I am *Lucia*, the much injure'd *Lucia*.

Omn. Ha!

Luc. The habit of a servant I put on,
That I might finde who 'twas I ought to pardon,
For all the wrongs done to me. I have found it,
Cosen, you know I have, and I forgive 'um.

Aur. Then all my plots are spoil'd. Pardon me, Cousin:
And, Mr. *Truman*, know you have a wife
That is as pure and innocent as the thoughts
Of dying Saints? 'Twas I that with the veile
Deceiv'd you in the Prison; it was I,
Who in that veile contracted my self to *Puny*.
Forgive me both; I do confess I've wrong'd you,
But Heav'n has seen you righted.

Tru. f. O this blest hour!
What shall I say? I know thou art all goodness,
But canst thou pardon, *Lucia*, that great sin,
That high and mighty sin which I have done
In doubting of thy faith? I fear thou canst not.

Luc. I do desire no more then that I may,
Deserve your better opinion, Sir, hereafter.
And uncle for your poyson—

Bla. Speak no more of it,
I do confess it, Neece; and shall most willingly
Surrender up the charge of your Estate.
It hath pleas'd Heav'n to restore me mine own
By marriage with this Widow.

Tru. p. Ha, ha, ha! To see how things are come about!
I thought *Dick* would not be such a fool as to marry one that
he knew not. He knew her well enough, I'll warrant you.
How do you, Captain? I was somewhat rash: I'm an old
man, alas.

Bla. *Cutter*, and M. *Dogrel*, you that sneak there;
You're precious witnesses. But no more o' that.
You have been to blame, *Aurelia*. But 'tis past.
We want your husband here: Where's *Puny*?

Pun. (I'll venture out amongst 'um.)   *Enter Puny.*
Nay ne'er laugh at me; I know I look like a door without
hinges. A pox upon you, *Dogrel*; are you there?

THE GUARDIAN

Bla. What? my son *John*? d'ye know this Gentlewoman?

Aur. D'ye know this piece of gold, Sir, which you broke?

Pun. Hum? Yes 'faith, 'tis the same: thou art my *Cynthia*, wench, my *Endymion*: we'll be married presently. O for a witty Parson to marry us two Wits!

Dog. 'Slife, one, two, three, i'faith four matches here at one time! What accursed fortune's this! there's three feasts lost: they'll dine all together.

Pun. I will not kiss thee, my little magazine, till I have washt my face. Ha, M. *Dogrel*, hast thou got no Spouse too?

Dog. The thrice three Sisters are my wives.

Pun. Well, because thou art a Poet, and my Jews-trump and I are Wits, thou shalt eat and drink at my pavilion always.

Aur. You shall ha' wine and serge. D'ye remember, *Dogrel*?

Dog. Thank you: but I'll ne'er lye for you again.

Bla. Come, let's all in to dinner.

The Epilogue.

THe Play is done, great Prince, which needs must fear,
    Though you brought all your fathers mercies here,
It may offend your Highness, and we've now
Three hours done treason here, for ought we know.
But pow'r your Grace can above Nature give;
It can give pow'r to make abortives live.
In which if our bold wishes should be crost,
'Tis but the life of one poor week that's lost.
Though it should fall beneath your present scorn,
It could not die sooner then it was born.

FINIS.

242

A

PROPOSITION

For the

ADVANCEMENT

Of

EXPERIMENTAL

Philosophy.

By A. Cowley.

[*design*]

LONDON,

Printed by *J. M.* for *Henry Herringman*; and are to be
sold at his Shop at the Sign of the *Blew-Anchor* in the
Lower-Walk of the New-Exchange, 1661.

To the Honourable Society for the Advancement of Experimental Philosophy.

THe Author of the following discourse, having since his going into *France* allowed me to make it publick, I thought I should do it most right by presenting it to Your Considerations; to the end that when it hath been fully examin'd by You, and receiv'd such Additions or Alterations as You shall think fit, the Design thereof may be promoted by Your recommending the Practice of it to the Nation. I am,

Your most humble Servant,

P. P.

The Preface.

ALL Knowledge must either be of God, or of his Creatures, that is, of Nature; the first is called from the Object, Divinity; *the latter,* Natural Philosophy, *and is divided into the Contemplation of the Immediate or Mediate Creatures of God, that is, the Creatures of his Creature Man. Of this latter kind are all Arts for the use of Humane Life, which are thus again divided: Some are purely Humane, or made by Man alone, and as it were intirely spun out of himself, without relation to other Creatures, such are* Grammar *and* Logick, *to improve his Natural Qualities of Internal and External speech; as likewise* Rhetorick *and* Politicks (*or* Law) *to fulfill and exalt his Natural Inclination to Society. Other are mixt, and are Mans Creatures no otherwise then by the Result which he effects by Conjunction and Application of the Creatures of God. Of these parts of Philosophy that which treats of God Almighty (properly called* Divinity) *which is almost only to be sought out of his revealed will, and therefore requires only the diligent and pious study of that, and of the best Interpreters upon it; and that part which I call purely Humane, depending solely* upon *Memory and Wit, that is, Reading and Invention, are both excellently well provided for by the Constitution of our Universities. But the other two Parts, the Inquisition into the Nature of Gods Creatures, and the Application of them to Humane Uses (especially the latter) seem to be very slenderly provided for, or rather almost totally neglected, except onely some small assistances to Physick, and the Mathematicks. And therefore the Founders of our Colledges have taken ample care to supply the Students with multitude of Books, and to appoint Tutors and frequent Exercises, the one to interpret, and the other to confirm their Reading, as also to afford them sufficient plenty and leisure for the opportunities of their private study, that the Beams which they receive by Lecture may be doubled by Reflections of their own Wit: But towards the Observation and Application, as I said, of the Creatures themselves, they have allowed no Instruments, Materials, or Conveniences. Partly, because the necessary expence thereof is much greater, then of the other; and partly from that idle and pernicious opinion which had long possest the World, that all things to be searcht in Nature, had been already found and discovered by the Ancients, and that it were a folly to travel about for that which others had before brought home to us. And the great Importer of all Truth they took to be Aristotle, as if (as Macrobius speaks foolishly of Hippocrates) he could neither deceive nor be deceived, or as if there had been not only no Lies in him, but all Verities. O true Philosophers in one sence! and contented with a very Little! Not that I would disparage the admirable Wit, and worthy labours of many of the Ancients, much less of Aristotle, the most eminent among them; but it were madness to imagine that the Cisterns of men should afford us as much, and as wholesome Waters, as the Fountains of Nature. As we understand the manners of men by conversation among them, and not by reading Romances, the same is our case in the true Apprehension & Judgement of Things. And no man can hope to make himself as rich by stealing out of others Truncks, as he might by opening and digging of new Mines. If he conceive that all are already exhausted, let him consider that many lazily thought so hundred years ago, and yet nevertheless since that time whole Regions of Art have been discovered, which the Ancients as little dreamt of as they did of America. There is yet many a Terra Incognita behind to exercise our diligence, and let us exercise it never so much, we shall leave work enough too for our Posterity.*

THE PREFACE

This therefore being laid down as a certain Foundation, that we must not content our selves with that Inheritance of Knowledge which is left us by the labour and bounty of our Ancestors, but seek to improve those very grounds, and adde to them new and greater Purchases ; it remains to be considered by what means we are most likely to attain the ends of this vertuous Covetousness.

And certainly the solitary and unactive Contemplation of Nature, by the most ingenious Persons living, in their own private Studies, can never effect it. Our Reasoning Faculty as well as Fancy, does but Dream, when it is not guided by sensible Objects. We shall compound where Nature has divided, and divide where Nature has compounded, and create nothing but either Deformed Monsters, or at best pretty but impossible Mermaids. 'Tis like Painting by Memory and Imagination which can never produce a Picture to the Life. Many Persons of admirable abilities (if they had been wisely managed and profitably employed) have spent their whole time and diligence in commentating upon Aristotles Philosophy, who could never go beyond him, because their design was only to follow, not grasp, or lay hold on, or so much as touch Nature, because they catcht only at the shadow of her in their own Brains. And therefore we see that for above a thousand years together nothing almost of Ornament or Advantage was added to the Uses of Humane Society, except only Guns and Printing, whereas since the Industry of Men has ventured to go abroad, out of Books and out of Themselves, and to work among Gods Creatures, instead of Playing among their Own, every age has abounded with excellent Inventions, and every year perhaps might do so, if a considerable number of select Persons were set apart, and well directed, and plentifully provided for the search of them. But our Universities having been founded in those former times that I complain of, it is no wonder if they be defective in their Constitution as to this way of Learning, which was not then thought on.

For the supplying of which Defect, it is humbly proposed to his Sacred Majesty, his most Honourable Parliament, and Privy Council, and to all such of his Subjects as are willing and able to contribute any thing towards the advancement of real and useful Learning, that by their Authority, Encouragement, Patronage, and Bounty, a Philosophical Colledge may be erected, after this ensuing, or some such like Model.

The Colledge.

THat the Philosophical Colledge be scituated within one, two, or (at farthest) three miles of *Lond[o]n*, and, if it be possible to find that convenience, upon the side of the River, or very near it.

That the Revenue of this Colledge amount to four thousand pounds a year.

That the Company received into it be as follows.

1. Twenty Philosophers or Professors. 2. Sixteen young Scholars, Servants to the Professors. 3. A Chaplain. 4. A Baily for the Revenue. 5. A Manciple or Purveyour for the provisions of the House. 6. Two Gardeners. 7. A Master-Cook. 8. An Under-Cook. 9. A Butler. 10. An Under-Butler. 11. A Chirurgeon. 12. Two Lungs, or Chymical Servants. 13. A Library-keeper who is likewise to be Apothecary, Druggist, and Keeper of Instruments, Engines, &c. 14. An Officer to feed and take care of all Beasts, Fowl, &c. kept by the Colledge. 15. A Groom of the Stable. 16. A Messenger to send up and down for all uses of the Colledge. 17. Four old Women, to tend the Chambers, keep the House clean, and such like services.

That the annual allowance for this Company be as follows.
1. To every Professor, and to the Chaplain, one hundred and twenty Pounds. 2. To the sixteen Scholars 20^l a piece, 10^l for their diet, and 10^l for their Entertainment. 3. To the Baily 30^l besides allowance for his Journeys. 4. To the Purveyour or Manciple thirty pounds. 5. To each of the Gardeners twenty Pounds. 6. To the Master-Cook twenty Pounds. 7. To the Under-Cook four Pounds. 8. To the Butler ten Pounds. 9. To the Under-Butler four Pounds. 10. To the Chirurgeon thirty Pounds. 11. To the Library-Keeper thirty Pounds. 12. To each of the Lungs twelve Pounds. 13. To the Keeper of the Beasts six Pounds. 14. To the Groom five Pounds. 15. To the Messenger twelve Pounds. 16. To the four necessary Women ten Pounds. For the Manciples Table at which all the Servants of the

THE COLLEDGE

House are to eat, except the Scholars, one hundred sixty Pounds. For 3 Horses for the Service of the Colledge, thirty Pounds.

All which amounts to three thousand two hundred eighty five Pounds. So that there remains for keeping of the House and Gardens, and Operatories, and Instruments, and Animals, and Experiments of all sorts, and all other expences, seven hundred & fifteen Pounds.

Which were a very inconsiderable sum for the great uses to which it is designed, but that I conceive the Industry of the Colledge will in a short time so enrich it self as to get a far better Stock for the advance and enlargement of the work when it is once begun; neither is the continuance of particular mens liberality to be despaired of, when it shall be encouraged by the sight of that publick benefit which will accrue to all Mankind, and chiefly to our Nation, by this Foundation. Something likewise will arise from Leases and other Casualties; that nothing of which may be diverted to the private gain of the Professors, or any other use besides that of the search of Nature, and by it the general good of the world, and that care may be taken for the certain performance of all things ordained by the Institution, as likewise for the protection and encouragement of the Company, it is proposed.

That some Person of Eminent Quality, a Lover of solid Learning, and no Stranger in it, be chosen Chancellour or President of the Colledge, and that eight Governours more, men qualified in the like manner, be joyned with him, two of which shall yearly be appointed Visitors of the Colledge, and receive an exact account of all expences even to the smallest, and of the true estate of their publick Treasure, under the hands and oaths of the Professors Resident.

That the choice of the Professors in any vacancy belong to the Chancellour and the Governours, but that the Professors (who are likeliest to know what men of the Nation are most proper for the duties of their Society) direct their choice by recommending two or three persons to them at every Election. And that if any learned Person within his Majesties Dominions discover or eminently improve any useful kind of knowledge, he may upon that ground for his reward and the encouragement of others, be preferr'd, if he pretend to the place, before any body else.

ABRAHAM COWLEY

That the Governours have power to turn out any Professor who shall be proved to be either scandalous or unprofitable to the Society.

That the Colledge be built after this, or some such manner: That it consist of three fair Quadrangular Courts, and three large grounds, enclosed with good walls behind them. That the first Court be built with a fair Cloyster, and the Professors Lodgings or rather little Houses, four on each side at some distance from one another, and with little Gardens behind them, just after the manner of the *Chartreux* beyond Sea. That the inside of the Cloyster be lined with a Gravel-walk, and that walk with a row of Trees, and that in the middle there be a Parterre of Flowers, and a Fountain.

That the second Quadrangle just behind the first, be so contrived, as to contain these parts. 1. A Chappel. 2. A Hall with two long Tables on each side for the Scholars and Officers of the House to eat at, and with a Pulpit and Forms at the end for the publick Lectures. 3. A large and pleasant Dining-Room within the Hall for the Professors to eat in, and to hold their Assemblies and Conferences. 4. A publick School-house. 5. A Library. 6. A Gallery to walk in, adorned with the Pictures or Statues of all the Inventors of any thing useful to Humane Life; as Printing, Guns, *America*, &c. and of late in Anatomy, the Circulation of the Blood, the Milky Veins, and such like discoveries in any Art, with short Elogies under the Portraictures: As likewise the Figures of all sorts of Creatures, and the stuft skins of as many strange Animals as can be gotten. 7. An Anatomy Chamber adorned with Skeletons and Anatomical Pictures, and prepared with all conveniences for Dissection. 8. A Chamber for all manner of Druggs, and Apothecaries Materials. 9. A Mathematical Chamber furnisht with all sorts of Mathematical Instruments, being an Appendix to the Library. 10. Lodgings for the Chaplain, Chirurgeon, Library-Keeper and Purveyour, near the Chappel, Anatomy Chamber, Library and Hall.

That the third Court be on one side of these, very large, but meanly built, being designed only for use and not for beauty too, as the others. That it contain the Kitchin, Butteries, Brew-house, Bake-house, Dairy, Lardry, Stables, &c. and especially great Laboratories for Chymical Operations, and Lodgings for the Under-servants.

THE COLLEDGE

That behind the second Court be placed the Garden, containing all sorts of Plants that our Soil will bear, and at the end a little House of pleasure, a Lodge for the Gardener, and a Grove of Trees cut out into Walks.

That the second enclosed ground be a Garden, destined only to the tryal of all manner of Experiments concerning Plants, as their Melioration, Acceleration, Retardation, Conservation, Composition, Transmutation, Coloration, or whatsoever else can be produced by Art either for use or curiosity, with a Lodge in it for the Gardener.

That the third Ground be employed in convenient Receptacles for all sorts of Creatures which the Professors shall judge necessary for their more exact search into the nature of Animals, and the improvement of their Uses to us.

That there be likewise built in some place of the Colledge where it may serve most for Ornament of the whole, a very high Tower for observation of Celestial Bodies, adorned with all sorts of Dyals and such like Curiosities; and that there be very deep Vaults made under ground, for Experiments most proper to such places, which will be undoubtedly very many.

Much might be added, but truly I am afraid this is too much already for the charity or generosity of this age to extend to ; and we do not design this after the Model of *Solomons* House in my Lord *Bacon* (which is a Project for Experiments that can never be Experimented) but propose it within such bounds of Expence as have often been exceeded by the Buildings of private Citizens.

Of the Professors, Scholars, Chaplain, and other Officers.

THat of the twenty Professors four be always travelling beyond Seas, and sixteen always Resident, unless by permission upon extraordinary occasions, and every one so absent, leaving a Deputy behind him to supply his Duties.

That the four Professors Itinerant be assigned to the four parts of the World, *Europe*, *Asia*, *Afrique*, and *America*, there

251

ABRAHAM COWLEY

to reside three years at least, and to give a constant account of all things that belong to the Learning, and especially Natural Experimental Philosophy of those parts.

That the expence of all Dispatches, and all Books, Simples, Animals, Stones, Metals, Minerals, &c. and all curiosities whatsoever, natural or artificial, sent by them to the Colledge, shall be defrayed out of the Treasury, and an additional allowance (above the 120¹) made to them as soon as the Colledges Revenue shall be improved.

That at their going abroad they shall take a solemn Oath never to write any thing to the Colledge, but what after very diligent Examination, they shall fully believe to be true, and to confess and recant it as soon as they find themselves in an Errour.

That the sixteen Professors Resident shall be bound to study and teach all sorts of Natural, Experimental Philosophy, to consist of the Mathematicks, Mechanicks, Medicine, Anatomy, Chymistry, the History of Animals, Plants, Minerals, Elements, &c. Agriculture, Architecture, Art Military, Navigation, Gardening; The Mysteries of all Trades, and Improvement of them; The Facture of all Merchandizes, all Natural Magick or Divination; and briefly all things contained in the Catalogue of Natural Histories annexed to My Lord *Bacon's Organon.*

That once a day from *Easter* till *Michaelmas*, and twice a week from *Michaelmas* to *Easter*, at the hours in the afternoon most convenient for Auditors from *London* according to the time of the year, there shall be a Lecture read in the Hall, upon such parts of Natural Experimental Philosophy, as the Professors shall agree on among themselves, and as each of them shall be able to perform usefully and honourably.

That two of the Professors by daily, weekly, or monethly turns shall teach the publick Schools according to the Rules hereafter prescribed.

That all the Professors shall be equal in all respects (except precedency, choice of Lodging, and such like priviledges, which shall belong to Seniority in the Colledge) and that all shall be Masters and Treasurers by annual turns, which two Officers for the time being shall take place of all the rest, and shall be *Arbitri duarum Mensarum.*

252

OF THE PROFESSORS, ETC.

That the Master shall command all the Officers of the Colledge, appoint Assemblies or Conferences upon occasion, and preside in them with a double voice, and in his absence the Treasurer, whose business is to receive and disburse all moneys by the Masters order in writing, (if it be an extraordinary) after consent of the other Professors.

That all the Professors shall sup together in the Parlour within the Hall every night, and shall dine there twice a week (to wit *Sundays* and *Thursdays*) at two round Tables for the convenience of discourse, which shall be for the most part of such matters as may improve their Studies and Professions, and to keep them from falling into loose or unprofitable talk shall be the duty of the two *Arbitri Mensarum*, who may likewise command any of the Servant-Scholars to read to them what he shall think fit, whilst they are at table: That it shall belong likewise to the said *Arbitri Mensarum* only, to invite Strangers, which they shall rarely do, unless they be men of Learning or great Parts, and shall not invite above two at a time to one table, nothing being more vain and unfruitful then numerous Meetings of Acquaintance.

That the Professors Resident shall allow the Colledge twenty Pounds a year for their Diet, whether they continue there all the time or not.

That they shall have once a week an Assembly or Conference concerning the Affairs of the Colledge and the progress of their Experimental Philosophy.

That if any one find out any thing which he conceives to be of consequence, he shall communicate it to the Assembly to be examined, experimented, approved or rejected.

That if any one be Author of an Invention that may bring in profit, the third part of it shall belong to the Inventor, and the two other to the Society ; and besides if the thing be very considerable, his Statue or Picture with an Elogy under it, shall be placed in the Gallery, and made a Denison of that Corporation of famous Men.

That all the Professors shall be always assigned to some particular Inquisition (besides the ordinary course of their Studies) of which they shall give an account to the Assembly, so that by this means there may be every day some operation or other made in all the Arts, as Chymistry, Anatomy, Me-

253

chanicks, and the like, and that the Colledge shall furnish for the charge of the operation.

That there shall be kept a Register under lock and key, and not to be seen but by the Professors, of all the Experiments that succeed, signed by the persons who made the tryall.

That the popular and received Errours in Experimental Philosophy (with which, like Weeds in a neglected Garden it is now almost all overgrown) shall be evinced by tryal, and taken notice of in the publick Lectures, that they may no longer abuse the credulous, and beget new ones by consequence or similitude.

That every third year (after the full settlement of the Foundation) the Colledge shall give an account in Print, in proper and ancient Latine, of the fruits of their triennial Industry.

That every Professor Resident shall have his Scholar to wait upon him in his Chamber and at Table, whom he shall be obliged to breed up in Natural Philosophy, and render an account of his progress to the Assembly, from whose Election he received him, and therefore is responsible to it, both for the care of his Education, and the just and civil usage of him.

That the Scholar shall understand Latine very well, and be moderately initiated in the Greek before he be capable of being chosen into the Service, and that he shall not remain in it above seven years.

That his Lodging shall be with the Professor whom he serves.

That no Professor shall be a married man, or a Divine, or a Lawyer in practice, only Physick he may be allowed to prescribe, because the study of that Art is a great part of the duty of his place, and the duty of that is so great, that it will not suffer him to lose much time in mercenary practice.

That the Professors shall in the Colledge wear the habit of ordinary Masters of Art in the Universities, or of Doctors, if any of them be so.

That they shall all keep an inviolable and exemplary friendship with one another, and that the Assembly shall lay a considerable pecuniary mulct upon any one who shall be proved to have entered so far into a quarrel as to give uncivil Language to his Brother-Professor ; and that the perseverance in any enmity shall be punish'd by the Governours with expulsion.

That the Chaplain shall eat at the Masters Table, (paying his twenty pounds a year as the others do) and that he shall read Prayers once a day at least, a little before Supper-time ; that he shall preach in the Chappel every *Sunday* Morning, and Catechize in the After-noon the Scholars and the School-boys; that he shall every moneth administer the Holy Sacrament; that he shall not trouble himself and his Auditors with the Controversies of Divinity, but only teach God in his just Commandments, and in his wonderful Works.

The Sch[o]ol.

THat the School may be built so as to contain about two hundred Boys.

That it be divided into four Classes, not as others are ordinarily into six or seven, because we suppose that the Children sent hither to be initiated in Things as well as Words, ought to have past the two or three first, and to have attained the age of about thirteen years, being already we[l]l advanced in the Latine Grammar, and some Authors.

That none, though never so rich, shall pay any thing for their teaching; and that if any Professor shall be convicted to have taken any money in consideration of his pains in the School, he shall be expelled with ignominie by the Governours; but if any persons of great estate and quality, finding their Sons much better Proficients in Learning here, then Boys of the same age commonly are at other Schools, shall not think fit to receive an obligation of so near concernment without returning some marks of acknowledgement, they may, if they please (for nothing is to be demanded) bestow some little rarity or curiosity upon the Society in recompence of their trouble.

And because it is deplorable to consider the loss which Children make of their time at most Schools, employing, or rather casting away six or seven years in the learning of words only, and that too very imperfectly :

That a Method be here established for the infusing Knowledge and Language at the same time into them; and that this may be their Apprenticeship in Natural Philosophy. This we conceive may be done, by breeding them up in Authors, or pieces of Authors, who treat of some parts of Nature, and who may be understood with as much ease and pleasure, as those which are commonly taught; Such are in Latine *Varro*, *Cato*, *Columella*, *Pliny*, part of *Celsus*, and of *Seneca*, *Cicero de Divinatione*, *de Naturâ Deorum*, and several scattered pieces, *Virgil's Georgicks*, *Grotius*, *Ne[m]esianus*, *Manilius*; and because the truth is we want good Poets (I mean we have but few) who have purposely treated of solid and learned, that is, Natural Matters (the most part indulging to the weakness of the world, and feeding it either with the follies of Love, or with the Fables of gods and Heroes) we conceive that one Book ought to be compiled of all the scattered little parcels among the ancient Poets that might serve for the advancement of Natural Science, and which would make no small or unuseful or unpleasant Volum[e]. To this we would have added the Morals and Rhetoricks of *Cicero*, and the Institutions of *Quintilian*; and for the Comœdians, from whom almost all that necessary part of common discourse, and all the most intimate proprieties of the Language are drawn, we conceive the Boys may be made Masters of them, as a part of their Recreation and not of their task, if once a moneth, or at least once in two, they act one of *Terences* Comœdies, and afterwards (the most advanced) some of *Plautus* his; and this is for many reasons one of the best exercises they can be enjoyned, and most innocent pleasures they can be allowed. As for the Greek Authors, they may study *Nicander*, *Oppianus* (whom *Scaliger* does not doubt to prefer above *Homer* himself, and place next to his adored *Virgil*) *Aristotles* History of Animals, and other parts, *Theophrastus* and *Dioscorides* of Plants, and a Collection made out of several both Poets and other Grecian Writers. For the Morals and Rhetorick *Aristotle* may suffice, or *Hermogenes* and *Longinus* be added for the latter; with the History of Animals they should be shewed Anatomy as a Divertisement, and made to know the Figures and Natures of those Creatures which are not common among us, disabusing them at the same time of those Errours which are universally admitted concerning many. The same Method should be used to make them acquainted with all Plants; and to this must be added a little of the ancient and modern Geography, the understanding of the Globes, and the Principles of Geometry and Astronomy. They should likewise use to declaim in Latine and English, as the Romans did in Greek and Latine; and in all this travel be rather led on by familiarity, encouragement, and emulation, then driven by severity, punishment, and terrour. Upon Festivals and playtimes they should exercise themselves in the Fields by riding, leaping, fencing, mustering and training after the manner of Souldiers, &c. and to prevent all dangers and all disorder, there should always be two of the Scholars with them to be as witnesses and directors of their actions; In foul weather it would not be amiss for them to learn to dance, that is, to learn just so much (for all beyond is superfluous, if not worse) as may give them a graceful comportment of their bodies.

Upon *Sundays*, and all days of Devotion, they are to be a part of the Chaplains Province.

That for all these ends the Colledge so order it, as that there may be some convenient & pleasant Houses thereabouts, kept by religious, discreet, and careful persons, for the lodging and boarding of young Scholars, that they have a constant eye over them to see that they be bred up there piously, cleanly, and plentifully, according to the proportion of their parents expences.

And that the Colledge, when it shall please God either by their own industry and success, or by the benevolence of Patrons, to enrich them so far, as that it may come to their turn and duty to be charitable to others, shall at their own charges erect and maintain some House or Houses for the Entertainment of such poor mens Sons whose good Natural Parts may promise either Use or Ornament to the Commonwealth, during the time of their abode at School, and shall take care that it shall be done with the same conveniences as are enjoyed even by rich mens Children (though they maintain the fewer for that cause) there being nothing of eminent and illustrious to be expected from a low, sordid, and Hospital-like Education.

ABRAHAM COWLEY

Conclusion.

IF I be not much abused by a natural fondness to my own Conceptions (that στοργή of the Greeks, which no other Language has a proper word for) there was never any Project thought upon, which deserves to meet with so few Adversaries as this; for who can without impudent folly oppose the establishment of twenty well selected persons in such a condition of Life, that their whole business and sole profession may be to study the improvement and advantage of all other Professions, from that of the highest General even to the lowest Artisan? Who shall be obliged to imploy their whole time, wit, learning, and industry, to these four, the most useful that can be imagined, and to no other Ends; first, to weigh, examine, and prove all things of Nature delivered to us by former ages, to detect, explode, and strike a censure through all false Monies with which the world has been paid and cheated so long, and (as I may say) to set the mark of the Colledge upon all true Coins that they may pass hereafter without any farther Tryal. Secondly, to recover the lost Inventions, and, as it were, Drown'd Lands of the Ancients. Thirdly, to improve all Arts which we now have; And lastly, to discover others which we yet have not. And who shall besides all this (as a Benefit by the by) give the best Education in the world (purely *gratis*) to as many mens Children as shall think fit to make use of the Obligation. Neither does it at all check or enterfere with any parties in State or Religion, but is indifferently to be embraced by all Differences in opinion, and can hardly be conceived capable (as many good Institutions have done) even of Degeneration into any thing harmful. So that, all things considered, I will suppose this Proposition shall encounter with no Enemies, the only Question is, whether it will find Friends enough to carry it on from Discourse and Design to Reality and Effect; the necessary Expences of the Beginning (for it will maintain it self well enough afterwards) being so great (though I have set them as low as is possible in order to so vast a work) that it may seem hopeless to raise such a sum out of those few dead Reliques of Humane Charity and Publick Generosity which are yet remaining in the World.

FINIS.

CUTTER

OF

COLEMAN-STREET.

A COMEDY.

The Scene *LONDON*,
in the year 1658.

Written by
ABRAHAM COWLEY.

LONDON,

Printed for *Henry Herringman* at the Sign of the
Anchor in the Lower walk in the New-Exchange.
Anno Dom. 1663.

PREFACE.

A *Comedy, called the* Guardian, *and made by me when I was very Young, was Acted formerly at* Camebridge, *and several times after privately during the troubles, as I am told, with good approbation, as it has been lately too at* Dublin. *There being many things in it which I disliked, and finding my self for some dayes idle, and alone in the Countrey, I fell upon the changing of it almost wholly, as now it is, and as it was play'd since at his Royal Highness's Theatre under this New name. It met at the first representation with no favourable reception, and I think there was something of* Faction *against it, by the early appearance of some men's disapprobation before they had seen enough of it to build their dislike upon their Judgment. Afterwards it got some ground, and found Friends as well as Adversarys. In which condition I should willingly let it dye, if the main imputations under which it suffered, had been shot only against my* Wit *or* Art *in these matters, and not directed against the tenderest parts of human reputation, good* Nature, *good* Manners, *and* Piety *it self. The first clamour which some malitious persons raised, and made a great noise with, was, That it was a piece intended for abuse and Satyre against the Kings party.* Good God! *Against the Kings party? After having served it twenty years during all the time of their misfortunes and afflictions, I must be a very rash and imprudent person if I chose out that of their Restitution to begin a Quarrel with them. I must be too much a* Madman *to be trusted with such an Edg'd Tool as Comedy. But first, why should either the whole party (as it was once distinguisht by that name, which I hope is abolisht now by Universal Loyalty) or any man of virtue or honour in it, believe themselves injured or at all concerned, by the representation of the faults and follies of a few who in the General division of the Nation had crowded in among them? In all mixt numbers (which is the case of Parties) nay, in the most entire and continued Bodies there are often some degenerate and corrupted parts, which may be cast away from that, and even cut off from this Unity, without any infection of scandal to the remaining Body. The Church of* Rome *with all her arrogance, and her wide pretences of certainty in all Truths, and exemption from all Errors, does not clap on this enchanted Armour of Infallibility upon all her particular Subjects, nor is offended at the reproof even of her greatest Doctors. We are not,*

261

ABRAHAM COWLEY

I hope, become such Puritans our selves as to assume the Name of the Congregation of the Spotless. It is hard for any Party to be so Ill as that no Good, Impossible to be so Good as that no Ill should be found among them. And it has been the perpetual privilege of Satyre and Comedy to pluck their vices and follies though not their Persons out of the Sanctuary of any Title. A Cowardly ranting Souldier, an Ignorant Charlatanical Doctor, a foolish Cheating Lawyer, a silly Pedantical Scholar, have alwayes been, and still are the Principal Subjects of all Comedy, without any scandal given to those Honourable Professions, or ever taken by their severest Professors; And, if any good Physician or Divine should be offended with me here for inveighing against a Quack, or for finding Deacon Soaker *too often in the Butteryes, my respect and reverence to their callings would make me troubled at their displeasure, but I could not abstain from taking them for very Cholerique and Quarrelsome persons. What does this therefore amount to, if it were true which is objected? But it is far from being so; for the representation of two Sharks about the Town (fellows merry and Ingenious enough, and therefore admitted into better companyes than they deserve, yet withall too very scoundrels, which is no unfrequent Character at* London) *the representation I say of these as Pretended Officers of the Royal Army, was made for no other purpose but to show the World, that the vices and extravagancies imputed vulgarly to the Cavaliers, were really committed by Aliens who only usurped that name, and endeavoured to cover the reproach of their Indigency or Infamy of their Actions with so honourable a Title. So that the business was not here to correct or cut off any natural branches, though never so corrupted or Luxuriant, but to separate and cast away that vermine which by sticking so close to them had done great and considerable prejudice both to the Beauty and Fertility of the Tree; And this is as plainly said, and as often inculcated as if one should write round about a Signe, This is a Dog, this is a Dog, out of over-much caution lest some might happen to mistake it for a Lyon, Therefore when this Calumny could not hold (for the case is cleer, and will take no colour) Some others sought out a subtiler hint to traduce me upon the same score, and were angry that the person whom I made a true Gentleman, and one both of considerable Quality and Sufferings in the Royal party, should not have a fair and noble Character throughout, but should submit in his great extremities to wrong his Niece for his own Relief. This is a refined*

PREFACE

exception, such as I little foresaw, nor should with the dulness of my usuul Charity, have found out against another man in twenty years. The truth is, I did not intend the Character of a Hero, one of exemplary virtue, and as Homer *often terms such men, Unblameable, but an ordinary jovial Gentleman, commonly called a Good Fellow, one not so conscientious as to sterve rather than do the least Injury, and yet endowed with so much sense of Honour as to refuse when that necessity was removed, the gain of five thousand pounds which he might have taken from his Niece by the rigour of a Forfeiture; And let the frankness of this latter generosity so expiate for the former frailty, as may make us not ashamed of his Company, for if his true Metal be but equal to his Allay, it will not indeed render him one of the Finest sorts of men, but it will make him Current, for ought I know, in any party that ever yet was in the World. If you be to choose parts for a Comedy out of any noble or elevated rank of persons, the most proper for that work are the worst of that kind. Comedy is humble of her Nature, and has alwayes been bred low, so that she knows not how to behave her self with the great or the accomplisht. She does not pretend to the brisk and bold Qualities of Wine, but to the Stomachal Acidity of Vinegar, and therefore is best placed among that sort of people which the* Romans *call The Lees of* Romulus. *If I had designed here the celebration of the Virtues of our Friends, I would have made the Scene nobler where I intended to erect their Statues. They should have stood in Odes, and Tragedies, and Epique Poems, (neither have I totally omitted those greater testimonies of my esteem of them)* Sed nunc non erat his Locus, &c. *And so much for this little spiny objection which a man cannot see without a Magnifying Glass. The next is enough to knock a man down, and accuses me of no less than Prophaness. Prophane, to deride the Hypocrisie of those men whose skuls are not yet bare upon the Gates since the publique and just punishment of it? But there is some imitation of Scripture Phrases; God forbid; There is no representation of the true face of Scripture, but only of that Vizard which these Hypocrites (that is, by interpretation Actors with a Vizard) draw upon it. Is it Prophane to speak of* Harrison's *return to Life again, when some of his friends really profest their belief of it, and he himself had been said to promise it? A man may be so imprudently scrupulous as to find prophaness in any thing either said or written by applying it under some similitude or other to some expressions in Scripture. This nicety is both vain and endless.*

263

ABRAHAM COWLEY

But I call God to witness, that rather than one tittle should remain among all my writings which according to my severest judgment should be found guilty of the crime objected, I would my self burn and extinguish them all together. Nothing is so detestably lewd and rechless as the derision of things sacred, and would be in me more unpardonable than any man else, who have endeavoured to root out the ordinary weeds of Poetry, and to plant it almost wholly with Divinity. I am so far from allowing any loose or irreverent expressions in matters of that Religion which I believe, that I am very tender in this point even for the grossest errors of Conscientious persons. They are the properest object (me thinks) both of our Pitty and Charity too; They are the innocent and white Sectaries, in comparison of another kind who engraft Pride upon Ignorance, Tyranny upon Liberty, and upon all their Heresies, Treason and Rebellion. These are Principles so destructive to the Peace and Society of Mankind that they deserve to be persued by our serious Hatred, and the putting a Mask of Sanctity upon such Devils is so Ridiculous, that it ought to be exposed to contempt and laughter. They are indeed Prophane, who counterfeit the softness of the voyce of Holiness to disguize the roughness of the hands of Impiety, and not they who with reverence to the thing which the others dissemble, deride nothing but their Dissimulation. If some piece of an admirable Artist should e ill Copyed even to ridiculousness by an ignorant hand, and another Painter should undertake to draw that Copy, and make it yet more ridiculous, to shew apparently the difference of the two works, and deformity of the latter, will not every man see plainly that the abuse is intended to the foolish Imitation, and not to the Excellent Original? I might say much more to confute and confound this very false and malitious accusation, but this is enough I hope to cleer the matter, and is I am afraid too much for a Preface to a work of so little consideration. As for all other objections which have been or may be made against the Invention or Elocution, or any thing else which comes under the Critical Jurisdiction, let it stand or fall as it can answer for it self, for I do not lay the great stress of my Reputation upon a Structure of this Nature, much less upon the slight Reparations only of an Old and unfashionable Building. There is no Writer but may fail sometimes in point of Wit, and it is no less frequent for the Auditors to fail in point of Judgment. I perceive plainly by dayly experience that Fortune is Mistris of the Theatre, as Tully sayes it is of all popular Assemblies. No man

PREFACE

can tell sometimes from whence the Invisible winds arise that move them. There are a multitude of people who are truly and onely Spectators at a play, without any use of their Understanding, and these carry it sometimes by the strength of their Number. There are others who use their Understanding too much, who think it a sign of weakness or stupidity to let anything pass by them unattaqued, and that the Honour of their Judgment (as some Brutals imagine of their Courage) consists in Quarrelling with every thing. We are therefore wonderfull wise men, and have a fine business of it, we who spend our time in Poetry, I do sometimes laugh, and am often angry with my self when I think on it, and if I had a Son inclined by Nature to the same folly, I believe I should bind him from it, by the strictest conjurations of a paternal Blessing. For what can be more ridiculous than to labour to give men delight, whilst they labour on their part more earnestly to take offence? to expose one's self voluntarily and frankly to all the dangers of that narrow passage to unprofitable Fame, which is defended by rude multitudes of the Ignorant, and by armed Troops of the Malitious? If we do ill many discover it and all despise us, if we do well but few men find it out, and fewer entertain it kindly. If we commit errors there is no pardon, if we could do wonders there would be but little thanks, and that too extorted from unwilling Givers. But some perhaps may say, Was it not always thus? Do you expect a particular privilege that was never yet enjoyed by any Poet? were the ancient Græcian, *or noble* Roman *Authors, was* Virgil *himself exempt from this Passibility,* Qui melior multis quam tu fuit, Improbe, rebus, *Who was in many things thy better far, Thou impudent Pretender? As was said by* Lucretius *to a person who took it ill that he was to Dye, though he had seen so many do it before him who better deserved Immortality; and this is to repine at the natural condition of a Living Poet, as he did at that of a Living Mortal. I do not only acknowledge the Præ-eminence of* Virgil *(whose Footsteps I adore) but submit to many of his* Roman Brethren, *and I confess that even they in their own times were not secure from the assaults of Detraction (though* Horace *brags at last,* Jam dente minus mordeor invido) *but then the Barkings of a few were drown'd in the Applause of all the rest of the* World, *and the Poison of their Bitings extinguisht by the Antidote of great rewards, and great encouragements, which is a way of curing now out of use, and I really profess that I neither expect, nor think I deserve it.*

Indolency would serve my turn instead of Pleasure; for though I comfort my self with some assurance of the favour and affection of very many candid and good natured (and yet too judicious and even Critical) persons, yet this I do affirm, that from all which I have written I never received the least benefit, or the least advantage, but on the contrary have felt sometimes the effects of Malice and Misfortune.

The Prologue.

AS when the Midland Sea is no where clear
   From dreadfull Fleets of *Tunis* and *Argier*,
Which coast about, to all they meet with Foes,
And upon which nought can be got but Blowes,
The Merchand Ships so much their passage doubt,
That, though full-freighted, none dares venture out,
And Trade decayes, and Scarcity ensues;
Just so the timerous Wits of late refuse,
Though laded, to put forth upon the Stage,
Affrighted by the Critiques of this age.
It is a Party numerous, watchfull, bold;
They can from nought, which sailes in sight, with-hold.
Nor doe their cheap, though mortal, Thunder spare;
They shoot, alas, with Wind-gunns, charg'd with Air.
But yet, Gentlemen Critiques of *Argier*,
For your own int'rest I'de advise ye here
To let this little Forlorn Hope goe by
Safe and untoucht; That must not be (you'l cry)
If ye be wise, it must; Ile tell yee why.
There are Seven, Eight, Nine, . . . stay . . . there are behind
Ten Playes at least, which wait but for a Wind,
And the glad News that we the Enemy miss;
And those are all your own, if you spare This.
Some are but new trim'd up, others quite New,
Some by known Shipwrights built, and others too
By that great Author made, whoere he be,
That stiles himself Person of Qualitie.

THE PROLOGUE

All these, if we miscarry here to-day,
Will rather till they Rot in th' Harbour stay,
Nay they will back again, though they were come,
Ev'n to their last safe Rode, the Tyring room.
Therefore again I say, if you be wise,
Let this for once pass free; let it suffise
That we your Soverai[gn] power here to avow,
Thus humbly ere we pass, strike sail to You.

Added at Court.

STay Gentlemen; what I have said, was all
 But forc'd submission, which I now recall.
Ye're all but Pirats now again; for here
Does the true Soveraign of the Seas appear.
The Soveraign of these Narrow Seas of wit;
'Tis his own *Thames*; He knows and Governs it.
'Tis his Dominion, and Domain; as Hee
Pleases, 'tis either Shut to us or Free.
Not onely, if his Pasport we obtain,
We fear no little Rovers of the Main,
But if our *Neptune* his calm visage show,
No Wave shall dare to Rise or Wind to Blow.

The Persons.

Colonel Jolly — { *A Gentleman whose Estate was confiscated in the late troubles.*

Mistris Aurelia — *His Daughter.*

Mistris Lucia — *His Niece, left to his Tuition.*

Cutter — { *A merry sharking fellow about the Town, pretending to have been a Colonel in the Kings Army.*

Worm — { *His Companion, and such another fellow, pretending to have been a Captain.*

Mr. Puny — { *A young, rich, brisk Fop, pretending to extraordinary wit, Suter to Mistris Lucia.*

Mr. Truman Senior — *An old, testy, Covetous Gentleman.*

Mr. Truman Junior — *His Son, in love with Mistris Lucia.*

Mistris Barebottle — { *A Sopeboyler's widdow, who had bought Jolly's Estate, A pretended Saint.*

Mistris Tabitha — *Her Daughter.*

Mistris Jane — { *Mistris Lucias Maid, a little laughing Fop.*

Mr. Soaker — *A little Fudling Deacon.*

Several Servants.

CUTTER

OF

COLEMAN-STREET.

Act 1.   Scene 1.

Truman Junior.

HOW hard, alas, is that young Lover's fate,
    Who has a father Covetous and Cholerique!
What has he made me swear?—
I dare not think upon the Oath, lest I should keep it—
Never to see my Mistris more, or hear her speak
Without his leave; And farewel then the use
Of Eyes and Ears;—
And all this Wickedness I submitted to,
For fear of being Disinherited;
For fear of losing Durt and Dross, I lose
My Mistris—There's a Lover! Fitter much
For Hell than thousand perjuries could make him;
Fit to be made th' Example which all Women
Should reproach Men with, when themselves grow false;
Yet she, the good and charitable *Lucia*,
With such a bounty as has onely been
Practis'd by Heaven, and Kings inspir'd from thence,
Forgives still, and still loves her perjur'd Rebel.
I 'le to my father strait, and swear to him
Ten thousand Oathes ne'r to observe that wicked one
Which he' has extorted from me—Here he comes;
And my weak heart, already us'd to falshood,
Begins to waver.

ABRAHAM COWLEY

Scene 2.

Truman Senior, Truman Junior.

Trum. Sen. Well, *Dick*, you know what you swore to me
yesterday, And solemnly.
I ha' been considering, and considering all Night, *Dick*, for
your good, and me-thinks, supposing I were a young man again,
and the case my own (for I love to be just in all things) me-
thinks 'tis hard for a young man, I say, who has been a Lover
so long as you ha' been, to break off on a suddain. Am I in
the right or no, *Dick?* Do you mark me?

Trum. Jun. Hard, Sir, 'tis harder much than any death
Prolong'd by Tortures.

Trum. Sen. Why so I thought; and therefore out o' my
care for your ease, I have hit upon an Expedient that I think
will salve the matter!

Trum. jun. And I will thank you for it more, Sir,
Than for the life you gave me.

Trum. sen. Why! well said, *Dick*, and I 'me glad with
all my
Heart, I thought upon 't; in brief, 'tis this, *Dick*;
I ha' found out another Mistris for you.

Trum. jun. Another? Heaven forbid, Sir!

Trum. sen. I; Another, Good-man Jack Sawce; marry
come up;
Won't one o' my choosing serve your turn, as well
As one o' your own; sure I 'me the older man,
Jack Sawce, and should be the Wiser!

Trum. jun. But Nature, Sir, that's wiser than all Mankind,
Is Mistris in the choice of our affections;
Affections are not rais'd from outward Reasons,
But inward Sympathies.

Trum. sen. Very well, Dick, if you be a dutiful son to me,
you shall have a good Estate, and so has she;
There's Sympathy for you now; but I perceive
You 'r hankring still after Mrs. *Lucy*,
Do, do! forswear your self; do, damn your self, and be a
beggar too; sure I would never undo my self, by perjury; if I

270

had a mind to go to hell, *Cromwel* should make me a Lord for 't ! I, and one of his Councel too, I 'de never be damn'd for nothing, for a Whim-wham in a Coif. But to be short, The person I design for you is Mrs. *Tabith[a Ba]rebottle,* our neighbour the Widow's daughter. What do you start at, Sirra ? I, Sirra, Jack-an-apes, if you start when your father speaks to you.

Trum. jun. You did not think her father once I 'me sure A person fit for your Alliance, when he plundred your House in *Hartfordshire,* and took away the very Hop-poles, pretending they were Arms too.

Trum. sen. He was a very Rogue, that 's the Truth on 't, as to the business between man and man, but as to God-ward he was always counted an Upright man, and very devout. But that 's all one, I 'me sure h 'as rais'd a fine Estate out o' nothing by his Industry in these Times : An' I had not been a Beast too—but Heaven's will be done, I could not ha' don 't with a good conscience. Well, *Dick,* I 'le go talk with her mother about this matter, and examine fully what her Estate is, for unless it prove a good one, I tell you true, *Dick,* I 'me o' your Opinion, not to marry such a Rogues daughter.

Trum. jun. I beseech you, Sir—   *Exit Trum. sen.*
It is in vain to speak to him—
Though I to save this Dung-hill an Estate
Have done a Crime like theirs,
Who have abjur'd their King for the same cause,
I will not yet, like them, persue the guilt,
And in thy place, *Lucia* my lawful Soverain,
Set up a low and scandalous Usurper !   *Enter Servant.*

Serv. 'Tis well the old man 's just gone. There 's a Gentlewoman without, Sir, desires to speak one word with you.

Trum. jun. With me ? who is 't ?

Serv. It should be Mrs. *Lucia* by her voice, Sir, but she 's veil'd all over. Will you please to see her, Sir ?

Trum. Will I see her, Blockhead ? yes ; go out and kneel to her
And pray her to come in.   *(Exit Serv.)*

ABRAHAM COWLEY

Scene 3.

Lucia (veil'd), Truman.

Trum. This is a favour, Madam!
That I as little hop'd, as I am able
To thank you for it—But why all this muffling?
Why a disguise, my Dearest, between us?
Unless to increase, my desire first, and then my joy to see thee
Thou cast this subtil night before thy beauty.
And now like one scorch'd with some raging Feaver,
Upon whose flames no dew of sleep has faln,
I do begin to quarrel with the Darkness,
And blame the sloathful rising of the Morn,
And with more joy shall welcome it, than they
Whose Icy dwellings the cold Bear o're-looks,
When after half the years Winter and Night,
Day and the Spring at once salutes their sight!
Thus it appears, thus like thy matchless beauty,
When this black Clowd is vanish'd.

> *[offers to pull off the Veil.*

Why d'e you shrink back, my Dearest?
I prethee let me look a little on thee:
'Tis all the pleasure Love has yet allow'd me,
And more than Nature does in all things else.
At least speak to me; well may I call it Night
When Silence too thus joyns it self with Darkness.
Ha! I had quite forgot the cursed Oath I made—
Pish! what's an Oath forc'd from a Lover's Tongue?
'Tis not recorded in Heaven's dreadful book,
But scatter'd loosely by the breath that made it:
Away with it; to make it was but a Rashness,
To keep it were a Sin—Dear Madam—

> *Offers agen, but she refuses, and gives him a Note.*

Ha! let's see this then first!

> *[He reads.*

You know I have forgiven your unkind Oath to your
Father, and shall never suffer you to be perjur'd.

272

I come onely to let you know, that the Physician and the
'Pothecary will do this morning what we propos'd; be ready
at hand, if there should be occasion for your presence; I dare
not stay one minute.   Farewel.
Now thousand Angels wait upon thee, *Lucia*,
And thousand Blessings upon all thou do'st.
Let me but kiss your hand, And I'le dismiss you.
Ah cruel father, when thou mad'st the Oath,
Thou little thought'st that thou had'st left
Such blessings for me out of it.   [*Exeunt*.

Scene 4.

Colonel Jolly, Will (his Man.)

Joll.   Give me the Pills; what said the Doctor, *Will?*
                    [*Col. Jolly in an Indian Gown and Night-cap.*
Will.   He said a great deal, Sir, but I was not Doctor
enough to understand half of it.
Joll.   A man may drink, he says, for all these Bawbles?
Will.   He's ill advised if he give your Worship drinking
Pills, for when you were drinking last together, a Fit took you
to beat the Doctor, which your Worship told him was a new
Disease.
Joll.   He was drunk then himself first, and spoke False
Latin, which becomes a Doctor worse than a beating.   But he
does not remember that, I hope, now?
Will.   I think he does, Sir, for he says the Pills
Are to purge Black Choler!
Joll.   I, Melancholy; I shall ha' need of them then, for my
old Purger of Melancholy, Canary, will grow too dear for me
shortly; my own Estate was sold for being with the King at
Oxford.   A Curse upon an old Dunce that needs must be
going to *Oxford* at my years!   My good Neighbor, I thank
him, Collonel *Fear-the-Lord-Barebottle*, a Saint and a Sope-
boyler, bought it; but he's dead, and boiling now himself,
that's the best of't; There's a Cavalier's comfort!   If his
damnable Wife now would marry me, it would return again, as

C. II.   S   273

I hope all things will at last; and even that too were as hard a Composition for ones own, as ever was made at *Habberdashers-Hall*; but hang her, she 'l ha' none o' me, unless I were True Rich and Counterfeit Godly; let her go to her husband; [*takes a Pill.*] (so much for that—It does not go down so glib as an Egg in Muskadine) Now when my Nieces Portion too goes out o' my hands, which I can keep but till a handsome Wench of eighteen pleases to marry (a pitiful slender Tenure that's the truth on 't) I ha' nothing to do but to live by Plots for the King, or at least to be hang'd by 'em. [*takes the two other Pills.*] (So, go thou too) well, something must be done, unless a man could get true Gems by drinking, or like a Mouse in a Cheese, make himself a house by eating.

Will, did you send for Colonel *Cutter* and Captain *Worm*, to come and keep me company this morning that I take Physick? They'l be loth to come to day, there's so little hope o' drinking here.

Will. They said they would be here, Sir, before this time; Some Morning's draught, I believe, has intercepted 'em.

Joll. I could Repent now heartily, but that 'twould look as if I were compell'd to 't, and besides if it should draw me to Amendment, 'twould undo me now, till I ha' gotten something. 'Tis a hard case to wrong my pretty Niece; but unless I get this wicked Widow, I and my daughter must starve else; and that's harder yet; Necessity is, as I take it, Fatality, and that will excuse all things, O! Here they are!

Scene 5.

Colonel Jolly, Colonel Cutter, Captain Worm.

Joll. Welcome! Men o' war, what news abroad in Town?

Cut. Brave news I faith! it arriv'd but yesterday by an Irish Priest, that came over in the habit of a Fish-wife; a cunning fellow, and a man o' business; he's to lie Leiger here for a whole Irish College beyond-Sea, and do all their Affairs of State. The Captain spoke with him last night at the Blew Anchor!

Joll. Well, and what is 't?

Worm. Why, Business is afloat again; the King has muster'd five and twenty thousand men in *Flanders*, as tall Fellows as any are in Christendom.

Joll. A pox upon you for a couple of gross Cheats! I wonder from what fools in what blind corners you get a dinner for this stuff.

Cut. Nay, there's another News that's stranger ye[t]; but for that let the Captain Answer.

Wor. I confess I should ha' thought it very ridiculous, but that I saw it from a good hand beyond Sea, under Black and White, and all in Cypher.

Joll. Oh it cann't miss then; what may it be, pray?

Wor. Why, that the Emperor of *Muscovy* has promis'd To land ten thousand Bears in *England* to Over-run the Country.

Joll. Oh! that's in revenge of the late barbarous Murder of their brethren here I warrant you!

Cut. Why, Colonel, things will come about again! We shall have another 'bout for 't!

Joll. Why all this to a friend that knows you? where were thy former Bouts, I prethee *Cutter?* where didst thou ever serve the King, or when?

Cut. Why every where; and the last time at *Worcester*. If I never serv'd him since, the faults not mine; an there had been any Action—

Joll. At *Worcester*, *Cutter?* prethee how got's thou thither?

Cut. Why as you and all other Gentlemen should ha' done; I carri'd him in a Troop of Reformado Officers; most of them had been under my command before!

Joll. I'le be sworn they were Reformado Tapsters then; but prethee how gots thou off?

Cut. Why as the King himself, and all the rest of the great ones; in a disguise, if you'l needs know't.

Wor. He's very cautious, Colonel, h'as kept it ever since.

Joll. That's too long 'ifaith, *Cutter*, prethee take one disguise now more at last, and put thy self into the habit of a Gentleman.

Cut. I'le answer no more Prethees; Is this the Mornings-draught you sent for me to?

Joll. No, I ha' better news for ye both, than ever ye had

from a good Irish hand; the truth is I have a Plot for yee, which if it take, ye Shall no more make monstrous Tales from *Bruges* to revive your sinking Credits in Loyal Ale-houses, nor inveigle into Taverns young Foremen of the Shop, or little beardless Blades of the Inns of Court, to drink to the Royal Family Parabolically, and with bouncing Oathes like Cannon at every Health; nor upon unlucky failing afternoons take melancholy turns in the Temple Walks, and when you meet acquaintance, cry, You wonder why your Lawyer stays so long with a pox to him.

Wor. This Physick has stirr'd ill humors in the Colonel, would they were once well purg'd, and we a Drinking again lovingly together as we were wont to do.

Joll. Nor make headless quarrels about the Reckoning time, and leave the house in confusion; nor when you go to bed produce ten several snuffs to make up one poor Pipe o' Tobacco!

Cut. Would I had one here now; I ha' n't had my morning Smoak yet, by this day!

Joll. Nor change your names and lodgings as often as a Whore: for as yet if ye liv'd like Tartars in a Cart (as I fear ye must die in one) your home could not be more uncertain. To day at *Wapping*, and to morrow you appear again upon *Mill-bank* (like a Duck that Dives at this end of the Pond, and rises unexpectedly at the other) I do not think *Pythagoras* his Soul e're chang'd so many dwellings as you ha' done within these two years.

Cut. Why, what then, Colonel? Soldiers must remove their Tents sometimes, *Alexander* the Great did it a thousand times.

Worm. Nine hundred, *Cutter*, you 'r but a Dunce in Story; But what's all this to th' matter, Noble Colonel?
You run a Wool-gathering like a zealous Teacher;
Where's the use of Consolation that you promis'd us?

Joll. Why thou shalt have it, little *Worm*, for these Damn'd Pills begin to make me horrible sick, and are not like to allow of long Digressions; Thus briefly then, as befits a man in my case!
When my brother the Merchant went into *Afrique*, to follow his great Trade there—

CUTTER OF COLEMAN-STREET

Wor. How o' Devil could he follow it? why he had quite lost his memory; I knew him when he was fain to carry his own Name in Writing about him for fear lest he should forget it.

Joll. Oh his man *John*, you know, did all, yet still he would go about with old *John*, and thought if he did Go, he did his business himself; well, when he went he left his Daughter with a Portion o' five thousand pounds to my Tuition, and if she married without my consent, she was to have but a thousand of it. When he was gon two years he dy'd—

Wor. He did a little forget himself me-thinks, when he left the Estate in your hands, Collonel.

Joll. Hold your tongue, Captain Coxcomb; now the case is this; ye shall give me a thousand pounds for my interest and favour in this business, settle the rest upon her, and her children, or me and mine, if she ha' none (d 'ee mark me? for I will not have one penny of the Principal pass through such glewy Fingers) upon these terms I 'le marry her to one of you; Always provided though, that he whom she shall choose (for she shall have as fair a choice as can be between two such fellows) shall give me good assurances of living afterwards like a Gentleman, as befits her husband, and cast off the t' others company!

Cut. The Conditions may be admitted of, though if I have her, she 'l ha' no ill bargain on 't when the King comes home; but how, Colonel, if she should prove a foolish fantastical Wench, and refuse to marry either of us?

Joll. Why! then she shall never ha' my consent to marry any body; and she 'l be hang'd, I think, first in the Friar's Rope, ere she turn Nun.

Wor. I 'l be a Carthusian an she do!

Joll. If 't were not for Chastity and Obedience thou mightest be so; their t' other Vow of never carrying any mony about them, thou hast kept from thy youth upwards.

Wor. I 'le have her; I 'me the better Scholar; and we 're both equal Soldiers, I' me sure.

Cut. Thou, Captain *Bobadil?* what with that Ember-week face o' thine? that Rasor o' thy Nose? thou look'st as if thou hadst never been fed since thou suck'st thy mother's milk.

277

ABRAHAM COWLEY

Thy cheeks begin to fall into thy mouth, that thou mightest eat them. Why thou very Lath, with a thing cut like a face at Top, and a slit at bottom. I am a man ha' serv'd my King and Country, a person of Honor, Dogbolt, and a Colonel.

Wor. Yes, as Priests are made now a daies, a Colonel made by thine own-self. I must confess thus much o' thy good parts, thou 'rt beholding to no body but thy self for what thou art. Thou a Soldier? Did not I see thee once in a quarrel at Nine-pins behind *Sodom*-lane disarm'd with one o' the pins? Alas, good *Cutter!* there 's difference, as I take it, betwixt the clattering o' Swords and Quart-pots, the effusion of Blood and Claret-wine—

Cut. (What a Barking little Curr 's this?)

Wor. The smoak o' Guns and Tobacco—nor can you, *Cutter*, fight the better, because you ha' beat an old Bawd or a Drawer; besides, what parts hast thou? Hast thou Scholarship enough to make a Brewers Clark? Canst thou read the Bible? I 'me sure thou hast not; canst thou write more than thine own name, and that in such vile Characters, that most men take 'em for Arabian Pot-hooks! Dost thou not live, *Cutter*, in the Chymærian darkness of Ignorance?

Joll. Cymmerian, Captain, prethee let it be Cymmerian!

Wor. I; I know some will have it so; but by this light I always call 't Chymærian!

Cut. O brave Scholar! has the Colonel caught you in false Latin, you dunce you? you 'd e'en as good stick to your Captainship; and that you may thank me for, you ingrateful Pimp you, was not I the first that ever call'd you so? and said you had serv'd stoutly in my Regiment at *Newberry?*

Joll. Thy Regiment?—well! leave your quarrelling, Baboons, and try your fortunes fairly; I begin to be very very sick; I 'le leave you, and send in my Niece to intertain you, upon my life, if you quarrel any more, As great Soldiers as you are, I 'le ha' you Cashier'd for ever out o' this Garrison o' mine, look to 't.   *Exit Col. Joll.*

Wor. Come *Cutter*, wee 'd e'en better play fair play with one another, than lose all to a third. Let 's draw Cuts who shall accost her first when she comes in, and the t' other void the room for a little while.

Cutt. Agreed! you may thank the Colonel for comming off

278

so easily; you know well enough I dare not offend him at such a time as this!

Wor. The longest first—   (*Draw Lots.*

Cut. Mine! Od 's my life! here she is already!

Scene 6.

Lucia, Cutter, Worm.

Luc. (*To her self at her Entrance.*)
Not choose amiss? indeed I must do, Uncle,
If I should choose again; especially,
If I should do 't out of your drinking Company;
Though I have seen these fellows here, I think
A hundred times, yet I so much despise 'em,
I never askt their names: But I must speak to 'em now.
My Uncle, Gentlemen, will wait upon you presently again, and sent me hither to desire your patience!

Cut. Patience, Madam, will be no virtue requisite for us, whilst you are pleas'd to stay here; Ha, ha! *Cutter!* that lit pretty pat 'ifaith for a beginning.   (*Worm goes out.*

Luc. Is your friend going, Sir?

Cut. Friend, Madam?—(I hope I shall be even with him presently) he 's a merry fellow that your Uncle and I divert our selves withall.

Luc. What is he? pray Sir.

Cut. That 's something difficult to tell you, Madam; But he has been all things. He was a Scholar once, and since a Merchant, but broke the first half year; after that he serv'd a Justice o' Peace, and from thence turn'd a kind o' Sollicitor at *Goldsmiths-hall*; h' as a pretty Smattering too in Poetry, and would ha' been my Lady Protectress's Poet; He writ once a Copy in praise of her Beauty, but her Highness gave him for it but an old Half-crown piece in Gold, which she had hoorded up before these troubles, and that discourag'd him from any further Applications to the Court. Since that, h 'as been a little Agitator for the Cavalier party, and drew in one of the 'Prentices that were hang'd lately; He 's a good ingenious fellow, that 's the truth on 't, and a pleasant Droll when h 'as got a cup o' Wine in his pate, which your Uncle and I supply him with; but for matters that concern the King neither of us trust him. Not that I can say h'as betraid any body, but he's so indigent a Varlet, that I'm afraid he would sell his Soul to *Oliver* for a Noble. But Madam, what a pox should we talk any more o' that Mole-catcher? (Now I'm out again—I am so us'd onely to ranting Whores, that an honest Gentlewoman puts me to a Non-plus!)

Luc. Why, my Uncle recommended him to me, Sir, as a Person of Quality, and of the same Condition with your self, onely that you had been a Collonel o' Foot, and he a Captain of Horse in his Majesty's Service.

Cut. You know your Uncle's Drolling humor, Madam; he thought there was no danger in the Raillerie, and that you'd quickly find out what he was; Here he comes again (*Enter Worm.*) I'le leave him with you, Madam, for a Minute, and wait upon you immediately, (I am at a loss, and must recover my self) Captain, I ha' dealt better by you than you deserv'd, and given you a high Character to her; see you do me right too, if there be occasion—I'l make bold though to hearken whether you do or no. (*Exit Cutter, and stands at the dore.*)

Wor. Madam, my Noble friend your Uncle has been pleas'd to honor me so far with his good Opinion, as to allow me the liberty to kiss your hands.

Luc. You'r welcome, Sir, but pray, Sir, give me leave
Before you enter into farther Complement
To ask one question of you.

Wor. I shall resolve you, Madam, with that truth
Which may, I hope, invite you to believe me
In what I'me to say afterwards.

Luc. 'Tis to tell me your friends Name, Sir, and his Quality, which, though I have seen him oft, I am yet ignorant of: I suppose him to be some honorable person, who has eminently serv'd the King in the late Wars.

Cut. (*at the door*) 'Tis a shrewd discerning Wench, she has hit me right already!

Wor. They call him Collonel *Cutter*, but to deal faithfully with you, Madam, he's no more a Colonel than you'r a Major General.

Cut. Ha! sure I mistake the Rogue!

Wor. He never serv'd his King, not he, no more than he

does his Maker; 'Tis true, h'as drunk his Health as often as any man, upon other men's charges, and he was for a little while, I think, a kind of Hector, 'till he was soundly beaten one day, and dragg'd about the room, like old *Hector* o' *Troy* about the Town.

Cut. What does this Dog mean, trow?

Wor. Once indeed he was very low for almost a twelve-month, and had neither mony enough to hire a Barber, nor buy Sizars, and then he wore a Beard (he said) for King *Charls*; he's now in pretty good cloathes, but would you saw the furniture of his Chamber! marry half a Chair, an Earthen Chamberpot without an Ear, and the bottom of an Ink-horn for a Candle-stick, the rest is broken foul Tobacco-pipes, and a dozen o' Gally-pots with Sawse in 'em.

Cut. Was there ever such a cursed Villain!

Wor. H'as been a known Cheat about the Town these twenty years.

Luc. What does my Uncle mean to keep him company, if he be such a one?

Wor. Why he's infatuated! I think, I ha' warn'd him on't a thousand times; he has some wit (to give the devil his due) and that 'tis makes us endure him, but however I'd advise your Uncle to be a little more cautious how he talks before him o' State matters, for he's shrewdly wrong'd if he be n't *Cromwel's* Agent for all the Taverns between *Kings-street* and the Devil at *Temple-bar*, indeed he's a kind o' Resident in 'em.

Cut. Flesh and blood can bear no longer—*Worm*, you'r a stinking, lying, perjur'd, damn'd Villain; and if I do not bring you, Madam, his Nose and both his Ears, and lay 'em at your feet here before night, may the Pillory and the Pox take mine; till then, suspend your judgment. *Exit Cutter.*

Luc. Nay, you'r both even; just such an excellent Character did he bestow on you; Why, thou vile Wretch, Go to the Stews, the Gaol, and there make love, Thou'lt find none there but such as will scorn thee!

Wor. Why here's brave work i'faith! I ha' carri'd it swimmingly, I'le e'en go steal away and drink a dozen before I venture to think one thought o' the business. *Exit.*

Luc. Go cursed race, which stick your loathsome crimes Upon the Honorable Cause and Party;

281

ABRAHAM COWLEY

And to the Noble Loyal Sufferers,
A worser suffering add of Hate and Infamy.
Go to the Robbers and the Parricides,
And fix your Spots upon their Painted Vizards,
Not on the native face of Innocence.
'Tis you retard that Industry by which
Our Country would recover from this sickness;
Which, whilst it fears th' eruption of such Ulcers,
Keeps a Disease tormenting it within,
But if kind Heav'n please to restore our Health,
When once the great Physician shall return,
He quickly will I hope restore our Beauty.

Act 2.   Scene 1.

Aurelia.

I See 'tis no small part of policy
    To keep some little Spies in an Enemies quarters :
The Parliament had reason—
I would not for five hundred pounds but ha' corrupted my
Cousin *Lucia's* Maid; and yet it costs me nothing but Sack-
possets, and Wine, and Sugar when her Mistris is a bed, and
tawd'ry Ribbonds, or fine Trimm'd Gloves sometimes, and
once I think a pair of Counterfeit Rubie Pendants
That cost me half a Crown. The poor Wench loves
Dy'd Glass like any Indian; for a Diamond Bob I'd have her
Ma[i]denhead if I were a Man and she a Maid. If her Mistris
did but talk in her sleep sometimes, o' my conscience she'd sit
up all night and watch her, onely to tell me in the morning
what she said; 'Tis the prettiest diligent Wretch in her
Calling, now she has undertaken't.
Her intelligence just now was very good, and
May be o' consequence; That young *Truman* is
Stoln up the back way into my Cousin's Chamber.
These are your grave Maids that study Romances, and will be
all *Mandanas* and *Cassandras*, and never spit but by the Rules
of Honor; Oh, here she comes, I hope, with fresh intelligence
from the Foe's Rendevouz.

Scene 2.

Aurelia, Jane.

Jane. Ha, ha, ha! for the love of goodness hold me, or I shall fall down with laughing, ha, ha, ha! 'Tis the best humor —no—I can't tell it you for laughing—ha, ha, ha! the prettiest sport, ha, ha, ha!

Aur. Why, thou hast not seen him lie with her, hast thou? The Wench is mad; prethee what is't?

Jane. Why (hee, hei, ha!) My Mistris sits by her Servant in a long Veil that covers her from Top to Toe, and says not one word to him, because of the Oath you know that the old man forc'd his son to take after your Father had forbid him the house, and he talks half an hour, like an Ass as he is, all alone, and looks upon her hand all the while, and kisses it. But that which makes me die with laughing at the conceit (ha, ha, ha!) is, that when he asks her anything, she goes to the Table, and writes her answer; you never saw such an innocent Puppet-play!

Aur. Dear *Jane* (kiss me, *Jane*,) how shall I do to see 'em?

Jan. Why, Madam, I'l go look the key of my Mistris Closet above, that looks into her Chamber, where you may see all, and not be seen.

Aur. Why that's as good as the trick o' the Veil; do, dear *Jane*, quickly, 'twill make us excellent sport at night, and we'l fuddle our Noses together, shall we, dear *Jane*?

Jane. I, dear Madam! I'l go seek out the key.

Exit Jane.

Aur. 'Tis strange, if this trick o' my Cousins should beget no trick o' mine, That would be pittiful dul doings.

Scene 3.

Aurelia, Mr. Puny.

Aur. Here comes another of her Servants; a young rich, fantastical Fop, that would be a Wit, and has got a new way of being so; he scorns to speak any thing that's common, and finds out some impertinent similitude for every thing. The Devil I think can't find out one for him. This Coxcomb has so little Brains too, as to make me the Confident of his Amours, I'le thank him for his Confidence ere I ha' done with him.

Pun. Whose here? O Madam! is your father out of his Metaphorical Grave yet? you understand my meaning, my dear Confident? you'r a Wit!

Aur. Like what, Mr. *Puny?*

Pun. Why—like—me!

Aur. That's right your way, Mr. *Puny*, its an odd similitude.

Pun. But where's your Father little Queen o' Diamonds? is he extant? I long like a Woman big with Twins to speak with him!

Aur. You can't now possibly: There was never any Creature so sick with a disease as he is with Physick, to day, the Doctor and the 'Pothecarie's with him, and will let no body come in. But, Mr. *Puny*, I have words o' comfort for you!

Pun. What, my dear Queen o' *Sheba!* and I have Ophir for thee if thou hast.

Aur. Why your Rival is forbid our house, and has sworn to his father never to see or hear your Mistris more.

Pun. I knew that yesterday as well as I knew my *Credo*, but I'm the very Jew of *Malta* if she did not use me since that, worse than I'de use a rotten Apple.

Aur. Why that can't be, Brother Wit, why that were uncivilly done of her!

Pun. O hang her, Queen of Fairies, (I'm all for Queens to day I think) she cares much for that; No, that Assyrian Crocodile *Truman* is still swimming in her præcordiums, but I'le so ferret him out; I'l beat him as a Bloomsbury Whore beats Hemp; I'l spoil his Grave Dominical Postures; I'l make him sneak, and look like a door off the hinges.

Aur. That's hard! but he deserves it truly, if he strive to Annihilate.

Pun. Why well said, Sister Wit, now thou speak'st oddly too!

Aur. Well, without wit or foolery, Mr. *Puny*, what will you give me, if this night, this very improbable night, I make you Marry my Cousin *Lucia?*

Pun. Thou talk'st like *Medusa's* head, thou astonishest me.

Aur. Well, in plain language as befits a Bargain; there's Pen and Inck in the next Chamber, give but a Bill under your hand to pay me five hundred pounds in Gold (upon forfeiture of a thousand if you fail) within an hour after the business is done, and I'l be bound Body for Body my Cousin *Lucia* shall be your Wife this night; if I deceive you, your Bond will do you no hurt, if, I do not, consider a little before-hand, whether the Work deserves the Reward, and do as you think fit.

Pun. There shall be no more considering than in a Hasty Pudding; I'l write it an' you will, in Short-hand, to dispatch immediately, and presently go put five hundred Mari-golds in a purse for you, Come away like an Arrow out of a Scythian Bow.

Aur. I'l do your business for you, I'l warrant you; *Allons Mon-Cher.*   *Exeunt.*

Scene 4.

Cutter, Worm.

Cut. Now I ha' thee at the place, where thou affronted'st me, here will I cut thy throat.

Wor. You'l be hang'd first.

Cut. No by this light.

Wor. You'l be hang'd after then.

Cut. Not so neither; for I'l hew thee into so many morsels, that the Crowner shall not be able to give his Verdict whether 'twas the Body of a Man or of a Beast, as thou art. Thou shalt be mince-meat, *Worm*, within this hour.

Wor. He was a Coward once, nor have I ever heard one syllable since of his Reformation, he shall not daunt me.

Cut. Come on; [*Draws.*] I'l send thee presently to *Erebus* without either Bail or Main-prize.

Wor. Have at you, *Cutter*, an' thou hadst as many lives as are in *Plutarch*, I'd make an end of 'em all.

Cut. Come on, Miscreant.

Wor. Do, do! strike an' thou dar'st.

Cut. Coward, I'l give thee the advantage of the first push, Coward.

Wor. I scorn to take anything o' thee, Jew.

Cut. If thou dar'st not strike first, thou submitt'st, and I give thee thy life.

Wor. Remember, *Cutter*, you were treacherous first to me, and therefore must begin. Come, pox upon 't, this quarrel will cost us quarts o' Wine a piece before the Treaty o' Peace be ended.

Cut. Here's company coming in; I'l hear o' no Treaties, *Worm*, we'l fight it out.

Scene 5.

Aurelia, Puny, Cutter, Worm.

Aur. [*Reading.*] Five hundred neat Gentlemen-like twenty-shilling pieces, though never wash'd nor barb'd—
A curse upon him, cann't he write a Bond without these sotteries?

Pun. Why how now Panims? fighting like two Sea-fish in the Map? Why how now my little Gallimaufry, my *Oleo-podrido* of Arts and Arms; Hold the feirce Gudgings!

Aur. 'Ods my life, *Puny*, let's go in again; that's the onely way to part 'em.

Pun. Do, do! kill one another and be hang'd like Ropes of Onyons.

Cut. At your command? no, *Puny*! I'le be forc'd by no

man; put up, *Worm*; we'l fight for no man's pleasure but our own.

Wor. Agreed! I won't make sport with murdering any man, an' he were a Turk.

Pun. Why now ye speak like the Pacifique Sea; we'l to the King's Poleanon, and drink all into *Pylades* again; we'l drink up a whole Vessel there to Redintegration, and that so big, that the Tun of *Heidelberg* shall seem but a Barel of Pickled Oisters to't; mean time, thou pretty little Smith o' my good fortune, beat hard upon the Anvil of your Plot, I'l go and provide the Spankers.   *Exit Puny.*

Cut. Your Cousin, Mrs. *Aurelia*, has abus'd us most irreverently.

Aur. Why what's the matter?

Cut. Your father recommended us two as Suters to her.

Aur. And she'd ha' none of you? What a foolish Girl 'tis, to stand in her own light so!

Wor. Nay, that's not all, but she us'd us worse than if we'd been the veriest Rogues upon the face of the whole Earth.

Aur. That's a little thought too much, but 'twas safer erring o' that hand.

Cut. I, we'r like to get much, I see, by complaining to you.

Enter Jane.

Jan. Ha, ha, ha! Here's the key o' the Closet, go up softly, Madam, ha, ha, ha! and make no noise, dear Madam, I must be gone.   *Exit.*

Aur. Why does this little Foppitee laugh always? 'tis such a Ninny that she betrays her Mistris, and thinks she does no hurt at all, no, not she; well, wretched Lovers, come along with me now, (but softly upon your lives, as you would steal to a Mistris through her Mothers Chamber) and I'l shew you this severe *Penelope*, lockt up alone in a Chamber with your Rival.

Cut. As softly as Snow falls.

Wor. Or Vapors rise.

Aur. What are you Punish too with your Similitudes? Mum—not a word—pull off your shoes at bottom of the stairs, and follow me.

Scene 6.

Enter Truman *junior.*

And presently Aurelia, Cutter, *and* Worm *appear at a little Window.*

Trum.   Why should her cruel Uncle seek t' oppose
A Love in all respects so good and equal?
He has some wicked end in 't, and deserves
To be deceiv'd!
    Cut.   Deceiv'd? pray mark that Madam.
    Trum.   She is gone in to see if things be ripe yet
To make our last attempt upon her Uncle;
If our Plot fail—
    Aur.   A Plot 'ifaith, and I shall Counter-plot ye.
    Trum.   In spight of our worst Enemies, our kindred,
And a rash Oath that's cancell'd in the making,
We will pursue our Loves to the last point,
And buy that Paradise though 't be with Martyrdom!

Scene 7.

Enter Lucia.

She goes to the Table and Writes whilst he Speaks, and gives him the Paper.

Trum.   She's come, me-thinks I see her through her Veil;
She's naked in my heart with all her Beauties.
    Wor.   Thou hast a Bawdy heart I'le warrant thee.
    Cut.   Hold your peace, Coxcomb.
    Trum.   That has, I think, taken an Oath
Quite contrary to mine, never to see
Any thing else!
He's extreme sick, and thinks he shall die, [*Reads a paper given him by* Lucia], the Doctor and 'Pothecary have acted very well;
I'le be with him presently, go into my little Oratory, and

pray for the success—[*A cry within, Mrs.* Aurelia.] I'l pray
with as much zeal as any sinner, converted just upon the point
of dea[t]h, prays his short time out.

[Exeunt Truman & Lucia.

Aur. What can this mean? [*They cry within.*] and the cry
within there? pray let's go down and see what's the matter.

Enter Will and Ralph crying.

Will. Ah, Lord! my poor Master! Mrs. *Aurelia*, Mrs.
Aurelia.

Aur. Here, what's the business?

Ralph. Oh Lord! the saddest accident.

Aur. For the love of Heaven speak quickly.

Will. I cannot speak for weeping; my poor Master's
poison'd.

Aur. Poison'd? how prethee, and by whom?

Will. Why by the strangest Accident, Mistris.
The Doctor prescrib'd one what dee' call it with a hard name,
and that careless Rogue the 'Pothecaries man (mistaking one
Glass for another that stood by it) put in another what dee' call
it, that is a mortal poison.

Aur. Oh then 'tis plain, this was the Plot they talk'd of;
ye heard, Gentlemen, what they said; pray follow me and
bear witness. *Exit* Aurelia.

Cut. Undoubtedly they had a hand in't; we shall be
brought to swear against them, *Worm.*

Worm. I'l swear what I heard, and what I heard not but
I'l hang 'em. I see I shall be revenged o' that proud Tit; but
it grieves me for the Colonel.

Scene 8.

Colonel Jolly (brought in a Chair) Aurelia, Cutter, Worm,
Will, Ralph, other Servants.

Joll. Oh! I ha' vomited out all my guts, and all my
entrails—

Aur. Oh my dear Father!

Joll. I'm going, daughter—ha' ye sent the pocky Doctor
and the plaguy 'Pothecary to a Justice o' Peace to be examin'd?

ABRAHAM COWLEY

Will. Yes, Sir, your Worship's Steward and the Constable are gone with 'em; does your Worship think they did it out o' malice, and not by a mistake? if I had thought they did, I'd a hang'd 'em presently, that you might ha' seen it done before you dy'd.

Joll. Huh, huh, huh! I think that Rogue the Doctor did it, because I beat him t' other day in our drinking! huh, huh, huh!

Aur. No, Sir, (O my dear father) no, Sir, you little think who were the Contrivers of your murder, e'en my Cousin *Luce* and her Gallant—Oh Lord—'tis discover'd by a miraculous providence—they'r both together in her Chamber now, and there we overheard 'em as it pleas'd—these two Gentlemen heard 'em as well as I—

Joll. Can they be such Monsters? Oh! I'm as hot as *Lucifer*—Oh—Oh—! what did you hear 'em say?—Oh my stomach!

Cut. Why that they had a Plot—

Aur. And that the Doctor and 'Pothecary had done it very well.

Wor. I and your Niece ask'd if he thought the Poison were strong enough.

Aur. There never was such an Impudence!

Will. How murder will out! I always thought, fellow *Ralph*, your Mistris *Lucia* was naught with that young smooth-fac'd Varlet; do you remember, *Ralph*, what I told you in the Butteries once?

Aur. Here she comes! O Impudence! [*Enter* Lucia.

Joll. Oh! Oh! Oh!—go all aside a little, and let me speak with her alone. Come hither, Niece—Oh! Oh—! you see by what accident 't has pleas'd—huh—huh—huh—to take away your loving Uncle, Niece! huh—

Luc. I see 't, Sir, with that grief which your misfortune and mine in the loss of you does require.

Cut. There's a Devil for you; but, Captain, (Joll. *and* Luc. *talk together.*) did you hear her speak o' poison, and whether it were strong enough?

Wor. No, but I love to strike home, when I do a business, I'm for through-stich; I'm through pac'd, what a pox should a man stand mincing?

Luc. I hope, Sir, and have faith, that you'l recover !
But, Sir, because the danger's too apparent,
And who (alas) knows how Heaven may dispose of you ? before
it grow too late (after your blessing) I humbly beg one Boon
upon my knees.

Joll. What is't (rise up Niece) Oh—I can deny you
nothing at this time sure !

Luc. It is (I wo' not rise, Sir, till you grant it)
That since the love 'twixt *Truman* and my self
Has been so fixt, and like our fortunes equal,
Ye would be pleas'd to sign before your death,
The confirmation of that Love, our Contract,
And when your Soul shall meet above, my fathers,
As soon as he has bid you welcome thither,
He'l thank you for this goodness to his daughter;
I do conjure you, Sir, by his memory !
By all your hopes of happiness hereafter !
In a better world ! and all your dearest wishes of happiness for
those whom ye love most, and leave behind you here !

Joll. You ha' deserv'd so well o' me Niece, that 'tis impos-
sible to deny you any thing; where's gentle Mr. *Truman?*

Luc. In the next room, Sir, waiting on your will
As on the Sentence of his life and death too.

Joll. Oh—I'm very sick—pray bring him in.

Luc. A thousand Angels guard your life, Sir !
Or if you die, carry you up to heaven.   [*Exit.*

Wor. Was there ever such a young dissembling Witch ?

Cut. Here's Woman in perfection !
The Devil's in their tails and in their tongues !
The[y're] possest both ways !

Joll. *Will, Ralph,* is *Jeremy* there too ? be ready when I
speak to you.

Enter Truman, Lucia, (*veil'd.*)

Trum. Our prayers are heard, 'tis as we wish'd, dear *Lucia,*
Oh this blest hour !

Joll. Take him and carry him up to the Green Chamber—
Oh my belly—lock him in sure there, till you see what becomes
of me; if I do die, he and his Mistris shall have but an ill

Match of it at *Tyburn*. Oh my Guts—lock up *Luce* too in her Chamber.

Trum. What do ye mean, Gentlemen? are ye mad?

Will. We mean to lock you up safe, Sir, for a great Jewel as you are!

Luc. Pray hear me all.

Joll. Away with 'em.

> *Exit all the Servants, with* Truman *and* Lucia
> *several ways.*

Aur. How do you, Sir? I hope you may o're-come it, your Nature's strong, Sir.

Joll. No, 'tis impossible; and yet I find a little ease, but 'tis but a flash—*Aurelia*—Oh there it wrings me again—fetch me the Cordial-glass in the Cabinet window, and the little Prayer-book; I would fain repent, but it comes so hardly—I am very unfit to die, if it would please Heaven—so, set down the Glass—there—give me—

Aur. The Prayer-book, Sir,'s all mouldy, I must wipe it first.

Joll. Lay it down too—so—it begins t' asswage a little—there lay down the Book; 'twill but trouble my Brains now I'm a dying.

Enter Will.

Will. Here's the Widow, Sir, without, and Mrs. *Tabitha* her daughter, they have heard o' your misfortune, and ha' brought Mr. *Knock-down* to comfort you.

Joll. How? everlasting *Knock-down!* will they trouble a Man thus when he's a dying? Sirrah! Blockhead! let in *Joseph Knock-down*, and I'l send thee to Heaven afore me; I have but an hour or two to live perhaps, and that's not enough for him I'm sure to preach in!

Will. Shall Mrs. *Barebottle* come in, Sir?

Joll. That's a She *Knock-down* too; well, let her come in —huh! huh! huh! I must bear all things patiently now; but Sirrah, Rogue! take heed o' *Joseph Knock-down*, thou shalt not live with ears if *Joseph Knock-down* enter.

Enter Widow, Tabitha.

Wid. How de' you Neighbour Colonel? how is't? take comfort.

CUTTER OF COLEMAN-STREET

Joll. Cut off in the flower o' my age Widow.

Wid. Why, Man's life is but a Flower, Mr. *Jolly*, and the Flower withers, and Man withers, as Mr. *Knock-down* observ'd last Sabbath-day at Evening Exercise; But, Neighbour, you'r past the Flower, you'r grown old as well as I—

Joll. I' the very flower; that damn'd Quack-salver—

Tabith. Me-thoughts he was the ugliest fellow, Mother, And they say he's a Papish too, forsooth.

Wid. I never liked a Doctor with a Red Nose; my Husband was wont to say—how do you, Mrs. *Aurelia?* comfort your self, we must all die sooner or later; to day here, to morrow gone.

Joll. Oh the torture of such a tongue! would I were dead already, and this my Funeral Sermon.

Wid. Alas poor man! his tongue I warrant yee is hot as passes; you have a better memory than I, *Tabitha*, tell him what Mr. *Knock-down* said was a Saints duty in tormenting sicknesses, now Poison's a great tormentor.

Joll. Oh! Oh!—this additional Poison will certainly make an end of me!

Wid. Why seek for spiritual Incomes, Mr. Colonel; I'l tell you what my Husband *Barebottle* was wont to observe (and he was a Colonel too) he never sought for Incomes but he had some Blessing followed immediately; once he sought for 'em in *Hartfordshire*, and the next day he took as many Horses and Arms in the Country as serv'd to raise three Troops; another time he sought for 'em in *Bucklersbury*, and three days after a friend of his, that he owed five hundred pounds too, was hang'd for a Malignant, and the Debt forgiven him by the Parliament; a third time he sought for 'em in *Hartford-shire*—

Tabith. No, Mother, 'twas in *Worcester-shire*, forsooth.

Wid. I, Child, it was indeed in *Worcester-shire;* and within two months after the Dean of *Worcester's* Estate fell to him.

Joll. He sought for 'em once out o' my Estate too, I thank him; Oh my head!

Wid. Why truly, Neighbour Colonel, he had that but for his Penny, and would have had but a hard Bargain of it, if he had not by a friend's means of the Councel hook'd in two thousand pounds of his Arrears.

Cut. For shame let's relieve him; Colonel, you said you had a mind to settle some affairs of your Estate with me, and Captain *Worm* here.

Wid. I'l leave you then for a while, pray send for me, Neighbor, when you have a mind to't Heaven strengthen you; come, *Tabitha.*

Joll. Aurelia, go out with them, and leave us three together for half an hour.   [*Exit* Wid. Tab. Aur.
Stay you, *Will*, and reach me the Cordial; I begin to hope that my extreme violent fit of Vomiting and Purging has wrought out all the Poison, and sav'd my life—my Pain's almost quite gone, but I'm so sore and faint—give me the Glass.

Wor. What d' you mean, Colonel? you will not doat, I hope, now you'r dying? drink I know not what there, made by a Doctor and a 'Pothecary? Drink a cup o' Sack, Man; healing Sack; you'l find your old Antidote best.

Cut. H'as reason, Colonel, it agrees best with your nature; 'tis good to recover your strength—as for the danger, that's past, I'm confident, already.

Jol. Dost thou think so, honest *Cutter?* fetch him a Bottle o' Sack, *Will*, for that news; I'le drink a little my self, one little Beer-glass.

Cut. Poor creature! he would try all ways to live!

Joll. Why if I do die, *Cutter*, a Glass o' Sack will do me no hurt I hope; I do not intend to die the Whining way, like a Girl that's afraid to lead Apes in Hell—[*Enter* Will, *with a Bottle and great Glass.*] So, give it me; a little fuller,—yet —it warms exceedingly—and is very Cordial.—So,—fill to the Gentlemen.

Wor. [*Sings.*] Let's drink, let's drink, whilst breath we
                 have;
You'l find but cold, but cold drinking in the Grave.

Cut. A Catch i' faith! Boy, go down, Boy, go down,
And fill us t'other quart,
That we may drink the Colonel's health.

Wor. That we may drink the Colonel's health.

Both. Before that we do part.

Wor. Why dost thou frown, thou arrant Clown?
Hey boyes—Tope—

Joll. Why this is very cheerly! pray let's ha' the Catch that we made t' other night against the Doctor.

Wor. Away with 't, *Cutter*; hum—
Come fill us the Glass o' Sack.

Cut. What Health do we lack?

Wor. Confusion to the Quack.

Both. Confound him, Confound him,
Diseases all around him.

Cut. And fill again the Sack,

Wor. That no man may Lack,

Cut. Confusion to the Quack,

Both. Confusion to the Quack,
Confound him, Confound him,
Diseases all around him.

Wor. He's a kind of Grave-maker,

Cut. A Urinal Shaker,

Wor. A wretched Groat-taker,

Cut. A stinking close-Stool raker,

Wor. He's a Quack that's worse than a Quaker.

Both. He's a Quack, etc.

Wor. Hey, Boys—*Gingo*—

Joll. Give me the Glass, *Will*. I 'le venture once more what e're come on 't, here's a Health to the Royal Travailer, and so *Finis Coronat.*

Wor. Come on Boys, *Vivat*; have at you agen then. Now a Pox on the Poll, of old Politique *Noll.*

Both. Wee'l drink till we bring,
In Triumph back the King.

[*Cut.*] May he Live till he see,
Old *Noll* upon a Tree.

Wor. And many such as he.

Both. May he Live till, etc.

Joll. I'me very Sick again; *Will*, help me into my Bed; rest you merry, Gentlemen.

Cut. Nay, we'l go in with him, Captain, he shall not die this bout.

Wor. It's pity but he should, he dos't so bravely; come along then, kiss me, *Cutter*; is not this better than quarrelling?

Both. May he live till he see, etc.
Hey for Fidlers now! [*Exeunt.*

Act 3. Scene 1.

Jolly, Aurelia.

Joll. 'Tis true, *Aurelia*, the Story they all agree in; 'twas nothing but a simple Plot o' the two Lovers to put me in fear o' death, in hope to work then upon my good Nature, or my Conscience, and Quack conspired with them out o' revenge; 'Twas a cursed Rogue though to give me such an unmerciful Dose of Scammony! It might ha' prov'd but an ill jest; but however, I will not be a loser by the business, ere I ha' done with 't.

Aur. Me-thinks there might be something extracted out of it.

Joll. Why so there shall; I 'le pretend, *Aurelia*, to be still desperately sick, and that I was really poison'd, no man will blame me after that, for whatsoever I do with my Niece. But that 's not all, I will be mightily troubled in Conscience, send for the Widow, and be converted by her: that will win her heart, joyn'd with the hopes of my swallowing *Lucia's* portion.

Aur. For that point I 'l assist you, Sir, Assure her that my Cousin *Lucia* is married privately this after-noon to Mr. *Puny*.

Joll. I would she were, Wench, (for thine and my sake) her Portion would be forfeited then indeed, and she would ha' no great need of 't, for that Fop's very rich.

Aur. Well, Sir, I 'l bring sufficient proofs of that, to satisfie the Widow, and that 's all you require; be pleas'd to let the secret of the business rest with me yet a while, to morrow you shall know 't. But for my own part, Sir, if I were in your place, I 'd rather patiently lose my Estate for ever, than take 't again with her.

Joll. Oh! hold your self contented, good frank-hearted *Aurelia;* would I were to marry such a one every week these two years: see how we differ now?

Aur. Bless us! what humming and hawing will be i' this house! what preaching, and houling, and fasting, and eating among the Saints! Their first pious work will be to banish *Fletcher* and *Ben Johnson* out 'o the Parlour, and bring in their rooms *Martin Mar-Prelate*, and Posies of Holy Hony-suckles,

and a Sawf-box for a Wounded Conscience, and a Bundle of
Grapes from *Canaan*. I cann't abide 'em; but I'l break my
sister *Tabitha's* heart within a month one way or other. But,
Sir, suppose the King should come in again, (as I hope he will
for all these Villains) and you have your own again o' course,
you'd be very proud of a Soap-boyler's Widow then in *Hide-
park*, Sir.

Joll. Oh! then the Bishops will come in too, and she'l
away to *New-England*; well, this does not do my business; I'l
about it, and send for her.   [*Exit.*

Enter Ralph.

Aur. And I'l about mine; *Ralph*, did you speak to Mr.
Puny to meet me an hour hence at the back-dore in the
Garden? he must not know the estate the house is in yet.

Ralph. Yes, forsooth, he bad me tell you, he'd no more
fail you than the Sun fails *Barnaby-day*, I know not what he
means by 't, but he charg'd me to tell you so, and he would
bring (forsooth) his Regiment of five hundred. He's a mad-
man, I think.

Aurel. Well, did you speak to Mr. *Soaker* to stay within
too, the little Deacon that uses to drink with *Will* and you?

Ral. Yes, forsooth, he's in the Buttery.

Aur. Pray Heaven he don't forget my Instructions there!
But first I have a little trick for my Lovers to begin withall,
they shall ha' twenty more before I ha' done with 'em.

[*Exit.*

Scene 2.

Enter Truman *junior*.

Trum. The Veil of this mistake will soon be cast away,
I would I could remove *Lucia's* as easily, and see her face again,
as fair, as shortly our Innocence will appear.

But if my angry father come to know our late Intelligence
in this unlucky business, though we ha' fulfill'd the Letter of
his Will, that which can satisfie a Lover's Conscience, will
hardly do so to an old man's Passion; Ye Heavenly Powers, or

take away my life, or give me quickly that for which I onely
am content to keep it.

Scene 3.

Enter Aurelia, (*veil'd.*)

Ha! I did but speak just now of Heavenly powers,
And my blest Angel enters, sure they have
Heard me, and promise what I prayed for.
My dear *Lucia*, I thought you'd been a kind of prisoner too.
      She gives him a Paper and embraces him.
She's kinder too than she was wont to be;
My prayers are heard and granted, I'm confirm'd in't.

              [*Reads.*

 By my Maid's means I have gotten Keys both of my own
Chamber and yours; we may escape if you please; but that I
fear would ruine you; We lie both now in the same house, a
good fortune that is not like to continue; since I have the
engagement of your faith, I account my self your Wife already,
and shall put my honor into your hands; about Midnight I
shall steal to you; If I were to speak this I should blush, but I
know whom I trust.

            Yours, *Lucia*.

 Trum. Thou dost not know me, *Lucia*,   [*aside.*
And hast forgot thy self: I am amaz'd.
Stay, here's a Postscript.
(Burn this Paper as soon as you have read it.)
Burn it? yes, would I had don't before,

        [*Burns it at the Candle.*

May all remembrance of thee perish with thee,
Unhappy paper!
Thy very ashes sure will not be innocent,
But flie about and hurt some chast man's eyes,
As they do mine.   [*weeps.*
Oh, *Lucia*, this I thought of all misfortunes
Would never have befaln me, to see thee
Forget the ways of Virtue and of Honor.
I little thought to see upon our love,

298

That flourish'd with so sweet and fresh a Beauty,
The slimy traces of that Serpent, Lust.
What Devil has poison'd her? I know not what to say to her.
Go, *Lucia*, retire, prethee, to thy Chamber,
And call thy wandring Virtue home again;
It is not yet far gone, but call it quickly,
'Tis in a dangerous way; I will forget thy error,
And spend this night in prayers that Heav'n may do so.

                                        Exit Aur.

Would she have had me been mine own Adulterer?
Before my Marriage?—Oh lust—Oh frailty—
Where in all human nature shall we miss
The ulcerous fermentations of thy heat,
When thus (alas) we find thee breaking out
Upon the comli'st Visage of perfection?   [*Exit.*

Scene 4.

Aurelia.

Aur. Pray Heaven, I ha'nt made my foolish Wit stay for me; if he talk with others of the house before me, I'm undone. Stay, have I my Paper ready? [*Pulls out a Paper.*] Oh! that's well! my Hand I'm sure's as like hers as the Left is to the Right; we were taught by the same Master, pure Italian, there's her *A*'s and her *G*'s I'l swear—Oh! are you come? that's well.

Scene . 5.

Enter Puny.

'Tis almost four o'clock and that's the precious hour.
Pun. My little *Heliogabalus*, here I am, *Præsto!*
Aur. You'r always calling me names, Mr. *Puny*, that's unkindly done to one that's labouring for you, as I am.
Pun. I ha' made more haste hither than a Parson does to a Living o' three hundred and fifty pounds a year.

Aur. *Puny*, you'r not a man o' business I see, that's not the style o' business; Well, I ha' done, I think, the work for you, 'tis as odd a Plot as ever you heard.

Pun. I like it better, I love odd things.

Aur. Why thus then, you know Mr. *Truman* took an Oath to his father never to see my Cousin more without his leave.

Pun. Pish, do I know that a Lawyer loves to take mony in *Michaelmas* Term?

Aur. A pies upon you: well, my father has made *Lucy* swear too, never to see *Truman* without his consent.

Pun. Good, there will be a good Bo-peep love.

Aur. For all this, they'r resolv'd to marry this afternoon, (nay don't interrupt me with your Fopperies, or I'l be gon) and to save their Oathes (like cunning Casuists, as all Lovers are) they'l be married in a dark room (do you mark me?), the Minister, Mr. *Soaker*, is to marry them without Book; and because thei'r bound not to speak to one another (for that I forgat to tell you) they'r to signifie their consent, when he asks 'em, Will you such a one— by reverences, and giving their hands; you never heard of such a humor, but the[y're] both mad—

Pun. Ha! ha! ha! Rare, as Fantastical as a Whirlgig— but how come you to know all this, my little pretty Witch of *Lancashire?*

Aur. Why that I'me coming to; her Maid you must know is my Pensioner, and betrays all Counsels; And to confirm all this to you, here's her last Letter to *Truman* about the business, which my Intelligencer ha's Deliver'd to me instead of him; you know her hand, Read it all over to your self.

Pun. Ile swear by her Foot, this is her Hand,—hum— [*Reads.*] my Uncle's sick, and no Body will be at this side o' the House,—the matted Chamber—hum—In at the Back door which shall be left only put to—(ha, ha, ha!) Mr. *Soaker* with you—just at four—you must not stay long with me—(ha, ha, ha!) when 'tis done and past recovery they'l release us of our Oaths—hum—I shall not fail—yours L. (ha, ha, ha.)

Aur. Now he knows nothing o' the time, for that he should ha' known by this Letter; and you conceive my design, I hope? you'r not a Wit for nothing.

Pun. My dear *Pythagorean*, that I should go in and Marry her instead of him?

Aur. Right! thou 'st a shrewd reach.

Pun. But where 's old *Soaker* all this while?

Aur. Why, I ha' told all this to him, only naming you in all things instead of *Truman*; and that 'twas my Contrivance all for my Cosens and your Sake; he 's within at a Call, Ile send for him; whose there? *Mary?* call hither Mr. *Soaker*; I ha' given him five Pounds, and for so much more he 'l Marry you to another to morrow, if you will.

Pun. I adore thee Queen *Solomon*; I had rather be Marri'd by such a Plot as this, than be Nephew to *Prester John*—Ile mak 't a thousand Spankers.

Enter Mr. *Soaker.*

Aur. Oh come 'tis time Mr. *Soaker*; as soon as you ha' done leave the Marri'd couple together; Ile lock this Door upon you, go out at the to'ther, where shee 'l come in to you.

Pun. 'Tis as dark as the Devil's conscience; but the best is, the Parson ha's a good *Fieri Facies*, like a Holiday, that will give some Light.

Aur. No! there's light enough to keep you from Stumbling within. Oh! I forgot to tell you, break a piece of Gold, and give her half, for a proof of the—do you understand me?

Pun. 'Tis well thought on; but *Domine Doctoribus*, can you say the Service without Book are you sure?

Soaker. I warrant you Sir; can you Lye with her without Book afterwards?

Pun. Hee's a Wit too by *Juno*; all are Wits that have a finger in this Venison pasty.

Aur. Shee 'l come immediately, go in; do not stay above half an hour; Mr. *Puny*, my Cozen will be mist else, and all spoil'd.

Pun. Ile warrant you, let 's in; dear Learning lead the way.
          [*They go in and* Aurelia *locks the Door o' the out-side.*

Aur. So, all 's sure this way; Ile be with you straight.
                              [*Exit.*

Scene 6.

Enter Jolly, Cutter.

Joll. So, now the Widdow's gone, I may breathe a little ; I believe really that true Devotion is a great Pleasure, but 'tis a damn'd constraint and drudgery methinks, this Dissimulation of it. I wonder how the new Saints can endure it, to be always at the work, Day and Night Acting ; But great Gain makes every thing seem easie ; And they have, I suppose, good Lusty Recreations in private. She's gone, the Little Holy thing, as proud as *Lucifer*, with the Imagination of having been the Chosen Instrument of my Conversion from *Popery*, *Prelacy*, and *Cavalerism;* she's gone to bragg of 't to *Joseph Knock-down*, and bring him to Confirm me. But *Cutter*, thine was the best Humor that ever was begot in a Rogue's Noddle, to be Converted in an instant, the Inspiration way, by my example ! It may hap to get thee *Tabitha*.

Cut. Nay, and I hit just pat upon her way, for though the Mother be a kind of *Brownist*, (I know not what the Devil she is indeed) yet *Tabitha* is o' the Fifth Monarchy Faith, and was wont to go every Sunday a-foot over the Bridge to hear Mr. *Feak*, when he was Prisoner in *Lambeth* house ; she has had a Vision too her self of Horns, and strange things.

Joll. Pish ! *Cutter*, for the way that's not material, so there be but enough of Nonsense and Hypocrisie ; But *Cutter*, you must reform your Habit too, a little ; Off with that Sword and Buff and greasie Plume o' Ribbons in your Hat. They'l be back here presently, do 't quickly.

Cut. Ile be chang'd in an instant, like a Scene, and then Ile fetch 'em to you.   (*Exit.*

Scene 7.

Enter Truman *Senior*.

Sen. Trum. I, there goes one of his Swaggerers ; I could ha' Swagger'd with him once—Oh ! Colonel, you'r finely Poison'd, are you not ? would I had the Poisoning o' you— where's my Son *Dick ?* what ha' you done with him ?

CUTTER OF COLEMAN-STREET

Joll. Mr. *Truman.*—

Trum. True me no more than I true you—come—Colonel you'r but a Swaggering—Ile ha' the Law to Swagger with you, that I will.

Joll. First leave your Raging ; though you should rage like *Tamerlain* at the Bull, 'twould do no good here.

Trum. Do you call me names too ? Ile have an Action o' *Scandalum.* Well Colonel, since you provoke me, the *Protector* shall know what you are, and what you would have had me done for the King in the time of the last rising.

Joll. Mr. *Truman*, I took you for a Person of Honour; and a Friend to his Majesty ; I little thought to hear you speak of betraying a Gentleman to the *Protector.*

Trum. s. Betraying ? no Sir, I scorn it as much as you, but Ile let him know what you are, and so forth, an' you keep my Son from me.

Joll. Mr. *Truman*, if you'l but hear me patiently, I shall propose a thing that will, I hope, be good and acceptable both to your Son and you.

Trum. Say you so Sir ? well ; but I won't be called *Tamerlain.*

Joll. My Niece, not only by her wicked design to Poison me, but by Marrying her self, without my consent this day to *Puny*, has (as you know very well, for you were a witness Sir to my Brother's will) lost all the right she had to a plentifull Portion. *Aurelia* shall have that and my Estate, (which now within few days I shall recover) after my Death ; she's not I think Unhandsome, and all that know her will confess she wants no Wit ; with these Qualities, and this Fortune, if your Son like her, (for though h'as injur'd me, Sir, I forget that, and attribute it only to the Enchantments of my Niece) I do so well approve both of his Birth and parts, and of that Fortune, which you I think will please to make him, that I should be extremely glad of the Alliance.

Trum. s. Good Colonel, you were always a kind Neighbour and loving Friend to our Family, and so were we to you, and had respects for you ; you know I would have had *Dick* marry your Niece, till you declar'd he should ha' no Portion with her.

Joll. For that I had a particular reason, Sir ; your Son's above in my House ; shall I call him, Sir, that we may know his mind ? I would not have him forc'd.

303

Trum. s. Pray send for him good Colonel; forc'd? no, Ile make him do't, Ile warrant you. Boys must not be their own choosers, Colonel, they must not 'ifaith, they have their Sympathies and Fiddle-come-faddles in their Brain, and know not what they would ha' themselves.

Scene 8.

Enter Lucia.

Joll. Why how now *Lucia*? how come you from your Chamber?

Luc. I hope you did not mean me a Prisoner, Sir, since now you'r satisfy'd sufficiently that you'r not Poison'd?

Joll. I am not Dead, that's true. But I may thank Heaven, and a strong Constitution for't; you did your weak endeavours; however, for the honour of our Family, and for your Father's sake, Ile speak no more o' that, but I could wish, for the security of my Life hereafter, that you would go home to your Husband, for they say you'r marri'd Niece this day without my knowledge—Nay,—I'm content,—go home to him when you please, you shall ha' your thousand Pounds.

Trum. s. Heark you, Colonel, she should not have a groat of 'em, not a groat; she can't recover't by Law; I know the Will.

Luc. I marry'd Sir? 'tis the first news I've heard of't.

Scene 9.

Enter Trum. Jun.

[Lucia *goes to put on her Veil.*

Joll. Nay, leave your pretty Jesuitical Love-tricks to salve an Oath; Mr. *Truman*, you may let your Son see her now.

Trum. s. I *Dick* you may see her as much as you please; she's marri'd.

Trum. j. Marri'd?

Trum. s. I marri'd, so I say, Marri'd this after-noon to Mr. *Puny.*

Luc. What do they mean ?

Trum. s. And *Dick* I ha' got a Wife too for you, you shall ha' pretty Mrs. *Aurelia.*

Trum. j. Lucia marri'd ?

Trum. s. Her Father and I are agreed of all things ; Heark you *Dick*, she has a brave Fortune now.

Trum. j. Marri'd to *Puny?*

Trum. s. You shall have her presently.

Trum. j. This after-noon ?

Trum. s. Come *Dick;* there's a Wife for you *Dick.*

Trum. j. I won't marry, Sir.

Trum. s. What do you say Sir ?

Trum. j. I wo' not marry Sir.

Trum. s. Get you out o' my sight you Rebel.

Joll. Nay, good Mr. *Truman.*

Trum. s. Ile ne're acknowledge him for my Son again ; I tell you Colonel, he's always thus with his wo' nots and his Cannots.

Scene 10.

Enter Puny.

Pun. We ha' made short work on 't ; t' was a brave quick Parsonides ; The little Skittish Philly got away from me I know not how, like an Eele out of a Basket.

Joll. Give him a little time Mr. *Truman,* he's troubl'd yet at my Niece's marriage, t' will over quickly.

Tru. s. Give my Son time, Mr. *Jolly?* marry come up—

Scene 11.

Enter Aurelia, (*after* Puny.)

Aur. What ha' you done already ? you 'r a sweet Husband indeed.

Pun. Oh ! my little Pimp of honour ! here, here's the five hundred Marigolds ; hold thy hand *Dido*—yonder's my Wife, by Satan ; how a Devil did that little *Mephistophilus* get hither before me ?

C. II.   U   305

Aur. To her *Puny;* never conceal the mystery any longer, 'tis too good a Jest to be kept close.

Trum. s. For your sake I will then, Colonel; Come prethee, *Dick*, be cheerfull.—

Trum. j. I beseech you,—Sir—

Trum. s. Look you there Colonel, now he should do what I would have him, now he's a beseeching—'tis the proudest stubborn'st Coxcomb—

Pun. And now my noble Uncle—[*to Jolly*], nay, never be angry at a Marriage i' the way of wit.—My fair Egyptian Queen, come to thine *Antony*.

Luc. What would this rude fellow have?

Trum. j. I am drown'd in wonder!

Pun. 'Twas I, my dear *Philoclea*, that marri'd thee e'en now in the dark room, like an amorous Cat; you may remember the Damask Bed by a better Token of Two than a bow'd *Philip* and *Mary*.

Luc. I call Heaven to witness,
Which will protect and justifie the Innocent;
I understand not the least word he utters,
But as I took him always for a Fool,
I now do for a Mad-man.

Aur. She's angry yet to have mistook her Man. [*to Jolly*.] 'Tis true, Sir, all that Mr. *Puny* says, I mean for the Marriage, for the rest, she's best able to answer for her self.

Luc. True, Cousin, then I see 'tis some conspiracy t' ensare my Honor and my Innocence.

Aur. The Parson, Mr. *Soaker*, that married 'em is still within.

Will. He's i' th' Buttery, shall I call him, Sir?

Joll. I, quickly.

Trum. j. 'Tis the sight of me, no doubt, confounds her with a shame to confess any thing; It seems that sudden fit of raging lust, that brought her to my Chamber, could not rest till it was satisfi'd, it seems I know not what.

Enter Mr. Soaker.

Joll. Mr. *Soaker*, did you marry my Niece this after-noon to Mr. *Puny* in the Matted Chamber?

Soak. Yes, Sir; I hope your Worship won't be angry, Marriage, your Worship knows, is honorable.

Luc. Hast thou no conscience neither?

Scene 12.

Enter Widow, Tabitha, Cutter *in a Puritanical habit.*

Joll. Niece, go in a little, I'l come t' you presently and examine this matter further; Mr. *Puny*, lead in your wife for shame.

Luc. Villain, come not near me,
I'l sooner touch a Scorpion or a Viper.   [*Exit.*

Pun. She's as humerous as a Bel-rope; she need not be so cholerique, I'm sure I behav'd my self like *Propria quæ maribus.*

Aur. Come in with me, Mr. *Puny*, I'l teach you how you shall handle her.   *Exeunt* Aur. Pun.

Joll. Mr. *Truman*, pray take your son home, and see how you can work upon him there; speak fairly to him.

Trum. s. Speak fairly to my son? I'l see him buried first.

Joll. I mean perswade him.—

Trum. s. Oh! that's another matter; I will perswade him, Colonel, but if ever I speak fair to him till he mends his manners—Come along with me, Jacksawce, come home.

                    Exeunt Trum. *sen.* Trum. *jun.*

Trum. j. I Sir, any whither.

Wid. What's the matter, brother Colonel, are there any broils here?

Joll. Why, Sister, my Niece has married without my consent, and so it pleases, it e'en pleases Heaven to bestow her Estate upon me.

Wid. Why, brother, there's a Blessing now already; If you had been a wicked Cavalier still she'd ha' done her duty, I warrant you, and defrauded you of the whole Estate; my brother *Cutter* here is grown the Heavenliest man o' the sudden, 'tis his work.

Cut. Sister *Barebottle*, I must not be called *Cutter* any more, that is a name of *Cavalero* darkness; the Devil was a

ABRAHAM COWLEY

Cutter from the beginning; my name is now *Abednego*, I had a Vision which whisper'd to me through a Key-hole, Go call thy self *Abednego*.

Tab. The wonderful Vocation of some Vessels!

Cut. It is a name that signifies Fiery Furnaces, and Tribulation, and Martyrdom, I know I am to suffer for the Truth.

Tab. Not as to death, Brother, if it be his will.

Cut. As to death, Sister, but I shall gloriously return.

Joll. What, Brother, after death? that were miraculous.

Cut. Why the wonder of it is, that it is to be miraculous.

Joll. But Miracles are ceas'd, Brother, in this wicked Age of Cavalerism.

Cut. They are not ceas'd, Brother, nor shall they cease till the Monarchy be establish'd.

I say again I am to return, and to return upon a Purple Dromadary, which signifies Magistracy, with an Ax in my hand that is called Reformation, and I am to strike with that Ax upon the Gate of *Westminster-hall*, and cry, down *Babylon*, and the Building called *Westminster-hall* is to run away and cast it self into the River, and then Major General *Harrison* is to come in Green sleeves from the North upon a Sky-colour'd Mule, which signifies heavenly Instruction.

Tab. Oh the Father! he's as full of Mysteries as an Egg is full of meat.

Cut. And he is to have a Trumpet in his mouth as big as a Steeple, and at the sounding of that Trumpet all the Churches in *London* are to fall down.

Wid. O strange, what times shall we see here in poor *England!*

Cut. And then *Venner* shall march up to us from the West in the figure of a Wave of the Sea, holding in his hand a Ship that shall be call'd the Ark of the Reform'd.

Joll. But when must this be, Brother *Abednego?*

Cut. Why all these things are to be when the Cat of the North has o're-come the Lion of the South, and when the Mouse of the West has slain the Elephant of the East. I do hear a silent Voice within me, that bids me rise up presently and declare these things to the Congregation of the Lovely in *Coleman-street*. *Tabitha, Tabitha, Tabitha*, I call thee thrice, come along with me, *Tabitha*. [*Exit.*

Tab. There was something of this, as I remember, in my last Vision of Horns the other day. Holy man ! I follow thee ; farewell, forsooth, Mother, till anon.

Joll. Come, let's go in too, Sister. [*Exeunt.*

Act 4. Scene 1.

Truman Junior.

WHat shall I think hence-forth of Woman-kind ?
    When I know *Lucia* was the best of it,
And see her what she is ? What are they made of ?
Their Love, their Faith, their Souls enslav'd to passion !
Nothing at their Command beside their Tears,
And we, vain men, whom such Heat-drops deceive !
Hereafter I will set my self at Liberty,
And if I sigh or grieve, it shall not be
For Love of One, but Pity of all the Sex.

Scene 2.

Enter Lucia.

Ha ! she will not let me see her sure ;
If ever, *Lucia*, a Veil befitted thee,
'Tis now, that thou maist hide thy guilty blushes.

Luc. If all their malice yet
Have not prevail'd on *Truman's* Constancy,
They'l miss their wicked end, and I shall live still.
I'l go and speak to him.

Trum. Forbear, *Lucia*, for I have made a second Oath, which I shall keep, I hope, with lesser trouble, never to see thy face more.

Luc. You were wont, Sir,
To say, you could not live without the sight of't.

Trum. I ; 'twas a good one then.

Luc. Has one day spoil'd it ?

Trum. O yes, more than a hundred years of time, made as much more by sorrow, and by sickness, could e'er have done.

Luc. Pray hear me, *Truman* :
For never innocent Maid was wrong'd as I am ;
Believe what I shall say to you, and confirm
By all the holiest Vows that can bind Souls.

   Trum. I have believ'd those Female tricks too long ;
I know thou canst speak willingly, but thy Words
Are not what Nature meant them, thy Mind's Picture ;
I 'l believe now what represents it better,
Thine own Hand, and the proof of mine own Eyes.

   Luc. I know not what you mean ; believe my Tears.

   Trum. They 'r idle empty Bubbles.
Rais'd by the Agitation of thy Passions,
And hollow as thy heart ; there is no weight in 'em.
Go thou once, *Lucia ;* Farewel,
Thou that wer 't dearer to me once, than all
The outward things of all the World beside,
Or my own Soul within me, farewel for ever ;
Go to thine Husband, and love him better than
Thou didst thy Lover.
I ne're will see thee more, nor shall, I fear,
Ere see my self again.

   Luc. [*kneels.*] Heare me but once.

   Trum. No, 'tis enough ; Heaven hear thee when thou
kneel'st to it.   [*Exit.*

   Luc. Will he ? he's gone ; now all the world has left me,
                                            [*rises.*

And I am desolately miserable ;
'Tis done unkindly, most unkindly, *Truman.*
Had a blest Angel come to me and said
That thou wert false, I should have sworn it li'd,
And thought that rather faln than thee.
Go, dear, false man, go seek out a new Mistris ;
But when you ha' talk'd, and lov'd, and vow'd, and sworn
A little while, take heed of using her
As you do me ; no, may your love to her
Be such as mine to you, which all thy injuries
Shall never change, nor death it self abolish.
May she be worthier of your bed than I,
And when the happy course of many years
Shall make you appear old to all but her,

May you in the fair Glass of your fresh Issue
See your own youth again ; but I would have 'em
True in their Loves, and kill no innocent Maids ;
For me it is no matter ; when I'm dead,
My busie soul shall flutter still about him,
'Twill not be else in Heaven ; it shall watch
Over his sleeps, and drive away all dreams
That come not with a soft and downy wing ;
If any dangers threaten, it shall becken
And call his spirit away, till they be past,
And be more diligent than his Guardian Angel ;
And when just Heaven, as I'm assur'd it will,
Shall clear my Honor and my Innocence,
He'l sigh, I know, and pity my misfortunes,
And blame himself, and curse my false Accusers,
And weep upon my Grave
For my wrong'd Virtue, and mistaken Truth,
And unjust Death ; I ask no more.   [*Exit.*

Scene 3.

Enter Truman *Junior.*

'Twas barbarously done to leave her so ;
Kneeling and weeping to me ; 'twas inhuman ;
I'l back and take my leave more civilly,
So as befits one who was once her Worshipper.
                    [*Goes over the Stage, and comes back.*
She's gone ; why let her go ; I feel her still ;
I feel the root of her, labouring within
To sprout afresh, but I will pluck it up,
Or tear my heart with 't.

Scene 4.

Enter Jolly, Truman *Senior.*

Joll.   He's there, Sir, pray let him now resolve you positively
what he means to do.

Trum. s.   What he means to do, Colonel ? that were fine
'Ifaith ; if he be my son he shall mean nothing ;

311

ABRAHAM COWLEY

Boys must not have their meanings, Colonel:
Let him mean what I mean with a Wennion.

Trum. j. I shall be prest, I see, by 'em, upon the hateful
Subject of a Marriage;
And to fill up the measure of Affliction,
Now I have lost that which I lov'd, compell'd
To take that which I hate.

Trum. s. I will not be troubled, Colonel, with his meanings,
if he do not marry her this very evening (for I 'le ha' none of
his Flim-flams and his May-be's) I 'le send for my son *Tom*
from St. *John's* College (he 's a pretty Scholar I can tell you,
Colonel, I have heard him syllogize it with Mr. *Soaker* in Mood
and Figure) and settle my Estate upon him with her; if he
have his Meanings too, and his Sympathies, I 'l disinherit 'em
both, and marry the Maid my self, if she can like me; I have
one Tooth yet left, Colonel, and that 's a Colt's one.

Trum. j. Did I submit to lose the sight of *Lucia*
Onely to save my unfortunate Inheritance;
And can there be impos'd a harder Article
For me to boggle at?
Would I had been born some wretched Peasant's son,
And never known what Love or Riches were.
Ha—I 'l marry her—why should I not? if I
Must marry somebody,
And hold my Estate by such a slavish Tenure,
Why not her as well as any else?
All Women are alike I see by *Lucia*,
'Tis but resolving to be miserable,
And that is resolv'd for me by my Destiny.

Joll. Well, try him pray, but do it kindly, Sir,
And artificially.

Trum. s. I warrant you; *Dick*, I 'l ha' you marry Mrs.
Aurelia to night.

Trum. j. To night? the warning 's short, Sir, and it may
be—

Trum. s. Why look you, Colonel, he 's at 's old lock, he 's
at 's May-bees again.

Trum. j. I know not, Sir—

Trum. s. I, and his Know-nots, you shall have him at his
Wo'nots presently; Sirra—I will have you know, Sir—

Joll. Nay, good Mr. *Truman*—you know not yet what answer he intends to make you.

Trum. j. Be pleas'd, Sir, to consider—

Trum. s. Look you, Sir, I must consider now, he upbraids his father with the want of consideration, like a Varlet as he is.

Trum. j. What shall I do? why should not I do any thing,
Since all things are indifferent?

Joll. I beseech you, Mr. *Truman*, have but a little patience—
Your father, Sir, desires to know—

Trum. s. I do not desire him, Colonel, nor never will desire him, I command him upon the duty of a Child—

Joll. Whether you can dispose your self to love and marry my daughter *Aurelia*, and if you can, for several reasons we desire it may be presently consummated.

Trum. j. Out with it, stubborn Tongue;
I shall obey my father, Sir, in all things.

Trum. s. Ha! what dee' you say, Sir?

Joll. This old testy Fool is angry, I think, to have no more occasion given him of being so.

Trum. j. I shall obey you, Sir.

Joll. You speak, Sir, like a vertuous Gentleman; the same obedience and resignation, to a father's will, I found in my *Aurelia*, and where two such persons meet, the issue cannot chuse but be successful.

Trum. s. Ah *Dick*, my son *Dick*, he was always the best natur'd Boy—he was like his father in that—he makes me weep with tenderness, like an old fool as I am—Thou shalt have all my Estate, *Dick*, I 'l put my self to a pension rather than thou shall want—go spruse up thy self a little presently, thou art not merry 'ifaith, *Dick*, prethee be merry *Dick*, and fetch fine Mrs. *Aurelia* presently to the little Church behind the Colonel's Garden, Mr. *Soaker* shall be there immediately and wait for you at the Porch (we 'l have it instantly, Colonel, done, lest the young fool should relapse) come, dear *Dick*, let 's go cheerily on with the business.

Trum. j. What have I said? what am I doing? the best is, it is no matter what I say or do.

313

Joll. I'l see *Aurelia* shall be ready, and all things on my part within this half hour.

Trum. s. Good, honest, noble Colonel, let me shake you by the hand. Come, dear *Dick*, we lose time. [*Exeunt.*

Scene 5.

Enter Cutter, Tabitha, *a Boy*.

Cut. And the Vision told me, sister *Tabitha*, that this same day, the first of the seventh month, in the year of Grace 1658, and of Revelation, and Confusion of Carnal Monarchies the tenth, that we two, who are both holy Vessels, should by an holy Man be joyned together in the holy Bond of sanctifi'd Matrimony.

Tab. I brother *Abednego*, but our friends consents—

Cut. Heaven is our friend, and, Sister, Heaven puts this into our thoughts; it is, no doubt, for propagation of the great Mystery; there shall arise from our two bodies, a great Confounder of *Gogmagog*, who shall be called the Pestle of Antichrist, and his children shall inherit the Grapes of *Canaan*.

Tab. My mother will be angry, I'm afraid.

Cut. Your Mother will rejoyce, the Vision says so, sister, the Vision says your Mother will rejoyce; how will it rejoyce her righteous heart to see you, *Tabitha*, riding behind me upon the Purple Dromedary? I would not for the world that you should do it, but that we are commanded from above; for to do things without the aforesaid Command is like unto the building of a Fire without the Bottom-cake.

Tab. I, I, that it is, he knows.

Cut. Now to confirm to you the truth of this Vision, there is to meet us at a zealous Shoomaker's habitation hard by here, by the command of a Vision too, our Brother *Zephaniah Fats*, an Opener of Revelations to the Worthy in *Mary White-chapel*, and he is the chosen Vessel to joyn our hands.

Tab. I would my Mother knew't; but if that holy man come too by a Vision, I shall have grace, I hope, not to resist.

Cut. Sister, let me speak one word of Instruction to yonder Babe.

Tab. Oh how my bowels yern!

Cut. Sirra, is my little Doctor already staying for me at *Tom Underleather* my Shoomaker's house?

Boy. Yes, Sir, but he's in so strange a Habit, that Mr. *Underleather's* Boy *Franck* and I were ready to die with laughing at him.

Cut. Oh so much the better; go you little piece of a Rogue and get every thing ready against I come back.   [*Exit Boy.*
Sister, that Babe you saw me speaking to is predestinated to Spiritual Mightiness, and is to be restorer of the Mystical Tribe of *Gad*—

Tab. Oh the Wonderous—but, Brother *Abednego,* will you not pronounce this Evening tide before the Congregation of the Spotless in *Coleman-street?*

Cut. The will of the latter Vision is to be fulfilled first, as a Preparatory Vision; let us not make the Messenger of Mystery, who is sent by a Vision so far as from *Mary White-chapel* for our sakes, to stay too long from his lawful Vocation of Basket-making. Come, Sister *Tabitha.*

Tab. Hei, ho! but I will not resist.   [*Exeunt.*

Scene 6.

Enter Jolly, Puny, Worm.

Joll. Mr. *Puny,* since you threaten me, I tell you plainly I think my Niece has undone her self by marrying thee, for though thou hast a fair Estate at present, I'm hainously mistaken if thou beest not cheated of it all within these three years by such Rabbit-suckers as these, that keep thee company, and like lying sons o' the Devil as they are, cry thee up for a Wit, when there's nothing so unlike, no not any of thy own Similitudes, thy odious Comparisons.

Pun. The Colonel's raging mad, like a Baker in the Suburbs, when his Oven's over-heated.

Wor. Good, very good i'faith.

Joll. I, that was one of 'em; as for her Portion, I thought to ha' given her a thousand pounds, but—

Pun. O magnanimous Colonel! what a portion for a Toothpick-maker's daughter!

Wor. Good, shoot him thick with similies like Hail-shot.

Joll. But now thou shalt not have a groat with her.

Pun. What not a poor old *Harry*-Groat that looks as thin as a Poet's Cloak? But however, my noble Mountain hearted Uncle, I ha' made her Maiden-head a Crack'd Groat already, and if I ha' nothing more from her, she shall ha' nothing more from me; no, she shall foot Stokins in a Stall for me, or make Children's Caps in a Garret fifteen stories high.

Joll. For that matter (for though thou speak'st no sense I guess thy brutish meaning) the Law will allow her honorable Alimony out o' your Foolship's Fortune.

Pun. And the Law will allow me her Portion too, good Colonel Uncle, you'r not too big to be brought into *West-minster*-hall; nay, Captain, his Niece uses me worse too, she will not let me touch the Nail of her little finger, and rails at me like a Flounder-mouth'd Fish-woman with a face like *Billingsgate.*

Joll. What flesh can support such an affected Widgen, who ha's not a design to cheat him of something as that Vermin ha's? well, I shall be able to Live now I hope as befits a Gentleman, and therefore I'le endure the company of Fopps and Knaves no longer.

Wor. Come Colonel, let's go in, and dispute the difference conscienciously over a Bottle o' Sack.

Joll. I keep no Tavern, *Worm*; or if I did, thy whole Estate would hardly reach to a Gill.

Wor. Colonel, thou art grown Unkind, and art Drunk this afternoon without me.

Joll. Without thee, Buffoon? why I tell thee, thou shall never shew that Odd, Pimping, Cheating face o' thine within my Doors agen, I'le turn away any man o' mine that shall disparage himself to drink with such a fellow as thou art.

Wor. As I? why what am I? pray? Mighty Colonel!

Joll. Thou art or hast been every thing that's ill, there is no Scandalous way of Living, no Vocation of the Devil, that thou hast not set up in at one time or other; Fortune ha's Whip'd thee about through all her streets; Thou'rt one that Lives like a Raven, by Providence and Rapin; now thou'rt feeding upon that raw young fellow, and doest Devour and Kaw him; thou'rt one that if thou should'st by chance go to Bed sober, would'st write it down in thy Almanack, for an Unlucky day; sleep is not the Image of Death to thee, unless thou bee'st Dead drunk; Thou art—I know not what—thou'rt any thing, and shall be to me hereafter nothing.

Pun. This Colonel pisses Vinegar to day.

Wor. This is uncivil Language Colonel to an old Camerade, and one of your own party.

Joll. My Comrade? o' my party thou? or any but the party of the Pick-purses!

Pun. This bouncing Bear of a Colonel will break the back o' my little Whelp of a Captain, unless I take him off; come away Captain, I'le firk his back with two Bum-baylies, till he spew up every Stiver of her Portion.

Joll. Fare-ye-well, Gentlemen, come not near these Doors if you love your own Leather, I'l ha' my Scullions batter you with Bones and Turneps, and the Maids drown you with Piss-pots, if you do but approach the Windows; these are sawcy Knaves indeed, to come to me for Pounds and Portions.

(Exit.

Wor. Poverty, the Pox, an ill Wife, and the Devil go with thee, Colonel.

Pun. I vex'd him to the Gills, *Worm*, when I put that bitter Bob o' the Baker upon him.

Wor. I? i'st e'n so? not come to your House? by *Jove* I'l turn him out of it himself by a trick that I have.

Pun. Pish! thou talk'st as Ravingly as a Costermonger in a Feaver.

Wor. I'l do't by *Jove*.

Pun. How, prethee, Captain? what does thy Pericranium mean?

Wor. Why here I ha't, by *Jove*; I'm ravish'd with the fancy of it; let me see—let me see—his Brother went seven years ago to *Guiny*.—

Pun. I, but the Merchants say he's Dead long since, and gon to the Blackamores below.

Wor. The more Knaves they; he Lives, and I'm the man.

Pun. Ha! ha! ha! thou talk'st like a Sowc'd Hoggs-face.

Wor. I knew him very well, and am pretty like him, liker than any of your Simil[i]tudes, *Puny;* by long Conversation with him, and the Colonel, I know all passages betwixt 'em; and

317

ABRAHAM COWLEY

what his Humor and his Estate was, much better than he him-
self, when he was Alive; he was a Stranger thing than any
Monster in *Afrique* where he Traded.

Pun. How! prethee Captain? I love these Odd fantastical
things as an Alderman loves Lobsters.

Wor. Why, you must know, he had quite lost his memory,
totally, and yet thought himself an able man for business, and
that he did himself all that was done by his man *John*, who
went always along with him; like a Dog with a Blind man.

Pun. Ha! ha! ha! Sublimely fantastical.

Wor. He carry'd a Scrowl about him of Memorandums,
even of his Daughters and his Brothers names, and where his
House stood; for as I told you, he remembred nothing; and
where his Scrowl failed, *John* was his remembrancer, we were
wont to call him Remembrancer *John*.

Pun. Ha, ha, ha! Rarely exotique! I'l Act that apple
John, never was such a *John* as I; not *John* o' *Gant*, or *John*
o' *Nokes*, I will turn Remembrancer *John*, as round as a Wedding
Ring, ha, ha, ha!

Wor. Well said! but you must lay aside conceits for a
while, and remote fancies. I'l teach you his humor instantly;
now will I and my man *John* swarthy our faces over as if that
Country's heat had made 'em so, (which will Disguise us
sufficiently) and attire our selves in some strange Habits o' those
Parts, (I know not how yet, but we shall see it in *Speed's*
Mapps) and come and take Possession of our House and Estate.

Pun. Dear *Ovid*, let's about thy Metamorphosis.

Wor. 'Twill be discover'd perhaps at last, but however, for
the present 'twill break off his match with the Widdow, (which
makes him so Proud now) and therefore it must be done in the
twinkling of an Eye, for they say he's to marry her this Night;
if all fail, 'twill be at least a merry 'bout for an hour, and a
mask to the Wedding.

Pun. Quick, dear Rogue! quick as Precipitation.

Wor. I know where we can ha' Cloaths, hard by here;
give me ten Pounds to hire 'em, and come away, but of all
things, man *John*, take heed of being witty.

Pun. I, that's the Devil on't; well, go; I'l follow you
behind like a long Rapier. [*Exeunt.*

Scene 7.

Aurelia.

Aur. If they would allow me but a little time, I could play such a trick with Mr. *Truman*, as should smart sorely for the rest of his Life, and be reveng'd abundantly on my Cozen, for getting of him from me, when I was such a foolish Girl three year ago as to be in Love with him.
But they would have us marri'd instantly,
The Parson stays for us at Church. I know not what to do—all must out—Odds my life he's coming to fetch me here to Church already.

Scene 8.

Enter Truman *Junior.*

Trum. j. I must go through with it now; I'l marry her,
And live with her according to the forms,
But I will never touch her as a Woman.
She stays for me—Madam—
Aur. Sir.
Trum. j. I cannot out with it—Madam.
Aur. Sir—
Trum. j. Must we go marry, Madam?
Aur. Our friends will have it so, it seems.
Trum. Why will you marry me? what is there in me
That can deserve your liking? I shall be
The most untoward and ill-favour'd Husband
That ever took a melting Maid t' his Bed;
The faculties of my Soul are all untuned,
And every Glory of my Springing youth
Is faln into a strange and suddain Winter,
You cannot Love me sure.
Aur. Not to Distraction, Sir.
Trum. No, nor I you; why should we marry then?
It were a folly, were it not, *Aurelia?*

Aur. Why they say, 'tis the best marriage, when like is
Joyn'd to like; now we shall make a very even match, for
neither you Love me, nor I Love you, and 'tis to be hop'd we
may get Children that will Love neither of us.

Trum. Nay, by my soul I love you, but alas,
Not in that way that Husbands should their Wives;
I cannot Toy, nor Kiss, nor do I know not what,
And yet I was a Lover, as true a Lover—

Aur. Alack a day!

Trum. 'Twas then, (me-thoughts) the only happiness
To sit and talk, and look upon my Mistriss,
Or if she was not by, to think upon her;
Then every Morning, next to my Devotion,
Nay often too (forgive me Heaven) before it,
She slipt into my fancy, and I took it
As a good Omen for the following day;
It was a pretty foolish kind of Life,
An honest, harmless Vanity; but now
The fairest Face moves me no more, than Snow
Or Lillies when I see 'em, and pass by;
And I as soon should deeply fall in Love
With the fresh Scarlet of an Eastern Cloud,
As the Red Lips and Cheeks of any Woman;
I do confess, *Aurelia*, thou art Fair,
And very Witty, and (I think) Well-natur'd,
But thou 'rt a Woman still.

Aur. The sight of you Sir,
Makes me not repent at all my being so.

Trum. And prethee now, *Aurelia*, tell me truly,
Are any Women constant in their Vows?
Can they continue a whole Moneth, a Week,
And never change their faith? Oh! if they could,
They would be excellent things; nay ne're dissemble;
Are not their Lusts unruly, and to them
Such Tyrants as their Beauties are to us?
Are their tears true, and solid when they weep?

Aur. Sure Mr. *Truman* you ha'nt slept of late,
If we should be marry'd to Night, what would you do for
Sleep?

Trum. Why? do not marry'd people sleep o' Nights?

320

Aur. Yes! yes! alas good innocence.

Trum. They have a scurvy Life on 't if they don't;
But wee 'l not Live as other people do,
Wee 'l find out some new handsome way of Love,
Some way of Love that few shall imitate,
Yet all admire; for 'tis a sordid thing,
That Lust should dare t' insinuate it self
Into the Marriage-bed; wee 'l get no Children,
The worst of Men and Women can do that;
Besides too, if our Issue should be Female,
They would all Learn to flatter and dissemble,
They would deceive with Promises and Vows
Some simple men, and then prove False and Kill 'em,
Would they not do 't, *Aurelia?*

Aur. I, any thing Mr. *Truman;* but what shall we do
Sir, when we are marry'd, pray?

Trum. Why! wee 'l live very Lovingly together,
Sometimes wee 'l sit and talk of excellent things,
And laugh at all the Nonsense of the world;
Sometimes wee 'l walk together,
Sometimes wee 'l read, and sometimes eat, and sometimes
       sleep;
And sometimes pray, and then at last, wee 'l dye,
And go to Heaven together; 'twill be rare!

Aur. We may do all this (me-thinks) and never marry for
the matter.

Trum. 'Tis true, we may so!
But since our Parents are resolv'd upon it,
In such a Circumstance let 'em have their humor.
My father sent me in to Complement,
And keep a Prating here, and play the Fool;
I cannot do 't, what should I say, *Aurelia?*
What do they use to say?

Aur. I believe you knew Sir, when you Woo'd my Cozen.

Trum. I, but those Days are past; they 'r gon for ever,
And nothing else, but Nights are to succeed 'em;
Gone like the faith and truth of Women kind,
And never to be seen again! O *Lucia!*
Thou wast a woundrous Angel in those days of thy blest state
      of Innocence.

There was a Cheek! a Fore-head! and an Eye!—
Did you observe her Eye, *Aurelia?*

Aur. O yes Sir! there were very pretty Babies in 't.

Trum. It was as glorious as the Eye of Heaven;
Like the souls Eye it peirc'd through every thing;
And then her Hands—her Hands of Liquid Ivory!
Did she but touch her Lute (the pleasing'st Harmony then
       upon Earth when she her self was silent)
The subtil motion of her Flying fingers
Taught Musique a New art, to take the Sight, as wel as Ear.

Aur. I, Sir, I! you 'd best go look her out, and marry
her, she has but one Husband yet.

Trum. Nay, prethee, good *Aurelia* be not angry,
For I will never Love or See her more.
I do not say she was more Fair than thou art,
Yet if I did? No, but I wo 'not say so!
Only allow me this one short last remembrance of one I lov'd
so long.   And now I think on 't, I 'l beg a favour of you, you
will Laugh at me I know, when you have heard it, but prethee
grant it; 'tis that you would be Veil'd, as *Lucia* was of late, for
this one day; I would fain marry thee so;
'Tis an odd foolish fancy, I confess,
But Love and Grief may be allow'd sometimes
A little Innocent folly.

Aur. Good! this Fool will help me I see to cheat himself;
At a dead lift, a little hint will serve me.
I 'l do 't for him to the Life.

Trum. Will you *Aurelia?*

Aur. That 's but a small Compliance; you 'l ha' power
anon to Command me greater things.

Trum. We shall be marry'd very privately;
None but our selves; and that 's e'en best, *Aurelia.*
Why do I stick here at a Fatal step
That must be made? *Aurelia*, are you ready?
The Minister stays for us.

Aur. I 'l but go in and take my Veil, as you Command me
Sir; Walk but a few turns in the Garden, in less than half an
hour I 'l come to you, ha, ha, ha!   [*Exit.*

Trum. I go, I am Condemn'd, and must Obey;
The Executioner stays for me at Church.   [*Exit.*

Act 5.   Scene 1.

Colonel Jolly, Will.

Joll. SO, I have her at last, and honest *Joseph Knock-down* married us, me-thinks, with convenient brevity; I have some hold now upon my Estate again (though she, I confess, be a clog upon it worse than a Mort-gage) that, my good Neighbour *Barebottle*, left wholly to his wife; almost all the rest of the Incomes upon his seeking, go to his daughter *Tabitha*, whom *Cutter* has got by this time, and promises me to live like an honest Gentleman hereafter; now he may do so comfortably and merrily. She marri'd me thus suddenly, like a good Housewife, purely to save charges; however though, we'l have a good Supper for her, and her eating Tribe; *Will,* is the Cook a doing according to my directions?

Will. Yes, Sir, he's very hard at his business; he's swearing and cursing in the Kitchin, that your Worship may hear him hither, he'l fright my new old Mistris out of the house.

Joll. 'Tis such an over-roasted coxcomb—bid him be sure to season well the Venison that came in luckily to day.

Will. Troth, Sir, I dare not speak to him now, unless I should put on your Worship's Armour that lies hid in the Barel below; he'd like to ha' spitted me just now, like a Goose as I was, for telling him he look'd like the Ox that's roasted whole in St. *James's* Fair. Who's there?

Joll. See who's at door. I shall ha' some plundred Plate, I hope, to entertain my friends with, when we come to visit the Truncks with Iron hoops; who is't.

Will. Nay, Heaven knows, Sir; two Fiends, I think, to take away the Cook for swearing. They ha' thrust in after me.

Scene 2.

Enter Worm *and* Puny *disguised like the Merchant and* John.

Wor. They 'l hardly know us at first in these forein habits.

Pun. I Sir, and as the Sun has us'd us in those hot Countries.

Wor. Why, this is my old house here, *John;* ha, ha! little thought I to see my old house upon *Tower-hill* again. Where 's my brother *Jolly?*

Joll. They call me Colonel *Jolly.*

Wor. Ha! let me see, [*Looks on his Note.*] A burly man of a moderate stature—a beard a little greyish—ha! a quick Eye, and a Nose inclining to red—

Pun. Nay, 'tis my Master's Worship, Sir, would we were no more alter'd since our Travels.

Wor. It agrees very well—Save you good brother, you little thought to see me here again, though I dare say you wish'd it; stay, let me see, how many years, *John*, is 't since we went from hence?

Pun. 'Tis now seven years, Sir.

Wor. Seven? me-thinks I was here but yesterday, how the what de-ye-call-it runs? how do you call it?

Pun. The Time, Sir.

Wor. I, I, the time, *John;* what was I saying? I was telling you, brother, that I had quite forgot you; was I not telling him so, *John?*

Joll. Faith we 'r both quits then; I 'l swear I ha' forgot you; why you were dead five years ago.

Wor. Was I? I ha' quite forgot it; *John*, was I dead five years ago? my memory fails me very much of late.

Pun. We were worse than dead, Sir, we were taken by a barbarous Nation, and there made slaves; *John*, quoth he? I was poor *John* I'm sure; they kept us three whole years with nothing but Water and Acorns, till we look'd like Wicker bottles.

Wor. What, Sirrah, did your Master look like? I 'l teach you to say your Master look'd like what de-ye-call 'ums.

Joll. Where did they take you prisoners?

Wor. Nay, ask *John*, he can tell you I warrant you; 'twas in—tell him, *John*, where it was.

Pun. In *Guiny*.

Joll. By what Country-men were you taken?

Wor. Why they were called—I ha' forgot what they call 'em, 'twas an odd kind o' name, but *John* can tell you.

Pun. Who I, Sir? do you think I can remember all things?

Wor. 'Tis i' my Book here I remember well. Name any Nation under the Sun.

Pun. I know the name, Sir, well enough; but I onely try'd my Master's memory, 'Twas the Tartarians.

Wor. I, I, those were the men.

Joll. How, *John*? why all the world man lies betwixt 'em, they live up in the North.

Pun. The North?

Joll. I the very North, *John*.

Pun. That's true indeed, but these were another Nation of Tartarians that liv'd in the South, they came antiently from the others.

Joll. How got you from 'em, *John*, at last?

Pun. Why faith, Sir, by a Ladie's means, who, to tell you the truth, fell in love with me; my Master has it all in his Book, 'tis a brave story.

Joll. In what Ship came you back?

Pun. A plague of 't, that question will be our ruine.

Wor. What Ship? 'twas call'd a thing that swims, what dee you call 't?

Joll. The *Mermaid*?

Wor. No, no, let me see.

Joll. The *Triton*?

Wor. No, no, a thing that in the water does—it swims in the water—

Joll. What is 't? the *Dolphin*?

Wor. No, no, I ha' quite forgot the name on 't, but 'tis no matter, it swims—

Joll. What say you, *John*?

Pun. I, Sir, my Master knows well enough; you cann't conceive the misery we endur'd, Sir.

Joll. Well, Brother, I'l but ask you one question more, where did you leave your Will?

Pun. 'Life, now he's pos'd again—we shall never carry't through.

Wor. I'l tell you presently, Brother—let me see, [*Reads in his Scrowl.*] Memorandums about my Will; left to my Brother the whole charge of my Estate—hum—hum—five thousand pounds—hum—What did you ask me, brother?

Joll. In what place you left your Will?

Wor. I that was it indeed—, that was the very thing you ask'd me; what a treacherous memory have I! my memory is so short—

Joll. This is no Answer to my Question yet.

Wor. 'Tis true indeed; what was your Question, brother?

Joll. Where you left your Will?

Wor. Good Lord, that I should forget you ask'd me that! I had forgot it, i' faith law that I had, you'l pardon, I hope, my Infirmity, for I alas—alas—I ha' forgot what I was going to say to you, but I was saying something, that I was.

Joll. Well, Gentlemen, I'm now in haste, walk but a while into the Parlour there, I'l come to you presently.

Wor. But where's my daughter—

Pun. *Lucia*, Sir?

Wor. I, *Lucia*—put me in mind to ask for her (a plague o' your Tartarians.)

Pun. And o' your What dee-ye-call-'ems.

Wor. 'Life, Tartarians!

[*Exeunt* Worm, Puny.

Joll. If these be Rogues, (as Rogues they seem to be) I will so exercise my Rogues, the tyranny of a new Beadle over a Beggar shall be nothing to't; what think'st thou of 'em, *Will?*

Will. Faith, Sir, I know not—h'as just my Masters Nose and Upper-lip; but if you think it be not he, Sir, I'l beat 'em worse than the Tartarians did.

Joll. No, let's try 'em first—trick for trick—Thou were wont to be a precious Knave, and a great Actor too, a very *Roscius;* did'st not thou play once the Clown in *Musidorus?*

Will. No, but I plaid the Bear, Sir.

Joll. The Bear! why that's as good a Part; thou'rt an

Actor then I'l warrant thee, the Bears a well-penn'd Part, and you remember my Brother's humor, don't you? They have almost hit it.

Will. I, Sir, I knew the shortness of his memory, he would always forget to pay me my Wages, till he was put in mind of't.

Joll. Well said, I'l dress thee within, and all the Servants shall acknowledge thee, you conceive the Design—be confident, and thou ca[n]st not miss; but who shall do trusty *John?*

Will. Oh, *Ralph* the Butler, Sir,'s an excellent try'd Actor, he play'd a King once; I ha' heard him speak a Play *ex tempore* in the Butteries.

Joll. O excellent *Ralph!* incomparable *Ralph* against the world! Come away *William,* I'l give you instructions within, it must be done in a moment. *[Exeunt.*

Scene 3.

Enter Aurelia, Jane.

Jane. Ha, ha, ha! this is the best Plot o' yours, dear Madam, to marry me to Mr. *Truman* in a Veil instead of your self; I cann't chuse but laugh at the very conceit of't; 'twill make excellent sport: My Mistris will be so mad when she knows that I have got her Servant from her, ha, ha, ha!

Aur. Well, are you ready? Veil your self all over, and never speak one word to him, what ever he says, (he'l ha' no mind to talk much) but give him your hand, and go along with him to Church; and when you come to, I take thee—mumble it over that he mayn't distinguish the voice.

Jane. Ha, ha, ha! I cann't speak for laughing—dear hony Madam, let me but go in and put on a couple o' Patches; you cann't imagine how much prettier I look with a Lozenge under the Left Eye, and a Half Moon o' this cheek; and then I'le but slip on the Silver-lac'd Shoes that you gave me, and be with him in a trice.

Aur. Don't stay, he's a fantastical fellow, if the whimsey take him he'l be gone. *[Exeunt.*

Scene 4.

Lucia.

They say he's to pass instantly this way
To lead his Bride to Church; ingrateful Man!
I'l stand here to upbraid his guilty Conscience,
And in that black attire in which he saw me
When he spoke the last kind words to me;
'Twill now befit my sorrows, and the Widow-hood of my
    Love;
He comes alone, what can that mean?

Scene 5.

Enter Truman *junior.*

Trum. Come, Madam, the Priest stays for us too long;
I ask your pardon for my dull delay,
And am asham'd of't.
 Luc. What does he mean? I'l go with him what e'er it
mean.   *[Exeunt.*

Scene 6.

Enter Cutter, Tabitha, Boy.

Cut. Come to my bed, my dear, my dear,   *[Sings.*
   My dear come to my bed,
  For the pleasant pain, and the loss with gain
   Is the loss of a Maidenhead.
  For the pleasant, etc.
 Tab. Is that a Psalm, Brother Husband, which you sing?
 Cut. No, Sister Wife, a short Ejaculation onely.
Well said, Boy, bring in the things,——(*Boy brings a Hat and
Feather, Sword and Belt, broad Lac'd Band, and Periwig.*
 Tab. What do you mean, Brother *Abednego?* you will not
turn Cavalier, I hope, again, you will not open before *Sion* in
the dressings of *Babylon?*

328

Cut. What do these cloathes befit Queen *Tabitha's* husband upon her day o' Nuptials? this Hat with a high black chimney for a crown, and a brim no broader than a Hatband? Shall I, who am to ride the Purple Dromedary, go drest like *Revelation Fats* the Basket-maker? Give me the Peruique, Boy; shall Empress *Tabitha's* husband go as if his head were scalded? or wear the Seam of a shirt here for a Band? Shall I who am zealous even to slaying, walk in the streets without a Sword, and not dare to thrust men from the wall, if any shall presume to take 't of Empress *Tabitha*? Are the Fidlers coming, Boy?

Tab. Pish, I cannot abide these doings; are you mad? there come no prophane Fidlers here.

Cut. Be peaceable gentle *Tabitha*; they will not bring the Organs with them hither; I say be peaceable, and conform to Revelations; It was the Vision bad me do this; Wil't thou resist the Vision?

Tab. An' these be your Visions! little did I think I wusse— O what shall I do? is this your Conversion? which of all the Prophets wore such a Map about their Ears, or such a Sheet about their Necks? Oh! my Mother! what shall I do? I'm undone.

Cut. What shalt thou do? why, thou shalt Dance, and Sing, and Drink, and be Merry; thou shalt go with thy Hair Curl'd, and thy Brests Open; thou shalt wear fine black Stars upon thy Face, and Bobs in thy Ears bigger than bouncing Pears; Nay, if thou do'st begin but to look rustily—I'l ha' thee Paint thy self, like the Whore o' *Babylon*.

Tab. Oh! that ever I was Born to see this day—

Cut. What, dost thou weep, Queen *Dido*? thou shalt ha' Sack to drive away thy Sorrows; bring in the Bottle, Boy, I'l be a Loving Husband, the Vision must be Obey'd; Sing *Tabitha*; Weep o' thy Wedding day? 'tis ominous; Come to my Bed my Dear, etc.
Oh, art thou come Boy? fill a Brimmer, nay, fuller yet, yet a little fuller! Here Lady Spouse, here's to our sport at Night.

Tab. Drink it your self, an you will; I'l not touch it, not I.

Cut. By this hand thou shal't pledge me, seeing the Vision said so; Drink, or I'l take a Coach, and carry thee to the *Opera* immediately.

Tab. Oh Lord, I can't abide it—   [*Drinks off.*

Cut. Why, this will chear thy Heart; Sack, and a Husband? both comfortable things; have at you agen.

Tab. I'l pledge you no more, not I.

Cut. Here take the Glass, and take it off—off every drop, or I'l swear a hundred Oaths in a breathing time.

Tab. Well! you'r the strangest man—   [*Drinks.*

Cut. Why, this is right; nay, off with 't; so—but the Vision said, that if we left our Drink behind us we should be Hang'd, as many other Honest men ha' been, only by a little negligence in the like case; Here's to you *Tabitha* once agen, we must fulfill the Vision to a Tittle.

Tab. What must I drink agen? well! you are such another Brother—Husband.

Cut. Bravely done, *Tabitha!* now thou Obey'st the Vision, thou wil't ha' Revelations presently.

Tab. Oh! Lord! my Head's giddy—nay, Brother, Husband, the Boy's taking away the Bottle, and there's another Glass or two in it still.

Cut. O Villainous Boy! fill out you Bastard, and squeeze out the last drop.

Tab. I'l drink to you now, my Dear; 'tis not handsome for you to begin always—[*Drinks.*] Come to my Bed my Dear, and how wast? 'twas a pretty Song, me-thoughts.

Cut. O Divine *Tabitha!* here come the Fidlers too, strike up ye Rogues.

Tab. What must we Dance too? is that the Fashion? I could ha' danc'd the Curranto when I was a Girl, the Curranto's a curious Dance.

Cut. We'l out-dance the Dancing disease; but *Tabitha*, there's one poor Health left still to be drunk with Musique.

Tab. Let me begin't; here Duck, here's to all that Love us.   [*Drinks.*

Cut. A Health, ye Eternal Scrapers, sound a Health; rarely done *Tabitha*, what think'st thou now o' thy Mother?

Tab. A fig for my Mother; I'l be a Mother my self shortly; Come Duckling, shall we go home?

Cut. Go home? the Bride-groom and his Spouse go home? no, we'l Dance home; afore us Squeakers, that way, and be Hang'd you Sempiternal Rakers. O brave! Queen *Tabitha!* Excellent Empress *Tabitha*, on ye Rogues!   [*Exeunt.*

Scene 7.

Enter Jolly, Worm, Puny.

Wor. But where's my what dee ye call her, Brother?
Joll. What Sir?
Wor. (*Reads.*) My Daughter—*Lucia*, a pretty fair Complexioned Girl, with a Black Eye, a Round Chin, a little Dimpled, and a Mole upon—I would fain see my daughter—Brother.
Joll. Why, you shall Sir presently, she's very well; what Noise is that? how now? what's the matter?

Enter Servant.

Serv. Ho! my old Master! my old Master's come, he's Lighted just now at the door with his man *John*; he's asking for you, he longs to see you; my Master, my old Master.
Joll. This fellow's Mad.
Serv. If you wo'nt believe me, go but in and see Sir; he's not so much alter'd, but you'l quickly know him, I knew him before he was Lighted, pray, go in Sir.
Joll. Why, this is strange—there was indeed some weeks since a report at the *Exchange* that he was Alive still, which was brought by a Ship that came from *Barbary;* but that he should be Split in two after his Death, and Live agen in both, is wonderfull to me. I'l go see what's the matter.
[Exeunt Jolly, Servant.
Pun. I begin to shake like a Plum-tree Leaf.
Wor. Tis a meer Plot o' the Devils to have us beaten, if he send him in just at this Nick.

Scene 8.

Enter Ralph (*as* John) *and two or three* Servants.

1. *Serv.* Ah Rogue, art thou come at last?
2. *Serv.* Why, you'l not look upon your Old friends! give me your Golls, *John*.

Ral. Thank ye all heartily for your Love ; thank you with all my Heart ; my old Bed-fellow, *Robin*, and how does little *Ginny* do ?

3. *Serv.* A murren take you, you 'l ne're leave your Waggery.

Pun. A murren take ye all, I shall be paid the Portion here with a witness.

Ral. And how does *Ralph ?* good honest *Ralph* ; there is not an honester Fellow in *Christendome*, though I say 't my self, that should not say 't.

2. *Serv.* Ha, ha, ha! Why *Ralph* the Rogue 's well still ; Come let 's go to him into the Buttery, he 'l be Overjoy'd to see thee, and give us a Cup o' the best Stingo there.

Ral. Well said ; Steel to the back still *Robin* ; that was your word you know ; my Master's coming in ! go, go, I 'l follow you.

1. *Serv.* Make haste, good *John.*

Ral. Here's a Company of as honest Fellow-servants ; I'm glad, I'm come among 'em agen.

Wor. And would I were got out from 'em, as honest as they are ; that *Robin* has a thrashing hand.

Pun. *John* with a Pox to him ! would I were hid like a Maggot in a Pescod.

Scene 9.

Enter Jolly, William.

Joll. Me-thinks you 'r not return'd, but born to us anew.

Will. Thank you good Brother ; truly we ha' past through many dangers ; my man *John* shall tell you all, I 'm Old and Crazie.

Enter Servant.

4. *Serv.* Sir, the Widdow (my Mistriss I should say) is coming in here with Mr. *Knock-down*, and four or five more.

Joll. O'ds my Life ! this farce is neither of Doctrine nor Use to them ! keep 'em here, *John*, till I come back.

(Exit Jolly.

CUTTER OF COLEMAN-STREET

Wor. I'm glad the Colonel's gone; now will I sneak away, as if I had stoln a Silver spoon.

Will. Who are those, *John?* by your leave Sir, would you speak with any body here?

Wor. The Colonel, Sir? but I'l take some other time to wait upon him, my occasions call me now.

Will. Pray stay, Sir, who did you say you would ha' spoken with?

Wor. The Colonel, Sir; but another time will serve; he has business now.

Will. Whom would he speak with, *John?* I forget still.

Ral. The Colonel, Sir.

Will. Colonel! what Colonel?

Wor. Your brother, I suppose he is Sir, but another time—

Will. 'Tis true indeed; I had forgot, Ifaith, my Brother was a Colonel; I cry you mercy Sir, he'l be here presently. Ye seem to be Foreiners by your habits, Gentlemen.

Wor. No Sir, we are English-men.

Will. English-men? law you there now! would you ha' spoke with me, Sir?

Wor. No Sir, your Brother; but my business requires no haste, and therefore—

Will. You'r not in haste, you say; pray Sir, sit down then, may I crave your name, Sir?

Wor. My name's not worth the knowing Sir—

Will. This Gentleman?

Wor. 'Tis my man, Sir, his name's *John.*

Pun. I'l be *John* no more, not I, I'l be Jackanapes first; No, my name's *Timothy* Sir.

Will. Mr. *John Timothy*, very well, Sir; ye seem to be Travellers.

Wor. We are just now as you see, arriv'd out of *Afrique*, Sir, and therefore have some business that requires—

Will. Of *Afrique?* law ye there now; what Country, pray?

Wor. *Prester-John's* Country; fare you well, Sir, for the present, I must be excus'd.

Will. Marry God forbid; what come from *Prester-John*, and we not Drink a Cup o' Sack together.

333

[*Pun.*] What shall I do? Friend, shall I trouble you to shew me a private place? I 'l wait upon you presently agen, Sir.

Will. You 'l stay here Master?—

Pun. I 'l only make a little Maid's water Sir, and come back to you immediately.

Ral. The door 's lock'd Sir, the Colonel ha's lock'd us in here—why do you shake Sir?

Pun. Nothing—only I have extreme list to make water. Here's the Colonel, I 'l sneak behind the Hangings.

Scene 10.

Enter Jolly, Widdow.

Joll. We 'l leave those Gentlemen within a while upon the point of Reprobation; but Sweet heart, I ha' two Brothers here, newly arriv'd, which you must be acquainted with.

Wid. Marry, Heaven fore-shield! not the Merchant I hope?

Joll. No, brethren in Love, only—How dee you Brother?

Wor. I your Brother; what de'e mean?

Joll. Why, are not you my brother *Jolly*, that was taken Prisoner by the Southern *Tartars?*

Wor. I Brother, I by *Tartars?*

Joll. What an impudent Slave is this? Sirra, Monster, did'st thou not come with thy man *John?*

Wor. I my man *John?* here 's no such person here; you see you 'r mistaken.

Joll. Sirra, I 'l strike thee Dead.

Wor. Hold, hold, Sir, I do remember now I was the Merchant *Jolly*, but when you ask'd me I had quite forgot it; alas, I 'm very Crasie.

Joll. That 's not amiss; but since thou art not he, I must know who thou art.

Wor. Why, do'nt you know me? I 'm Captain *Worm*, and *Puny* was my man *John*.

Joll. Where 's that fool, *Puny?* is he slipt away?

Pun. Yes, and no fool for 't neither for ought I know yet.

Wor. Why, we hit upon this frolique, Colonel, only for a

kind o' Mask (de' ye conceive me, Colonel?) to celebrate your Nuptials; Mr. *Puny* had a mind to reconcile himself with you in a merry way o' Drollery, and so had I too, though I hope you were not in earnest with me.

Joll. Oh! is that all? well said *Will*, bravely done *Will*, Ifaith; I told thee, *Will*, what 'twas to have Acted a Bear; and *Ralph* was an excellent *John* too.

Wor. How's this? then I'm an Ass agen; this damn'd *Punie's* fearfulness spoil'd all.

Pun. This cursed Coward *Worm*! I thought they were not the right ones.

Joll. Here's something for you to drink; go look to Supper, this is your Cue of Exit.   [*Ex.* Will *and* Ralph.

Wid. What need you, Love, ha' given 'em any thing? in truth, Love, you'r too lavish.

Wor. 'Twas wittily put off o' me however.

Scene II.

Enter Cutter, Tabitha, *with Fidlers.*

Joll. Here are more Maskers too, I think; this Masking is a Heavenly entertainment for the Widow, who ne'er saw any Shew yet but the Puppet-play o' *Ninive*.

Cut. Stay without, Scrapers.

Tab. Oh Lord, I'm as weary with Dancing as passes; Husband, husband, yonder's my Mother; O mother what do you think I ha' been doing to day?

Wid. Why what, Child? no hurt, I hope.

Tab. Nay nothing, I have onely been married a little, and my husband *Abednego* and I have so danc'd it since.

Cut. Brave *Tabitha* still; never be angry Mother, you know where Marriages are made, your Daughters and your own were made in the same place, I warrant you, they'r so like.

Wid. Well, his will be done—there's—no resisting Providence—but how, son *Abednego*, come you into that roaring habit of Perdition?

335

Cut. Mother, I was commanded by the Vision, there is some great end for it of Edification, which you shall know by the sequel.

Scene 12.

Enter Truman *senior,* Truman *junior,* Lucia *veil'd.*

Trum. sen. Come, *Dick,* bring in your wife to your t' other father, and ask hi[s] blessing handsomely;
Welcome, dear daughter; off with your Veil;

[Luc. unveils.

Heaven bless ye both.

Joll. Ha! what's this; more masking? why how now, Mr. *Truman?* you ha' not married my Niece, I hope, instead o' my daughter?

Trum. j. I onely did, Sir, as I was appointed,
And am amaz'd as much as you.

Trum. s. Villain, Rebel, Traitor, out o' my sight you son of a—

Joll. Nay, hold him; patience, good Mr. *Truman,* let's understand the matter a little—

Trum. s. I wo'not understand, no that I wo'not, I wo'not understand a word, whilst he and his Whore are in my sight.

Joll. Nay, good Sir—
Why, what Niece? two husbands in one afternoon? that's too much o' conscience.

Luc. Two, Sir? I know of none but this,
And how I came by him too, that I know not.

Joll. This is Ridle me ridle me—where's my Daughter? ho! *Aurelia.*

Scene 13.

Enter Aurelia.

Aur. Here, Sir, I was just coming in.
Joll. Ha' not you married young Mr. *Truman?*
Aur. No, Sir.

CUTTER OF COLEMAN-STREET

Joll. Why, who then has he marri'd?

Aur. Nay that, Sir, he may answer for himself,
If he be of age to marry.

Joll. But did not you promise me you'd marry him this afternoon, and go to Church with him presently to do't.

Aur. But, Sir, my Husband forbad the Banes.

Joll. They're all mad; your Husband?

Aur. I Sir, the truth o' the matter, Sir, is this, (for it must out I see) 'twas I that was married this afternoon in the Matted Chamber to Mr. *Puny*, instead o' my Cousin *Lucia*.

Joll. Stranger and stranger! what, and he not know't?

Aur. No, nor the Parson, Sir, himself.

Joll. Hey day!

Aur. 'Twas done in the dark, Sir, and I veil'd like my Cousin; 'twas a very clandestine marriage, I confess, but there are sufficient proofs of it; and for one, here's half the Piece of Gold he broke with me, which he'l know when he sees.

Pun. O rare, by *Hymen* I'm glad o' the change; 'tis a pretty Sorceress by my troath; Wit to Wit quoth the Devil to the Lawyer; I'l out amongst 'em presently, 't has sav'd me a beating too, which perhaps is all her Portion.

Joll. You turn my Head, you dizzie me; but wouldst thou marrie him without either knowing my mind, or so much as his?

Aur. His, Sir? he gave me five hundred pieces in Gold to make the Match; look, they are here still, Sir.

Joll. Thou hast lost thy senses, Wench, and wilt make me do so too.

Aur. Briefly the truth is this, Sir, he gave me these five hundred Pieces to marry him by a Trick to my Cousin *Lucia*, and by another Trick I took the money and married him my self; the manner, Sir, you shall know anon at leisure, onely your pardon, Sir, for the omission of my duty to you, I beg upon my knees.

Joll. Nay, Wench, there's no hurt done, fifteen hundred pounds a year is no ill match for the daughter of a Sequestred Cavalier—

Aur. I thought so, Sir.

Joll. If we could but cure him of some sottish affectations, but that must be thy task.

C. II. Y 337

Aur. My life on 't, Sir.

Pun. I 'l out ; Uncle Father your Blessing—my little *Matchivil*, I knew well enough 'twas you ; what did you think I knew not Cross from Pile ?

Aur. Did you i' faith ?

Pun. I, by this kiss of Amber-grees, or I 'm a Cabbage.

Aur. Why then you out-witted me, and I 'm content.

Pun. A pox upon you Merchant *Jolly*, are you there ?

Joll. But stay, how come you, Niece, to be marri'd to Mr. *Truman ?*

Luc. I know not, Sir, as I was walking in the Garden.

Trum. j. I thought 't had been . . . but blest be the mistake,
What ever prove the Consequence to all
The less important fortunes of my life.

Joll. Nay, there 's no hurt done here neither—

Trum. s. No hurt, Colonel ? I 'l see him hang'd at my door before he shall have a beggarly—

Joll. Hark you, Mr. *Truman*, one word aside [*Talk aside.*] (for it is not necessary yet my wife should know so much.)

Aur. This foolish *Jane* (as I perceive by the story) has lost a Husband by staying for a Black patch.

Joll. Though I in rigour by my brothers Will might claim the forfeiture of her Estate, yet I assure you she shall have it all to the utmost farthing ; in a day like this, when Heaven bestows on me and on my daughter so unexpected and so fair a fortune, it were an ill return to rob an Orphan committed to my Charge.

Aur. My father's in the right.
And as he clears her Fortune, so will I
Her Honor. Hark you, Sir.

Trum. s. Why you speak, Sir, like a Vertuous Noble Gentleman, and do just as I should do my self in the same case ; it is—

Aur. 'Twas I upon my credit in a Veil ; [*to* Trum. *jun.* I 'l tell, if you please, all that you said, when you had read the Letter. But d' you hear, Mr. *Truman*, do not you believe now that I had a design to lie with you (if you had consented to my coming at midnight) for upon my faith I had not, but did it purely to try upon what terms your two Romantique Loves stood.

Cut. Ha, ha, ha ! but your Farce was not right methinks at the end.

Pun. Why how, pray ?

Cut. Why there should ha' been a Beating, a lusty Cudgeling to make it come off smartly with a twang at the tail.

Wor. Say you so ? h' as got a set of damnable brawny Servingmen.

Cut. At least *John Pudding* here should ha' been basted.

Wor. A curse upon him, he sav'd himself like a Rat behind the Hangings.

Trum. j. O *Lucia*, how shall I beg thy pardon
For my unjust suspitions of thy Virtue ?
Can you forgive a very Repentant sinner ?
Will a whole life of Penitence absolve me ?

Trum. s. 'Tis enough, good noble Colonel, I'm satisfi'd ; Come, *Dick*, I see 'twas Heaven's will, and she's a very worthy virtuous Gentlewoman ; I'm old and testy, but 'tis quickly over ; my blessing upon you both.

Cut. Why so, all's well of all sides then ; let me see, here's a brave Coupling day, onely poor *Worm* must lead a Monkish life of 't.

Aur. I'l have a Wife for him too, if you will, fine Mrs. *Jane* within ; [*aside.*] I'le undertake for her, I ha' set her a gog to day for a husband, the first comer has her sure.

Wor. I, but what Portion has she, Mrs. *Puny?* for we Captains o' the King's side ha' no need o' Wives with nothing.

Aur. Why Lozenges, and Half-moons, and a pair of Silverlac'd Shoes ; but that Tropes lost to you ; well, we'l see among us what may be done for her.

Joll. Come, let's go in to Supper; there never was such a day of Intrigues as this in one Family. If my true Brother had come in at last too after his being five years dead, 'twould ha' been a very Play. [*Exeunt.*

FINIS.

ABRAHAM COWLEY

EPILOGUE,

Spoken by

CUTTER.

[Without his Peruique.

ME-thinks a Vision bids me silence break,
    And some words to this Congregation speak,
So great and gay a one I ne'er did meet
At the Fifth Monarch's Court in Coleman-street.
But yet I wonder much not to espy a
Brother in all this Court call'd Zephaniah.
Bless me! where are we? What may this place be?
For I begin by Vision now to see
That this is a meer Theater; well then,
If't be e'en so I'l Cutter be again.

[Puts on his Peruique.

Not Cutter the pretended Cavaleer:
For to confess ingenuously here
To you who always of that Party were,
I never was of any; up and down
I rowld, a very Rakehell of this Town.
But now my Follies and my Faults are ended,
My Fortune and my Mind are both amended,
And if we may believe one who has fail'd before,
Our Author says He'l mend, that is, He'l write no more.

EPILOGUE.

At Court.

THe Madness of your People, and the Rage,
      You've seen too long upon the Publique Stage,
'Tis time at last (great Sir) 'tis time to see
Their Tragique Follies brought to Comedy.
If any blame the Lowness of our Scene,
We humbly think some Persons there have been
On the World's Theatre not long ago,
Much more too High, than here they are too Low.
And well we know that Comedy of old,
Did her Plebeian rank with so much Honour hold,
That it appear'd not then too Base or Light,
For the Great Scipio's Conquering hand to Write.
How e're, if such mean Persons seem too rude,
When into Royal presence they intrude,
Yet we shall hope a pardon to receive
From you, a Prince so practis'd to forgive;
A Prince, who with th' applause of Ear[t]h and Heaven,
The rudeness of the Vulgar has Forgiven.

FINIS.

A

DISCOURSE

By way of

VISION,

Concerning the Government of *Oliver Cromwell.*

I T was the Funeral day of the late man who made himself
to be called *Protectour*. And though I bore but little
affection, either to the memory of him, or to the trouble and
folly of all publick Pageantry, yet I was forced by the im-
portunity of my company to go along with them, and be a
Spectator of that solemnity, the expectation of which had been
so great, that it was said to have brought some very curious
persons (and no doubt singular Virtuoso's) as far as from the
Mount in *Cornwall*, and from the *Orcades*. I found there had
been much more cost bestowed than either the dead man, or
indeed Death it self could deserve. There was a mighty train
of black assistants, among which too divers Princes in the
persons of their Ambassadors (being infinitely afflicted for the
loss of their Brother) were pleased to attend ; the Herse was
Magnificent, the Idol Crowned, and (not to mention all other
Ceremonies which are practised at Royal interments, and
therefore by no means could be omitted here) the vast
multitude of Spectators made up, as it uses to do, no small
part of the Spectacle it self. But yet I know not how, the
whole was so managed, that, methoughts, it somewhat repre-
sented the life of him for whom it was made ; Much noise,
much tumult, much expence, much magnificence, much vain-
glory ; briefly, a great show, and yet after all this, but an
ill sight. At last, (for it seemed long to me, and like his short

Reign too, very tedious) the whole Scene past by, and I retired back to my Chamber, weary, and I think more melancholy than any of the Mourners. Where I began to reflect on the whole life of this Prodigious Man, and sometimes I was filled with horror and detestation of his actions, and sometimes I inclined a little to reverence and admiration of his courage, conduct and success; till by these different motions and agitations of mind, rocked, as it were, a sleep, I fell at last into this Vision, or if you please to call it but a Dream, I shall not take it ill, because the Father of Poets tells us, Even Dreams too are from God.

But sure it was no Dream; for I was suddenly transported afar off (whether in the body, or out of the body, like St. *Paul*, I know not) and found my self on the top of that famous Hill in the Island *Mona*, which has the prospect of three Great, and Not-long-since most happy Kingdoms. As soon as ever I lookt on them, the Not-long-since strook upon my Memory, and called forth the sad representation of all the Sins, and all the Miseries that had overwhelmed them these twenty years. And I wept bitterly for two or three hours, and when my present stock of moisture was all wasted, I fell a sighing for an hour more, and as soon as I recovered from my passion the use of speech and reason, I broke forth, as I remember (looking upon *England*) into this complaint.

1.

Ah, happy Isle, how art thou chang'd and curst,
        Since I was born, and knew thee first!
When Peace, which had forsook the World around,
(Frighted with noise, and the shrill Trumpets sound)
        Thee for a private place of rest,
        And a secure retirement chose
        Wherein to build her *Halcyon* Nest;
No wind durst stir abroad the Air to discompose.

2.

When all the riches of the Globe beside
        Flow'd in to Thee with every Tide;
When all that Nature did thy Soil deny,
The Growth was of thy fruitfull Industry,

ABRAHAM COWLEY

When all the proud and dreadfull Sea,
And all his Tributary-streams,
A constant Tribute paid to Thee.
When all the liquid World was one extended Thames.

3.

When Plenty in each Village did appear,
And Bounty was it's Steward there;
When Gold walkt free about in open view,
Ere it one Conquering parties Prisoner grew;
When the Religion of our State
Had Face and Substance with her Voice,
Ere she by 'er foolish Loves of late,
Like Eccho (once a Nymph) turn'd onely into Noise.

4.

When Men to Men respect and friendship bore,
And God with Reverence did adore;
When upon Earth no Kingdom could have shown
A happier Monarch to us than our own,
And yet his Subjects by him were
(Which is a Truth will hardly be
Receiv'd by any vulgar Ear,
A secret known to few) made happi'r ev'n than He.

5.

Thou doest a *Chaos*, and Confusion now,
A *Babel*, and a *Bedlam* grow,
And like a Frantick person thou doest tear
The Ornaments and Cloaths which thou shouldst wear,
And cut thy Limbs; and if we see
(Just as thy Barbarous *Britons* did)
Thy Body with Hypocrisie
Painted all o're, thou think'st, Thy naked shame is hid.

6.

The Nations, which envied thee erewhile,
Now laugh (too little 'tis to smile)
They laugh, and would have pitty'd thee (alas!)
But that thy Faults all Pity do surpass.

OLIVER CROMWEL

Art thou the Country which didst hate,
And mock the *French* Inconstancy?
And have we, have we seen of late
Less change of Habits there, than Governments in Thee?

7.

Unhappy Isle! No ship of thine at Sea,
    Was ever tost and torn like thee.
Thy naked Hulk loose on the Waves does beat,
The Rocks and Banks around her ruin threat;
        What did thy foolish Pilots ail,
        To lay the Compass quite aside?
        Without a Law or Rule to sail,
And rather take the winds, then Heavens to be their Guide?

8.

Yet, mighty God, yet, yet, we humbly crave,
    This floating Isle from shipwrack save;
And though to wash that Bloud which does it stain,
It well deserves to sink into the Main;
        Yet for the Royal Martyr's prayer
        (The Royal Martyr pray's we know)
        This guilty, perishing Vessel spare;
Hear but his Soul above, and not his bloud below.

I think, I should have gone on, but that I was interrupted
by a strange and terrible Apparition, for there appeared to me
(arising out of the earth, as I conceived) the figure of a man
taller than a Gyant, or indeed, than the shadow of any Gyant
in the evening. His body was naked, but that nakedness
adorn'd, or rather deform'd all over, with several figures, after
the manner of the antient *Britons*, painted upon it: and I
perceived that most of them were the representation of the late
battels in our civil Wars, and (if I be not much mistaken) it
was the battle of *Naseby* that was drawn upon his Breast. His
Eyes were like burning Brass, and there were three Crowns of
the same metal (as I guest) and that lookt as red-hot too, upon
his head. He held in his right hand a Sword that was yet
bloody, and never the less the Motto of it was *Pax quæritur
bello*, and in his left hand a thick Book, upon the back of

345

which was written in Letters of Gold, Acts, Ordinances, Protestations, Covenants, Engagements, Declarations, Remonstrances, &c. Though this suddain, unusual, and dreadful object might have quelled a greater courage than mine, yet so it pleased God (for there is nothing bolder then a man in a Vision) that I was not at all daunted, but askt him resolutely and briefly, What art thou? And he said, I am called The North-west Principality, His Highness, the Protector of the Common-wealth of *England, Scotland* and *Ireland,* and the Dominions belonging thereunto, for I am that Angell, to whom the Almighty has committed the Government of those three Kingdoms which thou seest from this place. And I answered and said, If it be so, Sir, it seems to me that for almost these twenty years past, your highness has been absent from your charge : for not only if any Angel, but if any wise and honest M[a]n had since that time been our Governour, we should not have wandred thus long in these laborious and endless Labyrinths of confusion, but either not have entered at all into them, or at least have returned back ere we had absolutely lost our way ; but in stead of your Highness, we have had since such a Protector as was his Predecessor *Richard* the Third to the King his Nephew ; for he presently slew the Common-wealth, which he pretended to protect, and set up himself in the place of it : a little less guilty indeed in one respect, because the other slew an Innocent, [and] this Man did but murder a Murderer. Such a Protector we have had as we would have been glad to have changed for any Enemy, and rather received a constant Turk, than this every moneths Apostate ; such a Protector as Man is to his Flocks, which he sheers, and sells, or devours himself ; and I would fain know, what the Wolf, which he protects him from, could do more. Such a Protector—and as I was proceeding, me-thoughts, his Highness began to put on a displeased and threatning countenance, as men use to do when their dearest Friends happen to be traduced in their company, which gave me the first rise of jealousy against him, for I did not believe that *Cromwel* among all his forein Correspondences had ever held any with Angels. However, I was not hardned enough yet to venture a quarrel with him then ; and therefore (as if I had spoken to the Protector himself in White-hall) I desired him that his Highness would please to pardon me, if I had unwittingly spoken any thing to the disparagement of a person, whose relations to his Highness I had not the honour to know. At which he told me, that he had no other concernment for his late Highness, than as he took him to be the greatest man that ever was of the *English* Nation, if not (said he) of the whole World, which gives me a just title to the defence of his reputation, since I now account my self, as it were a naturalized *English* Angel, by having had so long the management of the affairs of that Country. And pray Countryman, (said he, very kindly and very flatteringly) for I would not have you fall into the general errour of the World, that detests and decryes so extraordinary a Virtue, what can be more extraordinary than that a person of mean birth, no fortune, no eminent qualities of Body, which have sometimes, or of Mind, which have often raised men to the highest dignities, should have the courage to attempt, and the happiness to succeed in so improbable a design, as the destruction of one of the most antient, and most solidly founded Monarchies upon the Earth? that he should have the power or boldness to put his Prince and Master to an open and infamous death? to banish that numerous, and strongly-allied Family? to do all this under the name and wages of a Parliament; to trample upon them too as he pleased, and spurn them out of dores when he grew weary of them; to raise up a new and un-heard of Monster out of their Ashes; to stifle that in the very infancy, and set up himself above all things that ever were called Sovereign in *England*; to oppress all his Enemies by Armes, and all his Friends afterwards by Artifice; to serve all parties patiently for a while, and to command them victoriously at last; to over-run each corner of the three Nations, and overcome with equal facility both the riches of the South, and the poverty of the North; to be feared and courted by all forein Princes, and adopted a Brother to the gods of the earth; to call together Parliaments with a word of his Pen, and scatter them again with the Breath of his Mouth; to be humbly and daily petitioned that he would please to be hired at the rate of two millions a year, to be the Master of those who had hired him before to be their Servant; to have the Estates and Lives of three Kingdomes as much at his disposal, as was the little inheritance of his Father, and to be as noble and liberal in the spending of them ; and lastly (for there is no end of all the particulars of his glory) to bequeath all this with one word to his Posterity ; to die with peace at home, and triumph abroad; to be buried among Kings, and with more than Regal solemnity; and to leave a name behind him, not to be extinguisht, but with the whole World, which as it is now too little for his praises, so might have been too for his Conquests, if the short line of his Humane Life could have been stretcht out to the extent of his immortal designs?

By this speech I began to understand perfectly well what kind of Angel his pretended Highness was, and having fortified my self privately with a short mental Prayer, and with the sign of the Cross (not out of any superstition to the sign, but as a recognition of my Baptism in Christ) I grew a little bolder, and replyed in this manner; I should not venture to oppose what you are pleased to say in commendation of the late great, and (I confess) extraordinary person, but that I remember Christ forbids us to give assent to any other doctrine but what himself has taught us, even though it should be delivered by an Angel; and if such you be, Sir, it may be you have spoken all this rather to try than to tempt my frailty: For sure I am, that we must renounce or forget all the Laws of the New and Old Testament, and those which are the foundation of both, even the Laws of Moral and Natural Honesty, if we approve of the actions of that man whom I suppose you commend by Irony. There would be no end to instance in the particulars of all his wickedness; but to sum up a part of it briefly; What can be more extraordinarily wicked, than for a person, such as your self, qualifie him rightly, to endeavour not only to exalt himself above, but to trample upon all his equals and betters? to pretend freedom for all men, and under the help of that pretence to make all men his servants? to take Armes against Taxes of scarce two hundred thousand pounds a year, and to raise them himself to above two Millions? to quarrel for the losse of three or four Eares, and strike off three or four hundred Heads? to fight against an imaginary suspition of I know not what, two thousand Guards to be fetcht for the King, I know not from whence, and to keep up for himself no less than fourty thousand? to pretend the defence of Parliaments, and violently to dissolve all even of his own calling, and almost choosing? to undertake the Reformation of Religion, to rob it even to the very skin, and then to expose it naked to the rage of all Sects and Heresies? to set up Counsels of Rapine, and Courts of Murder? to fight against the King under a commission for him; to take him forceably out of the hands of those for whom he had conquered him; to draw him into his Net, with protestations and vows of fidelity, and when he had caught him in it, to butcher him, with as little shame, as Conscience, or Humanity, in the open face of the whole World? to receive a Commission for King and Parliament, to murder (as I said) the one, and destroy no less impudently the other? to fight against Monarchy when he declared for it, and declare against it when he contrived for it in his own person? to abase perfideously and supplant ingratefully his own General first, and afterwards most of those Officers, who with the loss of their Honour, and hazard of their Souls, had lifted him up to the top of his unreasonable ambitions? to break his faith with all Enemies, and with all friends equally? and to make no less frequent use of the most solemn Perjuries than the looser sort of People do of customary Oaths? to usurp three Kingdoms without any shadow of the least pretensions, and to govern them as unjustly as he got them? to set himself up as an Idol (which we know as St. *Paul* sayes, in it self is nothing) and make the very streets of *London*, like the Valley of *Hinnon*, by burning the bowels of men as a sacrifice to his *Moloch-ship*? to seek to entail this usurpation upon his Posterity, and with it an endless War upon the Nation? And lastly, by the severest Judgment of Almighty God, to dye hardned, and mad, and unrepentant, with the curses of the present Age, and the detestation of all to succeed.

Though I had much more to say (for the Life of man is so short, that it allows not time enough to speak against a Tyrant) yet because I had a mind to hear how my strange Adversary would behave himself upon this subject, and to give even the Devil (as they say) his right, and fair play in a Disputation, I stopt here, and expected (not without the frailty of a little fear) that he should have broke into a violent passion in behalf of his Favourite; but he on the contrary very calmly, and with the Dove-like innocency of a Serpent that was not yet warm'd enough to sting, thus replyed to me;

It is not so much out of my affection to that person whom

we discourse of (whose greatness is too solid to be shaken by the breath of any Oratory) as for your own sake (honest Countryman) whom I conceive to err, rather by mistake than out of malice, that I shall endeavour to reform your uncharitable and unjust opinion. And in the first place I must needs put you in mind of a Sentence of the most antient of the Heathen Divines, that you men are acquainted withall,

οὐχ [ὁσίη] κταμένοισιν ἐπ' ἀνδράσιν εὐχετάασθαι,

Tis wicked with insulting feet to tread
Upon the Monuments of the Dead.

And the intention of the reproof there, is no less proper for this Subject; for it is spoken to a person who was proud and insolent against those dead men to whom he had been humble and obedient whilst they lived. Your Highness may please (said I) to add the Verse that follows, as no less proper for this Subject,

Whom God's just doom and their own sins have sent
Already to their punishment.

But I take this to be the rule in the case, that when we fix any infamy upon deceased persons, it should not be done out of hatred to the Dead, but out of love and charity to the Living, that the curses which onely remain in mens thoughts, and dare not come forth against Tyrants (because they are Tyrants) whilst they are so, may at least be for ever setled and engraven upon their Memories, to deterr all others from the like wickedness, which else in the time of their foolish prosperity, the flattery of their own hearts, and of other mens Tongues, would not suffer them to perceive. Ambition is so subtil a Tempter, and the corruption of humane nature so susceptible of the temptation, that a man can hardly resist it, be he never so much forewarn'd of the evil consequences, much less if he find not onely the concurrence of the present, but the approbation too of following ages, which have the liberty to judge more freely. The mischief of Tyranny is too great, even in the shortest time that it can continue; it is endless and insupportable, if the Example be to reign too, and if a *Lambert* must be invited to follow the steps of a *Cromwell* as well by the voice

OLIVER CROMWEL

of Honour, as by the sight of power and riches. Though it may seem to some fantastically, yet was it wisely done of the *Syracusians*, to implead with the forms of their ordinary justice, to condemn, and destroy even the Statues of all their Tyrants; If it were possible to cut them out of all History, and to extinguish their very names, I am of opinion that it ought to be done; but since they have left behind them too deep wounds to be ever closed up without a Scar, at least let us set such a Mark upon their memory, that men of the same wicked inclinations may be no less affrighted with their lasting Ignominy, than enticed by their momentary glories. And that your Highness may perceive that I speak not all this out of any private animosity against the person of the late *Protector*, I assure you upon my faith, that I bear no more hatred to his name, than I do to that of *Marius* or *Sylla*, who never did me or any friend of mine the least injury; and with that transported by a holy fury, I fell into this sudden rapture.

1.

Curst be the Man (what do I wish? as though
    The wretch already were not so;
But curst on let him be) who thinks it brave
    And great, his Countrey to enslave.
    Who seeks to overpoise alone
    The Balance of a Nation;
    Against the whole but naked State,
Who in his own light Scale makes up with Arms the weight.

2.

Who of his Nation loves to be the first,
    Though at the rate of being worst.
Who would be rather a great Monster, than
    A well-proportion'd Man.
    The Son of Earth with hundred hands
    Upon his three-pil'd Mountain stands,
    Till Thunder strikes him from the sky;
The Son of Earth again in his Earths womb does lie.

ABRAHAM COWLEY

3.

What Bloud, Confusion, Ruine, to obtain
      A short and miserable Reign?
In what oblique and humble creeping wise
        Does the mischievous Serpent rise?
        But even his forked Tongue strikes dead,
        When h'as rear'd up his wicked Head,
        He murders with his mortal frown,
A *Basilisk* he grows if once he get a Crown.

4.

But no Guards can oppose assaulting Ears,
      Or undermining Tears.
No more than doors, or close-drawn Curtains keep
        The swarming Dreams out when we sleep.
        That bloudy Conscience too of his
        (For, oh, a Rebel Red-Coat 'tis)
        Does here his early Hell begin,
He sees his Slaves without, his Tyrant feels within.

5.

Let, Gracious God, let never more thine hand
      Lift up this rod against our Land.
A Tyrant is a Rod and Serpent too,
        And brings worse Plagues than *Egypt* knew.
        What Rivers stain'd with blood have been?
        What Storm and Hail-shot have we seen?
        What Sores deform'd the Ulcerous State?
What darkness to be felt has buried us of late?

6.

How has it snatcht our Flocks and Herds away?
      And made even of our Sons a prey?
What croaking Sects and Vermin has it sent
        The restless Nation to torment?
        What greedy Troups, what armed power
        Of Flies and Locusts to devour
        The Land which every where they fill?
Nor flie they, Lord, away; no, they devour it still.

OLIVER CROMWEL

7.

Come the eleventh Plague, rather than this should be;
    Come sink us rather in the Sea.
Come rather Pestilence and reap us down;
    Come Gods sword rather than our own.
    Let rather *Roman* come again,
    Or *Saxon*, *Norman*, or the *Dane*,
    In all the bonds we ever bore,
We griev'd, we sigh'd, we wept; we never blusht before.

8.

If by our sins the Divine Justice be
    Call'd to this last extremity,
Let some denouncing *Jonas* first be sent,
    To try if *England* can repent.
    Methinks at least some Prodigy,
    Some dreadful Comet from on high,
    Should terribly forewarn the Earth,
As of good Princes Deaths, so of a Tyrants birth.

Here the spirit of Verse beginning a little to fail, I stopt, and his Highness smiling, said, I was glad to see you engaged in the Enclosures of *Meeter*, for if you had staid in the open plain of Declaiming against the word Tyrant, I must have had patience for half a dozen hours, till you had tired your self as well as me. But pray, Countrey-man, to avoid this sciomachy, or imaginary Combat with words, let me know sir, what you mean by the name of Tyrant, for I remember that among your ancient Authors, not only all Kings, but even *Jupiter* himself (your *Juvans Pater*) is so termed, and perhaps as it was used formerly in a good sence, so we shall find it upon better consideration to be still a good thing for the benefit and peace of mankind, at least it will appear whether your interpretation of it may be justly applied to the person who is now the subject of our Discourse. I call him (said I) a Tyrant, who either intrudes himself forcibly into the Government of his fellow Citizens without any legal Authority over them, or who having a just Title to the Government of a people, abuses it to the destruction, or tormenting of them. So that all Tyrants are at the same time Usurpers, either of the whole or at least of a part of that power which they assume to themselves, and no less are they to be accounted Rebels, since no man can usurp Authority over others, but by rebelling against them who had it before, or at least against those Laws which were his Superiors; and in all these sences no History can afford us a more evident example of Tyranny, or more out of all possibility of excuse, or palliation, than that of the person whom you are pleased to defend, whether we consider his reiterated rebellions against all his Superiors, or his usurpation of the Supream power to himself, or his Tyranny in the exercise of it; and if lawful Princes have been esteemed Tyrants by not containing themselves within the bounds of those Laws which have been left them as the sphere of their Authority by their fore-fathers, what shall we say of that man, who having by right no power at all in this Nation, could not content himself with that which had satisfied the most ambitious of our Princes? nay, not with those vastly extended limits of Soveraity, which he (disdaining all that had been prescribed and observed before) was pleased (but of great modesty) to set to himself? not abstaining from Rebellion and Usurpation even against his own Laws as well as those of the Nation?

Hold friend (said his Highness, pulling me by my Arm) for I see your zeal is transporting you again; whether the Protector were a Tyrant in the exorbitant exercise of his power we shall see anon, it is requisite to examine first whether he were so in the usurpation of it. And I say, that not only He, but no man else ever was, or can be so; and that for these reasons. First, Because all power belongs only to God, who is the source and fountain of it, as Kings are of all Honours in their Dominions. Princes are but his Viceroys in the little Provinces of this World, and to some he gives their places for a few years, to some for their lives, and to others (upon ends or deserts best known to himself, or meerly for his undisputable good pleasure) he bestows as it were Leases upon them, and their posterity, for such a date of time as is prefixt in that Patent of their Destiny, which is not legible to you men below. Neither is it more unlawful for *Oliver* to succeed *Charles* in the Kingdom of *England*, when God so disposes of it, than it had been for him to have succeeded the Lord *Strafford* in the Lieutenancy of *Ireland*, if he had been appointed to it by the King then reigning. Men are in both the cases obliged to obey him whom they see actually invested with the Authority by that Sovereign from whom he ought to derive it, without disputing or examining the causes, either of the removal of the one, or the preferment of the other. Secondly, because all power is attained either by the Election and Consent of the people, and that takes away your objection of forcible intrusion; or else by a Conquest of them, and that gives such a legal Authority as you mention to be wanting in the usurpation of a Tyrant; so that either this Title is right, and then there are no Usurpers, or else it is a wrong one, and then there are none else but Usurpers, if you examine the Original pretences of the Princes of the World. Thirdly, (which quitting the dispute in general, is a particular justification of his Highness) the Government of *England* was totally broken and dissolved, and extinguisht by the confusions of a Civil War, so that his Highness could not be accused to have possest himself violently of the antient building of the Common-wealth, but to have prudently and peaceably built up a new one out of the ruines and ashes of the former; and he who after a deplorable shipwrack can with extraordinary Industry gather together the disperst and broken planks and pieces of it, and with no less wonderful Art and Felicity so rejoyn them as to make a new Vessel more tight and beautiful than the old one, deserves, no doubt, to have the command of her (even as his Highness had) by the desire of the Seamen and Passengers themselves. And do but consider Lastly (for I omit a multitude of weighty things that might be spoken upon this noble argument) do but consider seriously and impartially with your self, what admirable parts of wit and prudence, what indefatigable diligence and invincible courage must of necessity have concurred in the person of that man who from so contemptible beginnings (as I observed before) and through so many thousand difficulties, was able not only to make himself the greatest and most absolute Monarch of this Nation, but to add to it the entire Conquest of *Ireland* and *Scotland* (which the whole force of the World joyned with the *Roman* virtue could never attain to) and to Crown all this with illustrious and Heroical undertakings, and successes upon all our foreign Enemies; do but (I say again) consider this, and you will confess, that his prodigious merits were a better Title to Imperial Dignity, than the bloud of an hundred Royal Progenitors; and will rather lament that he lived not to overcome more Nations, than envy him the Conquest and Dominion of these. Who ever you are (said I, my indignation making me somewhat bolder) your discourse (methinks) becomes as little the person of a Tutelar Angel, as *Cromwels* actions did that of a Protector. It is upon these Principles, that all the great Crimes of the world have been committed, and most particularly those which I have had the misfortune to see in my own time, and in my own Countrey. If these be to be allowed, we must break up humane society, retire into the Woods, and equally there stand upon our Guards against our Brethren Mankind, and our Rebels the Wild Beasts. For if there can be no Usurpation upon the rights of a whole Nation, there can be none most certainly upon those of a private person; and if the robbers of Countreys be Gods Vice-gerents, there is no doubt but the Thieves and Bandito's, and Murderers, are his under Officers. It is true which you say, that God is the [source] and fountain of all power, and it is no less true that he is the Creator of Serpents as well as Angels; nor does his goodness fail of its ends even in the malice of his own Creatures. What power he suffers the Devil to exercise in this world, is too apparent by our daily experience, and by nothing more than the late monstrous iniquities which you dispute for, and patronize in *England*; but would you inferr from thence, that the power of the Devil is a just and lawful one, and that all men ought, as well as most men do, obey him? God is the fountain of all powers; but some flow from the right hand (as it were) of his Goodness, and others from the left hand of his Justice; and the World, like an Island between these two Rivers, is sometimes refresh[t] and nourisht by the one, and sometimes overrun and ruined by the other; and (to continue a little farther the Allegory) we are never overwhelmed with the latter, till either by our malice or negligence we have stopt and damm'd up the former. But to come a little closer to your argument, or rather the Image of an Argument, your similitude; If *Cromwell* had come to command in *Ireland* in the place of the late Lord *Strafford*, I should have yielded obedience, not for the equipage, and the strength, and the guards which he brought with him, but for the Commission which he should first have shewed me from our common Sovereign that sent him; and if he could have done that from God Almighty, I would have obeyed him too in *England*; but that he was so far from being able to do, that on the contrary, I read nothing but commands, and even publick Proclamations from God Almighty, not to admit him. Your second Argument is, that he had the same right for his Authority, that is the foundation of all others even the right of Conquest. Are we then so unhappy as to be conquered by the person, whom we hired at a daily rate, like a labourer, to conquer others for us? did we furnish him with Arms, onely to draw and try upon our Enemies (as we, it seems, falsely thought them) and keep them for ever sheath'd in the bowels of his Friends? did we fight for Liberty against our Prince, that we might become Slaves to our Servant? this is such an impudent pretence, as neither He nor any of his flatterers for him had ever the face to mention. Though it can hardly be spoken or thought of without passion, yet I shall, if you please, argue it more calmly than the case deserves. The right certainly of Conquest can only be exercised upon those against whom the War is declared, and the Victory obtained. So that no whole Nation can be said to be conquered but by foreign force. In all Civil wars men are so far from stating the quarrel against their Countrey, that they do it only against a person or party which they really believe, or at least pretend to be pernicious to it, neither can there be any just cause for the destruction of a part of the body, but when it is done for the preservation and safety of the whole. 'Tis our Countrey that raises men in the quarrel, our Countrey that arms, our Countrey that pays them, our Countrey that authorises the undertaking, and by that distinguishes it from rapine and murder; Lastly, 'tis our Countrey that directs and commands the Army, and is indeed their General. So that to say in Civil Wars that the prevailing party conquers their Countrey, is to say, the Countrey conquers it self. And if the General only of that party be the Conquerour, the Army by which he is made so, is no less conquered than the Army which is beaten, and have as little reason to triumph in that Victory, by which they lose both their Honour and Liberty. So that if *Cromwel* conquer'd any party, it was only that against which he was sent, and what that was, must appear by his Commission. It was (says that) against a company of evil Counsellors, and disaffected persons, who kept the King from a good intelligence and conjunction with his People. It was not then against the People. It is so far from being so, that even of that party which was beaten, the Conquest did not belong to *Cromwel* but to the Parliament which employed him in their Service, or rather indeed to the King and Parliament, for whose Service, (if there had been any faith in mens vows and protestations) the Wars were undertaken. Merciful God! did the right of this miserable Conquest remain then in His Majesty, and didst thou suffer him to be destroyed with more barbarity than if he had been conquered even by Savages and Cannibals? was it for King and Parliament that we fought, and has it fared with them just as with the Army which we fought against, the one part being slain, and the other fled? It appears therefore plainly, that *Cromwel* was not a Conqueror, but a Thief and Robber of the Rights of the King and Parliament, and an Usurper upon those of the People. I do not here deny Conquest to be sometimes (though it be very rarely) a true title, but I deny this to be a true Conquest. Sure I am, that the race of our Princes came not in by such a one. One Nation may conquer another sometimes justly, and if it be unjustly, yet still it is a true Conquest, and they are to answer for the injustice only to God Almighty (having nothing else in authority above them) and not as particular Rebels to their Countrey, which is, and ought always to be their Superior and their Lord. If perhaps we find Usurpation in stead of Conquest in the Original Titles of some Royal Families abroad (as no doubt there have been many Usurpers before ours, though none in so impudent and execrable a manner) all I can say for them is, that their Title was very weak, till by length of time, and the death of all juster pretenders, it became to be the true, because it was the onely one. Your third defence of his Highness (as your Highness pleases to call him) enters in most seasonably after his pretence of Conquest, for then a man may say any thing. The Government was broken; Who broke it? It was dissolved; Who dissolved it? It was extinguisht; Who was it but *Cromwell*, who not onely put out the Light, but cast away even the very snuff of it? As if a man should murder a whole

OLIVER CROMWEL

Family, and then possesse himself of the House, because 'tis better that He, than that onely Rats should live there. Jesus God! (said I, and at that word I perceived my pretended Angel to give a start and trembled, but I took no notice of it, and went on) this were a wicked pretension even though the whole Family were destroyed, but the Heirs (blessed be God) are yet surviving, and likely to out-live all Heirs of their dispossessors, besides their Infamy. *Rode Caper vitem*, &c. There will be yet wine enough left for the Sacrifice of those wild Beasts that have made so much spoil in the Vineyard. But did *Cromwell* think, like *Nero*, to set the City on fire, onely that he might have the honour of being founder of a new and more beautiful one? He could not have such a shadow of Virtue in his wickedness; he meant onely to rob more securely and more richly in midst of the combustion; he little thought then that he should ever have been able to make himself Master of the Palace, as well as plunder the Goods of the Common-wealth. He was glad to see the publick Vessel (the Sovereign of the Seas) in as desperate a condition as his own little Canon, and thought onely with some scattered planks of that great ship-wrack to make a better Fisherboat for himself. But when he saw that by the drowning of the Master (whom he himself treacherously knockt on the head as he was swimming for his life) by the flight and dispersion of others, and cowardly patience of the remaining company, that all was abandoned to his pleasure, with the old Hulk and new mis-shapen and disagreeing pieces of his own, he made up with much adoe that Piratical Vessel which we have seen him command, and which, how tight indeed it was, may best be judged by it's perpetual Leaking. First then (much more wicked than those foolish daughters in the Fable, who cut their old Father into pieces, in hope by charms and witchcraft to make him young and lusty again) this man endeavoured to destroy the Building, before he could imagine in what manner, with what materials, by what workmen, or what Architect it was to be rebuilt. Secondly, if he had dreamt himself to be able to revive that body which he had killed, yet it had been but the insupportable insolence of an ignorant Mountebanck; And Thirdly (which concerns us nearest) that very new thing which he made out of the ruines of the old, is no more like the Original, either for beauty, use, or duration, than an artificial Plant raised by the fire of a Chymist is comparable to the true and natural one which he first burnt, that out of the ashes of it he might produce an imperfect similitude of his own making. Your last argument is such (when reduced to Syllogism) that the Major Proposition of it would make strange work in the World, if it were received for truth; to wit, that he who has the best parts in a Nation, has the right of being King over it. We had enough to do here of old with the contention between two branches of the same Family, what would become of us when every man in *England* should lay his claim to the Government? and truely if *Cromwell* should have commenced his plea when he seems to have begun his ambition, there were few persons besides that might not at the same time have put in theirs too. But his Deserts I suppose you will date from the same terme that I do his great Demerits, that is, from the beginning of our late calamities, (for, as for his private faults before, I can onely wish (and that with as much Charity to him as to the publick) that he had continued in them till his death, rather than changed them for those of his latter dayes) and therefore we must begin the consideration of his greatness from the unlucky *Æra* of our own misfortunes, which puts me in mind of what was said less truely of *Pompey* the Great, *Nostra Miseria Magnus es*. But because the general ground of your argumentation consists in this, that all men who are the effecters of extraordinary mutations in the world, must needs have extraordinary forces of Nature by which they are enabled to turn about, as they please, so great a Wheel; I shall speak first a few words upon this universal proposition, which seems so reasonable, and is so popular, before I descend to the particular examination of the eminences of that person which is in question.

I have often observed (with all submission and resignation of spirit to the inscrutable mysteries of Eternal Providence) that when the fulness and maturity of time is come that produces the great confusions and changes in the World, it usually pleases God to make it appear by the manner of them, that they are not the effects of humane force or policy, but of the Divine Justice and Predestination, and though we see a Man, like that which we call Jack of the Clock-house, striking, as it were, the Hour of that fulness of time, yet our reason must needs be convinced, that his hand is moved by some secret, and to us who stand without, invisible direction. And the stream of the Current is then so violent, that the strongest men in the World cannot draw up against it, and none are so weak, but they may sail down with it. These are the Spring-Tides of publick affairs which we see often happen, but seek in vain to discover any certain causes,

> ——*Omnia fluminis*
> *Ritu feruntur, nunc medio alveo*
> *Cum pace delabentis Hetruscum*
> *In mare, nunc lapides adesos*
> *Stirpesque raptas, & pecus & domos*
> *Volventis una, non sine montium*
> *Clamore, vicinæque silvæ;*
> *Cum fera Diluvies quietos*
> *Irritat amnes,*—— .

Hor. Car.
3. 29.

and one man then, by malitiously opening all the Sluces that he can come at, can never be the sole Author of all this (though he may be as guilty as if really he were, by intending and imagining to be so) but it is God that breaks up the Flood-Gates of so general a Deluge, and all the art then and industry of mankind is not sufficient to raise up Dikes and Ramparts against it. In such a time it was as this, that not all the wisdom and power of the Roman Senate, nor the wit and eloquence of *Cicero*, nor the Courage and Virtue of *Brutus* was able to defend their Country or themselves against the unexperienced rashness of a beardless Boy, and the loose rage of a voluptuous Madman. The valour and prudent Counsels on the one side are made fruitless, and the errours and cowardize on the other ha[r]mless, by unexpected accidents. The one General saves his life, and gains the whole World, by a very dream; and the other loses both at once by a little mistake of the shortness of his sight. And though this be not alwaies so, for we see that in the translation of the great Monarchies from one to another, it pleased God to make choice of the most Eminent men in Nature, as *Cyrus, Alexander, Scipio* and his contemporaries, for his chief instruments and actors in so admirable a work (the end of this being not only to destroy or punish one Nation, which may be done by the worst of mankind, but to exalt and bless another, which is only to be effected by great and virtuous persons) yet when God only intends the temporary chastisement of a people, he does not raise up his servant *Cyrus* (as he himself is pleased to call him) or an *Alexander* (who had as many virtues to do good, as vices to do harm) but he makes the *Massanelloes*, and the *Johns* of *Leyden* the instruments of his vengeance, that the power of the Almighty might be more evident by the weakness of the means which he chooses to demonstrate it. He did not assemble the Serpents and the Monsters of Afrique to correct the pride of the *Egyptians*, but called for his Armies of Locusts out of *Æthiopia*, and formed new ones of Vermine out of the very dust; and because you see a whole Country destroyed by these, will you argue from thence they must needs have had both the craft of the Foxes, and the courage of Lions? It is easie to apply this general observation to the particular case of our troubles in *England*, and that they seem only to be meant for a temporary chastisement of our sins, and not for a total abolishment of the old, and introduction of a new Government, appears probabl[e] to me from these considerations, as far as we may be bold to make a judgment of the will of God in future events. First, because he has suffered nothing to settle or take root in the place of that which hath been so unwisely and unjustly removed, that none of these untempered Mortars can hold out against the next blast of Wind, nor any stone stick to a stone, till that which these Foolish Builders have refused, be made again the Head of the Corner. For when the indisposed and long tormented Commonwealth has wearied and spent it self almost to nothing with the chargeable, various, and dangerous experiments of several Mountebanks, it is to be supposed, it will have the wit at last to send for a true Physician, especially when it sees (which is the second consideration) most evidently (as it now begins to do, and will do every day more and more, and might have done perfectly long since) that no usurpation (under what name or pretext soever) can be kept up without open force, nor force without the continuance of those oppressions upon the people, which will at last tire out their patience, though it be great even to stupidity. They cannot be so dull (when poverty and hunger begins to whet their understanding) as not to find out this no extraordinary mystery, that 'tis madness in a Nation to pay three Millions a year for the maintaining of their servitude under Tyrants, when they might live free for nothing under their Princes. This, I say, will not alwayes ly hid, even to the slowest capacities, and the next truth they will discover afterwards, is, that a whole people can never have the will without having at the same time the power to redeem themselves. Thirdly, it does not look (me-thinks) as if God had forsaken the family of that man, from whom he has raised up five Children, of as Eminent virtue, and all other commendable qualities, as ever lived perhaps (for so many together, and so young) in any other family in the whole world. Especially, if we adde hereto this consideration, that by protecting and preserving some of them already through as great danger[s] as ever were past with safety, either by Prince or private person, he has given them already (as we may reasonably hope it to be meant) a promise and earnest of his future favours. And lastly (to return closely to the discourse from which I have a little digrest) because I see nothing of those excellent parts of nature, and mixture of Merit with their Vices in the late disturbers of our peace and happiness, that uses to be found in the persons of those who are born for the erection of new Empires. And I confess I finde nothing of that kind, no not any shadow (taking away the false light of some prosperity) in the man whom you extol for the first example of it. And certainly all Virtues being rightly devided into Moral and Intellectual, I know not how we can better judge of the former than by mens actions, or of the latter than by their Writings or Speeches. As for these latter (which are least in merit, or rather which are only the instruments of mischief where the other are wanting) I think you can hardly pick out the name of a man who ever was called Great, besides him we are now speaking of, who never left the memory behinde him of one wise or witty Apothegm even amongst his Domestique Servants or greatest Flatterers. That little in print which remains upon a sad record for him, is such, as a Satyre against him would not have made him say, for fear of transgressing too much the rules of Probability. I know not what you can produce for the justification of his parts in this kind, but his having been able to deceive so many particular persons, and so many whole parties; which if you please to take notice of for the advantage of his Intellectuals, I desire you to allow me the liberty to do so too, when I am to speak of his Morals. The truth of the thing is this, That if Craft be Wisdom, and Dissimulation Wit, (assisted both and improved with Hypocrisies and Perjuries) I must not deny him to have been singular in both; but so gross was the manner in which he made use of them, that as wise-men ought not to have believed him at first, so no man was Fool enough to believe him at last; neither did any man seem to do it, but those who thought they gained as much by that dissembling, as he did by his. His very actings of Godliness grew at last as ridiculous, as if a Player, by putting on a Gown, should think he represented excellently a Woman, though his Beard at the same time were seen by all the Spectators. If you ask me why they did not hiss, and explode him off the stage, I can only answer, that they durst not do so, because the Actors and the Door-keepers were too strong for the Company. I must confess that by these arts (how grosly soever managed, as by Hypocritical praying, and silly preaching, by unmanly tears and whinings, by falshoods and perjuries even Diabolical) he had at first the good fortune (as men call it, that is the ill-Fortune) to attain his ends; but it was because his ends were so unreasonable, that no humane reason could foresee them; which made them who had to do with him believe that he was rather a well meaning and deluded Bigot, than a crafty and malicious Impostor, that these arts were helpt by an Indefatigable industry (as you term it) I am so far from doubting, that I intended to object that diligence as the worst of his Crimes. It makes me almost mad when I hear a man commended for his diligence in wickedness. If I were his Son, I should wish to God he had been a more lazy person, and that we might have found him sleeping at the hours when other men are ordinarily waking, rather than waking for those ends of his when other men were ordinarily asleep; how diligent the wicked are the Scripture often tell[s] us; *Their feet run to evill, and they make haste to shed innocent bloud, Isa.* 59. 7. *He travels with iniquity, Psal.* 7. 14. *He deviseth mischief upon his bed, Psal.* 34. 4. *They search out iniquity, they accomplish a diligent search, Psal.* 64. 6. and in

OLIVER CROMWEL

a multitude of other places. And would it not seem ridiculous to praise a Wolf for his watchfulness, and for his indefatigable industry in ranging all night about the Country, whilst the sheep, and perhaps the shepherd, and perhaps the very Dogs too are all asleep?

The *Chartreux* wants the warning of a Bell
To call him to the duties of his Cell;
There needs no noise at all t'awaken sin,
Th' Adulterer and the Thief his Larum has within.

And if the diligence of wicked persons be so much to be blamed, as that it is only an Emphasis and Exaggeration of their wickedness, I see not how their courage can avoid the same censure. If the undertaking bold, and vast, and unreasonable designs can deserve that honourable name, I am sure *Faux* and his fellow Gun-powder Fiends will have cause to pretend, though not an equal, yet at least the next place of Honour, neither can I doubt but if they too had succeeded, they would have found their Applauders and Admirers. It was bold unquestionably for a man in defiance of all Humane and Divine Laws (and with so little probability of a long impunity) so publiquely and so outragiously to murder his Master; It was bold with so much insolence and affront to expel and disperse all the chief Partners of his guilt, and Creators of his power; It was bold to violate so openly and so scornfully all Acts and Constitutions of a Nation, and afterwards even of his own making; it was bold to Assume the Authority of calling, and bolder yet of breaking so many Parliaments; it was bold to trample upon the patience of his own, and provoke that of all neighbouring Countreys; It was bold, I say, above all boldnesses, to Usurp this Tyranny to himself, and impudent above all impudences to endeavour to transmit it to his posterity. But all this boldness is so far from being a sign of manly courage, (which dares not transgress the rules of any other Virtue) that it is only a Demonstration of Brutish Madness or Diabolical Possession. In both which last cases there uses frequent examples to appear of such extraordinary force as may justly seem more wonderful and astonishing than the actions of *Cromwel*, neither is it stranger to believe that a whole Nation should not be able to govern

365

ABRAHAM COWLEY

Him and a Mad Army, than that five or six Men should not be strong enough to bind a distracted Girl. There is no man ever succeeds in one wickedness but it gives him the boldness to attempt a greater; 'Twas boldly done of *Nero* to kill his Mother, and all the chief Nobility of the Empire; 'twas boldly done to set the Metropolis of the Whole world on fire, and undauntedly play upon his Harp whilst he saw it burning; I could reckon up five hundred boldnesses of that great person (for why should not He too be called so?) who wanted when he was to die, that courage which could hardly have failed any Woman in the like necessity. It would look (I must confess) like Envy or too much partiality if I should say that personal kind of courage had been deficient in the man we speak of; I am confident it was not, and yet I may venture I think to affirm, that no man ever bore the honour of so many victories, at the rate of fewer wounds or dangers of his own body, and though his valour might perhaps have given him a just pretension to one of the first charges in an Army, it could not certainly be a sufficient ground for a Title to the command of three Nations. What then shall we say? that he did all this by Witchcraft? He did so indeed in a great measure by a sin that is called like it in the Scriptures. But truely and unpassionately reflecting upon the advantages of his person which might be thought to have produced those of his Fortune, I can espy no other but extraordinary Diligence and infinite Dissimulation; and believe he was exalted above his Nation, partly by his own Faults, but chiefly for Ours. We have brought him thus briefly (not through all his Labyrinths) to the Supreme Usurpt Authority, and because you say it was great pity he did not live to command more Kingdoms, be pleased to let me represent to you in a few words, how well I conceive he governed these. And we will divide the consideration into that of his foreign and domestique Actions. The first of his foreign was a peace with our Brethren of *Holland* (who were the first of our neighbours that God chastised for having had so great a hand in the encouraging and abetting our troubles at home) who would not imagine at first glympse that this had been the most virtuous and laudable deed that his whole life could have made any parade of? but no man can look upon all the circumstances without perceiving,

366

that it was purely the sale and sacrificing of the greatest
advantages that this Countrey could ever hope, and was ready
to reap from a foreign War, to the private Interests of his
Covetousness and Ambition, and the security of his new and
unsetled Usurpation. No sooner is that danger past, but this
Beatus Pacificus is kindling a fire in the Northern World, and
carrying a War two thousand miles off Westwards. Two
millions a year (besides all the Vales of his Protectorship) is
as little capable to suffice now either his Avarice or Prodigality,
as the two hundred pounds were that he was born to. He
must have his prey of the whole *Indies* both by Sea and Land,
this great Aligator. To satisfie our Anti-*Solomon* (who has
made Silver almost as rare as Gold, and Gold as precious stones
in his new *Jerusalem*) we must go, ten thousand of his slaves,
to fetch him riches from his fantastical *Ophir*. And because
his flatterers brag of him as the most fortunate Prince (the
Faustus as well as *Sylla* of our Nation, whom God never
forsook in any of his undertakings) I desire them to consider,
how since the *English* name was ever heard of, it never
received so great and so infamous a blow as under the
imprudent conduct of this unlucky *Faustus* ; and herein let
me admire the justice of God in this circumstance, that they
who had enslaved their Countrey (though a great Army, which
I wish may be observed by ours with trembling) should be so
shamefully defeated by the hands of forty slaves. It was very
ridiculous to see how prettily they endeavoured to hide this
ignominy under the great name of the Conquest of *Jamaica*,
as if a defeated Army should have the impudence to brag
afterwards of the Victory, because, though they had fled out
of the Field of Battel, yet they quartered that night in a
Village of the Enemies. The War with *Spain* was a necessary
consequence of this folly, and how much we have gotten by it,
let the Custom-house and Exchange inform you ; and if he
please to boast of the taking a part of the Silver Fleet, (which
indeed no body else but he, who was the sole gainer, has cause
to do) at least, let him give leave to the rest of the Nation
(which is the only loser) to complain of the loss of twelve
hundred of her ships. But because it may here perhaps be
answered, that his successes nearer home have extinguisht the
disgrace of so remote miscarriages, and that *Dunkirk* ought

more to be remembred for his glory, than St. *Domingo* for his disadvantage ; I must confess, as to the honour of the *English* courage, that they were not wanting upon that occasion (excepting only the fault of serving at least indirectly against their Master) to the upholding of the renown of their warlike Ancestors. But for his particular share of it, who sate still at home, and exposed them so frankly abroad, I can only say, that for less money than he in the short time of his Reign exacted from his fellow Subjects, some of our former Princes (with the daily hazard of their own persons) have added to the Dominion of *England* not only one Town, but even a greater Kingdom than it self. And this being all considerable as concerning his enterprises abroad, let us examine in the next place, how much we owe him for his Justice and good Government at home. And first he found the Common-wealth (as they then called it) in a ready stock of about 800ᵐ pounds, he left the Common-wealth (as he had the impudent raillery still to call it) some two Millions and an half in debt. He found our Trade very much decayed indeed, in comparison of the golden times of our late Princes ; he left it as much again more decay'd than he found it ; and yet not only no Prince in *England*, but no Tyrant in the World ever sought out more base or infamous means to raise moneys. I shall only instance in one that he put in practice, and another that he attempted, but was frighted from the execution (even He) by the infamy of it. That which he put in practice was Decimation ; which was the most impudent breach of all publick Faith that the whole Nation had given, and all private capitulations which himself had made, as the Nations General and Servant, that can be found out (I believe) in all History, from any of the most barbarous Generals of the most barbarous People. Which because it has been most excellently and most largely laid open by a whole Book written upon that Subject, I shall only desire you here to remember the thing in general, and to be pleased to look upon that Author when you would recollect all the particulars and circumstances of the iniquity. The other design of raising a present sum of money, which he violently persued, but durst not put in execution, was by the calling in and establishment of the *Jews* at *London* ; from which he was rebuted by the universal outcry of the Divines, and even of

OLIVER CROMWEL

the Citizens too, who took it ill that a considerable number at least amongst themselves were not thought *Jews* enough by their own *Herod*. And for this design, they say, he invented (Oh Antichrist! Πονηρόν and ὁ Πονηρός!) to sell St. *Pauls* to them for a Synagogue, if their purses and devotions could have reacht to the purchase. And this indeed if he had done only to reward that Nation which had given the first noble example of crucifying their King, it might have had some appearance of Gratitude, but he did it only for love of their Mammon; and would have sold afterwards for as much more St. *Peters* (even at his own *Westminster*) to the Turks for a *Mosquito*. Such was his extraordinary Piety to God, that he desired he might be worshipped in all manners, excepting only that heathenish way of the Common-Prayer Book. But what do I speak of his wicked inventions for getting money? when every penny that for almost five years he took every day from every man living in *England*, *Scotland* and *Ireland*, was as much Robbery as if it had been taken by a Thief upon the High-ways. Was it not so? or can any man think that *Cromwell* with the assistance of his Forces and Mosse-Troopers, had more right to the command of all mens purses, than he might have had to any ones whom he had met and been too strong for upon a Road? and yet when this came in the case of Mr. *Coney*, to be disputed by a legal tryal, he (which was the highest act of Tyranny that ever was seen in *England*) not only discouraged and threatned, but violently imprisoned the Council of the Plaintiff; that is, he shut up the Law it self close Prisoner, that no man might have relief from, or access to it. And it ought to be remembred, that this was done by those men, who a few years before had so bitterly decried, and openly opposed the Kings regular and formal way of proceeding in the trial of a little Ship-money. But though we lost the benefit of our old Courts of Justice, it cannot be denied that he set up new ones; and such they were, that as no virtuous Prince before would, so no ill one durst erect. What, have we lived so many hundred years under such a form of Justice as has been able regularly to punish all men that offended against it, and is it so deficient just now, that we must seek out new ways how to proceed against offenders? The reason which can only be given in nature for a necessity of this, is, because those things are now made Crimes, which were never esteemed so in former ages; and there must needs be a new Court set up to punish that, which all the old ones were bound to protect and reward. But I am so far from declaiming (as you call it) against these wickednesses (which if I should undertake to do, I should never get to the Peroration) that you see I only give a hint of some few, and pass over the rest as things that are too many to be numbred, and must onely be weighed in gross. Let any man shew me (for though I pretend not to much reading, I will defie him in all History) let any man shew me (I say) an Example of any Nation in the World (though much greater than ours) where there have in the space of four years been made so many Prisoners only out of the endless jealousies of one Tyrants guilty imagination. I grant you that *Marius* and *Sylla*, and the accursed Triumvirate after them, put more People to death, but the reason I think partly was, because in those times that had a mixture of some honour with their madness, they thought it a more civil revenge against a *Roman* to take away his life, than to take away his Liberty. But truly in the point of murder too, we have little reason to think that our late Tyranny has been deficient to the examples that have ever been set it in other Countreys. Our Judges and our Courts of Justice have not been idle; And to omit the whole reign of our late King (till the beginning of the War) in which no drop of blood was ever drawn but from two or three Ears, I think the longest time of our worst Princes scarce saw many more Executions than the short one of our blest Reformer. And we saw, and smelt in our open streets, (as I markt to you at first) the broyling of humane bowels as a burnt Offering of a sweet Savour to our Idol; but all murdering, and all torturing (though after the subtilest invention of his Predecessors of *Sicilie*) is more Humane and more Supportable, than his selling of Christians, Englishmen, Gentlemen; his selling of them (oh monstrous! oh incredible!) to be slaves in *America*. If his whole life could be reproacht with no other action, yet this alone would weigh down all the multiplicity of Crimes in any of our Tyrants; and I dare only touch, without stopping or insisting upon so insolent and so execrable a cruelty, for fear of falling into so violent (though a just) Passion, as would make me exceed that temper and moderation which I resolve to observe in this Discourse with you. These are great calamities; but even these are not the most insupportable that we have endured; for so it is, that the scorn and mockery and insultings of an Enemy, are more painful than the deepest wounds of his serious fury. This Man was wanton and merry (unwittily and ungracefully merry) with our sufferings; He loved to say and do senceless and fantastical things, onely to shew his power of doing or saying any thing. It would ill befit mine, or any civil Mouth, to repeat those words which he spoke concerning the most sacred of our *English* Laws, the Petition of Right, and *Magna Charta*. To day you should see him ranting so wildly, that no body durst come near him, the morrow flinging of cushions, and playing at Snow-balls with his Servants. This moneth he assembles a Parliament, and professes himself with humble tears to be onely their Servant and their Minister; the next moneth he swears By the Living God, that he will turn them out of dores, and he does so, in his princely way of threatning, bidding them, Turn the buckles of their girdles behind them. The representative of a whole, nay of three whole Nations, was in his esteem so contemptible a meeting, that he thought the affronting and expelling of them to be a thing of so little consequence, as not to deserve that he should advise with any mortal man about it. What shall we call this? Boldness, or Bruitishness? Rashness, or Phrensie? there is no name can come up to it, and therefore we must leave it without one. Now a Parliament must be chosen in the new manner, next time in the old form, but all cashiered still after the newest mode. Now he will govern by Major Generals, now by One House, now by Another House, now by No House; now the freak takes him, and he makes seventy Peers of the Land at one clap (*Extempore*, and *stans pede in uno*) and to manifest the absolute power of the Potter, he chooses not onely the worst Clay he could find, but picks up even the Durt and Mire, to form out of it his Vessels of Honour. It was said antiently of Fortune, that when she had a mind to be merry and to divert her self, she was wont to raise up such kind of people to the highest Dignities. This Son of fortune, *Cromwell* (who was himself one of the primest of her Jests) found out the true haut-goust of this pleasure, and rejoyced in the extravagance of his wayes as the fullest demonstration of his uncontroulable Soveraity. Good God! What have we seen? and what have we suffer'd? What do all these actions signifie? What do they say aloud to the whole Nation, but this (even as plainly as if it were proclaimed by Heralds through the streets of *London*) You are Slaves and Fools, and so Ile use you? These are briefly a part of those merits which you lament to have wanted the reward of more Kingdomes, and suppose that if he had lived longer he might have had them; Which I am so far from concurring to, that I believe his seasonable dying to have been a greater good fortune to him than all the victories and prosperities of his Life. For he seemed evidently (methinks) to be near the end of his deceitfull Glories; his own Army grew at last as weary of him as the rest of the People; and I never past of late before his Palace (His, do I call it? I ask God and the King pardon) but I never past of late before Whitehall without reading upon the Gate of it, *Mene, Mene, Tekel, Upharsin*. But it pleased God to take him from the ordinary Courts of Men, and Juries of his Peers, to his own High Court of Justice, which being more mercifull than Ours below, there is a little room yet left for the hope of his friends, if he have any; though the outward unrepentance of his death afford but small materials for the work of Charity, especially if he designed even then to Entail his own injustice upon his Children, and by it inextricable confusions and Civil Wars upon the Nation. But here's at last an end of him; And where's now the fruit of all that blood and calamity which his ambition has cost the World? Where is it? Why, his Son (you'l say) has the whole Crop; I doubt he will find it quickly Blasted; I have nothing to say against the Gentleman, or any living of his family, on the contrary I wish him better fortune than to have a long and unquiet possession of his Masters inheritance. Whatsoever I have spoken against his Father, is that which I should have thought (though Decency perhaps might have hindred me from saying it) even against mine Own, if I had been so unhappy, as that Mine by the same wayes should have left me three Kingdoms.

Here I stopt; and my pretended Protector, who, I expected, should have been very angry, fell a laughing; it seems at the simplicity of my discourse, for thus he replied: You seem to pretend extremely to the old obsolete rules of Virtue and

OLIVER CROMWEL

Conscience, which makes me doubt very much whether from this vast prospect of three Kingdoms you can show me any acres of your own. But these are so far from making you a Prince, that I am afraid your friends will never have the contentment to see you so much as a Justice of Peace in your own Countrey. For this I perceive which you call Virtue, is nothing else but either the frowardness of a Cynick, or the laziness of an Epicurean. I am glad you allow me at least Artfull Dissimulation, and unwearied Diligence in my *Hero*, and I assure you that he whose Life is constantly drawn by those two, shall never be misled out of the way of Greatness. But I see you are a Pedant, and Platonical Statesman, a Theoretical Common-wealths-man, an Utopian Dreamer. Was ever Riches gotten by your Golden Mediocrities? or the Supreme place attained to by Virtues that must not stir out of the middle? Do you study *Aristotles* Politiques, and write, if you please, Comments upon them, and let another but practise *Machiavil*, and let us see then which of you two will come to the greatest preferments. If the desire of rule and superiority be a Virtue (as sure I am it is more imprinted in human Nature than any of your Lethargical Morals; and what is the Virtue of any Creature but the exercise of those powers and Inclinations which God has infused into it?) if that (I say) be Virtue, we ought not to esteem any thing Vice, which is the most proper, if not the onely means of attaining of it.

> It is a Truth so certain, and so clear,
> That to the first-born Man it did appear;
> Did not, the mighty Heir, the noble *Cain*,
> By the fresh Laws of Nature taught, disdain
> That (though a Brother) any one should be
> A greater Favourite to God than He?
> He strook him down; and, so (said He) so fell
> The Sheep which thou didst Sacrifice so well.
> Since all the fullest Sheaves which I could bring,
> Since all were Blasted in the Offering,
> Lest God should my next Victime too despise,
> The acceptable Priest I'le Sacrifice.
> Hence Coward Fears; for the first Blood so spilt
> As a Reward, He the first City built.

ABRAHAM COWLEY

'Twas a beginning generous and high,
Fit for a Grand-Child of the Deity.
So well advanc'd, 'twas pity there he staid;
One step of Glory more he should have made,
And to the utmost bounds of Greatness gone;
Had *Adam* too been kill'd, He might have Reign'd Alone.
One Brother's death, What do I mean to name,
A small Oblation to Revenge and Fame?
The mighty-soul'd *Abimelec* to shew
What for high place a higher Spirit can do,
A Hecatomb almost of Brethren slew,
And seventy times in nearest blood he dy'd
(To make it hold) his Royal Purple Pride.
Why do I name the Lordly Creature Man?
The weak, the mild, the Coward Woman, can,
When to a Crown she cuts her sacred way,
All that oppose with Manlike Courage slay.
So *Athaliah*, when she saw her Son,
And with his Life her dearer Greatness gone,
With a Majestique fury slaughter'd all
Whom high birth might to high pretences call.
Since he was dead who all her power sustain'd,
Resolv'd to reign alone; Resolv'd, and Reign'd.
In vain her Sex, in vain the Laws withstood,
In vain the sacred plea of *David*'s Blood,
A noble, and a bold contention, She,
(One Woman) undertook with Destiny.
She to pluck down, Destiny to uphold
(Oblig'd by holy Oracles of old)
The great *Jessæan* race on *Juda*'s Throne;
Till 'twas at last an equal Wager grown,
Scarce Fate, with much adoe, the Better got by One.
Tell me not she her self at last was slain;
Did she not first seven years (a Life-time) reign?
Seven royal years t' a publick spirit will seem
More than the private Life of a *Methusalem*.
'Tis Godlike to be Great; and as they say
A thousand years to God are but a day:
So to a Man, when once a Crown he wears,
The Coronation Days more than a thousand years.

OLIVER CROMWEL

He would have gone on I perceiv'd in his blasphemies, but
that by Gods Grace I became so bold as thus to interrupt him.
I understand now perfectly (which I guest at long before) what
kind of Angel and Protector you are; and though your stile in
verse be very much mended since you were wont to deliver
Oracles, yet your Doctrine is much worse than ever you had
formerly (that I heard of) the face to publish; whether your
long practice with mankind has encreast and improved your
malice, or whether you think Us in this age to be grown so
impudently wicked, that there needs no more Art or Disguises
to draw us to your party. My Dominion (said he hastily, and
with a dreadful furious look) is so great in this World, and I
am so powerful a Monarch of it, that I need not be ashamed
that you should know me; and that you may see I know you
too, I know you to be an obstinate and inveterate Malignant;
and for that reason I shall take you along with me to the next
Garrison of Ours; from whence you shall go to the Tower,
and from thence to the Court of Justice, and from thence you
know whither. I was almost in the very pounces of the great
Bird of prey,

When, Lo, e're the last words were fully spoke,
From a fair Cloud, which rather ope'd, than broke,
A flash of Light rather than Lightning came,
So swift, and yet so gentle was the Flame.
Upon it rode, and in his full Career,
Seem'd to my Eyes no sooner There than Here,
The comliest Youth of all th' Angelique Race;
Lovely his shape, ineffable his Face.
The Frowns with which he strook the trembling Fiend,
All smiles of Humane Beauty did transcend,
His Beams of Locks fell part dishevel'd down,
Part upwards curld, and form'd a nat'ral Crown,
Such as the *Brittish* Monarchs us'd to wear;
If Gold might be compar'd with Angels Hair.
His Coat and flowing Mantle were so bright,
They seem'd both made of woven Silver Light:
Across his Breast an azure Ruban went,
At which a Medal hung that did present

In wondrous living figures to the sight,
The mystick Champions, and old Dragon's fight,
And from his Mantles side there shone afar,
A fixt, and, I believe, a real Star.
In his fair hand (what need was there of more?)
No Arms but th' *English* bloody Cross he bore,
Which when he towards th' affrighted Tyrant bent,
And some few words pronounc'd (but what they meant,
Or were, could not, alas, by me be known,
Only I well perceiv'd Jesus was one)
He trembled, and he roar'd, and fled away;
Mad to quit thus his more than hop'd-for prey.
Such Rage inflames the Wolves wild heart and eyes
(Rob'd as he thinks unjustly of his prize)
Whom unawares the Shepherd spies, and draws
The bleating Lamb from out his ravenous jaws.
The Shepherd fain himself would he assail,
But Fear above his Hunger does prevail,
He knows his Foe too strong, and must be gone;
He grins as he looks back, and howls as he goes on.

Several Discourses by way of Essays, in Verse and Prose.

1. Of Liberty.

THE Liberty of a people consists in being governed by Laws which they have made themselves, under whatsoever form it be of Government. The Liberty of a private man in being Master of his own Time and Actions, as far as may consist with the Laws of God and of his Country. Of this latter only we are here to discourse, and to enquire what estate of Life does best seat us in the possession of it. This Liberty of our own Actions is such a Fundamental Priviledge of human Nature, that God himself notwithstanding all his infinite power and right over us, permits us to enjoy it, and that too after a Forfeiture made by the Rebellion of *Adam*. He takes so much care for the intire preservation of it to us, that he suffers neither his Providence nor Eternal Decree to break or infringe it. Now for our Time, the same God, to whom we are but Tenants-at-will for the whole, requires but the seventh part to be paid to him as a small Quit-Rent in acknowledgment of his Title. It is man only that has the impudence to demand our whole time, though he neither gave it, nor can restore it, nor is able to pay any considerable valew for the least part of it. This Birth-right of mankind above all other creatures, some are forced by hunger to sell, like *Esau*, for Bread and Broth, but the greatest part of men make such a Bargain for the delivery up of themselves, as *Thamar* did with *Judah*, instead of a Kid, the necessary provisions for humane life, they are contented to do it for Rings and Bracelets. The great dealers in this world may be divided into the Ambitious, the Covetous, and the Voluptuous, and that all these men sell themselves to be slaves, though to the vulgar it may seem a Stoical Paradox, will appear to the wise so plain and obvious that they will scarce think it deserves the labour of Argumentation. Let us first consider the Ambitious, and those both in their progress to Greatness, and after the attaining of it. There is nothing truer than what *Salust* saies, *Dominationis in alios servitiam suam Mercedem dant*, They are content to pay so great a price as their own Servitude to purchase the domination over others. The first thing they must resolve to sacrifice, is their whole time, they must never stop, nor ever turn aside whilst they are in the race of Glory, no not like *Atalanta* for Golden Apples. Neither indeed can a man stop himself if he would when he's in this Career. *Fertur equis Auriga neque audit Currus habenas.*

Pray, let us but consider a little, what mean servil things men do for this Imaginary Food. We cannot fetch a greater example of it, then from the chief men of that Nation which boasted most of Liberty. To what pitiful baseness did the noblest *Romans* submit themselves for the obtaining of a Prætorship, or the Consular dignity: they put on the Habit of Suppliants, and ran about on foot, and in durt, through all the Tribes to beg voices, they flattered the poorest Artisans, and carried a *Nomenclator* with them, to whisper in their ear every mans name, least they should mistake it in their salutations: they shook the hand, and kist the cheek of every popular Tradesman ; they stood all day at every Market in the publick places to shew and ingratiate themselves to the rout ; they imploy'd all their friends to sollicite for them, they kept open Tables in every street, they distributed wine and bread and money, even to the vilest of the people. *En Romanos rerum Dominos! Behold the Masters of the World begging from door to door.* This particular humble way to Greatness is now out of fashion, but yet every Ambitious person is still in some sort a *Roman* Candidate. He must feast and bribe, and attend and flatter, and adore many Beasts, though not the Beast with many heads. *Cat[i]line* who was so proud that he could not content himself with a less power than *Sylla's*, was yet so humble for the attaining of it, as to make himself the most contemptible of all Servants, to be a publique Bawd, to provide whores, and something worse, for all the young Gentlemen of

Rome, whose hot lusts and courages, and heads he thought he might make use of. And since I happen here to propose *Cat[i]line* for my instance (though there be thousand of Examples for the same thing) give me leave to transcribe the Character which *Cicero* gives of this noble Slave, because it is a general description of all Ambitious men, and which *Machiavil* perhaps would say ought to be the rule of their life and actions. This man (saies he, as most of you may well *Orat. pro* remember) had many artificial touches and stroakes that look'd *M. Cælio.* like the beauty of great Virtues, his intimate conversation was with the worst of men, and yet he seem'd to be an Admirer and Lover of the best, he was furnish't with all the nets of Lust and Luxury, and yet wanted not the Arms of Labour and Industry: neither do I believe that there was ever any monster in nature, composed out of so many different and disagreeing parts. Who more acceptable, sometimes, to the most honorable persons, who more a favourite to the most Infamous? who, sometimes, appear'd a braver Champion, who at other times, a bolder Enemy to his Country? who more dissolute in his pleasures, who more patient in his toiles? who more rapacious in robbing, who more profuse in giving? Above all things, this was remarkable and admirable in him, The arts he had to acquire the good opinion and kindness of all sorts of men, to retain it with great complaisance, to communicate all things to them, to watch and serve all the occasions of their fortune, both with his money and his interest, and his industry; and if need were, not by sticking at any wickedness whatsoever that might be useful to them, to bend and turn about his own Nature and laveer with every wind, to live severely with the melancholy, merrily with the pleasant, gravely with the aged, wantonly with the young, desperately with the bold, and debauchedly with the luxurious: with this variety and multiplicity of his nature, as he had made a collection of friendships with all the most wicked and reckless of all Nations, so by the artificial simulation of some vertues, he made a shift to ensnare some honest and eminent persons into his familiarity; neither could so vast a design as the destruction of this Empire have been undertaken by him, if the immanity of so many vices had not been covered and disguised by the appearances of some excellent qualities.

ABRAHAM COWLEY

I see, methinks, the Character of an *Anti-Paul*, who became all things to all men, that he might destroy all; who only wanted the assistance of Fortune to have been as great as his Friend *Cæsar* was a little after him. And the ways of *Cæsar* to compass the same ends (I mean till the Civil War, which was but another manner of setting his Country on Fire) were not unlike these, though he used afterward his unjust Dominion with more moderation then I think the other would have done. *Salust* therefore who was well acquainted with them both, and with many such like Gentlemen of his time, saies, That it is the nature of Ambition (*Ambitio multos mortales falsos fieri coegit &*) to make men Lyers and Cheaters, to hide the Truth in their breasts, and show, like juglers, another thing in their Mouths, to cut all fri[e]ndships and enmities to the measure of their own Interest, and to make a good Countenance without the help of good will. And can there be Freedom with this perpetual constraint? What is it but a kind of Rack that forces men to say what they have no mind to? I have wondred at the extravagant and barbarous stratagem of *Zopirus*, and more at the praises which I finde of so deformed an action; who though he was one of the seven Grandees of *Persia*, and the Son of *Megabises*, who had freed before his Country from an ignoble Servitude, slit his own Nose and Lips, cut off his own Ears, scourged and wounded his whole body, that he might, under pretence of having been mangled so inhumanly by *Darius*, be received into *Babylon* (then beseiged by the *Persians*) and get into the command of it by the recommendation of so cruel a Sufferance, and their hopes of his endeavouring to revenge it. It is great pity the *Babylonians* suspected not his falshood, that they might have cut off his hands too, and whipt him back again. But the design succeeded, he betrayed the City, and was made Governour of it. What brutish master ever punished his offending Slave with so little mercy as Ambition did this *Zopirus*? and yet how many are there in all nations who imitate him in some degree for a less reward? who though they indure not so much corporal pain for a small preferment or some honour (as they call it) yet stick not to commit actions, by which they are more shamefully and more lastingly stigmatized? But you may say, Though these be the most ordinary and open waies to greatness, yet there are

De Bel. Catil.

380

narrow, thorney, and little-trodden paths too, through which some men finde a passage by vertuous industry. I grant, sometimes they may; but then that Industry must be such, as cannot consist with Liberty, though it may with Honesty.

Thou 'rt careful, frugal, painful; we commend a Servant so, but not a Fr[ie]nd.

Well then, we must acknowledg the toil and drudgery which we are forced to endure in this Ascent, but we are Epicures and Lords when once we are gotten up into the High Places. This is but a short Apprentiship after which we are made free of a Royal Company. If we fall in love with any beautious woman, we must be content that they should be our Mistresses whilst we woo them, as soon as we are wedded and enjoy, 'tis we shall be the Masters.

I am willing to stick to this similitude in the case of Greatness; we enter into the Bonds of it, like those of Matrimony; we are bewitcht with the outward and painted Beauty, and take it for Better or worse, before we know its true nature and interiour Inco[n]veniences. A great Fortune (saies *Seneca*) is a great servitude, But many are of that Opinion which *Brutus* imputes (I hope untruly) even to that Patron of Liberty, his Friend *Cicero*, We fear (saies he to *Atticus*) Death, and Banishment, and Poverty, a great deal too much. *Cicero*, I am afraid, thinks these to be the worst of evils, and if he have but some persons, from whom he can obtain what he has a mind to, and others who will flatter and worship him, seems to be well enough contented with an honorable servitude, if any thing indeed ought to be called honorable, in so base and contumelious a condition. This was spoken as became the bravest man who was ever born in the bravest Commonwealth : But with us generally, no condition passes for servitude, that is accompanied with great riches, with honors, and with the service of many Inferiours. This is but a Deception of the sight through a false medium, for if a Groom serve a Gentleman in his chamber, that Gentleman a Lord, and that Lord a Prince; The Groom, the Gentleman, and the Lord, are as much servants one as the other : the circumstantial difference of the ones getting only his Bread and wages, the second a plentiful, and the third a superfluous estate, is no more intrinsical to this matter then the difference between a plain, a rich and gaudy Livery. I do not say, That he who sells his whole time, and his own will for one hundred thousand, is not a wiser Merchant than he who does it for one hundred pounds, but I will swear, they are both Merchants, and that he is happier than both, who can live contentedly without selling that estate to which he was born. But this Dependance upon Superiors is but one chain of the Lovers of Power, *Amatorem Trecentæ [Pirithoum] cohibent catenæ.* Let's begin with him by break of day : For by that time he's besieged by two or three hundred Suitors ; and the Hall and Antichambers (all the Outworks) possest by the Enemy as soon as his Chamber opens, they are ready to break into that, or to corrupt the Guards, for entrance. This is so essential a part of Greatness, that whosoever is without it, looks like a Fallen Favorite, like a person disgraced, and condemned to do what he please all the morning. There are some who rather then want this, are contented to have their rooms fild up every day with murmuring and cursing Creditors, and to charge bravely through a Body of them to get to their Coach. Now I would fain know which is the worst duty, that of any one particular person who waits to speak with the Great man, or the Great mans, who waits every day to speak with all the company. *Aliena negotia centum Per caput & circum saliunt latus,* A hundred businesses of other men (many unjust and most impertinent) fly continually about his Head and Ears, and strike him in the Face like Dorres ; Let's contemplate him a little at another special Scene of Glory, and that is, his Table. Here he seems to be the Lord of all Nature : The Earth affords him her best Metals for his dishes, her best Vegetables and Animals for his food ; the Air and Sea supply him with their choicest Birds and Fishes : and a great many men who look like Masters, attend upon him, and yet when all this is done, even all this is but Table d'Hoste, 'Tis crowded with people for whom he cares not, for with many Parasites, and some Spies, with the most burdensome sort of Guests, the Endeavourers to be witty.

But every body pays him great respect, every body commends his Meat, that is, his Mony ; every body admires the exquisite dressing & ordering of it, that is, his Clark of the kitchin, or his Cook ; every body loves his Hospitality, that is, his Vanity.

ESSAYS, IN VERSE AND PROSE

But I desire to know why the honest In-keeper who provides a publick Table for his Profit, should be but of a mean profession; and he who does it for his Honour, a munificent Prince, You'l say, Because one sels, and the other gives: Nay, both sell, though for different things, the one for plain Money, the other for I know not what Jewels, whose value is in Custom and in Fancy. If then his Table be made a Snare (as the Scripture speakes) to his Liberty, where can he hope for Freedom, there is alwaies, and every where some restraint upon him. He's guarded with Crowds, and shackled with Formalities. The half hat, the whole hat, the half smile, the whole smile, the nod, the embrace, the Positive parting with a little bow, the Comparative at the middle of the room, the Superlative at the door; and if the person be *Pan huper sebastus*, there's a *Hupersuperlative* ceremony then of conducting him to the bottome of the stairs, or to the very gate: as if there were such Rules set to these *Leviathans* as are to the Sea, *Hitherto shalt thou go, and no further. Perditur hæc inter miser[o] Lux*, Thus wretchedly the precious day is lost.

How many impertinent Letters and Visits must he receive, and sometimes answer both too as impertinently? he never sets his foot beyond his Threshold, unless, like a Funeral, he have a train to follow him, as if, like the dead Corps, he could not stir, till the Bearers were all ready. My life, (sayes *Horace*, speaking to one of these *Magnifico's*) is a great deal more easie and commodious then thine, In that I can go into the Market and cheapen what I please without being wondred at; and take my Horse and ride as far as *Tarentum*, without being mist. 'Tis an unpleasant constraint to be alwayes under the sight and observation, and censure of others; as there may be Vanity in it, so methinks, there should be Vexation too of spirit: And I wonder how Princes can endure to have two or three hundred men stand gazing upon them whilst they are at dinner, and taking notice of every bit they eat. Nothing seems greater and more Lordly then the multitude of Domestick Servants; but, even this too, if weighed seriously, is a piece of Servitude; unless you will be a Servant to them (as many men are) the trouble and care of yours in the Government of them all, is much more then that of every one of them in their observance of you. I take the Profession of a School-

Master to be one of the most usefull, and which ought to be of the most honourable in a Commonwealth, yet certainly all his Fasces and Tyrannical Aut[h]ority over so many Boys, takes away his own Liberty more than theirs.

I do but slightly touch upon all these particulars of the slavery of Greatness: I shake but a few of their outward Chains; their Anger, Hatred, Jealousie, Fear, Envy, Grief, and all the *Etcætera* of their Passions, which are the secret, but constant Tyrants and Torturers of their life, I omit here, because though they be symptomes most frequent and violent in this Disease; yet they are common too in some degree to the Epidemical Disease of Life it self. But, the Ambitious man, though he be so many wayes a slave (*O toties servus!*) yet he bears it bravely and heroically; he struts and looks big upon the Stage; he thinks himself a real Prince in his Masking Habit, and deceives too all the foolish part of his Spectators: He's a slave in *Saturnalibus*. The Covetous Man is a down-right Servant, a Draught Horse without Bells or Feathers; *ad Metalla damnatus*, a man condemned to work in Mines, which is the lowest and hardest condition of servitude; and, to encrease his Misery, a worker there for he knows not whom: He heapeth up Riches and knows not who shall enjoy them; 'Tis onely sure that he himself neither shall nor can injoy them. He's an indigent needy slave, he will hardly allow himself Cloaths, and Board-Wages; *Unciatim vix demenso de suo suum defraudans Genium comparsit miser*; He defrauds not only other Men, but his own Genius; He cheats himself for Mony. But the servile and miserable condition of this wretch is so apparent, that I leave it, as evident to every mans sight, as well as judgment. It seems a more difficult work to prove that the Voluptuous Man too is but a servant: What can be more the life of a Freeman, or as we say ordinarily, of a Gentleman, then to follow nothing but his own pleasures? Why, I'le tell you who is that true Freeman, and that true Gentleman; Not he who blindly follows all his pleasures (the very name of Follower is servile) but he who rationally guides them, and is not hindred by outward impediments in the conduct and enjoyment of them. If I want skill or force to restrain the Beast that I ride upon, though I bought it, and call it my own, yet in the truth of the matter I am at that

Phorm.
Act. 1.
Sect. 1.

time rather his Man, then he my Horse. The Voluptuous Men (whom we are fallen upon) may be divided, I think, into the Lustful and Luxurious, who are both servants of the Belly; the other whom we spoke of before, the Ambitious and the Covetous, were κακὰ θηρία, Evil wilde Beasts, these are Γαστέρες ἀργαὶ, slow Bellies, as our Translation renders it; but the word Ἀργαὶ (which is a fantastical word, with two directly opposite significations) will bear as well the translation of Quick or Diligent Bellies, and both Interpretations may be applyed to these men. *Metrodorus* said, That he had learnt Ἀληθῶς γαστρὶ χαρίζεσθαι, to give his Belly just thanks for all his pleasures. This by the Calumniators of *Epicurus* his Philosophy was objected as one of the most scandalous of all their sayings; which, according to my Charitable understanding may admit a very virtuous sence, which is, that he thanked his own Belly for that moderation in the customary appetites of it, which can only give a Man Liberty and Happiness in this World. Let this suffice at present to be spoken of those great Triumviri of the World; the Covetous Man, who is a mean villain, like *Lepidus*; the Ambitious, who is a brave one, like *Octavius*, and the Voluptuous, who is a loose and debauched one, like *Mark Antony*. *Quisnam igitur Liber? Sapiens, sibi qui Imperiosus:* Hor. L. 2. Not *Oenomaus*, who commits himself wholly to a Chariotteer Sat. 7. that may break his Neck, but the Man, Serm.

> Who governs his own course with steddy hand,
> Who does Himself with Sovereign Pow'r command;
> Whom neither Death, nor Poverty does fright,
> Who stands not aukwardly in his own light
> Against the Truth: who can when Pleasures knock
> Loud at his door, keep firm the bolt and lock.
> Who can though Honour at his gate should stay
> In all her Masking Cloaths, send her away,
> And cry, be gone, I have no mind to Play.

This I confess is a Freeman: but it may be said, That many persons are so shackled by their Fortune, that they are hindred from enjoyment of that Manumission which they have obtained from Virtue. I do both understand, and in part feel the weight of this objection: All I can Answer to it, is, That we must

get as much Liberty as we can, we must use our utmost
endeavours, and when all that is done, be contented with the
Length of that Line which is allow'd us. If you ask me
in what condition of Life I think the most allow'd; I should
pitch upon that sort of People whom King *James* was wont
to call the Happiest of our Nation, the Men placed in the
Countrey by their Fortune above an High-Constable, and yet
beneath the trouble of a Justice of Peace, in a moderate plenty,
without any just argument for the desire of encreasing it by
the care of many relations, and with so much knowledge and
love of Piety and Philosophy (that is of the study of Gods
Laws, and of his Creatures) as may afford him matter enough
never to be Idle though without Business; and never to be
Melancholy though without Sin or Vanity.

I shall conclude this tedious Discourse with a Prayer of
mine in a Copy of Latin Verses, of which I remember no
other part, and (*pour faire bonne bouche*) with some other Verses
upon the same Subject.

Magne Deus, quod ad has vitæ brevis attinet horas,
Da mihi, da Panem Libertatemque, nec ultrà
Sollicitas effundo preces, siquid datur ultrà
Accipiam gratus; si non, Contentus abibo.

For the few Houres of Life allotted me,
Give me (great God) but Bread and Liberty,
I'le beg no more; if more thou'rt pleas'd to give,
I'le thankfully that Overplus receive:
If beyond this no more be freely sent,
I'le thank for this, and go away content.

Martial. Lib. 2.

Vota tui breviter, &c.

WEll then, Sir, you shall know how far extend
    The Prayers and Hopes of your Poetick Friend;
He does not Palaces nor Manors crave,
Would be no Lord, but less a Lord would have.
The ground he holds, if he his own, can call,
He quarrels not with Heaven because 'tis small:

Let gay and toilsome Greatness others please,
He loves of homely Littleness the Ease.
Can any Man in guilded rooms attend,
And his dear houres in humble visits spend;
When in the fresh and beauteous Fields he may
With various healthful pleasures fill the day?
If there be Man (ye Gods) I ought to Hate
Dependance and Attendance be his Fate.
Still let him Busie be, and in a crowd,
And very much a Slave, and very Proud:
Thus he perhaps Pow'rful and Rich may grow;
No matter, O ye Gods! that I'le allow.
But let him Peace and Freedome never see;
Let him not love this Life, who loves not Me.

Martial. L. [2.]

Vis fieri Liber? &c.

WOuld you be Free? 'Tis your chief wish, you say,
  Come on; I'le shew thee, Friend, the certain way,
If to no Feasts abroad thou lov'st to go,
Whilst bounteous God does Bread at home bestow,
If thou the goodness of thy Cloaths dost prize
By thine own Use, and not by others Eyes.
(If onely safe from Weathers) thou can'st dwell,
I[n] a small House, but a convenient Shell,
If thou without a Sigh, or Golden wish,
Canst look upon thy Beechen Bowl, and Dish;
If in thy Mind such power and greatness be,
The *Persian* King's a Slave compar'd with Thee.

Mart. L. 2.

Quod te nomine? &c.

THat I do you with humble Bowes no more,
  And danger of my naked Head adore.
That I who Lord and Master cry'd erewhile,
Salute you in a new and different Stile,

ABRAHAM COWLEY

By your own Name, a scandal to you now,
Think not that I forget my self or you:
By loss of all things by all others sought
This Freedome, and the Freemans Hat is bought.
A Lord and Master no man wants but He
Who o're Himself has no Autoritie.
Who does for Honours and for Riches strive,
And Follies, without which Lords cannot Live.
If thou from Fortune dost no Servant crave,
Believe it, thou no Master need'st to have.

Ode.

Upon Liberty.

I.

FReedome with Virtue takes her seat,
   Her proper place, her onely Scene,
    Is in the Golden Mean,
She lives not with the Poor, nor with the Great.
The Wings of those Necessity has clipt,
    And they'r in Fortunes Bridewell whipt,
    To the laborious task of Bread;
Those are by various Tyrants Captive lead.
Now wild Ambition with imperious force
Rides, raines, and spurs them like th' unruly Horse.
    And servile Avarice yoakes them now
    Like toilsome Oxen to the Plow.
And sometimes Lust, like the Misguiding Light,
Drawes them through all the Labyrinths of Night.
If any Few among the Great there be
    From these insulting Passions free,
    Yet we ev'n those too fetter'd see
By Custom, Business, Crowds, and formal Decency.
And whereso'ere they stay, and whereso'ere they go,
    Impertinencies round them flow:
    These are the small uneasie things
    Which about Greatness still are found,
    And rather it Molest then Wound:

Like Gnats which too much heat of summer brings;
But Cares do swarm there too, and those have stings:
As when the Honey does too open lie,
      A thousand Wasps about it fly:
Nor will the Master ev'n to share admit;
The Master stands aloof, and dares not Tast of it.

2.

'Tis Morning; well; I fain would yet sleep on;
      You cannot now; you must be gone
      To Court, or to the noisy Hall:
Besides, the Rooms without are crowded all;
      The st[r]eam of Business does begin,
And a Spring-Tide of Clients is come in.
Ah cruel Guards, which this poor Prisoner keep!
      Will they not suffer him to sleep?
Make an Escape; out at the Postern flee,
And get some blessed Houres of Libertie,
With a few Friends, and a few Dishes dine,
      And much of Mirth and moderate Wine.
To thy bent Mind some relaxation give,
And steal one day out of thy Life to Live.
Oh happy man (he cries) to whom kind Heaven
      Has such a Freedome alwayes given!
Why, mighty Madman, what should hinder thee
      From being every day as Free?

3.

In all the Freeborn Nations of the Air,
Never did Bird a spirit so mean and sordid bear,
As to exchange his Native Liberty
Of soaring boldly up into the sky,
His Liberty to Sing, to Perch, or Fly,
      When, and where'ver he thought good,
And all his innocent pleasures of the Wood,
For a more plentiful or constant Food.
      Nor ever did Ambitious rage
      Make him into a painted Cage;
Or the false Forest of a well-hung Room,
      For Honour and Preferment come.

ABRAHAM COWLEY

Now, Blessings on ye all, ye Heroick Race,
Who keep their Primitive powers and rights so well
   Though Men and Angels fell.
Of all Material Lives the highest place,
   To you is justly given;
   And wayes and walkes the neerest Heaven.
Whilst wretched we, yet vain and proud, think fit
   To boast, That we look up to it.
Even to the Universal Tyrant Love,
   You Homage pay but once a year:
None so degenerous and unbirdly prove,
   As his perpetual yoke to bear.
None but a few unhappy Houshold Foul,
   Whom human Lordship does controul;
   Who from their birth corrupted were
By Bondage, and by mans Example here.

4.

He's no small Prince who every day
   Thus to himself can say,
Now will I sleep, now eat, now sit, now walk,
Now meditate alone, now with Acquaintance talk.
This I will do, here I will stay,
Or if my Fancy call me away,
My Man and I will presently go ride;
(For we before have nothing to provide,
Nor after are to render an account)
To *Dover*, *Barwick*, or the *Cornish* Mount.
   If thou but a short journey take,
   As if thy last thou wert to make,
Business must be dispatch'd e're thou canst part,
   Nor canst thou stirr unless there be
   A hundred Horse and Men to wait on thee,
   And many a Mule, and many a Cart;
   What an [unwieldy] man thou art?
   The *Rhodian Colossus* so
   A Journey too might go.

5.

Where Honour or where Conscience does not bind
   No other Law shall shackle me,
   Slave to my self I will not be,

Nor shall my future Actions be confin'd
    By my own present Mind.
Who by Resolves and Vows engag'd does stand
    For days that yet belong to Fate,
Does like an unthrift Mor[t]gage his Estate
    Before it falls into his Hand,
    The Bondman of the Cloister so
All that he does receive does always owe.
And still as Time comes in, it goes away
    Not to Enjoy, but Debts to pay.
Unhappy Slave, and Pupil to a Bell!
Which his hours work as well as hours does tell!
Unhappy till the last, the kind releasing Knell.

6.

If Life should a well-order'd Poem be
    (In which he only hits the white
Who joyns true Profit with the best Delight)
The more Heroique strain let others take,
    Mine the Pindarique way I'le make.
The Matter shall be Grave, the Numbers loose and free.
It shall not keep one setled pace of Time,
In the same Tune it shall not always Chime,
Nor shall each day just to his Neighbour Rhime,
A thousand Liberties it shall dispense,
And yet shall mannage all without offence;
Or to the sweetness of the Sound, or greatness of the Sence,
Nor shall it never from one Subject start,
    Nor seek Transitions to depart,
Nor its set way o're Stiles and Bridges make,
    Nor thorough Lanes a Compass take
As if it fear'd some trespass to commit,
    When the wide Air's a Road for it.
So the Imperial Eagle does not stay
    Till the whole Carkass he devour
    That's fallen into its power.
As if his generous Hunger understood
That he can never want plenty of Food,
    He only sucks the tastful Blood.
And to fresh Game flies cheerfully away;
To Kites and meaner Birds he leaves the mangled Prey.

ABRAHAM COWLEY

[2.] *Of Solitude.*

NUnquam *minus solus, quam cum solus,* is now become a
very vulgar saying.   Every Man and almost every Boy
for these seventeen hundred years, has had it in his mouth.   But
it was at first spoken by the Excellent *Scipio,* who was without
question a most Eloquent and Witty person, as well as the
most Wise, most Worthy, most Happy, and the Greatest of
all Mankind.   His meaning no doubt was this, That he found
more satisfaction to his mind, and more improvement of it by
Solitude then by Company, and to shew that he spoke not
this loosly or out of vanity, after he had made *Rome,* Mistriss
of almost the whole World, he retired himself from it by a
voluntary exile, and at a private house in the middle of a wood
Epist. 86. neer *Linternum,* passed the remainder of his Glorious life no
less Gloriously.   This House *Seneca* went to see so long after
with great veneration, and among other things describes his
Baths to have been of so mean a structure, that now, says he,
the basest of the people would despise them, and cry out, poor
Scipio understood not how to live.   What an Authority is here
for the credit of Retreat? and happy had it been for *Hannibal,*
if Adversity could have taught him as much Wisdom as was
learnt by *Scipio* from the highest prosperities.   This would be
no wonder if it were as truly as it is colourably and wittily
said by Monsieur *de Montagne.*   That Ambition it self might
teach us to love Solitude; there's nothing does so much hate
to have Companions.   'Tis true, it loves to have its Elbows
free, it detests to have Company on either side, but it delights
above all Things in a Train behind, I, and Ushers too before
it.   But the greatest part of men are so far from the opinion
of that noble *Roman,* that if they chance at any time to be
without company, they'r like a becalmed Ship, they never
move but by the wind of other mens breath, and have no Oars
of their own to steer withal.   It is very fantastical and contra-
dictory in humane Nature, that Men should love themselves
above all the rest of the world, and yet never endure to be
with themselves.   When they are in love with a Mistriss,
all other persons are importunate and burdensome to them.
Tecum vivere amem, tecum obeam Lubens, They would live and
dye with her alone.

ESSAYS, IN VERSE AND PROSE

Sic ego secretis possum benè vivere silvis
Quà nulla humano sit via trita pedè,
Tu mihi curarum requies, tu noĉte vel atrâ
Lumen, & in solis tu mihi turba locis.

With thee for ever I in woods could rest,
Where never humane foot the ground has prest,
Thou from all shades the darkness canst exclude,
And from a Desart banish Solitude.

And yet our Dear Self is so wearisome to us, that we can
scarcely support its conversation for an hour together. This
is such an odd temper of mind as *Catullus* expresses towards
one of his Mistresses, whom we may suppose to have been of
a very unsociable humour.

Odi & Amo, quanàm id faciam ratione requiris?
Nescio, sed fieri sentio, & excrucior.

I Hate, and yet I Love thee to[o];
How can that be? I know not how;
Only that so it is I know,
And feel with Torment that 'tis so.

It is a deplorable condition, this, and drives a man sometimes
to pittiful shifts in seeking how to avoid Himself.
The truth of the matter is, that neither he who is a Fop
in the world, is a fit man to be alone; nor he who has set
his heart much upon the world, though he have never so much
understanding; so that Solitude can be well fitted and set right,
but upon a very few persons. They must have enough know-
ledge of the World to see the vanity of it, and enough Virtue
to despise all Vanity; if the Mind be possest with any Lust
or Passions, a man had better be in a Faire, then in a Wood
alone. They may like petty Thieves cheat us perhaps, and
pick our pockets in the midst of company, but like Robbers
they use to strip and bind, or murder us when they catch us
alone. This is but to retreat from Men, and fall into the
hands of Devils. 'Tis like the punishment of Parricides among
the *Romans*, to be sow'd into a Bag with an Ape, a Dog, and
a Serpent. The first work therefore that a man must do to
make himself capable of the good of Solitude, is, the very
Eradication of all Lusts, for how is it possible for a Man to

393

enjoy himself while his Affections are tyed to things without Himself? In the second place, he must learn the Art and get the Habit of Thinking; for this too, no less than well speaking, depends upon much practice, and Cogitation is the thing which distinguishes the Solitude of a God from a wild Beast. Now because the soul of Man is not by its own Nature or observation furnisht with sufficient Materials to work upon; it is necessary for it to have continual recourse to Learning and Books for fresh supplies, so that the solitary Life will grow indigent, and be ready to starve without them; but if once we be throughly engaged in the Love of Letters, instead of being wearied with the length of any day, we shall only complain of the shortness of our whole Life.

> *O vita, stulto longa, sapienti brevis!*
> O Life, long to the Fool, short to the Wise!

The first Minister of State has not so much business in publique, as a wise man has in private; if the one have little leisure to be alone, the other has less leisure to be in company; the one has but part of the affairs of one Nation, the other all the works of God and Nature under his consideration. There is no saying shocks me so much as that which I hear very often, That a man does not know how to pass his Time. 'Twould have been but ill spoken by *Methusalem* in the Nine hundred sixty ninth year of his Life, so far it is from us, who have not time enough to attain to the utmost perfection of any part of any Science, to have cause to complain that we are forced to be idle for want of work. But this you'l say is work only for the Learned, others are not capable either of the employments or divertisements that arrive from Letters; I know they are not; and therefore cannot much recommend Solitude to a man totally illiterate. But if any man be so unlearned as to want entertainment of the little Intervals of accidental Solitude, which frequently occurr in almost all conditions (except the very meanest of the people, who have business enough in the necessary provisions for Life) it is truly a great shame both to his Parents and Himself, for a very small portion of any Ingenious Art will stop up all those gaps of our Time, either Musique, or Painting, or Designing, or Chymistry, or History, or Gardening, or twenty other things will do it usefully and pleasantly; and if he happen to set his affections upon Poetry (which I do not advise him too immoderately) that will over do it; no wood will be thick enough to hide him from the importunities of company or business, which would abstract him from his Beloved.

> ——*O quis me gelidis sub montibus Æmi*
> *Sistat, & ingenti ramorum protegat umbrâ?*

Virg.
Georg.

I.

Hail, old *Patrician* Trees, so great and good!
    Hail ye *Plebeian* under wood!
    Where the Poetique Birds rejoyce,
And for their quiet Nests and plentious Food,
    Pay with their grateful voice.

2.

Hail, the poor Muses richest Mannor Seat!
    Ye Countrey Houses and Retreat,
    Which all the happy Gods so Love,
That for you oft they quit their Bright and Great
    Metropolis above.

3.

Here Nature does a House for me erect,
    Nature the wisest Architect,
    Who those fond Artists does despise
That can the fair and living Trees neglect;
    Yet the Dead Timber prize.

4.

Here let me careless and unthoughtful lying,
    Hear the soft winds above me flying,
    With all their wanton Boughs dispute,
And the more tuneful Birds to both replying
    Nor be my self too Mute.

5.

A Silver stream shall roul his waters neer,
    Guilt with the Sun-beams here and there
    On whose enamel'd Bank I'll walk,
And see how prettily they Smile, and hear
    How prettily they Talk.

395

ABRAHAM COWLEY

6.

Ah wretched, and too Solitary Hee
Who loves not his own Company!
He'l feel the weight of't many a day
Unless he call in Sin or Vanity
To help to bear't away.

7.

Oh Solitude, first state of Human-kind!
Which blest remain'd till man did find
Even his own helpers Company.
As soon as two (alas!) together joyn'd,
The Serpent made up Three.

8.

Though God himself, through countless Ages Thee
His sole Companion chose to be,
Thee, Sacred Solitude alone,
Before the Branchy head of Numbers Tree
Sprang from the Trunk of One.

9.

Thou (though men think thine an unactive part)
Dost break and tame th'unruly heart,
Which else would know no setled pace,
Making it move, well mannag'd by thy Art,
With Swiftness and with Grace.

10.

Thou the faint beams of Reasons scatter'd Light,
Dost like a Burning-glass unite,
Dost multiply the feeble Heat,
And fortifie the strength, till thou dost bright
And noble Fires beget.

11.

Whilst this hard Truth I teach, methinks, I see
The Monster *London* laugh at me,
I should at thee too, foolish City,
If it were fit to laugh at Misery,
But thy Estate I pity.

12.

Let but thy wicked men from out thee go,
　　And all the Fools that crowd the[e] so,
　　Even thou who dost thy Millions boast,
A Village less then *Islington* wilt grow,
　　A Solitude almost.

3.　*Of Obscurity.*

N*AM neque Divitibus contingunt gaudia solis,*
　Nec vixit male, qui natus moriensque Fefellit.

Hor. Epist.
l. 1. 1[7].

God made not pleasures only for the Rich,
Nor have those men without their share too liv'd,
Who both in Life and Death the world deceiv'd.

This seems a strange Sentence thus literally translated, and looks as if it were in vindication of the men of business (for who else can Deceive the world?) whereas it is in commendation of those who live and dye so obscurely, that the world takes no notice of them. This *Horace* calls deceiving the world, and in another place uses the same phrase.

Secretum iter & Fallentis semita vitæ.
The secret tracks of the Deceiving Life.

Ep. 18.

It is very elegant in Latine, but our English word will hardly bear up to that sence, and therefore Mr. *Broom* translates it very well,

Or from a Life, led as it were by stealth.

Yet we say in our Language, a thing deceives our sight, when it passes before us unperceived, and we may say well enough out of the same Authour,

Sometimes with sleep, somtimes with wine we strive,
The cares of Life and troubles to Deceive.

But that is not to deceive the world, but to deceive our selves, as *Quintilian* saies, *Vitam fallere*, To draw on still, and amuse, and deceive our Life, till it be advanced insensibly to the fatal Period, and fall into that Pit which Nature hath prepared for it. The meaning of all this is no more then that most vulgar

Declam.
de Apib.

ABRAHAM COWLEY

saying, *Bene qui latuit, bene vixit*, He has lived well, who has lain well hidden. Which if it be a truth, the world (I'le swear) is sufficiently deceived: For my part, I think it is, and that the pleasantest condition of Life, is *in Incognito*. What a brave Privilege is it to be free from all Contentions, from all Envying or being Envyed, from recieving and from paying all kind of Ceremonies? It is in my mind, a very delightful pastime, for two good and agreeable friends to travail up and down together, in places where they are by no body known, nor know any body. It was the case of *Æneas* and his *Achates*, when they walkt invisibly about the fields and streets of *Carthage*, *Venus* her self

Virg. 1.
Æn.

> *A vail of thickned Air around them cast,*
> *That none might know, or see them as they past.*

The common story of *Demosthenes*'s confession that he had taken great pleasure in hearing of a Tanker-woman say as he past; This is that *Demosthenes*, is wonderful ridiculous from so solid an Orator. I my self have often met with that temptation to vanity (if it were any) but am so far from finding it any pleasure, that it only makes me run faster from the place, till I get, as it were out of sight-shot. *Democritus* relates, and in such a manner, as if he gloried in the good fortune and commodity of it, that when he came to *Athens* no body there did so much as take notice of him; and *Epicurus* lived there very well, that is, Lay hid many years in his Gardens, so famous since that time, with his friend *Metrodorus*: after whose death, making in one of his letters a kind commemoration of the happiness which they two had injoyed together, he adds at last, that he thought it no disparagement to those great felicities of their life, that in the midst of the most talk'd-of and Talking Country in the world, they had lived so long, not only without Fame, but almost without being heard of. And yet within a very few years afterward, there were no two Names of men more known or more generally celebrated. If we engage into a large Acquaintance and various familiarities, we set open our gates to the Invaders of most of our time: we expose our life to a *Quotidian Ague* of frigid impertinencies, which would make a wise man tremble to think of. Now, as for being known much by sight, and pointed at, I cannot comprehend the

398

honour that lies in that: Whatsoever it be, every Mountebank
has it more then the best Doctor, and the Hangman more then
the Lord Chief Justice of a City. Every creature has it both
of Nature and Art if it be any ways extraordinary. It was as
often said, This is that *Bucephalus*, or, This is that *Incitatus*,
when they were led prancing through the streets, as, this is that
Alexander, or this is that *Domitian*; and truly for the latter, I
take *Incitatus* to have bin a much more Honourable Beast then
his Master, and more deserving the Consulship, then he the
Empire. I love and commend a true good Fame, because it is
the shadow of Virtue, not that it doth any good to the Body
which it accompanies, but 'tis an efficacious shadow, and like
that of St. *Peter* cures the Diseases of others. The best kinde
of Glory, no doubt, is that which is reflected from Honesty,
such as was the Glory of *Cato* and *Aristides*, but it was harmful
to them both, and is seldom beneficial to any man whilst he
lives, what it is to him after his death, I cannot say, because, I
love not *Philosophy* merely notional and conjectural, and no
man who has made the Experiment has been so kind as to
come back to inform us. Upon the whole matter, I account a
person who has a moderate Minde and Fortune, and lives in
the conversation of two or three agreeable friends, with little
commerce in the world besides, who is esteemed well enough
by his few neighbours that know him, and is truly irreproach-
able by any body, and so after a healthful quiet life, before the
great inconveniences of old age, goes more silently out of it
then he came in, (for I would not have him so much as Cry in
the *Exit*). This Innocent Deceiver of the world, as *Horace*
calls him, this *Muta persona*, I take to have been more happy
in his Part, then the greatest Actors that fill the Stage with
show and noise, nay, even then *Augustus* himself, who askt with
his last breath, Whether he had not played his *Farce* very well.

Seneca, ex Thyeste,
Act. 2. Chor.

Stet quicunque volet, potens
Aulæ culmine lubrico, &c.

Upon the slippery tops of humane State,
The guilded Pinnacles of Fate,

Let others proudly stand, and for a while
  The giddy danger to beguile,
With Joy, and with disdain look down on all,
  Till their Heads turn, and down they fall.
Me, O ye Gods, on Earth, or else so near
  That I no Fall to Earth may fear,
And, O ye gods, at a good distance seat
  From the long Ruines of the Great.
Here wrapt in th' Arms of Quiet let me ly;
Quiet, Companion of Obscurity.
Here let my Life, with as much silence slide,
  As Time that measures it does glide.
Nor let the Breath of Infamy or Fame,
From town to town Eccho about my Name.
Nor let my homely Death embroidered be
   With Scutcheon or with Elegie.
   An old *Plebean* let me Dy,
Alas, all then are such as well as I.
   To him, alas, to him, I fear,
The face of Death will terrible appear:
Who in his life flattering his senceless pride
By being known to all the world beside,
Does not himself, when he is Dying know
Nor what he is, nor Whither hee's to go.

4. *Of Agriculture.*

THE first wish of *Virgil* (as you will find anon by his
  Verses) was to be a good Philosopher; the second, a good
Husbandman; and God (whom he seem'd to understand better
then most of the most learned Heathens) dealt with him just
as he did with *Solomon*; because he prayed for wisdom in the
first place, he added all things else which were subordinately to
be desir'd. He made him one of the best Philosophers, and
best Husbandmen, and to adorn and communicate both those
faculties, the best Poet: He made him besides all this a rich
man, and a man who desired to be no richer. *O Fortunatus
nimium, & bona qui sua novit:* To be a Husbandman, is but a

retreat from the City; to be a Philosopher, from the world, or rather, a Retreat from the world, as it is mans; into the world, as it is Gods. But since Nature denies to most men the capacity or appetite, and Fortune allows but to a very few the opportunities or possibility of applying themselves wholy to Philosophy, the best mixture of humane affairs that we can make, are the employments of a Country life. It is, as *Columella* calls it, *Res sine dubitatione proxima, & quasi Consanguinea Sapientiæ*, The nearest Neighbour, or rather next in *lib. 1. c. 1.* Kindred to Philosophy. *Varro* sayes, the Principles of it are the same which *Ennius* made to be the Principles of all Nature: Earth, Water, Air, and the Sun. It does certainly comprehend more parts of Philosophy then any one Profession, Art or Science in the world besides: and therefore *Cicero* saies, The pleasures of a Husbandman, *Mihi ad sapientis vitam proxime videntur accedere*, Come very nigh to those of a Philosopher. There is *De senect.* no other sort of life that affords so many branches of praise to a Panegyrist: The Utility of it to a mans self: The Usefulness, or rather Necessity of it to all the rest of Mankind: The Innocence, the Pleasure, the Antiquity, the Dignity. The Utility (I mean plainly the Lucre of it) is not so great now in our Nation as arises from Merchandise and the trading of the City, from whence many of the best Estates and chief Honours of the Kingdom are derived: we have no men now fetcht from the Plow to be made Lords, as they were in *Rome* to be made Consuls and Dictators, the reason of which I conceive to be from an evil Custom, now grown as strong among us, as if it were a Law, which is, that no men put their Children to be bred up Apprentices in Agriculture, as in other Trades, but such who are so poor, that when they come to be men, they have not wherewithall to set up in it, and so can only Farm some small parcel of ground, the Rent of which devours all but the bare Subsistence of the Tenant: Whilst they who are Proprietors of the Land, are either too proud, or, for want of that kind of Education, too ignorant to improve their Estates, though the means of doing it be as easie and certain in this as in any other track of Commerce: If there were alwaies two or three thousand youths, for seven or eight years bound to this Profession, that they might learn the whole Art of it, and afterwards be enabled to be Masters in it, by a moderate stock:

ABRAHAM COWLEY

I cannot doubt but that we should see as many Aldermens Estates made in the Country, as now we do out of all kind of Merchandizing in the City. There are as many wayes to be Rich, and which is better, there is no Possibility to be poor, without such negligence as can neither have excuse nor Pity; for a little ground will without question feed a little family, and the superfluities of Life (which are now in some cases by custome made almost necessary) must be supplyed out of the superabundance of Art and Industry, or contemned by as great a Degree of Philosophy. As for the Necessity of this Art, it is evident enough, since this can live without all others, and no one other without this. This is like Speech, without which the Society of men cannot be preserved; the others like Figures and Tropes of Speech which serve only to adorn it. Many Nations have lived, and some do still, without any Art but this; not so Elegantly, I confess, but still they Live, and almost all the other Arts which are here practised, are beholding to this for most of their Materials. The Innocence of this Life is the next thing for which I commend it, and if Husbandmen preserve not that, they are much to blame, for no men are so free from the Temptations of Iniquity. They live by what they can get by Industry from the Earth, and others by what they can catch by Craft from men. They live upon an Estate given them by their Mother, and others upon an Estate cheated from their Brethren. They live like Sheep and Kine, by the allowances of Nature, and others like Wolves and Foxes by the acquisitions of Rapine. And, I hope, I may affirm (without any offence to the Great) that Sheep and Kine are very useful, and that Wolves and Foxes are pernicious creatures. They are without dispute of all men the most quiet and least apt to be inflamed to the distaurbance of the Common-wealth: their manner of Life inclines them, and Interest binds them to love Peace: In our late mad and miserable Civil Wars, all other Trades, even to the meanest, set forth whole Troopes, and raised up some great Commanders, who became famous and mighty for the mischiefs they had done: But, I do not remember the Name of any one Husbandman who had so considerable a share in the twenty years ruine of his Country, as to deserve the Curses of his Country-men: And if great delights be joyn'd with so much Innocence, I think it is ill done of men not to take them here where they are so tame, and ready at hand, rather then hunt for them in Courts and Cities, where they are so wild, and the chase so troublesome and dangerous.

We are here among the vast and noble Scenes of Nature; we are there among the pitiful shifts of Policy: We walk here in the light and open wayes of the Divine Bounty; we grope there in the dark and confused Labyrinths of Human Malice: Our Senses are here feasted with the clear and genuine taste of their Objects, which are all Sophisticated there, and for the most part overwhelmed with their contraries. Here Pleasure looks (methinks) like a beautiful, constant, and modest Wife ; it is there an impudent, fickle, and painted Harlot. Here is harmless and cheap Plenty, there guilty and expenseful Luxury.

I shall onely instance in one Delight more, the most natural and best natur'd of all others, a perpetual companion of the Husbandman; and that is, the satisfaction of looking round about him, and seeing nothing but the effects and improvements of his own Art and Diligence; to be always gathering of some Fruits of it, and at the same time to behold others ripening, and others budding: to see all his Fields and Gardens covered with the beauteous Creatures of his own Industry; and to see, like God, that all his Works are Good.

> ——*Hinc atque hinc glomerantur Oreades ; ipsi*
> *Agricolæ tacitum pertentant gaudia pectus.*

On his heart-strings a secret Joy does strike.

The Antiquity of his Art is certainly not to be contested by any other. The three first Men in the World, were a Gardner, a Ploughman, and a Grazier; and if any man object, That the second of these was a Murtherer, I desire he would consider, that as soon as he was so, he quitted our Profession, and turn'd Builder. It is for this reason, I suppose, that *Ecclesiasticus* forbids us to hate Husbandry; because (sayes he) the most High has created it. We were all Born to this Art, *Cap. 7.* and taught by Nature to nourish our Bodies by the same Earth out of which they were made, and to which they must return, and pay at last for their sustenance.

ABRAHAM COWLEY

Behold the Original and Primitive Nobility of all those great Persons, who are too proud now, not onely to till the Ground, but almost to tread upon it. We may talke what we please of Lilies, and Lions Rampant, and Spread-Eagles in Fields d' Or, or d' Argent; but if Heraldry were guided by Reason, a Plough in a Field Arable, would be the most Noble and Antient Armes.

All these considerations make me fall into the wonder and complaint of *Columella*, How it should come to pass that all Arts or Sciences, (for the dispute, which is an Art, and which a Science, does not belong to the curiosity of us Husbandmen) *Metaphysick*, *Physick*, *Morality*, *Mathematicks*, *Logick*, *Rhetorick*, &c. which are all, I grant, good and usefull faculties, (except onely *Metaphysick* which I do not know whether it be any thing or no) but even *Vaulting*, *Fencing*, *Dancing*, *Attiring*, *Cookery*, *Carving*, and such like Vanities, should all have publick Schools and Masters; and yet that we should never see or hear of any man who took upon him the Profession of teaching this so pleasant, so virtuous, so profitable, so honourable, so necessary Art.

A man would think, when he's in serious humour, that it were but a vain, irrational and ridiculous thing, for a great company of Men and Women to run up and down in a Room together, in a hundred several postures and figures, to no purpose, and with no design; and therefore Dancing was invented first, and onely practised anciently in the Ceremonies of the Heathen Religion, which consisted all in Mommery and Madness; the latter being the chief glory of the Worship, and accounted Divine Inspiration: This, I say, a severe Man would think, though I dare not determine so far against so customary a part now of good breeding. And yet, who is there among our Gentry, that does not entertain a Dancing Master for his Children as soon as they are able to walk? But, Did ever any Father provide a Tutor for his Son to instruct him betimes in the Nature and Improvements of that Land which he intended to leave him? That is at least a superfluity, and this a Defect in our manner of Education; and therefore I could wish (but cannot in these times much hope to see it) that one Colledge in each University were erected, and appropriated to this study, as well as there are to Medecin, and the Civil Law: There

ESSAYS, IN VERSE AND PROSE

would be no need of making a Body of Scholars and Fellowes, with certain endowments, as in other Colledges; it would suffice, if after the manner of Halls in *Oxford*, there were only four Professors constituted (for it would be too much work for onely one Master, or Principal, as they call him there) to teach these four parts of it. First, *Aration*, and all things relating to it. Secondly, *Pasturage*. Thirdly, *Gardens, Orchards, Vine-yards* and *Woods*. Fourthly, All parts of *Rural Oeconomy*, which would contain the Government of *Bees, Swine, Poultry, Decoys, Ponds*, &c. and all that which *Varro* calls *Villaticas Pastiones*, together with the Sports of the Field (which ought to be looked upon not onely as Pleasures, but as parts of House-keeping) and the Domestical conservation and uses of all that is brought in by Industry abroad. The business of these Pro-fessors should not be, as is commonly practised in other Arts, onely to read Pompous and Superficial Lectures out of *Virgils Georgickes, Pliny, Varro* or *Columella*, but to instruct their Pupils in the whole Method and course of this study, which might be run through perhaps with diligence in a year or two; and the continual succession of Scholars upon a moderate taxa-tion for their Diet, Lodging, and Learning, would be a sufficient constant revenue for Maintenance of the House and the Pro-fessors, who should be men not chosen for the Ostentation of Critical Literature, but for solid and experimental Knowledge of the things they teach such Men; so industrious and publick-spirited as I conceive Mr. *Hartlib* to be, if the Gentleman be yet alive: But it is needless to speak farther of my thoughts of this Design, unless the present Disposition of the Age allowed more probability of bringing it into execution. What I have further to say of the Country Life, shall be borrowed from the Poets, who were alwayes the most faithful and affectionate friends to it. Poetry was Born among the Shepherds.

Nescio qua Natale solum dulcedine Musas
Ducit, & immemores non sinit esse sui.

The Muses still love their own Native place,
T'has secret Charms which nothing can deface.

The truth is, no other place is proper for their work; one might as well undertake to Dance in a Crowd, as to make good Verses in the midst of Noise and Tumult.

ABRAHAM COWLEY

As well might Corn as Verse in Cities grow;
In vain the thankless Glebe we Plow and Sow,
Against th' unnatural Soil in vain we strive;
'Tis not a Ground in which these Plants will thrive.

It will bear nothing but the Nettles or Thornes of *Satyre*, which grow most naturally in the worst Earth; And therefore almost all Poets, except those who were not able to eat Bread without the bounty of Great men, that is, without what they could get by Flattering of them, have not onely withdrawn themselves from the Vices and Vanities of the Grand World (*Pariter vitiisque Jocisque Altius humanis exeruere caput*) into the innocent happiness of a retired Life; but have commended and adorned nothing so much by their Ever-living Poems. *Hesiod* was the first or second Poet in the World that remains yet extant (if *Homer*, as some think, preceded him, but I rather believe they were Contemporaries) and he is the first Writer too of the Art of Husbandry: He has contributed (sayes *Columella*) not a little to our Profession; I suppose he means not a little Honour, for the matter of his Instructions is not very important: His great Antiquity is visible through the Gravity and Simplicity of his Stile. The most Acute of all his sayings concerns our purpose very much, and is couched in the reverend obscurity of an Oracle. Πλεόν ἥμισυ Παντὸς. The half is more then the whole. The occasion of the speech is this; His Brother *Perses* had by corrupting some great men (Βασιλῆας Δωροφάγους, Great Bribe-eaters he calls them) gotten from him the half of his Estate. It is no Matter, (says he) they have not done me so much prejudice, as they imagine.

Νήπιοι, οὐδὲ ἴσασιν ὅσῳ Πλέον Ἥμισυ Παντός,
Οὐδ' ὅσον ἐν μαλάχῃ τε καὶ ἀσφοδέλῳ μέγ' ὄνειαρ,
Κρύψαντες γὰρ ἔχουσι θεοὶ βίον ἀνθρώποισι.

Unhappy they to whom God has not reveal'd
By a strong Light which must their sence controle,
That halfe a great Estate's more then the whole:
Unhappy, from whom still conceal'd does lie
Of Roots and Herbs, the wholesome Luxurie.

ESSAYS, IN VERSE AND PROSE

This I conceive to have been Honest *Hesiods* meaning.
From *Homer* we must not expect much concerning our affairs.
He was Blind and could neither work in the Countrey, nor
enjoy the pleasures of it, his helpless Poverty was likeliest to be
sustained in the richest places, he was to delight the *Grecians*
with fine tales of the Wars and adventures of their Ancestors;
his Subject removed him from all Commerce with us, and yet,
methinks, he made a shift to show his good will a little. For
though he could do us no Honour in the person of his *Hero*
Ulisses (much less of *Achilles*) because his whole time was con-
sumed in Wars and Voyages, yet he makes his Father *Laertes* a
Gardener all that while, and seeking his Consolation for the
absence of his son in the pleasure of Planting and even Dunging
his own grounds. Ye see he did not contemn us Peasants,
nay, so far was he from that insolence, that he always stiles
Eumæus, who kept the Hogs with wonderful respect Δῖον
ὑφορβόν. The Divine Swine-herd he could ha' done no more
for *Menelaus* or *Agamemnon*. And *Theocritus* (a very ancient
Poet, but he was one of our own Tribe, for he wrote nothing
but Pastorals) gave the same Epithete to an Husbandman
Ἀμείβετο Δῖος ἀγρώτης. The Divine Husbandman replyed
to *Hercules*, who was but Δῖος Himself. These were Civil
Greeks! and who understood the Dignity of our Calling!
among the *Romans* we have in the first place, our truly Divine
Virgil, who, though by the favour of *Mecænas* and *Augustus*, he
might have been one of the chief men of *Rome*, yet chose
rather to employ much of his time in the exercise, and much of
his immortal wit in the praise and instructions of a Rustique
Life, who though he had written before whole Books of
Pastorals and *Georgiques* could not abstain in his great and
Imperial Poem from describing *Evander*, one of his best Princes,
as living just after the homely manner of an ordinary Countrey-
man. He seats him in a Throne of Maple, and lays him but
upon a Bears skin, the Kine and Oxen are lowing in his Court
yard, the Birds under the Eeves of his Window call him up in
the morning, and when he goes abroad, only two Dogs go
along with him for his guard: at last when he brings *Æneas*
into his Royal Cottage, he makes him say this memorable
complement, greater then ever yet was spoken at the *Escurial*,
the *Louvre*, or our *Whitehall*.

ABRAHAM COWLEY

———— *Hæc (inquit) limina victor*
Alcides subiit, hæc illum Regia cepit,
Aude, Hospes, contemnere opes, & te quoque dignum
Finge Deo, rebusque veni non asper egenis.

This humble Roof, this rustique Court (said He)
Receiv'd *Alcides* crown'd with victory.
Scorn not (Great Guest) the steps where he has trod,
But contemn Wealth, and imitate a God.

The next Man whom we are much obliged to, both for his Doctrine and Example, is the next best Poet in the world to *Virgil*; his dear friend *Horace*, who when *Augustus* had desired *Mecænas* to perswade him to come and live domestically, and at the same Table with him, and to be Secretary of State of the whole World under him, or rather joyntly with him, for he says, *ut nos in Epistolis scribendis adjuvet*, could not be tempted to forsake his *Sabin*, or *Tiburtin* Mannor, for so rich and so glorious a trouble. There was never, I think, such an example as this in the world, that he should have so much moderation and courage as to refuse an offer of such greatness, and the Emperour so much generosity and good Nature as not to be at all offended with his refusal, but to retain still the same kindness, and express it often to him in most friendly and familiar Letters, part of which are still extant. If I should produce all the passages of this excellent Author upon the several Subjects which I treat of in this Book, I must be obliged to translate half his works; of which I may say more truly than in my opinion he did of *Homer, Qui quid sit pulchrum, quid Turpe, quid utile, quid non, plenius & melius Chrysippo, & Crantore dicit.* I shall content my self upon this particular Theme with three only, one out of his *Odes*, the other out of his *Satyrs*, the third out of his [*E*]*pistles*, and shall forbear to collect the suffrages of all other Poets, which may be found scattered up and down through all their writings, and especially in *Martials*. But I must not omit to make some excuse for the bold undertaking of my own unskilful Pencil upon the beauties of a Face that has been drawn before by so many great Masters, especially, that I should dare to do it in *Latine* verses (though of another kind) and have the confidence to Translate them. I can only say that I love the Matter, and that ought to cover many faults; and that I run not to contend with those before me, but follow to applaud them.

Virg. Georg.

O fortunatus nimium, &c.

A Translation out of *Virgil.*

OH happy, (if his Happiness he knows)
   The Country Swain, on whom kind Heav'n bestows
At home all Riches that wise Nature needs;
Whom the just earth with easie plenty feeds.
'Tis true, no morning Tide of Clients comes,
And fills the painted Chanels of his rooms,
Adoring the rich Figures, as they pass,
In Tap'stry wrought, or cut in living brass;
Nor is his Wooll superfluously dy'd
With the dear Poyson of *Assyrian* pride:
Nor do *Arabian* Perfumes vainly spoil
The Native Use, and Sweetness of his Oyl.
Instead of these, his calm and harmless life
Free from th' Alarms of Fear, and storms of Strife,
Does with substantial blessedness abound,
And the soft wings of Peace cover him round:
Through artless Grots the murmuring waters glide;
Thick Trees both against Heat and Cold provide,
From whence the Birds salute him; and his ground
With lowing Herds, and bleeting Sheep does sound;
And all the Rivers, and the Forests nigh,
Both Food and Game, and Exercise supply.
Here a well hard'ned active youth we see,
Taught the great Art of chearful Poverty.
Here, in this place alone, there still do shine
Some streaks of Love, both humane and Divine;
From hence *Astræa* took her flight, and here
Still her last Foot-steps upon Earth appear.
'Tis true, the first desire which does controul
All the inferiour wheels that move my Soul,
Is, that the Muse me her high Priest would make;
Into her holyest Scenes of Myst'ry take,

ABRAHAM COWLEY

And open there to my mind's purged eye
Those wonders which to Sense the Gods deny;
How in the Moon such change of shapes is found:
The Moon, the changing Worlds eternal bound.
What shakes the solid Earth, what strong disease
Dares trouble the firm Centre's antient ease;
What makes the Sea retreat, and what advance:
Varieties too regular for chance.
What drives the Chariot on of Winters light,
And stops the lazy Waggon of the night.
But if my dull and frozen Blood deny,
To send forth Sp'rits that raise a Soul so high;
In the next place, let Woods and Rivers be
My quiet,· though unglorious destiny.
In Life's cool vale let my low Scene be laid;
Cover me Gods, with *Tempe's* thickest shade.
Happy the Man, I grant, thrice happy he
Who can through gross effects their causes see:
Whose courage from the deeps of knowledg springs,
Nor vainly fears inevitable things;
But does his walk of virtue calmly go,
Through all th' allarms of Death and Hell below.
Happy! but next such Conquerours, happy they,
Whose humble Life lies not in fortunes way.
They unconcern'd from their safe distant seat,
Behold the Rods and Scepters of the great.
The quarrels of the mighty without fear,
And the descent of forein Troops they hear.
Nor can even *Rome* their steddy course misguide,
With all the lustre of her perishing Pride.
Them never yet did strife or avarice draw,
Into the noisy markets of the Law,
The Camps of Gowned War, nor do they live
By rules or forms that many mad men give.
Duty for Natures Bounty they repay,
And her sole Laws religiously obey.
    Some with bold Labour plow the faithless main,
Some rougher storms in Princes Courts sustain.
Some swell up their sleight sails with pop'ular fame,
Charm'd with the foolish whistlings of a Name.

ESSAYS, IN VERSE AND PROSE

Some their vain wealth to Earth again commit;
With endless cares some brooding o're it sit.
Country and Friends are by some Wretches sold,
To lie on *Tyrian* Beds and drink in Gold;
No price too high for profit can be shown;
Not Brothers blood, nor hazards of their own.
Around the World in search of it they roam,
It makes ev'n their Antipodes their home;
Mean while, the prudent Husbandman is found,
In mutual duties striving with his ground,
And half the year he care of that does take,
That half the year grateful returns does make.
Each fertil moneth does some new gifts present,
And with new work his industry content.
This, the young Lamb, that the soft Fleece doth yield,
This, loads with Hay, and that, with Corn the Field:
All sorts of Fruit crown the rich *Autumns* Pride:
And on a swelling Hill's warm stony side,
The powerful Princely Purple of the Vine,
Twice dy'd with the redoubled Sun, does shine.
In th' Evening to a fair ensuing day,
With joy he sees his Flocks and Kids to play;
And loaded Kyne about his Cottage stand,
Inviting with known sound the Milkers hand;
And when from wholsom labour he doth come,
With wishes to be there, and wish't for home,
He meets at door the softest humane blisses,
His chast Wives welcom, and dear Childrens kisses.
When any Rural Holy dayes invite
His Genius forth to innocent delight,
On Earth's fair bed beneath some sacred shade,
Amidst his equal friends carelesly laid,
He sings thee *Bacchus* Patron of the Vine,
The Beechen Boul fomes with a floud of Wine,
Not to the loss of reason or of strength:
To active games and manly sport at length,
Their mirth ascends, and with fill'd veins they see,
Who can the best at better trials be.
Such was the Life the prudent *Sabins* chose,
From such the old *Hetrurian* virtue rose.

ABRAHAM COWLEY

Such, *Remus* and the God his Brother led,
From such firm footing *Rome* grew the World's head.
Such was the Life that ev'n till now does raise
The honour of poor *Saturns* golden dayes:
Before Men born of Earth and buried there,
Let in the Sea their mortal fate to share.
Before new wayes of perishing were sought,
Before unskilful Death on Anvils wrought.
Before those Beasts which humane Life sustain,
By Men, unless to the Gods use were slain.

Horat. Epodon.

Beatus ille qui procul, &c.

HAppy the Man whom bounteous Gods allow
     With his own Hands Paternal Grounds to plough!
Like the first golden Mortals Happy he
From Business and the cares of Money free!
No humane storms break off at Land his sleep.
No loud Alarms of Nature on the Deep,
From all the cheats of Law he lives secure,
Nor does th' affronts of Palaces endure;
Sometimes the beauteous Marriagable Vine
He to the lusty Bridegroom Elm does joyn;
Sometimes he lops the barren Trees around,
And grafts new Life into the fruitful wound;
Sometimes he sheers his Flock, and sometimes he
Stores up the Golden Treasures of the Bee.
He sees his lowing Herds walk o're the Plain,
Whilst neighbouring Hills low back to them again:
And when the Season Rich as well as Gay,
All her Autumnal Bounty does display.
How is he pleas'd th' encreasing Use to see,
Of his well trusted Labours bend the tree?
Of which large shares, on the glad sacred daies
He gives to Friends, and to the Gods repays.
With how much joy do's he beneath some shade
By aged trees rev'rend embraces made,

His careless head on the fresh Green recline,
His head uncharg'd with Fear or with Design.
By him a River constantly complaines,
The Birds above rejoyce with various strains
And in the solemn Scene their *Orgies* keep
Like Dreams mixt with the Gravity of sleep,
Sleep which does alwaies there for entrance wait
And nought within against it shuts the gate.
  Nor does the roughest season of the sky,
Or sullen *Jove* all sports to him deny,
He runs the *Mazes* of the nimble Hare,
His well-mouth'd Dogs glad concert rends the air,
Or with game bolder, and rewarded more,
He drives into a Toil, the foaming Bore,
Here flies the Hawk t' assault, and there the Net
To intercept the travailing foul is set.
And all his malice, all his craft is shown
In innocent wars, on beasts and birds alone.
This is the life from all misfortunes free,
From thee the Great one, Tyrant Love, from Thee;
And if a chaste and clean, though homely wife
Be added to the blessings of this Life,
Such as the antient Sun-burnt *Sabins* were,
Such as *Apulia*, frugal still, does bear,
Who makes her Children and the house her care,
And joyfully the work of Life does share,
Nor thinks herself too noble or too fine
To pin the sheepfold or to milch the Kine,
Who waits at door against her Husband come
From rural duties, late, and wearied home,
Where she receives him with a kind embrace,
A chearful Fire, and a more chearful Face:
And fills the Boul up to her homely Lord,
And with domestique plenty loads the board.
Not all the lustful shel-fish of the Sea,
Drest by the wanton hand of Luxurie,
Nor *Ortalans* nor *Godwits* nor the rest
Of costly names that glorify a Feast,
Are at the Princely tables better cheer,
Then Lamb and Kid, Lettice and Olives here.

ABRAHAM COWLEY

The Country Mouse.

A Paraphrase upon Horace 2 *Book*, Satyr. 6.

AT the large foot of a fair hollow tree,
    Close to plow'd ground, seated commodiously,
His antient and Hereditary House,
There dwelt a good substantial Country-Mouse:
Frugal, and grave, and careful of the main,
Yet, one, who once did nobly entertain
A City Mouse well coated, sleek, and gay,
A Mouse of high degree, which lost his way,
Wantonly walking forth to take the Air,
And arriv'd early, and belighted there,
For a days lodging: the good hearty Hoast,
(The antient plenty of his hall to boast)
Did all the stores produce, that might excite,
With various tasts, the Courtiers appetite.
Fitches and Beans, Peason, and Oats, and Wheat,
And a large Chesnut, the delicious meat
Which *Jove* himself, were he a Mouse, would eat.
And for a *Haut goust* there was mixt with these
The swerd of Bacon, and the coat of Cheese.
The precious Reliques, which at Harvest, he
Had gather'd from the Reapers luxurie.
Freely (said he) fall on and never spare,
The bounteous Gods will for to morrow care.
And thus at ease on beds of straw they lay,
And to their Genius sacrific'd the day.
Yet the nice guest's Epicurean mind,
(Though breeding made him civil seem and kind)
Despis'd this Country feast, and still his thought
Upon the Cakes and Pies of *London* wrought.
Your bounty and civility (said he)
Which I'm surpriz'd in these rude parts to see,
Shews that the Gods have given you a mind,
Too noble for the fate which here you find.

ESSAYS, IN VERSE AND PROSE

Why should a Soul, so virtuous and so great,
Lose it self thus in an Obscure retreat?
Let savage Beasts lodg in a Country Den,
You should see Towns, and Manners know, and men:
And taste the generous Lux'ury of the Court,
Where all the Mice of quality resort;
Where thousand beauteous shees about you move,
And by high fare, are plyant made to love.
We all e're long must render up our breath,
No cave or hole can shelter us from death.
    Since Life is so uncertain, and so short,
Let's spend it all in feasting and in sport.
Come, worthy Sir, come with me, and partake,
All the great things that mortals happy make.
    Alas, what virtue hath sufficient Arms,
T'oppose bright Honour, and soft Pleasures charms?
What wisdom can their magick force repel?
It draws this reverend Hermit from his Cel.
It was the time, when witty Poets tell,
That Phœbus *into* Thetis *bosom fell:*
She blusht at first, and then put out the light,
And drew the modest Curtains of the night.
Plainly, the troth to tell, the Sun was set,
When to the Town our wearied Travellers get,
To a Lords house, as Lordly as can be
Made for the use of Pride and Luxury,
They come; the gentle Courtier at the door
Stops and will hardly enter in before.
But 'tis, Sir, your command, and being so,
I'm sworn t'obedience, and so in they go.
Behind a hanging in a spacious room,
(The richest work of *Mortclakes* noble Loom)
They wait awhile their wearied limbs to rest,
Till silence should invite them to their feast.
About the hour that Cynthia's *Silver light,*
Had touch'd the pale Meridies of the night;
At last the various Supper being done,
It happened that the Company was gone,
Into a room remote, Servants and all,
To please their nobles fancies with a Ball.

ABRAHAM COWLEY

Our host leads forth his stranger, and do's find,
All fitted to the bounties of his mind.
Still on the Table half fill'd dishes stood,
And with delicious bits the floor was strow'd.
The courteous mouse presents him with the best,
And both with fat varieties are blest,
Th' industrious Peasant every where does range,
And thanks the gods for his Life's happy change.
Loe, in the midst of a well fraited Pye,
They both at last glutted and wanton lye.
When see the sad Reverse of prosperous fate,
And what fierce storms on mortal glories wait.
With hideous noise, down the rude servants come,
Six dogs before run barking into th' room;
The wretched gluttons fly with wild affright,
And hate the fulness which retards their flight.
Our trembling Peasant wishes now in vain,
That Rocks and Mountains cover'd him again.
Oh how the change of his poor life he curst!
This, of all lives (said he) is sure the worst.
Give me again, *ye gods*, my Cave and wood;
With peace, let tares and acorns be my food.

A Paraphrase upon the 10th *Epistle of the first
Book of* Horace.

Horace *to* Fuscus Aristius.

HEalth, from the lover of the Country me,
    Health, to the lover of the City thee,
A difference in our souls, this only proves,
In all things else, w' agree like marryed doves.
But the warm nest, and crowded dove-house thou
Dost like; I loosly fly from bough to bough,
And Rivers drink, and all the shining day,
Upon fair Trees, or mossy Rocks I play;

In fine, I live and reign when I retire
From all that you equal with Heaven admire.
Like one at last from the Priests service fled,
Loathing the honie'd Cakes, I long for Bread.
Would I a house for happines erect,
Nature alone should be the Architect.
She'd build it more convenient, then great,
And doubtless in the Country choose her seat.
Is there a place, doth better helps supply,
Against the wounds of Winters cruelty?
Is there an Ayr that gentl'er does asswage
The mad Celestial Dogs, or Lyons rage?
Is it not there that sleep (and only there)
Nor noise without, nor cares within does fear?
Does art through pipes, a purer water bring,
Then that which nature straines into a spring?
Can all your Tap'stries, or your Pictures show
More beauties then in herbs and flowers do grow?
Fountains and trees our wearied Pride do please,
Even in the midst of gilded Palaces.
And in your towns that prospect gives delight,
Which opens round the country to our sight.
Men to the good, from which they rashly fly,
Return at last, and their wild Luxury
Does but in vain with those true joyes contend,
Which Nature did to mankind recommend.
The man who changes gold for burnisht Brass,
Or small right Gems, for larger ones of glass:
Is not, at length, more certain to be made
Ridiculous, and wretched by the trade,
Than he, who sells a solid good, to buy
The painted goods of Pride and Vanity.
If thou be wise, no glorious fortune choose,
Which 'tis but pain to keep, yet grief to loose.
For, when we place even trifles, in the heart,
With trifles too, unwillingly we part.
An humble Roof, plain bed, and homely board,
More clear, untainted pleasures do afford,
Then all the Tumult of vain greatness brings
To Kings, or to the favorites of Kings.

ABRAHAM COWLEY

The horned Deer by Nature arm'd so well,
Did with the Horse in common pasture dwell;
And when they fought, the field it alwayes wan,
Till the ambitious Horse begg'd help of Man,
And took the bridle, and thenceforth did reign
Bravely alone, as Lord of all the plain:
But never after could the Rider get
From off his back, or from his mouth the bit.
So they, who poverty too much do fear,
T' avoid that weight, a greater burden bear;
That they might Pow'r above their equals have,
To cruel Masters they themselves enslave.
For Gold, their Liberty exchang'd we see,
That fairest flow'r, which crowns Humanity.
And all this mischief does upon them light,
Only, because they know not how, aright,
That great, but secret, happiness to prize,
That's laid up in a Little, for the Wise:
That is the best, and easiest Estate,
Which to a man sits close, but not too strait;
'Tis like a shooe; it pinches, and it burns,
Too narrow; and too large it overturns.
My dearest friend, stop thy desires at last,
And chearfully enjoy the wealth thou hast.
And, if me still seeking for more you see,
Chide, and reproach, despise and laugh at me.
Money was made, not to command our will,
But all our lawful pleasures to fulfil.
Shame and wo to us, if we' our wealth obey;
The Horse doth with the Horse man run away.

The Country Life.

Libr. 4. Plantarum.

Blest be the man (and blest he is) whom[e're]
  (Plac'd far out of the roads of Hope or Fear)
A little Field, and little Garden feeds;
The Field gives all that Frugal Nature needs,
The wealthy Garden liberally bestows
All she can ask, when she luxurious grows.
The specious inconveniences that wait
Upon a life of Business, and of State,
He sees (nor does the sight disturb his rest)
By Fools described, by wicked men possest.
Thus, thus (and this deserv'd great *Virgils* praise)
The old *Corycian* Yeom[a]n past his daies,
Thus his wise life *Abdolonymus* spent:
Th' Ambassadours which the great Emp'rour sent
To offer him a Crown, with wonder found
The reverend Gard'ner howing of his Ground,
Unwillingly and slow and discontent,
From his lov'd Cottage, to a Throne he went?
And oft he stopt in his tryumphant way,
And oft lookt back, and oft was heard to say
Not without sighs, Alas, I there forsake
A happier Kingdom then I go to take.
Thus *Aglaüs* (a man unknown to men,
But the gods knew and therefore lov'd him Then)
Thus liv'd obscurely then without a Name,
Aglaüs now consign'd t' eternal Fame.
For *Gyges*, the rich King, wicked and great,
Presum'd at wise *Apollos Delphick* seat
Presum'd to ask, Oh thou, the whole Worlds Eye,
See'st thou a Man, that Happier is then I?
The God, who scorn'd to flatter Man, reply'd,
Aglaüs Happier is. But *Gyges* cry'd,
In a proud rage, Who can that *Aglaüs* be?
We have heard as yet of no such King as Hee.

And true it was through the whole Earth around
No King of such a Name was to be found.
Is some old *Hero* of that name alive,
Who his high race does from the Gods derive?
Is it some mighty General that has done,
Wonders in fight, and God-like honours wone?
Is it some m[a]n of endless wealth, said he?
None, none of these; who can this *Aglaüs* bee?
After long search and vain inquiries past,
In an obscure *Arcadian* Vale at last,
('The *Arcadian* life has always shady been.
Near *Sopho's* Town (which he but once had seen)
This *Aglaüs* who Monarchs Envy drew,
Whose Happiness the Gods stood witness too,
This mighty *Aglaüs* was labouring found,
With his own Hands in his own little ground.
   So, gracious God, (if it may lawful be,
Among those foolish gods to mention Thee)
So let me act, on such a private stage,
The last dull Scenes of my declining Age;
After long toiles and Voyages in vain,
This quiet Port let my tost Vessel gain,
Of Heavenly rest, this Earnest to me lend,
Let my Life sleep, and learn to love her End.

The Garden.

To J. Evelyn *Esquire.*

I Never had any other desire so strong, and so like to
Covetousness as that one which I have had always, that
I might be master at last of a small house and large garden,
with very moderate conveniencies joyned to them, and there
dedicate the remainder of my life only to the culture of them
and study of Nature,

   And there (with no design beyond my wall) whole and
      intire to lye,
   In no unactive Ease, and no unglorious Poverty.

ESSAYS, IN VERSE AND PROSE

Or as *Virgil* has said, Shorter and Better for me, that I might there *Studiis florere ignobilis otii* (though I could wish that he had rather said, *Nobilis otii*, when he spoke of his own) But several accidents of my ill fortune have disappointed me hitherto, and do still, of that felicity; for though I have made the first and hardest step to it, by abandoning all ambitions and hopes in this World, and by retiring from the noise of all business and almost company, yet I stick still in the Inn of a hired House and Garden, among Weeds and Rubbish; and without that plesantest work of Human Industry, the Improvement of something which we call (not very properly, but yet we call) Our Own. I am gone out from *Sodom*, but I am not yet arrived at my Little *Zoar*. *O let me escape thither (Is it not a Little one?) and my Soul shall live.* I do not look back yet; but I have been forced to stop, and make too many halts. You may wonder, Sir, (for this seems a little too extravagant and Pindarical for *Prose*) what I mean by all this Preface; It is to let you know, That though I have mist, like a Chymist, my great End, yet I account my affections and endeavours well rewarded by something that I have met with by the By; which is, that they have procured to me some part in their kindness and esteem; and thereby the honour of having my Name so advantagiously recommended to Posterity, by the *Epistle* you are pleased to prefix to the most useful Book that has been written in that kind, and which is to last as long as Moneths and Years.

Among many other *Arts* and *Excellencies* which you enjoy, I am glad to find this Favourite of mine the most predominant, That you choose this for your Wife, though you have hundreds of other Arts for your Concubines; Though you know them, and beget Sons upon them all (to which you are rich enough to allow great Legacies) yet the issue of this seemes to be designed by you to the main of the Estate; you have taken most pleasure in it, and bestow'd most charges upon its Education: and I doubt not to see that Book, which you are pleased to Promise to the World, and of which you have given us a Large Earnest in your Calendar, as Accomplisht, as any thing can be expected from an *Extraordinary Wit*, and no ordinary Expences, and a long Experience. I know no body that possesses more private happiness then you do in your Garden; and yet no

man who makes his happiness more publick, by a free com-
munication of the Art and Knowledge of it to others. All that
I my self am able yet to do, is onely to recommend to Mankind
the search of that Felicity, which you Instruct them how to
Find and to Enjoy.

1.

Happy art Thou, whom God does bless
With the full choice of thine own Happiness;
    And happier yet, because thou'rt blest
    With prudence, how to choose the best:
In Books and Gardens thou hast plac'd aright
    (Things which thou well dost understand;
And both dost make with thy laborious hand)
    Thy noble, innocent delight:
And in thy virtuous Wife, where thou again dost meet
    Both pleasures more refin'd and sweet:
    The fairest Garden in her Looks,
    And in her Mind the wisest Books.
Oh, Who would change these soft, yet solid joys,
    For empty shows and senceless noys;
    And all which rank Ambition breeds,
Which seem such beauteous Flowers, and are such poisonous
    Weeds?

2.

When God did Man to his own Likeness make,
As much as Clay, though of the purest kind,
    By the great Potters art refin'd;
    Could the Divine Impression take,
    He thought it fit to place him, where
    A kind of Heaven too did appear,
As far as Earth could such a Likeness bear:
    That man no happiness might want,
Which Earth to her first Master could afford;
    He did a Garden for him plant
By the quick Hand of his Omnipotent Word.
As the chief Help and Joy of human life,
He gave him the first Gift; first, ev'n before a Wife.

3.

For God, the universal Architect,
    'Thad been as easie to erect
A Louvre or Escurial, or a Tower
That might with Heav'n communication hold,
As *Babel* vainly thought to do of old:
    He wanted not the skill or power,
    In the Worlds Fabrick those were shown,
And the Materials were all his own.
But well he knew what place would best agree
With Innocence, and with Felicity:
And we elsewhere still seek for them in vain,
If any part of either yet remain;
If any part of either we expect,
This may our Judgment in the search direct;
God the first Garden made, and the first City, *Cain*.

4.

Oh blessed shades! O gentle cool retreat
    From all th' immoderate Heat,
In which the frantick World does Burn and Sweat!
This does the Lion-Star, Ambitions rage;
This Avarice, the Dogstars Thirst asswage;
Every where else their fatal power we see,
They make and rule Mans wretched Destiny:
    They neither Set, nor Disappear,
    But tyrannize o're all the Year;
Whilst we ne're feel their Flame or Influence here.
    The Birds that dance from Bough to Bough,
    And Sing above in every Tree,
    Are not from Fears and Cares more free,
Then we who Lie, or Sit, or Walk below,
    And should by right be Singers too.
What Princes Quire of Musick can excell
    That which within this shade does dwell?
    To which we nothing Pay or Give,
    They like all other Poets live,
Without reward, or thanks for their obliging pains;
    'Tis well if they become not Prey:

The whis[t]ling Winds add their less artfull strains,
And a grave Base the murmuring Fountains play;
Nature does all this Harmony bestow,
  But to our Plants, Arts Musick too,
The Pipe, Theorbo, and Guitarr we owe;
The Lute it self, which once was Green and Mute,
  When *Orpheus* strook th' inspired Lute,
  The Trees danc'd round, and understood
  By Sympathy the Voice of Wood.

5.

These are the Spels that to kind Sleep invite,
And nothing does within resistance make,
  Which yet we moderately take;
  Who would not choose to be awake,
While he's encompast round with such delight,
To th' Ear, the Nose, the Touch, the Tast & Sight?
When *Venus* would her dear *Ascanius* keep
A Prisoner in the Downy Bands of Sleep,
She Od'rous Herbs and Flowers beneath him spread
  As the most soft and sweetest Bed;
Not her own Lap would more have charm'd his Head.
Who, that has Reason, and his Smell,
Would not among Roses and Jasmin dwell,
  Rather then all his Spirits choak
With Exhalations of Durt and Smoak?
  And all th' uncleanness which does drown
In Pestilential Clouds a populous Town?
The Earth it self breaths better Perfumes here,
Then all the Femal Men or Women there,
Not without cause, about them bear.

6.

When *Epicurus* to the World had taught,
  That Pleasure was the chiefest Good,
(And was perhaps i'th' right, if rightly understood)
  His Life he to his Doctrine brought,
And in a Gardens shade that Sovereign Pleasure sought:
Whoever a true Epicure would be,
May there find cheap and virtuous Luxurie.

Vitellius his Table, which did hold
As many Creatures as the Ark of old:
That Fiscal Table, to which every day
All Countries did a constant Tribute pay,
Could nothing more delicious afford,
  Then Natures Liberalitie,
Helpt with a little Art and Industry,
Allows the meanest Gard'ners board.
The wanton Tast no Fish, or Fowl can choose,
For which the Grape or Melon she would lose,
Though all th' Inhabitants of Sea and Air
Be listed in the Gluttons bill of Fare;
  Yet still the Fruits of Earth we see
Plac'd the Third Story high in all her Luxury.

7.

But with no Sence the Garden does comply;
None courts, or flatters, as it does the Eye:
When the great *Hebrew* King did almost strain
The wond'rous Treasures of his Wealth and Brain,
His Royal Southern Guest to entertain;
  Though she on Silver Floores did tread,
With bright *Assyrian* Carpets on them spread,
   To hide the Metals Poverty.
  Though she look'd up to Roofs of Gold,
 And nought around her could behold
   But Silk and rich Embrodery,
    And *Babylonian* Tapestry,
  And wealthy *Hirams* Princely Dy:
Though *Ophirs* Starry Stones met every where her Eye;
Though She her self, and her gay Host were drest
With all the shining glories of the East;
When lavish Art her costly work had done,
  The honour and the Prize of Bravery
Was by the Garden from the Palace won;
And every Rose and Lilly there did stand
  Better attir'd by Natures hand:
The case thus judg'd against the King we see,
By one that would not be so Rich, though Wiser far then He.

8.

Nor does this happy place onely dispence
    Such various Pleasures to the Sence;
        Here Health it self does live,
That Salt of Life, which does to all a relish give,
Its standing Pleasure, and Intrinsick Wealth,
The Bodies Virtue, and the Souls good Fortune Health.
The Tree of Life, when it in *Eden* stood,
Did its immortal Head to Heaven rear;
It lasted a tall Cedar till the Flood;
Now a small thorny Shrub it does appear;
    Nor will it thrive too every where:
    It alwayes here is freshest seen;
    'Tis onely here an Ever-green.
    If through the strong and beauteous Fence
    Of Temperance and Innocence,
And wholsome Labours, and a quiet Mind,
    Any Diseases passage find,
    They must not think here to assail
A Land unarm'd, or without a Guard;
They must fight for it, and dispute it hard,
    Before they can prevail:
    Scarce any Plant is growing here
Which against Death some Weapon does not bear.
    Let Cities boast, That they provide
    For Life the Ornaments of Pride;
    But 'tis the Country and the Field,
    That furnish it with Staffe and Shield.

9.

Where does the Wisdom and the Power Divine
In a more bright and sweet Reflection shine?
Where do we finer strokes and colours see
Of the Creators Real Poetry,
    Then when we with attention look
Upon the Third Dayes Volume of the Book?
If we could open and intend our Eye,
    We all like *Moses* should espy
Ev'n in a Bush the radiant Deitie.

But we despise these his Inferiour wayes,
(Though no less full of Miracle and Praise)
    Upon the Flowers of Heaven we gaze;
The Stars of Earth no wonder in us raise,
    Though these perhaps do more then they,
      The life of Mankind sway.
Although no part of mighty Nature be
More stor'd with Beauty, Power, and Mysterie;
Yet to encourage human Industrie,
God has so ordered, that no other part
Such Space, and such Dominion leaves for Art.

10.

We no where Art do so triumphant see,
    As when it Grafs or Buds the Tree:
In other things we count it to excell,
If it a Docile Schollar can appear
To Nature, and but imitate her well;
It over-rules, and is her Master here.
It imitates her Makers Power Divine,
And changes her sometimes, and sometimes does refine:
It does, like Grace, the Fallen Tree restore
To its blest state of Paradise before:
Who would not joy to see his conquering hand
Ore all the Vegetable World command?
And the wild Giants of the Wood receive
    What Law he's pleas'd to give?
He bids th' il-natur'd Crab produce
The gentler Apples Winy Juice;
    The golden fruit that worthy is
    Of *Galatea*'s purple kiss;
    He does the savage Hawthorn teach
    To bear the Medlar and the Pear,
    He bids the rustick Plum to rear
    A noble Trunk, and be a Peach.
    Even *Daphnes* coyness he does mock,
    And weds the Cherry to her stock,
    Though she refus'd *Apolloes* suit;
    Even she, that chast and Virgin Tree,
    Now wonders at her self, to see
That she's a mother made, and blushes in her fruit.

ABRAHAM COWLEY

11.

Methinks I see great *Dioclesian* walk
In the *Salonian* Gardens noble shade,
Which by his own Imperial hands was made:
I see him smile (methinks) as he does talk
With the Ambassadors, who come in vain,
 T'entice him to a throne again.
If I, my Friends (said he) should to you show
All the delights, which in these Gardens grow;
'Tis likelier much, that you should with me stay,
Than 'tis that you should carry me away:
And trust me not, my Friends, if every day,
 I walk not here with more delight,
Then ever after the most happy fight,
In Triumph, to the Capitol, I rod,
To thank the gods, & to be thought, my self almost a god.

6. *Of Greatness.*

SInce we cannot attain to Greatness, (saies the *Sieur de Montagn*) let's have our revenge by railing at it: this he spoke but in Jest. I believe he desired it no more then I do, and had less reason, for he enjoyed so plentiful and honourable a fortune in a most excellent Country, as allowed him all the real conveniences of it, seperated and purged from the Incommodities. If I were but in his condition, I should think it hard measure, without being convinced of any crime, to be sequestred from it and made one of the Principal Officers of State. But the Reader may think that what I now say, is of small authority, because I never was, nor ever shall be put to the tryal: I can therefore only make my Protestation,

> *If ever I more Riches did desire*
> *Then Cleanliness and Quiet do require.*
> *If e're Ambition did my Fancy cheat,*
> *With any wish, so mean as to be great,*
> *Continue, Heav'n, still from me to remove*
> *The Humble Blessings of that Life I love.*

428

ESSAYS, IN VERSE AND PROSE

I know very many men will despise, and some pity me, for this humour, as a poor spirited fellow; but I'me content, and like *Horace* thank God for being so. *Dii bene fecerunt inopis me quodque pusilli Finxerunt animi.* I confess, I love Littleness almost in all things. A little convenient Estate, a little chearful House, a little Company, and a very little Feast, and if I were ever to fall in love again (which is a great Passion, and therefore, I hope, I have done with it) it would be, I think, with Prettiness, rather than with Majestical Beauty. I would neither wish that my Mistress, nor my Fortune, should be a *Bona Roba*, nor as *Homer* uses to describe his Beauties, like a Daughter of great *Jupiter* for the stateliness and largeness of her person, but as *Lucretius* saies,

 Parvula, pumilio, Χαρίτων μία, *tota merum sal.*

Where there is one man of this, I believe there are a thousand of *Senecio's* mind, whose ridiculous affectation of Grandeur, *Seneca* the Elder describes to this effect. *Senecio* was a man of a turbid and confused wit, who could not endure to speak any but mighty words and sentences, till this humour grew at last into so notorious a Habit, or rather Disease, as became the sport of the whole Town: he would have no servants, but huge, massy fellows, no plate or houshold-stuff, but thrice as big as the fashion: you may believe me, for I speak it without Railery, his extravagancy came at last into such a madness, that he would not put on a pair of shooes, each of which was not big enough for both his feet: he would eat nothing but what was great, nor touch any Fruit but Horseplums and Pound-pears: he kept a Concubine that was a very Gyantess, and made her walk too alwaies in *Chiopins*, till at last, he got the Surname of *Senecio Grandio*, which, *Messala* said, was not his *Cognomen*, but his *Cognomentum*: when he declamed for the three hundred *Lacedæmonians*, who alone opposed *Xerxes* his Army of above three hundred thousand, he stretch'd out his armes, and stood on tiptoes, that he might appear the taller, and cryed out, in a very loud voice; I rejoyce, I rejoyce— We wondred, I remember, what new great fortune had befaln his Eminence. *Xerxes* (saies he) is All mine own. He who took away the sight of the Sea, with the Canvas Vailes of so many ships— and then he goes on so, as I know not what to make of the rest, whither it be the fault of the Edition, or the Orators own burly way of Non-sence.

This is the character that *Seneca* gives of this *Hyperbolical* Fop, whom we stand amazed at, and yet there are very few men who are not in some things, and to some degrees *Grandio's*. Is any thing more common, then to see our Ladies of quality wear such high shooes as they cannot walk in, without one to lead them? and a Gown as long again as their Body, so that they cannot stir to the next room without a Page or two to hold it up? I may safely say, That all the ostentation of our Grandees is just like a Train of no use in the world, but horribly cumbersome and incommodious. What is all this, but a spice of *Grandio*? how tædious would this be, if we were always bound to it? I do believe there is no King, who would not rather be deposed, than endure every day of his Reign all the Ceremonies of his Coronation. The mightiest Princes are glad to fly often from these Majestique pleasures (which is, me-thinks, no small disparagement to them) as it were for refuge, to the most contemptible divertisements, and meanest recreations of the vulgar, nay, even of Children. One of the most power-ful and fortunate Princes of the world, of late, could finde out no delight so satisfactory, as the keeping of little singing Birds, and hearing of them, and whistling to them. What did the Emperours of the whole world? If ever any men had the free and full enjoyment of all humane Greatness (nay that would not suffice, for they would be gods too) they certainly possess it: and yet, one of them who stiled himself Lord and God of the Earth, could not tell how to pass his whole day pleasantly, without spending constant two or three hours in catching of Flies, and killing them with a bodkin, as if his Godship had been *Beelzebub*. One of his Predecessors, *Nero* (who never put any bounds, nor met with any stop to his Appetite) could divert himself with no pastime more agreeable, than to run about the streets all night in a disguise, and abuse the women, and affront the men whom he met, and sometimes to beat them, and some-times to be beaten by them: This was one of his Imperial nocturnal pleasures. His chiefest in the day, was to sing and play upon a Fiddle, in the habit of a Minstril, upon the publick stage: he was prouder of the Garlands that were given to his Divine voice (as they called it then) in those kinde of Prizes,

than all his Forefathers were, of their Triumphs over nations:
He did not at his death complain, that so mighty an Emperour
and the last of all the *Cæsarian* race of Deities, should be
brought to so shameful and miserable an end, but only cryed out,
Alas, what pity 'tis that so excellent a Musician should perish in
this manner! His Uncle *Claudius* spent half his time at playing
at Dice, that was the main fruit of his Soveraignty. I omit the
madnesses of *Caligula*'s delights, and the execrable sordidness of
those of *Tiberius*. Would one think that *Augustus* himself, the
highest and most fortunate of mankind, a person endowed too
with many excellent parts of Nature, should be so hard put to
it sometimes for want of recreations, as to be found playing at
Nuts and bounding stones, with little *Syrian* and *Moorish* Boyes,
whose company he took delight in, for their prating and their
wantonness?

> Was it for this, that *Romes* best blood he spilt,
>   With so much Falshood, so much guilt?
> Was it for this that his Ambition strove,
> To æqual *Cæsar* first, and after *Jove*?
> Greatness is barren sure of solid joyes;
> Her Merchandize (I fear) is all in toyes,
> She could not else sure so uncivil be,
> To treat his universal Majesty,
>   His new-created Deity,
> With Nuts and Bounding-stones and Boys.

But we must excuse her for this meager entertainment, she
has not really wherewithall to make such Feasts as we imagine,
her Guests must be contented sometimes with but slender
Cates, and with the same cold meats served over and over
again, even till they become Nauseous. When you have pared
away all the Vanity what solid and natural contentment does
there remain which may not be had with five hundred pounds a
year? not so many servants or horses; but a few good ones,
which will do all the business as well: not so many choice
dishes at every meal, but at several meals, all of them, which
makes them both the more healthy, and the more pleasant: not
so rich garments, nor so frequent changes, but as warm and as
comely, and so frequent change too, as is every jot as good for
the Master, though not for the Tailor, or *Valet de chamber*: not

such a stately Palace, nor guilt rooms, or the costliest sorts of Tapestry ; but a convenient brick house, with decent Wainscot, and pretty Forest-work hangings. Lastly, (for I omit all other particulars, and will end with that which I love most in both conditions) not whole Woods cut in walks, nor vast Parks, nor Fountain, or Cascade-Gardens ; but herb, and flower, and fruit-Gardens which are more useful, and the water every whit as clear and wholesome, as if it darted from the breasts of a marble Nymph, or the Urn of a River-God. If for all this, you like better the substance of that former estate of Life, do but consider the inseparable accidents of both : Servitude, Disquiet, Danger, and most commonly Guilt, Inherent in the one; in the other Liberty, Tranquility, Security and Innocence, and when you have thought upon this, you will confess that to be a truth which appeared to you before, but a ridiculous *Paradox*, that a low Fortune is better guarded and attended than an high one, If indeed we look only upon the flourishing Head of the Tree, it appears a most beautiful object,

——Sed quantum vertice ad aur[a]s
Æther[ias] tantum radice ad Tartara tendit.

As far as up to'wards He'ven the Branches grow,
So far the Root sinks down to Hell below.

Another horrible disgrace to greatness is, that it is for the most part in pitiful want and distress : what a wonderful thing is this ? unless it degenerate into Avarice, and so cease to be Greatness : It falls perpetually into such Necessities, as drive it into all the meanest and most sordid ways of Borrowing, Cousinage, and Robbery, *Mancipiis locuples eget æris Cappadocum Rex*, This is the case of almost all Great men, as well as of the poor King of *Cappadocia*. They abound with slaves, but are indigent of Money. The ancient Roman Emperours, who had the Riches of the whole world for their Revenue, had wherewithal to live (one would have thought) pretty well at ease, and to have been exempt from the pressures of extream Poverty. But yet with most of them, it was much otherwise, and they fell perpetually into such miserable penury, that they were forced to devour or squeeze most of their friends and servants, to cheat with infamous projects, to ransack and pillage all their Provinces. This fashion of Imperial Grandeur, is imitated by all inferiour and subordinate sorts of it, as if it were a point of Honour. They must be cheated of a third part of their Estates, two other thirds they must expend in Vanity, so that they remain Debtors for all the Necessary Provisions of life, and have no way to satisfie those debts, but out of the succours and supplies of Rapine, as Riches encreases (says Solomon) so do the Moaths that devour it. The Master Moath has no more than before. The Owner, methinks, is like *Ocnus* in the [F]able, who is perpetually winding a Rope of Hay and an Ass at the end perpetually eating it. Out of these inconveniences arises natur-. ally one more, which is, that no Greatness can be satisfied or contented with it self: still if it could mount up a little higher, it would be Happy, if it could gain but that point, it would ob-tain all it's desires; but yet at last, when it is got up to the very top of the Pic of Tenarif, it is in very great danger of breaking its neck downwards, but in no possibility of ascending upwards into the seat of Tranquility above the Moon. The first am-bitious men in the world, the old Gyants are said to have made an Heroical attempt of scaling Heaven in despight of the gods, and they cast *Ossa* upon *Olympus* and *Pelion* upon *Ossa* : two or three mountains more they thought would have done their Business, but the Thunder spoil'd all the work, when they were come up to the third story.

> And what a noble plot was crost,
> And what a brave design was lost.

A famous person of their Off-spring, the late Gyant of our Nation, when from the condition of a very inconsiderable Cap-tain, he had made himself Lieutenant General of an Army of little *Titans*, which was his first Mountain, and afterwards General, which was his second, and after that, absolute Tyrant of three Kingdoms, which was the third, and almost touch'd the Heaven which he affected, is believed to have dyed with grief and discontent, because he could not attain to the honest name of a King, and the old formality of a Crown, though he had before exceeded the power by a wicked Usurpation. If he could have compast that, he would perhaps have wanted some-thing else that is necessary to felicity, and pined away for want of the Title of an Emperour or a God. The reason of this is, that Greatness has no reallity in Nature, but a Creature of the Fancy, a Notion that consists onely in Relation and Comparison: It is indeed an Idol; but St. *Paul* teaches us, *That an Idol is nothing in the World*. There is in truth no Rising or Meridian of the Sun, but onely in respect to several places: there is no Right or Left, no Upper-Hand in Nature; every thing is Little, and every thing is Great, according as it is diversly compared. There may be perhaps some Village in *Scotland* or *Ireland* where I might be a Great Man; and in that case I should be like *Cæsar*. (you would wonder how *Cæsar* and I, should be like one another in any thing) and choose rather to be the First man of the Village, then Second at *Rome*. Our Country is called *Great Britany*, in regard onely of a Lesser of the same Name; it would be but a ridiculous Epithete for it, when we consider it together with the Kingdom of *China*. That too, is but a pitifull Rood of ground in comparison of the whole Earth besides: and this whole Globe of Earth, which we account so immense a Body, is but one Point or Atome in relation to those numberless Worlds that are scattered up and down in the Infinite Space of the Skie which we behold. The other many Inconveniences of grandeur I have spoken of disperstly in several Chapters, and shall end this with an *Ode* of *Horace*, not exactly copyed, but rudely imitated.

Horace. L. 3. Ode 1.

Odi profanum vulgus, &c.

1.

HEnce, ye Profane; I hate ye all;
    Both the Great, Vulgar, and the small.
To Virgin Minds, which yet their Native whiteness hold,
Not yet Discolour'd with the Love of Gold,
    (That Jaundice of the Soul,
Which makes it look so Guilded and so Foul)
To you, ye very Few, these truths I tell;
The Muse inspires my Song, Heark, and observe it well.

ESSAYS, IN VERSE AND PROSE

2.

We look on Men, and wonder at such odds
    'Twixt things that were the same by Birth;
We look on Kings as Giants of the Earth,
These Giants are but Pigmeys to the Gods.
    The humblest Bush and proudest Oak,
Are but of equal proof against the Thunder-stroke.
Beauty, and Strength, and Wit, and Wealth, and Power
    Have their short flourishing hour;
    And love to see themselves, and smile,
And joy in their Preeminence a while;
    Even so in the same Land,
Poor Weeds, rich Corn, gay Flowers together stand;
Alas, Death Mowes down all with an impartial Hand.

3.

And all you Men, whom Greatness does so please,
    Ye feast (I fear) like *Damocles:*
    If you your eyes could upwards move,
(But you (I fear) think nothing is above)
You would perceive by what a little thread
    The Sword still hangs over your head.
No Title of Wine would drown your cares;
No Mirth or Musick over-noise your feares.
The fear of Death would you so watchfull keep,
As not t' admit the Image of it, sleep.

4.

Sleep is a God too proud to wait in Palaces
And yet so humble too as not to scorn
    The meanest Country Cottages;
    His Poppey grows among the Corn.
The Halcyon sleep will never build his nest
    In any stormy breast.
    'Tis not enough that he does find
    Clouds and Darkness in their Mind;
    Darkness but half his work will do.
'Tis not enough; he must find Quiet too.

5.

The man, who in all wishes he does make,
    Does onely Natures Counsel take.
That wise and happy man will never fear
    The evil Aspects of the Year;
Nor tremble, though two Comets should appear;
He does not look in Almanacks to see,
    Whether he Fortunate shall be;
Let *Mars* and *Saturn* in th' Heavens conjoyn,
And what they please against the World design,
    So *Jupiter* within him shine.

6.

If of your pleasures and desires no end be found,
God to your Cares and Fears will set no bound.
    What would content you? Who can tell?
Ye fear so much to lose what you have got,
    As if you lik'd it well.
Ye strive for more, as if ye lik'd it not.
    Go, level Hills, and fill up Seas,
Spare nought that may your wanton Fancy please
    But trust Me, when you 'have done all this,
Much will be Missing still, and much will be Amiss.

7. *Of Avarice.*

THere are two sorts of *Avarice*, the one is but of a Bastard
kind, and that is, the rapacious Appetite of Gain; not for
its own sake, but for the pleasure of refunding it immediately
through all the Channels of Pride and Luxury. The other is
the true kind, and properly so called; which is a restless and
unsatiable desire of Riches, not for any farther end or use, but
onely to hoard, and preserve, and perpetually encrease them.
The Covetous Man, of the first kind, is like a greedy *Ostrich*,
which devours any Metall, but 'tis with an intent to feed upon
it, and in effect it makes a shift to digest and excern it. The
second is like the foolish Chough, which loves to steal Money
onely to hide it. The first does much harm to Mankind, and

a little good too to some few: The second does good to
none; no, not to himself. The first can make no excuse to
God, or Angels, or Rational Men for his actions; The second
can give no Reason or colour, not to the Devil himself for
what he does; He is a slave to Mammon without wages.
The first makes a shift to be beloved; I, and envyed too by
some People: The second is the universal Object of Hatred
and Contempt. There is no Vice has been so pelted with
good Sentences, and especially by the Poets, who have pursued
it with Stories and Fables, and Allegories, and Allusions; and
moved, as we say, every Stone to fling at it: Among all
which, I do not remember a more fine and Gentleman-like
Correction, then that which was given it by one Line of
Ovids.

> *Desunt Luxuriæ multa, Avaritiæ Omnia.*

> Much is wanting to Luxury, All to Avarice.

To which saying, I have a mind to add one Member, and
render it thus,

> Poverty wants some, Luxury Many, Avarice
> All Things.

Some body sayes of a virtuous and wise Man, That having
nothing, he has all: This is just his Antipode, Who, having
All things, yet has Nothing. He's a Guardian Eunuch to his
beloved Gold; *Audivi eos Amatores esse maximos sed nil potesse.*
They'r the fondest Lovers, but impotent to Enjoy.

> And, oh, What Mans condition can be worse
> Then his, whom Plenty starves, and Blessings curse;
> The Beggars but a common Fate deplore,
> The Rich poor Man's Emphatically Poor.

I wonder how it comes to pass, that there has never been
any Law made against him: Against him, do I say? I mean,
For him; as there are publick Provisions made for all other
Madmen: It is very reasonable that the King should appoint
some persons (and I think the Courtiers would not be against
this proposition) to manage his Estate during his Life (for his
Heires commonly need not that care) and out of it to make
it their business to see, that he should not want Alimony

ABRAHAM COWLEY

befitting his condition, which he could never get out of his own cruel fingers. We relieve idle Vagrants, and counterfeit Beggars, but have no care at all of these really Poor men, who are (methinks) to be respectfully treated in regard of their quality. I might be endless against them, but I am almost choakt with the super-abundance of the Matter; Too much Plenty impoverishes me as it does Them. I will conclude this odious Subject with part of *Horace's* first *Satyre*, which take in his own familiar stile.

I 'dmire, *Mecænas*, how it comes to pass,
That no man ever yet contented was,
Nor is, nor perhaps will be with that state
In which his own choice plants him or his Fate
Happy their Merchant, the old Soldier cries;
The Merchant beaten with tempestuous skies,
Happy the Soldier one half hour to thee
Gives speedy Death or Glorious victory.
The Lawyer, knockt up early from his rest
By restless Clyents, calls the Peasant blest,
The Peasant when his Labours ill succeed,
Envys the Mouth which only Talk does feed,
'Tis not (I think you'l say) that I want store
Of Instances, if here I add no more,
They are enough to reach at least a mile
Beyond long *Orator Fabias* his Stile,
But, hold, you whom no Fortune e're endears
Gentlemen, Malecontents, and Mutineers,
Who bounteous *Jove* so often cruel call,
Behold, *Jove's* now resolv'd to please you all.
Thou Souldier be a Merchant, Merchant, Thou
A Souldier be; and, Lawyer, to the Plow.
Change all their stations strait, why do they stay?
The Devil a man will change, now when he may,
Were I in General *Jove's* abused case,
By *Jove* I'de cudgel this rebellious race:
But he's too good; Be all then as you were,
However make the best of what you are,
And in that state be chearful and rejoyce,
Which either was your Fate, or was your Choice.

No, they must labour yet, and sweat and toil,
And very miserable be a while.
But 'tis with a Design only to gain
What may their Age with plenteous ease maintain.
The prudent Pismire does this Lesson teach
And industry to Lazy Mankind preach.
The little Drudge does trot about and sweat,
Nor does he strait devour all he can get,
But in his temperate Mouth carries it home
A stock for Winter which he knows must come.
And when the rowling World to Creatures here
Turns up the deform'd wrong side of the Year,
And shuts him in, with storms, and cold, and wet,
He chearfully does his past labours eat:
O, does he so? your wise example, th' Ant,
Does not at all times Rest, and Plenty want.
But weighing justly 'a mortal Ants condition
Divides his Life 'twixt Labour and Fruition.
Thee neither heat, nor storms, nor wet, nor cold
From thy unnatural diligence can withhold,
To th' *Indies* thou wouldst run rather then see
Another, though a Friend, Richer then Thee.
Fond man! what Good or Beauty can be found
In heaps of Treasure buried under ground?
Which rather then diminisht e're to see
Thou wouldst thy self too buried with them be:
And what's the difference, is't not quite as bad
Never to Use, as never to have Had?
In thy vast Barns millions of Quarters store,
Thy Belly for all that will hold no more
Then Mine does; every Baker makes much Bread,
What then? He's with no more then others fed.
Do you within the bounds of Nature Live,
And to augment your own you need not strive,
One hundred Acres will no less for you
Your Life's whole business then ten thousand do.
But pleasant 'tis to take from a great store;
What, Man? though you'r resolv'd to take no more
Then I do from a small one? if your Will
Be but a Pitcher or a Pot to fill,

ABRAHAM COWLEY

To some great River for it must you go,
When a clear spring just at your feet does flow?
Give me the Spring which does to humane use
Safe, easie, and untroubled stores produce,
He who scorns these, and needs will drink at *Nile*
Must run the danger of the Crocodile,
And of the rapid stream it self which may
At unawares bear him perhaps away.
In a full Flood *Tantalus* stands, his skin
Washt o're in vain, for ever, dry within;
He catches at the Stream with greedy lips,
From his toucht Mouth the wanton Torment slips:
You laugh now, and expand your careful brow;
Tis finely said, but what's all this to you?
Change but the Name, this Fable is thy story,
Thou in a Flood of useless Wealth dost Glory,
Which thou canst only touch but never taste;
Th' abundance still, and still the want does last.
The Treasures of the Gods thou wouldst not spare,
But when they'r made thine own, they Sacred are,
And must be kept with reverence, as if thou
No other use of precious Gold didst know,
But that of curious Pictures to delight
With the fair stamp thy *Virtuoso* sight.
The only true, and genuine use is this,
To buy the things which *Nature* cannot miss
Without discomfort, Oyl, and vital Bread,
And Wine by which the Life of Life is fed.
And all those few things else by which we live;
All that remains is Giv'n for thee to Give;
If Cares and Troubles, Envy, Grief and Fear,
The bitter Fruits be, which fair Riches bear,
If a new Poverty grow out of store;
The old plain way, ye Gods, let me be Poor.

A Paraphrase on an Ode in Horace's *third Book,* *beginning thus,* Inclusam Danaen ˙turris ahenea.

A Tower of Brass, one would have said,
  And Locks, and Bolts, and Iron bars,
And Guards, as strict as in the heat of wars,
Might have preserv'd one Innocent Maiden-head.
The jealous Father thought he well might spare,
    All further jealous Care,
And as he walkt, t'himself alone he smil'd,
    To think how *Venus* Arts he had beguil'd;
    And when he slept, his rest was deep,
But *Venus* laugh'd to see and hear him sleep.
    She taught the Amorous *Jove*
    A Magical receit in Love,
Which arm'd him stronger, and which help'd him more,
Than all his Thunder did, and his Almighty-ship before.

2.

She taught him Loves Elixar, by which Art,
His Godhead into Gold he did convert,
    No Guards did then his passage stay,
    He pass'd with ease; Gold was the Word;
Subtle as Lightning, bright and quick and fierce,
    Gold through Doors and Walls did pierce;
And as that works sometimes upon the sword,
    Melted the Maiden-head away,
Even in the secret scabbard where it lay.
    The prudent *Macedonian* King,
To blow up Towns, a Golden Mine did spring.
    He broke through Gates with this *Petar*,
'Tis the great Art of Peace, the Engine 'tis of War;
    And Fleets and Armies follow˙it afar,
The Ensign 'tis at Land, and 'tis the Seamans Star.

3.

Let all the World, slave to this Tyrant be,
Creature to this Disguised Deitie,
      Yet it shall never conquer me.
A Guard of Virtues will not let it pass,
And wisdom is a Tower of stronger brass.
The Muses Lawrel round my Temples spread,
'T does from this Lightnings force secure my head.
      Nor will I lift it up so high,
As in the violent Meteors way to lye.
Wealth for its power do we honour and adore?
The things we hate, ill Fate, and Death, have more.

4.

From Towns and Courts, Camps of the Rich and Great,
The vast *Xerxean* Army I retreat,
And to the small Laconick forces fly,
      Which hold the straights of Poverty.
Sellars and Granaries in vain we fill,
      With all the bounteous Summers store,
If the Mind thirst and hunger still.
      The poor rich Man's emphatically poor.
      Slaves to the things we too much prize,
We Masters grow of all that we despise.

5.

A Field of Corn, a Fountain and a Wood,
      Is all the Wealth by Nature understood,
The Monarch on whom fertile *Nile* bestows
      All which that grateful Earth can bear,
      Deceives himse[l]f, if he suppose
That more than this falls to his share.
Whatever an Estate does beyond this afford,
      Is not a rent paid to the Lord;
But is a Tax illegal and unjust,
Exacted from it by the Tyrant Lust.
      Much will always wanting be,
      To him who much desires. Thrice happy He
To whom the wise indulgency of Heaven,
  With sparing hand, but just enough has given.

[8.] *The dangers of an Honest man in much Company.*

IF twenty thousand naked *Americans* were not able to resist the assaults of but twenty well-armed *Spaniards*, I see little possibility for one Honest man to defend himself against twenty thousand Knaves, who are all furnisht *Cap a pe*, with the defensive arms of worldly prudence, and the offensive too of craft and malice. He will find no less odds than this against him, if he have much to do in humane affairs. The only advice therefore which I can give him, is, to be sure not to venture his person any longer in the open Campagn, to retreat and entrench himself, to stop up all Avenues, and draw up all bridges against so numerous an Enemy. The truth of it is, that a man in much business must either make himself a Knave, or else the world will make him a Fool: and if the injury went no farther then the being laught at, a wise man would content himself with the revenge of retaliation; but the case is much worse, for these civil *Cannibals* too, as well as the wild ones, not only dance about such a taken stranger, but at last devour him. A sober man cannot get too soon out of drunken company, though they be never so kind and merry among themselves, 'tis not unpleasant only, but dangerous to him. Do ye wonder that a vertuous man should love to be alone? It is hard for him to be otherwise; he is so, when he is among ten thousand: neither is the Solitude so uncomfortable to be alone without any other creature, as it is to be alone, in the midst of wild Beasts. Man is to man all kinde of Beasts, a fauning Dog, a roaring Lion, a theiving Fox, a robbing Wolf, a dissembling Crocodile, a treacherous Decoy, and a rapacious Vulture. The civilest, methinks, of all Nations, are those whom we account the most barbarous, there is some moderation and good Nature in the *Toupinambaltians* who eat no men but their Enemies, whilst we learned and polite and Christian *Europeans*, like so many Pikes and Sharks prey upon every thing that we can swallow. It is the great boast of Eloquence and Philosophy, that they first congregated men disperst, united them into Societies, and built up the Houses and the walls of Cities.

443

ABRAHAM COWLEY

I wish they could unravel all they had wooven; that we might have our Woods and our Innocence again instead of our Castles and our Policies. They have assembled many thousands of scattered people into one body: 'tis true, they have done so, they have brought them together into Cities, to cozen, and into Armies to murder one another: They found them Hunters and Fishers of wild creatures, they have made them Hunters and Fishers of their Brethren, they boast to have reduced them to a State of Peace, when the truth is, they have only taught them an Art of War; they have framed, I must confess, wholesome laws for the restraint of Vice, but they rais'd first that Devil which now they Conjure and cannot Bind; though there were before no punishments for wickednes, yet there was less committed because there were no Rewards for it. But the men who praise Philosophy from this Topick are much deceived; let Oratory answer for it self, the tinckling perhaps of that may unite a Swarm: it never was the work of Philosophy to assemble multitudes, but to regulate onely, and govern them when they were assembled, to make the best of an evil, and bring them, as much as is possible, to Unity again. Avarice and Ambition only were the first Builders of Towns, *Gen. 11. 4.* and Founders of Empire; They said, *Go to, let us build us a City and a Tower whose top may reach unto heaven, and let us make us a name, least we be scattered abroad upon the face of the Earth.* What was the beginning of *Rome,* the *Metropolis* of all the World? what was it, but a concourse of Theives, and a Sanctuary of Criminals? it was justly named by the *Augury* of no less then twelve Vultures, and the Founder cimented his walls with the blood of his Brother; not unlike to this was the beginning even of the first Town too in the world, and such is the Original sin of most Cities: their Actual encrease daily with their Age and growth; the more people, the more wicked all of them; every one brings in his part to enflame the contagion, which becomes at last so universal and so strong, that no Precepts can be sufficient Preservatives, nor any thing secure our safety, but flight from among the Infected. We ought in the choice of a Scituation to regard above all things the Healthfulness of the place, and the healthfulness of it for the Mind rather than for the Body. But suppose (which is hardly to be supposed) we had Antidote enough against this

444

Poison; nay, suppose farther, we were alwaies and at all pieces armed and provided both against the Assaults of Hostility, and the Mines of Treachery, 'twill yet be but an uncomfortable life to be ever in Alarms, though we were compast round with Fire, to defend ourselves from wild Beasts, the Lodging would be unpleasant, because we must always be obliged to watch that fire, and to fear no less the defects of our Guard, then the diligences of our Enemy. The summe of this is, that a virtuous man is in danger to be trod upon and destroyed in the crowd of his Contraries, nay, which is worse, to be changed and corrupted by them, and that 'tis impossible to escape both these inconveniences without so much caution, as will take away the whole Quiet, that is, the Happiness of his Life. Ye see then, what he may lose, but, I pray, What can he get there? *Quid Romæ faciam? Mentiri nescio.* What should a *Juv. Sat. 3.* man of truth and honesty do at Rome? he can neither understand, nor speak the Language of the place; a naked man may swim in the Sea, but 'tis not the way to catch Fish there; they are likelier to devour him, then he them, if he bring no Nets, and use no Deceits. I think therefore it was wise and friendly advice which *Martial* gave to *Fabian*, when he met him newly arrived at *Rome*. *Mart. L. 3.*

> Honest and Poor, faithful in word and thought;
> What has thee, *Fabian*, to the City brought?
> Thou neither the B[u]ffoon, nor Bawd canst play,
> Nor with false whispers th' Innocent betray:
> Nor corrupt Wives, nor from rich Beldams get
> A living by thy industry and sweat;
> Nor with vain promises and projects cheat,
> Nor Bribe or Flatter any of the Great.
> But you'r a Man of Learning, prudent, just;
> A Man of Courage, firm, and fit for trust.
> Why you may stay, and live unenvyed here;
> But (faith) go back, and keep you where you were.

Nay, if nothing of all this were in the case, yet the very sight of Uncleanness is loathsome to the Cleanly; the sight of Folly and Impiety vexatious to the Wise and Pious.

Lucretius, by his favour, though a good Poet; was but an *Lucr. Lib. 2.* ill-natur'd Man, when he said, It was delightful to see other

ABRAHAM COWLEY

Men in a great storm: And no less ill-natur'd should I think *Democritus*, who laught at all the World, but that he retired himself so much out of it, that we may perceive he took no great pleasure in that kind of Mirth. I have been drawn twice or thrice by company to go to *Bedlam*, and have seen others very much delighted with the fantastical extravagancie of so many various madnesses, which upon me wrought so contrary an effect, that I alwayes returned, not onely melancholy, but ev'n sick with the sight. My compassion there was perhaps too tender, for I meet a thousand Madmen abroad, without any perturbation; though, to weigh the matter justly, the total loss of Reason is less deplorable then the total depravation of it. An exact Judge of human blessings, of Riches, Honours, Beauty, even of Wit it self, should pity the abuse of them more then the want.

Briefly, though a wise man could pass never so securely through the great Roads of human Life, yet he will meet perpetually with so many objects and occasions of compassion, grief, shame, anger, hatred, indignation, and all passions but envy (for he will find nothing to deserve that) that he had better strike into some private path; nay, go so far, if he could, out of the common way, *Ut nec facta audiat Pelopidarum*; that he might not so much as hear of the actions of the Sons of *Adam*. But, Whither shall we flye then? into the Deserts, like the antient Hermites?

Metam. 1.

> *Quia terra patet sera regnat Erynnis,*
> *In facinus jurasse putes.*

One would think that all Mankind had bound themselves by an Oath to do all the wickedness they can; that they had all (as the Scripture speaks) sold themselves to Sin: the difference onely is, that some are a little more crafty (and but a little God knows) in making of the bargain. I thought when I went first to dwell in the Country, that without doubt I should have met there with the simplicity of the old Poetical Golden Age: I thought to have found no Inhabitants there, but such as the Shepherds of Sir *Phil. Sydney* in *Arcadia*, or of *Monsieur d'Urfe* upon the Banks of *Lignon*; and began to consider with my self, which way I might recommend no less to Posterity the Happiness and Innocence of the Men of *Chertsea*: but to confess the truth, I perceived quickly, by infallible demonstrations, that I was still in Old *England*, and not in *Arcadia*, or *La Forrest*; that if I could not content my self with any thing less then exact Fidelity in human conversation, I had almost as good go back and seek for it in the Court, or the Exchange, or Westminster-Hall. I ask again then Whither shall we fly, or what shall we do? The World may so come in a Mans way, that he cannot choose but Salute it, he must take heed though not to go a whoring after it. If by any lawful Vocation, or just necessity men happen to be Married to it, I can onely give them St. *Pauls* advice. *Brethren, the time is short, it remaines* ¹ Cor. 7. 29. *that they that have Wives be as though they had none. But I would* Verse 7. *that all Men were even as I my self.*

In all cases they must be sure that they do *Mundum ducere*, and not *Mundo nubere*. They must retain the Superiority and Headship over it: Happy are they who can get out of the sight of this Deceitful Beauty, that they may not be led so much as into Temptation ; who have not onely quitted the Metropolis, but can abstain from ever seeing the next Market Town of their Country.

Claudian's Old Man of *Verona*.

HAppy the Man, who his whole time doth bound
    Within th' enclosure of his little ground.
Happy the Man, whom the same humble place,
(Th' hereditary Cottage of his Race)
From his first rising infancy has known,
And by degrees sees gently bending down,
With natural propension to that Earth
Which both preserv'd his Life, and gave him birth.
Him no false distant lights by fortune set,
Could ever into foolish wandrings get.
He never dangers either saw, or fear'd:
The dreadful stormes at Sea he never heard.
He never heard the shrill allarms of War,
Or the worse noises of the Lawyers Bar.

447

No change of Consuls marks to him the year,
The change of seasons is his Calendar.
The Cold and Heat, Winter and Summer shows,
Autumn by Fruits, and Spring by Flow'rs he knows.
He measures Time by Land-marks, and has found
For the whole day the Dial of his ground.
A neighbouring Wood born with himself he sees,
And loves his old contemporary Trees.
H'as only heard of near *Verona's* Name,
And knows it like the *Indies*, but by Fame.
Does with a like concernment notice take
Of the Red-Sea, and of *Benacus* Lake.
Thus Health and Strength he to' a third age enjoyes,
And sees a long Posterity of Boys.
About the spacious World let others roam,
The Voyage Life is longest made at home.

9. *The shortness of Life and uncertainty of Riches.*

IF you should see a man who were to cross from *Dover* to *Calais*, run about very busie and sollicitous, and trouble himselfe many weeks before in making provisions for his voyage, would you commend him for a cautious and discreet person, or laugh at him for a timerous and impertinent Coxcomb? A man who is excessive in his pains and diligence, and who consumes the greatest part of his time in furnishing the remainder with all conveniencies and even superfluities, is to Angels and wise men no less ridiculous; he does as little consider the shortness of his passage that he might proportion his cares accordingly. It is, alas, so narrow a streight betwixt the Womb and the Grave, that it might be called the *Pas de Vie*, as well as that the *Pas de Calais*. We are all Ἐφήμεροι (as *Pindar* calls us) Creatures of a day, and therefore our Saviour bounds our desires to that little space; as if it were very probable that every day should be our last, we are taught to demand even Bread for no longer a time. The Sun ought not to set upon our Covetousness no more then upon our Anger, but as to God Almighty a thousand years are as one day, so in direct opposition, one day to the covetous man is as a thousand years; *Tam brevi fortis jaculatur ævo multa,* so far he shoots beyond his Butt: One would think he were of the opinion of the *Millenaries,* and hoped for so long a Reign upon Earth. The Patriarchs before the Flood, who enjoy'd almost such a Life, made, we are sure, less stores for the maintaining of it; they who lived Nine hundred years scarcely provided for a few days; we who live but a few days, provide at least for Nine hundred years; what a strange alteration is this of Humane Life and Manners? and yet we see an imitation of it in every mans particular experience, for we begin not the cares of Life till it be half spent, and still encrease them as that decreases. What is there among the actions of Beasts so illogical and repugnant to Reason? when they do any thing which seems to proceed from that which we call Reason, we disdain to allow them that perfection, and attribute it only to a Natural Instinct; and are not we Fools too by the same kind of Instinct? If we could but learn to number our days (as we are taught to pray that we might) we should adjust much better our other accounts, but whilst we never consider an end of them, it is no wonder if our cares for them be without end too. *Horace* advises very wisely, and in excellent good words, *spacio brevi spem longam reseces,* From a short Life cut off all Hopes that grow too long. They must be pruned away like suckers that choak the Mother-Plant, and hinder it from bearing fruit. And in another place to the same sence, *Vit[æ] summa brevis spem nos vetat inc[h]oare longam,* which *Seneca* does not mend when he says, *Oh quanta dementia est spes longas inchoantium*! but he gives an example there of an acquaintance of his named *Senecio,* who from a very mean beginning by great industry in turning about of Money through all ways of gain, had attained to extraordinary Riches but died on a suddain after, having supped merrily, *In ipso actu bene cedentium rerum, in ipso procurrentis fortunæ impetu,* In the full course of his good Fortune, when she had a high Tide and a stiff Gale and all her Sails on; upon which occasion he cries, out of *Virgil*

Insere nunc Melib[æ]e pyros, pone ordine vites,

Go *Melib[æ]us,* now,
Go graff thy Orchards and thy Vineyards plant;
Behold the Fruit!

For this *Senecio* I have no compassion, because he was taken as we say, in *ipso facto*, still labouring in the work of Avarice, but the poor rich man in St. *Luke* (whose case was not like this) I could pity, methinks, if the Scripture would permit me, for he seems to have been satisfied at last, he confesses he had enough for many years, he bids his soul take its ease, and yet for all that, God says to him: *Thou Fool, this night thy soul shall be required of thee,* and the things thou hast laid up, whom shall they belong to? where shall we find the causes of this bitter Reproach and terrible Judgement? we may find, I think, Two, and God perhaps saw more. First, that he did not intend true Rest to his Soul, but only to change the employments of it from Avarice to Luxury, his design is to eat and to drink, and to be merry. Secondly, that he went on too long before he thought of resting; the fulness of his old Barns had not sufficed him, he would stay till he was forced to build new ones; and God meted out to him in the same measure; Since he would have more Riches then his Life could contain, God destroy'd his Life and gave the Fruits of it to another.

Thus God takes away sometimes the Man from his Riches, and no less frequently Riches from the Man; what hope can there be of such a Marriage, where both parties are so fickle and uncertain? by what Bonds can such a couple be kept long together?

Luk. 12. 20.

1.

Why dost thou heap up Wealth, which thou must quit,
    Or, what is worse, be left by it?
Why dost thou load thy self, when thou'rt to flie,
    Oh Man ordain'd to die?

2.

Why dost thou build up stately Rooms on high,
    Thou who art under Ground to lie?
Thou Sow'st and Plantest, but no Fruit must see,
    For Death, alas! is sowing Thee.

3.

Suppose, thou Fortune couldst to tameness bring,
    And clip or pinion her wing;
Suppose thou couldst on Fate so far prevail
    As not to cut off thy Entail.

4.

Yet Death at all that subtilty will laugh,
    Death will that foolish Gardner mock,
Who does a slight and annual Plant engraff,
    Upon a lasting stock.

5.

Thou dost thy self Wise and Industrious deem ;
    A mighty Husband thou wouldst seem ;
Fond Man ! like a bought slave, thou all the while
    Dost but for others Sweat and Toil.

6.

Officious Fool ! that needs must medling be
    In business that concerns not thee !
For when to Future years thou' extendst thy cares
    Thou deal'st in other mens affairs.

7.

Even aged men, as if they truly were
    Children again, for Age prepare,
Provisions for long travail they design,
    In the last point of their short Line.

8.

Wisely the Ant against poor Winter hoords
    The stock which Summers wealth affords,
In Grashoppers that must at Autumn die,
    How vain were such an Industry ?

9.

Of Power and Honour the deceitful Light
    Might halfe excuse our cheated sight,
If it of Life the whole small time would stay,
    And be our Sun-shine all the day,

10.

Like Lightning that, begot but in a Cloud
    (Though shining bright, and speaking loud)
Whilst it begins, concludes its violent Race,
    And where it Guilds, it wounds the place.

ABRAHAM COWLEY

11.

Oh Scene of Fortune, which dost fair appear,
    Only to men that stand not near !
Proud Poverty, that Tinsel brav'ry wears !
    And, like a Rainbow, Painted Tears !

12.

Be prudent, and the shore in prospect keep,
    In a weak Boat trust not the deep.
Plac'd beneath Envy, above envying rise ;
    Pity Great Men, Great Things despise.

13.

The wise example of the Heavenly Lark,
    Thy Fellow-Poet, *Cowley* mark,
Above the Clouds let thy proud Musique sound,
    Thy humble Nest build on the Ground.

10. The danger of Procrastination.

A Letter to Mr. S. L.

I Am glad that you approve and applaud my design, of with-
drawing my self from all tumult and business of the world ;
and consecrating the little rest of my time to those studies, to
which Nature had so Motherly inclined me, and from which
Fortune, like a Step-mother has so long detained me. But never-
theless (you say, which, *But*, is *Ærugo mera*, a rust which spoils
the good Metal it grows upon. But you say) you would advise
me not to precipitate that resolution, but to stay a while longer
with patience and complaisance, till I had gotten such an Estate
as might afford me (according to the saying of that person whom
you and I love very much, and would believe as soon as another
man) *Cum dignitate otium.* This were excellent advice to *Josua*,
who could bid the Sun stay too. But there's no fooling with Life
when it is once turn'd beyond Forty. The seeking for a Fortune
then, is but a desperate After-game, 'tis a hundred to one, if a
man fling two Sixes and recover all ; especially, if his hand be no
luckier than mine. There is some help for all the defects of

Horat.

452

Fortune, for if a man cannot attain to the length of his wishes, he may have his Remedy by cutting of them shorter. *Epicurus* writes a Letter to *Idomeneas* (who was then a very powerful, wealthy, and (it seems) bountiful person) to recommend to Him who had made so many men Rich, one *Pythocles*, a friend of his, whom he desired might be made a rich man too ; But I intreat you that you would not do it just the same way as you have done to many less deserving persons, but in the most Gentlemanly manner of obliging him, which is not to adde any thing to his Estate, but to take something from his desires. The summ of this is, That for the uncertain hopes of some Conveniences we ought not to defer the execution of a work that is Necessary, especially, when the use of those things which we would stay for, may otherwise be supplyed, but the loss of time, never recovered : Nay, farther yet, though we were sure to obtain all that we had a mind to, though we were sure of getting never so much by continuing the Game, yet when the light of Life is so near going out, and ought to be so precious, *Le jeu ne vaut pas la Chandele*, The play is not worth the expence of the Candle : after having been long tost in a Tempest, if our Masts be standing, and we have still Sail and Tackling enough to carry us to our Port, it is no matter for the want of Streamers and Top-Gallants ; *Utere velis, Totos pande sinus.* A Gentleman in our late Civil Wars, when his Quarters were beaten up by the Enemy, was taken Prisoner, and lost his life afterwards, only by staying to put on a Band, and adjust his Periwig : He would escape like a person of quality, or not at all, and dyed the noble Martyr of Ceremony, and Gentility. I think your counsel of *Festina lente* is as ill to a man who is flying from the world, as it would have been to that unfortunate wel-bred Gentleman, who was so cautious as not to fly undecently from his Enemies, and therefore I prefer *Horace*'s advice before yours.

— Sapere Aude, Incipe —

Begin ; the Getting out of doors is the greatest part of the *Libr.* 1. *Agric.* Journey. *Varro* teaches us that *Latin* Proverb, *Portam itineri longissimam esse :* But to return to *Horace*,

> *— Sapere aude,*
> *Incipe, vivendi qui reɛte prorogat horam*
> *Rusticus expeɛtat dum labitur Amnis, at ille*
> *Labitur, & labetur in omne volubilis ævum.*

ABRAHAM COWLEY

Begin, be bold, and venture to be wise;
He who defers this work from day to day,
Does on a Rivers Bank expecting stay,
Till the whole stream, which stopt him, should be gon,
That runs, and as it runs, forever will run on.

Cæsar (the man of Expedition above all others) was so far
from this Folly, that whensoever, in a journey he was to cross
any River, he never went one foot out of his way for a Bridge,
or a Foord, or a Ferry, but flung himself into it immediately, and
swam over; and this is the course we ought to imitate, if we
meet with any stops in our way to Happiness. Stay till the
waters are low, stay till some Boats come by to transport you,
stay till a Bridge be built for you; You had even as good stay
till the River be quite past. *Persius* (who, you use to say, you
do not know whether he be a good Poet or no, because you
cannot understand him, and whom therefore (I say) I know to be
not a good Poet) has an odd expression of these Procrastinators,
which, methinks, is full of Fancy.

Pers.
Satyr. 5.
Jam Cras Hesternum consumpsimus, Ecce aliud Cras
Egerit hos annos.

> Our Yesterdays To morrow now is gone,
> And still a new Tomorrow does come on,
> We by Tomorrows draw up all our store,
> Till the exhausted Well can yield no more.

And now, I think, I am even with you, for your *Otium cum*
dignitate, and *Festina lente,* and three or four other more of your
New Latine Sentences: if I should draw upon you all my
forces out of *Seneca* and *Plutarch* upon this subject, I should over-
whelm you, but I leave those as Triary for your next charge.
I shall only give you now a light skirmish out of an Epigram-
matist, your special good Friend, and so, *Vale.*

Mart. Lib. 5. Epigr. 59.

To morrow you will Live, you always cry;
In what far Country does this morrow lye,
That 'tis so mighty long 'ere it arrive?
Beyond the *Indies* does this Morrow live?

'Tis so far fetcht this Morrow, that I fear
'Twill be both very Old and very Dear.
To morrow I will live, the Fool does say ;
To Day it self's too Late, the wise liv'd Yesterday.

Mart. Lib. 2. Ep. 90.

Wonder not, Sir (you who instruct the Town
In the true Wisdom of the Sacred Gown)
That I make haste to live, and cannot hold
Patiently out, till I grow Rich and Old.
Life for Delays and Doubts no time does give,
None ever yet, made Haste enough to Live.
Let him defer it, whose preposterous care
Omits himself, and reaches to his Heir.
Who does his Fathers bounded stores despise,
And whom his own too never can suffice :
My humble thoughts no glittering roofs require,
Or Rooms that shine with ought but constant Fire.
I well content the Avarice of my sight
With the fair guildings of reflected Light :
Pleasures abroad, the sport of Nature yeilds
Her living Fountains, and her smiling Fields :
And then at home, wha[t] pleasure is't to see
A little cleanly chearful Familie ?
Which if a chast Wife crown, no less in Her
Then Fortune, I the Golden Mean prefer.
Too noble, nor too wise, she should not be,
No, not too Rich, too Fair, too fond of me.
Thus let my life slide silently away,
With Sleep all Night, and Quiet all the Day.

11. *Of My self.*

IT is a hard and nice Subject for a man to write of himself, it
grates his own heart to say any thing of disparagement, and
the Readers Eares to hear any thing of praise from him. There
is no danger from me of offending him in this kind ; neither my

Mind, nor my Body, nor my Fortune, allow me any materials for that Vanity. It is sufficient, for my own contentment, that they have preserved me from being scandalous, or remarkable on the defective side. But besides that, I shall here speak of myself, only in relation to the subject of these precedent discourses, and shall be likelier thereby to fall into the contempt, then rise up to the estimation of most people. As far as my Memory can return back into my past Life, before I knew, or was capable of guessing what the world, or glories, or business of it were, the natural affections of my soul gave me a secret bent of aversion from them, as some Plants are said to turn away from others, by an Antipathy imperceptible to themselves, and inscrutable to mans understanding. Even when I was a very young Boy at School, instead of running about on Holy-daies and playing with my fellows; I was wont to steal from them, and walk into the fields, either alone with a Book, or with some one Companion, if I could find any of the same temper. I was then too, so much an Enemy to all constraint, that my Masters could never prevail on me, by any perswasions or encouragements, to learn without Book the common rules of Grammar, in which they dispensed with me alone, because they found I made a shift to do the usual exercise out of my own reading and observation. That I was then of the same mind as I am now (which I confess, I wonder at my self) may appear by the latter end of an Ode, which I made when I was but thirteen years old, and which was then printed with many other Verses. The Beginning of it is Boyish, but of this part which I here set down (if a very little were corrected) I should hardly now be much ashamed.

9.

This only grant me, that my means may lye
Too low for Envy, for Contempt too high.
　　Some Honor I would have
Not from great deeds, but good alone.
The unknown are better than ill known.
　　Rumour can ope' the Grave,
Acquaintance I would have, but when 't depends
Not on the number, but the choice of Friends.

10.

Books should, not business entertain the Light,
And sleep, as undisturb'd as Death, the Night.
    My House a Cottage, more
Then Palace, and should fitting be
For all my Use, no Luxury.
    My Garden painted o're
With Natures hand, not Arts; and pleasures yeild,
Horace might envy in his Sabine field.

11.

Thus would I double my Lifes fading space,
For he that runs it well, twice runs his race.
    And in this true delight,
These unbought sports, this happy State,
I would not fear nor wish my fate,
    But boldly say each night,
To morrow let my Sun his beams display,
Or in clouds hide them; I have liv'd to Day.

You may see by it, I was even then acquainted with the Poets
(for the Conclusion is taken out of *Horace* ;) and perhaps it was
the immature and immoderate love of them which stampt first,
or rather engraved these Characters in me : They were like
Letters cut into the Bark of a young Tree, which with the
Tree still grow proportionably.   But, how this love came to be
produced in me so early, is a hard question : I believe I can tell
the particular little chance that filled my head first with such
Chimes of Verse, as have never since left ringing there : For I
remember when I began to read, and to take some pleasure in
it, there was wont to lie in my Mothers Parlour (I know not by
what accident, for she her self never in her life read any Book
but of Devotion) but there was wont to lie *Spencers* Works;
this I happened to fall upon, and was infinitely delighted with
the Stories of the Knights, and Giants, and Monsters, and brave
Houses, which I found every where there : (Though my under-
standing had little to do with all this) and by degrees with the
tinckling of the Rhyme and Dance of the Numbers, so that I
think I had read him all over before I was twelve years old, and

ABRAHAM COWLEY

was thus made a Poet as immediately as a Child is made an Eunuch. With these affections of mind, and my heart wholly set upon Letters, I went to the University ; But was soon torn from thence by that violent Publick storm which would suffer nothing to stand where it did, but rooted up every Plant, even from the Princely Cedars to Me, the Hyssop. Yet I had as good fortune as could have befallen me in such a Tempest ; for I was cast by it into the Family of one of the best Persons, and into the Court of one of the best Princesses of the World. Now though I was here engaged in wayes most contrary to the Original design of my life, that is, into much company, and no small business, and into a daily sight of Greatness, both Militant and Triumphant (for that was the state then of the *English* and *French* Courts) yet all this was so far from altering my Opinion, that it onely added the confirmation of Reason to that which was before but Natural Inclination. I saw plainly all the Paint of that kind of Life, the nearer I came to it ; and that Beauty which I did not fall in Love with, when, for ought I knew, it was reall, was not like to bewitch, or intice me, when I saw that it was Adulterate. I met with several great Persons, whom I liked very well, but could not perceive that any part of their Greatness was to be liked or desired, no more then I would be glad, or content to be in a Storm, though I saw many Ships which rid safely and bravely in it : A storm would not agree with my stomach, if it did with my Courage. Though I was in a croud of as good company as could be found any where, though I was in business of great and honourable trust, though I eate at the best Table, and enjoyed the best conveniences for present subsistance that ought to be desired by a man of my condition in banishment and publick distresses ; yet I could not abstain from renewing my old School-boys Wish in a Copy of Verses to the same effect.

Well then ; I now do plainly see
This busie World and I shall ne're agree, *&c.*

And I never then proposed to my self any other advantage from His Majesties Happy Restoration, but the getting into some moderately convenient Retreat in the Country, which I thought in that case I might easily have compassed, as well as some others, with no greater probabilities or pretences have arrived to extraordinary fortunes: But I had before written a shrewd Prophesie against my self, and I think *Apollo* inspired me in the Truth, though not in the Elegance of it.

Pindar. Od.
Destiny.

Thou, neither great at Court nor in the War,
Nor at th' Exchange shal't be, nor at the wrangling Barr;
Content thy self with the small barren praise
Which neglected Verse does raise, *&c.*

However by the failing of the Forces which I had expected, I did not quit the Design which I had resolved on, I cast my self into it *A Corps Perdue*, without making capitulations, or taking counsel of Fortune. But God laughs at a Man, who sayes to his Soul, *Take thy ease* : I met presently not onely with many little encumbrances and impediments, but with so much sickness (a new misfortune to me) as would have spoiled the happiness of an Emperour as well as Mine: Yet I do neither repent nor alter my course. *Non ego perfidum Dixi Sacramentum;* Nothing shall separate me from a Mistress, which I have loved so long, and have now at last married; though she neither has brought me a rich Portion, nor lived yet so quietly with me as I hoped from Her.

———— *Nec vos, dulcissima mundi*
Nomina, vos Musæ, Libertas, Otia, Libri,
Hortique Sylvæq; anima remanente relinquam.

Nor by me ere shall you,
You of all Names the sweetest, and the best,
You Muses, Books, and Liberty and Rest;
You Gardens, Fields, and Woods forsaken be,
As long as Life it self forsakes not Me.

But this is a very petty Ejaculation; because I have concluded all the other Chapters with a Copy of Verses, I will maintain the Humour to the last.

ABRAHAM COWLEY

Martial. L. 10. Ep. 47.

Vitam quæ faciunt beatio[r]em, &c.

SInce, dearest Friend, 'tis your desire to see
   A true Receipt of Happiness from Me ;
These are the chief Ingredients, if not all ;
Take an Estate neither too great nor small,
Which *Quantum Sufficit* the Doctors call.
Let this Estate from Parents care descend ;
The getting it too much of Life does spend.
Take such a Ground, whose gratitude may be
A fair Encouragement for Industry.
Let constant Fires the Winters fury tame ;
And let thy Kitchens be a Vestal Flame.
Thee to the Town let never Suit at Law ;
And rarely, very rarely Business draw.
Thy active Mind in equal Temper keep,
In undisturbed Peace, yet not in sleep.
Let Exercise a vigorous Health maintain,
Without which all the Composition's vain.
In the same weight Prudence and Innocence take,
And of each does the just mixture make.
But a few Friendships wear, and let them be
By Nature and by Fortune fit for thee.
In stead of Art and Luxury in food,
Let Mirth and Freedome make thy Table good.
If any cares into thy Day-time creep,
At night, without Wines Opium, let them sleep.
Let rest, which Nature does to Darkness wed,
And not Lust, recommend to thee thy Bed,
Be satisfi'd, and pleas'd with what thou art ;
Act chearfully and well th' alotted part,
Enjoy the present Hour, be thankful for the Past,
And neither fear, nor wish th' approaches of the last.

ESSAYS, IN VERSE AND PROSE

Martial Book 10.   *Epigram* 96.

ME who have liv'd so long among the great,
    You wonder to hear talk of a Retreat:
And a retreat so distant, as may show
No thoughts of a return when once I go.
Give me a Country, how remote so e're,
Where happiness a mod'rate rate does bear,
Where poverty it self in plenty flowes,
And all the solid use of Riches knowes.
The ground about the house maintains it there,
The House maintains the ground about it here.
Here even Hunger's dear, and a full board,
Devours the vital substance of the Lord.
The Land it self does there the feast bestow,
The Land it self must here to Market go.
Three or four suits one Winter here does wast,
One suit does there three or four winters last.
Here every frugal Man must oft be cold,
And little Luke-warm-fires are to you sold.
There Fire's an Element as cheap and free,
Almost as any of the other Three.
Stay you then here, and live among the Great,
Attend their sports, and at their tables eat.
When all the bounties here of Men you score:
The Places bounty there, shall give me more.

Epitaphium Vivi Auctoris.

HIc, O *Viator*, sub *Lare parvulo*
    Couleius *Hic est Conditus*, *Hic Jacet*;
  Defunctus humani Laboris
      Sorte, supervacuâque vitâ.
Non Indecorâ pauperie *Nitens*,
Et Non inerti *nobilis* otio,
  Vanôque dilectis popello
      Divitiis animosus hostis.

461

ABRAHAM COWLEY

Possis ut illum dicere mortuum ;
En Terra jam nunc Quantula *sufficit ?*
Exempta sit Curis, viator,
  Terra sit illa Levis, precare.
Hic sparge Flores, *sparge breves* Rosas,
Nam vita gaudet Mortua Floribus,
  Herbisque Odoratis Corona
    Vatis adhuc Cinerem Calentem.

To the Duke of Buckingham, *upon his Marriage
with the Lord* Fairfax *his Daughter.*

1.

BEauty and strength together came,
  Even from the Birth with *Buckingham* ;
The little active Seeds which since are grown
  So fair, so large and high,
With Life it self were in him sown;
Honour and wealth stood like the Midwifes by,
  To take the Birth into their happy Hands,
And wrapt him warme in their rich swaddling Bands:
To the great Stock the thriving Infant soon
  Made greater Acquisitions of his own;
With Beauty generous Goodness he Combin'd,
Courage to Strength, Judgment to Wit he joyn'd;
He pair'd, and match'd his Native Virtues right,
Both to improve their use, and their Delight.

2.

O blest Conjunction of the fairest Stars,
  That Shine in Humane Natures Sphere !
But O ! what envious Cloud your Influence bars,
  Ill fortune, what dost thou do there ?
  Hadst thou the least of Modesty,
Thou'dst be asham'd that we should see

TO THE DUKE OF BUCKINGHAM

Thy deform'd Looks, and Dress, in such a Company:
Thou wert deceiv'd, rash Goddess, in thy hate,
    If thou dist foolishly believe
That thou could'st him of ought deprive,
    But, what men hold of thee, a great Estate.
And here indeed thou to the full did shew
    All that thy Tyrant Deity could do,
His Virtues never did thy power obey,
In dissipating Storms, and routed Battles they
Did close and constant with their Captain stay;
    They with him into Exile went,
    And kept their Home in Banishment.
The Noble Youth was often forc'd to flee
    From the insatiate Rage of thee,
    Disguised, and Unknown;
In all His shap'es they always kept their own,
Nay, with the Foil of darkness, brighter shone,
    And might Unwillingly have don,
But, that just Heaven thy wicked Will abhor'd,
What Virtues most detest, might have betrayd their Lord.

3.

Ah slothful *Love*, could'st thou with patience see
Fortune usurp that flowry Spring from thee;
And nip thy rosy Season with a Cold,
That comes too soon, when Life's short year grows old,
    Love his gross Error saw at last,
And promis'd large amends for what was past,
He promis'd, and has don it, which is more
Than I, who knew him long, e'er knew him do before.
H' has done it Nobly, and we must confess
Could do no more, though h' ought to do no less.
What has he don? he has repair'd
The Ruines which a luckless War did make,
    And added to it a Reward
Greater than Conquest for its share could take.
His whole Estate could not such gain produce,
Had it layd out a hundred years at use.

4.

Now blessings to thy Noble choice betide,
  Happy, and Happy-making Bride.
Though thou art born of a Victorious Race,
And all their rougher Victorie dost grace
  With gentle Triumphs of thy Face,
Permit us in this milder War to prize
No less thy yeilding Heart, than thy Victorious Eyes.
  Nor doubt the honour of that field,
Where thou didst first overcome, e'er thou didst yield.
  And tho' thy Father's Martial Name
  Has fill'd the Trumpets and the Drums of Fame,
Thy Husband triumphs now no less than He,
  And it may justly question'd be,
  Which was the Happiest Conqueror of the Three.

5.

There is in Fate (which none but Poets see)
  There is in Fate the noblest Poetry,
And she has shown, Great Duke, her utmost Art in Thee;
  For after all the troubles of thy Scene,
  Which so confus'd, and intricate have been,
She has ended with this Match thy Tragicomedy;
We all admire it, for the truth to tell,
Our Poet Fate ends not all Plays so well;
But this she as her Master-piece does boast,
  And so indeed She may;
For in the middle Acts, and turnings of the Play,
  Alas! we gave our Hero up for lost.
All men, I see, this with Applause receive,
  And now let me have leave,
A Servant of the Person, and the Art,
To Speak this Prologue to the second part.

A

POEM

ON THE LATE

CIVIL WAR.

By Mr. *ABRAHAM COWLEY*.

[Design]

LONDON, Printed 1679.

The Publisher

TO THE

READER.

Eeting *accidentally with this* Poem *in Manuscript, and being informed that it was a Piece of the incomparable* Mr. A C's, *I thought it unjust to hide such a* Treasure *from the* World. *I remember'd that our Author in his Preface to his* Works, *makes mention of some* Poems *written by him on the* late Civil War, *of which the following Copy is questionably a part. In his most imperfect and unfinish'd* Pieces, *you will discover the Hand of so great a Master. And (whatever his own Modesty might have advised to the contrary) there is not one careless stroke of his but what should be kept sacred to Posterity. He could write nothing that was not worth the preserving, being habitually a* Poet *and* Always Inspired. *In this Piece the Judicious Reader will find the Turn of the Verse to be his, the same Copious and Lively Imagery of* Fancy, *the same Warmth of* Passion *and Delicacy of* Wit *that sparkles in all his* Writings. *And certainly no Labours of a* Genius *so Rich in its self, and so Cultivated with* Learning *and* Manners, *can prove an unwelcome* Present *to the* World.

A

POEM

On the late

CIVIL WAR.

WHat Rage does *England* from it self divide,
    More than the Seas from all the World beside.
From every part the roaring Cannons play,
From every part Blood roars as loud as they.
What *English* Ground but still some Moisture bears,
Of Young Mens Blood, and more of Mothers Tears!
What Airs unthickened with the Sighs of Wives,
Tho' more of Maids for their dear Lovers Lives.
Alas, what Triumphs can this Victory shew,
That dies us Red in Blood and Blushes too!
How can we wish that Conquest, which bestows
Cypress, not Bays, upon the Conquering Brows,
It was not so when *Henry*'s dreadful Name,
Not Sword, nor Cause, whole Nations overcame.
To farthest West did his swift Conquests run,
Nor did his Glory set but with the Sun.
In vain did *Roderic* to his Hold retreat,
In vain had wretched *Ireland* call'd him Great.
Ireland! which now most basely we begin
To labour more to lose than he to win,
It was not so when in the happy East,
Richard our *Mars*, *Venus*'s Isle possest.
'Gainst the proud Moon, he the *English* Cross display'd,
Ecclips'd one Horn, and the other paler made.
When our dear Lives we ventured bravely there,
And digg'd our own to gain Christs Sepulchre.
That sacred Tomb which should we now enjoy,
We should with as much zeal fight to destroy.

ABRAHAM COWLEY

The precious Signs of our dead Lord we scorn,
And see his Cross worse than his Body torn.
We hate it now both for the *Greek* and *Jew*,
To us 'tis Fo[o]lishness and Scandal to[o].
To what with Worship the fond Papist falls,
That the fond Zealot a cursed Idol calls.
So, 'twixt their double Madness here's the odds,
One makes false Devils, t'other makes false Gods.

  It was not so when *Edward* prov'd his Cause,
By a Sword stronger than the *Salique* Laws.
Tho fetched from *Pharamond*, when the *French* did fight,
With Womens Hearts against the Womens Right.
The afflicted Ocean his first Conquest bore,
And drove Red Waves to the sad *Gallique* Shore:
As if he had Angry with that Element been,
Which his wide Soul bound with an Island in.
Where's now that spirit with which at *Cressey* we,
And *Poictiers* forced from fate a Victory?
Two Kings at once we brought sad Captives home,
A Triumph scarcely known to ancient *Rome*;
Two Foreign Kings, but now alas we strive,
Our own, our own good Soveraign to Captive!

  It was not so when *Agincourt* was won,
Under great *Henry* served the Rain and Sun,
A Nobler Fight the Sun himself ne'r knew,
Not when he stop'd his Course a Fight to view!
Then Death's old Archer did more skilful grow,
And learned to shoot more sure from th' *English* bow;
Then *France* was her own story sadly taught,
And felt how *Cæsar* and how *Edward* fought.

  It was not so when that vast Fleet of *Spain*,
Lay torn and scatter'd on the *English* Main;
Through the proud World, a Virgin, terror struck,
The *Austrian* Crowns and *Rome*'s seven hills she shook:
To her great *Neptune* Homaged all his Streams
And all the wide-stretched Ocean was her *Thames*.
Thus our Fore-Fathers Fought, Thus bravely bled,
Thus still they live, whil'st we alive are dead;
Such Acts they did that *Rome* and *Cæsar* too,
Might Envy those, whom once they did subdue.

ON THE LATE CIVIL WAR

We're not their off-spring, sure our Heralds Lie,
But Born we know not how, as now we Die;
Their precious Blood we could not venture thus:
Some *Cadmus* sure sow'd *Serpents* teeth for us;
We could not else by mutual Fury fall,
Whilst *Rhine* and *Sequan* for our Armies call:
Chuse War or Peace, you have a Prince you know,
As fit for both, as both are fit for you.
Furious as Lightning when Wars Tempest came,
But Calm in Peace, Calm as a Lambent Flame.
  Have you forgot those happy years of late,
That saw nought ill, but us that were Ingrate;
Such years, as if Earths youth Return'd had been,
And that old Serpent Time had Cast his Skin:
As Gloriously, and Gently did they move,
As the bright Sun that Measures them above;
Then onely in Books the Learn'd could misery see,
And the Unlearned ne're heard of Misery.
Then happy *James* with as deep Quiet Reigned,
As in His heavenly Throne, by Death, he gained.
And least this blessing with his Life should Cease,
He left us *Charles* the Pledge of future Peace.
Charles under whom, with much ado, no less
Than sixteen years, we endur'd our happiness;
Till in a Moment, in the *North* we find,
A Tempest Conjured up without a Wind.
As soon the *North* her Kindness did Repent,
First the Peace-Maker, and next War she sent:
Just *Tweed* that now had with long Peace forgot
On which side dwelt the *English*, which the Scot:
Saw glittering Arms shine sadly on his face;
Whil'st all the affrighted Fish sank down apace;
No blood did then from this dark Quarrel grow,
It gave blunt wounds, that bled not out till now!
For *Jove*, who might have us'd his thundring power,
Chose to fall calmly in a Golden showre!
A way we found to Conquer, which by none
Of all our thrifty Ancestors was known;
So strangly Prodigal of late we are,
We there buy Peace, and here at home buy War.

ABRAHAM COWLEY

How could a war so sad and barbarous please,
But first by slandring those blest days of Peace?
Through all the Excrements of State they pry,
Like Emp'ricks to find out a Malady;
And then with Desperate boldness they endeavor,
Th' Ague to cure by bringing in a Feavor:
The way is sure to expel some ill no doubt,
The Plague we know, drives all Diseases out.
What strange wild fears did every Morning breed,
Till a strange fancy made us sick indeed?
And Cowardise did Valours place supply,
Like those that kill themselves for fear to die!
What frantick Diligence in these Men appears,
That fear all Ills, and act o'r all their Fears?
Thus into War we scared ourselves; and who
But *Aaron*'s Sons, that the first Trumpet blew.
Fond Men! who knew not that they were to keep
For God, and not for Sacrifice, their Sheep.
The Churches first this Murderous Doctrine sow,
And learn to Kill as well as Bury now.
The Marble Tombs where our Fore-fathers lie,
Sweated with dread of too much company:
And all their sleeping Ashes shook for fear,
Least thousand Ghosts should come and shroud them there.
   Petitions next from every Town they frame,
To be restored to them from whom they came.
The same stile all, and the same sense does pen,
Alas, they allow set Forms of Prayer to Men.
Oh happy we, if Men would neither hear
Their studied Form, nor God their sudden Prayer.
They will be heard, and in unjustest wise,
The many-Headed Rout for Justice cries.
They call for Blood, which now I fear does call
For Blood again, much louder than they all.
In sensless Clamours, and confused Noise,
We lost that rare, and yet unconquer'd Voice:
So when the sacred *Thracian* Lyre was drown'd,
In the *Bistonian* Womens mixed sound.
The wondring Stones, that came before to hear,
Forgot themselves, and turn'd his Murderers there.

ON THE LATE CIVIL WAR

The same loud Storm, blew the *Grave Mitre* down;
It blew down that, and with it shook the *Crown*.
Then first a *State*, without a *Church* begun;
Comfort thy self dear *Church*, for then 'twas done.
The same great Storm, to Sea great *Mary* drove,
The Sea could not such dangerous Tempests move.
The same drove *Charles* into the North, and then
Would Readilier far have driven him back agen.
To fly from noise of Tumults is no shame,
Ne'r will their Armies force them to the same:
They all his Castles, all his Towns invade,
He's a large Prisoner in all *England* made!
He must not pass to *Irelands* weeping Shore,
The Wounds these Surgeons make must yield them more:
He must not conquer his lewd Rebels there,
Least he should learn by that to do it here.
The Sea they subject next to their command,
The Sea that Crowns our Kings and all their Land.
Thus poor they leave him, their base Pride and Scorn,
As poor as these, now mighty Men, were born.
When straight whole Armies meet in *Charle[s]*'s Right,
How no Man knows, but here they are and Fight.
A Man would swear that saw this altered State,
Kings were called Gods, because they could Create
Vain Men; 'tis Heaven this first Assistance brings,
The same is Lord of Hosts, that's King of Kings.
Had Men forsook him, Angels from above,
(The Assyrian did less their Justice move.)
Would all have mustered in his Righteous Aid,
And Thunder against your Cannon would have play'd.
It needs not so, for Man desires to right
Abused Mankind, and wretches you must fight.
    Worster first saw't, and trembled at the view,
Too well the Ills of *Civil War* she knew.
Twice did the Flames of old her Towers invade,
Twice call'd she in vain for her own *Severn's* Aid.
Here first the Rebel Winds began to roar,
Brake loose from the just Fetters which they bore.
Here Mutinous Waves above their shore did swell,
And the first Storm of that Dire Winter fell.

But when the two great Brethren once appeared,
And their bright Heads like *Leda*'s off-spring rear'd,
When those Sea-calming Sons, from *Jove* were spied,
The Winds all fled, the Waves all sunk and died!
How fought great *Rupert*, with what Rage and Skill?
Enough to have Conquered had his Cause been ill!
Comely Young Man; and yet his dreadful sight,
The Rebels Blood to their faint Hearts does fright.
In vain alas it seeks so weak defence;
For his keen Sword brings it again from thence:
Yet grieves he at the Lawrels thence he bore;
Alas poor Prince, they'll fight with him no more.
His Vertue will be eclipsed with too much Fame,
Henceforth he will not Conquer, but his Name:
Here —— with tainted Blood the Field did stain,
By his own Sacriledge, and's Countrys Curses slain.
The first Commander did Heavens Vengeance shew,
And led the Rebels Van to shades below.

On two fair Hills both Armies next are seen,
The affrighted Valley sighs and sweats between;
Here *Angels* did, with fair Expectance stay,
And wish'd good things to a King as mild as they;
There *Fiends* with hunger waiting did abide,
And Cursed both, but spurr'd on the guilty side.
Here stood *Religion*, her looks gently sage,
Aged, but much more comely for her Age!
There *Schism* Old Hagg, tho' seeming young appears,
As Snakes by casting skins, Renew their years;
Undecent Rags of several Dies she wore,
And in her hand torn *Liturgies* she bore.
Here *Loyalty* an humble *Cross* display'd,
And still as *Charles* pass'd by, she bow'd and pray'd.
Sedition there her Crimson Banner spreads,
Shakes all her Hands, and roars with all her Heads.
Her knotty Hairs were with dire Serpents twist,
And every Serpent at each other hist.
Here stood *White Truth*, and her own Host does bless,
Clad with those Armes of Proof her Nakedness.
There *Perjuries* like Cannons roar aloud,
And *Lies* flew thick, like Cannons smoaky Cloud.

ON THE LATE CIVIL WAR

Here *Learning* and th' *Arts* met, as much they fear'd
As when the *Hunns* of old and *Goths* appear'd.
What should they do, unapt themselves to fight,
They promised noble Pens the Acts to write.
There *Ignorance* advanced, and joy'd to spy
So many that durst fight they know not why.
From those, who most the slow-soul'd *Monks* disdain,
From those she hopes the *Monks* dull Age again,
Here *Mercy* waits with sad but gentle look,
Never alass had she her *Charles* forsook!
For *Mercy* on her Friends, to *Heaven* she cries,
Whilst *Justice* pulls down *Vengeance* from the Skies.
Oppression there, *Rapine* and *Murder* stood
Ready as was the Field to drink their Blood.
A thousand wronged Spirits amongst them moan'd,
And thrice the Ghost of mighty *Strafford* groan'd.
  Now flew their Cannon thick through wounded Air,
Sent to defend, and kill their Soveraign there.
More than he them, the Bullets feared his Head,
And at his Feet lay innocently Dead.
They knew not what those Men that sent them meant,
And acted their pretence not their intent.
  This was the Day, this the first Day that shew'd
How much to *Charles* for our long Peace we ow'd:
By his Skill here, and Spirit we understood,
From War naught kept him but his Countries good.
In his great Looks, what chearful Anger shone,
Sad *War*, and joyful *Triumphs* mixed in one.
In the same Beams of his Majestick Eye,
His own Men Life, his Foes did Death espy.
Great *Rupert* this, that Wing great *Willmott* leads,
White-feathered Conquest, flies o'r both their Heads.
They charge, as if alone, they'd beat the Foe;
Whether their Troops followed them up or no.
They follow close and haste into the fight,
As swift as strait the Rebels made their flight.
So swift the Miscreants fly, as if each fear
And jealousie they framed, had met them there.
They heard Wars Musick, and away they flew,
The Trumpets fright worse than the Organs do.

473

Their Souls which still, new by-ways do invent,
Out at their wounded Backs perversly went.
Pursue no more, ye *Noble Victors* stay,
Least too much Conquest lose so brave a day:
For still the Battail sounds behind, and Fate
Will not give all; but sets us here a Rate:
Too dear a rate she sets, and we must pay
One honest Man, for ten such Knaves as they.
Streams of Black tainted Blood the Field besmear,
But pure well coloured drops shine here and there:
They scorn to mix with flouds of baser veines,
Just as the nobler moisture, Oyl disdains.
Thus fearless *Lindsey*, thus bold *Aubigny*,
Amid'st the Corps of slaughtered Rebels lie:
More honourably than — — e'r was found,
With troops of living Traytors circled round.
Rest valiant Souls in peace, ye sacred pair,
And all whose Deaths attended on you there:
You'r kindly welcomed to Heavens peaceful coast,
By all the reverend Martyrs Noble Host.
Your soaring Souls they meet with triumph, all
Led by great *Stephen* their old General.
Go — — now prefer thy flourishing State,
Above those murdered Heroes doleful fate.
Enjoy that life which thou durst basely save,
And thought'st a Saw-pit nobler than a Grave,
Thus many saved themselves, and *Night* the rest,
Night that agrees with their dark Actions best.
A dismal shade did *Heavens* sad Face o'r flow,
Dark as the night, slain *Rebels* found below.
No gentle Stars their chearful Glories rear'd,
Ashamed they were at what was done, and fear'd
Least wicked Men their bold excuse should frame
From some strange Influence, and so vail their shame.
To Duty thus, Order and Law incline,
They who ne'r Err from one eternal Line.
As just the Ruin of these Men they thought,
As *Sisera*'s was, 'gainst whom themselves had fought.
Still they Rebellions ends remember well
Since *Lucifer* the Great, their shining Captain fell.

ON THE LATE CIVIL WAR

For this the Bells they ring, and not in vain,
Well might they all ring out for thousands slain.
For this the Bonefires, their glad Lightness spread,
When Funeral Flames might more befit their dead.
For this with solemn thanks they tire their *God*,
And whilst they feel it, mock th' Almighties Rod.
They proudly now abuse his Justice more,
Than his long Mercies they abu'sd before.
Yet these the Men that true Religion boast,
The Pure and Holy, Holy, Holy, Host!
What great reward for so much Zeal is given?
Why, Heaven has thank'd them since as they thank'd Heaven.
    Witness thou *Brainford*, say thou Ancient Town,
How many in thy Streets fell grovelling down.
Witness the *Red Coats* weltering in their Gore,
And died anew into the Name they bore.
Witness their Men blowed up into the Air,
All Elements their Ruins joyed to share.
In the wide Air quick Flames their Bodies tore,
Then drown'd in Waves, thei'r tost by Waves to shore.
Witness thou *Thames*, thou wast amazed to see
Men madly run to save themselves in thee.
In vain, for *Rebels Lives* thou woul[d]st not save,
And down they sunk beneath thy conquering Wave.
Good reverend *Thames*, the best beloved of all
Those noble Blood, that meet at *Neptune*'s Hall;
London's proud *Towers*, which do thy Head adorn,
Are not thy Glory now, but Grief and Scorn.
Thou grievest to see the *White named Palace* shine,
Without the Beams of it's own Lord and thine:
Thy Lord which is to all as good and free,
As thou kind Flood to thine own Banks can be.
How does thy peaceful Back disdain to bear
The *Rebels* busie Pride at *Westminster*.
Thou who thy self doest without murmuring pay
Eternal Tribute to thy Prince the Sea.
    To *Oxford* next Great *Charles* in Triumph came,
Oxford the *British* Muses second Fame.
Here Learning with some State and Reverence looks,
And dwells in Buildings lasting as her Books;

ABRAHAM COWLEY

Both now Eternal, but they had Ashes been,
Had these *Religious Vandals* once got in.
Not *Bodley*'s *Noble Work* their *Rage* would spare,
For *Books* they know the chief *Malignants* are.
In vain they silence every Age before,
For Pens of Time to come will wound them more.
The Temples decent Wealth, and modest State,
Had suffered, this their Avarice, that their Hate.
Beggary and Scorn into the Church they'd bring,
And make God Glorious, as they made the King.
O happy Town, that to Lov'd *Charles*'s Sight,
In those sad Times givest Safety and Delight.
The Fate which *Civil War* it self doth bless,
Scarce wouldst thou change; for *Peace* this happiness.
Amidst all Joys which Heaven allows thee here,
Think on thy *Sister*, and then shed a tear.

What Fights did this sad Winter see each day,
Her Winds and Storms came not so thick as they!
Yet nought these far lost Rebels could recall,
Not *Marlborough*'s nor *Cirencester*'s fall.
Yet still for Peace the *Gentle Conqueror* sues,
By his Wrath they Perish, yet his Love refuse.
Nor yet is the plain Lesson understood,
Writ by kind Heaven, in *B——* and *H——*'s Blood.
Chad and his Church saw where their Enemy lay,
And with just Red, new marked their Holy day.
Fond Men, this Blow the injured *Crosier* strook,
Naught was more fit to perish but thy Book.
Such fatal Vengeance did wronged *Charlegrove* shew,
Where —— both begun and ended to[o].
His cursed Rebellion, where his Soul's repaid
With separation, great as that he made.
—— Whose Spirit moved o'r this mighty Frame,
O' th Brittish Isle, and out this Chaos came.
—— The Man that taught Confusions Art,
His Treasons restless and yet noisless Heart.
His Active Brain, like *Ætna*'s Top appear'd,
Where Treason's forged, yet no noise outward heard.
'Twas he continued what e'r bold *M——* said,
And all the popular noise that *P——* has made.

476

ON THE LATE CIVIL WAR

'Twas he that taught the *Zealous Rout* to rise,
And be his Slaves for some feigned Liberties.
Him for this Black Design, Hell thought most fit,
Ah! wretched Man, cursed by too good a Wit.

If not all this your stubborn Hearts can fright,
Think on the *West*, think on the *Cornish* might:
The *Saxon* Fury, to that far stretch'd place,
Drove the torn Reliques of great *Brutus* Race.
Here they of old, did in long safety lie,
Compassed with Seas, and a worse Enemy.
Ne'r till this time, ne'r did they meet with Foes
More Cruel and more Barbarous than those.
Ye noble *Brittains*, who so oft with Blood
Of *Pagan Hosts*, have died old *Tamar*'s Flood,
If any drop of mighty *Uther* still,
Or *Uther*'s mighty'r Son your Veins does fill,
Shew then that Spirit, till all Men think by you
The doubtful Tales of your great *Arthur* true.
You have shewn it *Britains*, and have often done
Things that have cheared the weary setting Sun.
Again did *Tamar* your dread Arms behold,
As just and as successful as the Old:
It kissed the *Cornish Banks*, and vow'd to bring
His richest Waves to feed the ensuing Spring;
But murmur'd sadly, and almost deny'd
All fruitful Moisture to the *Devon* side.
Ye Sons of War, by whose bold Acts we see
How great a thing exalted Man may be;
The World remains your Debtor, that as yet
Ye have not all gone forth and conquerd it.
I knew that Fate some wonders for you meant,
When matchless *Hopton* to your Coasts she sent.
Hopton! so wise, he needs not Fortunes Aid,
So fortunate his Wisdom's useless made.
Should his so often tryed Companions fail,
His *Spirit*, alone, and *Courage* would prevail.
Miraculous Man! how would I sing thy praise,
Had any Muse crowned me with half the *Bays*
Conquest hath given to thee; and next thy Name
Should *Berkly, Stanning, Digby* press to Fame.

ABRAHAM COWLEY

Godolphin thee, thee *Greenvil* I'd rehearse,
But Tears break off my Verse,
How oft has vanquished *Stamford* backward fled,
Swift as the parted Souls of those he led!
How few did his huge Multitudes defeat,
For most are Ciphers when the Number's great.
Numbers alass of Men, that made no more,
Than he himself Ten Thousand times told o'r.
Who hears of *Stratton* Fight, but must confess
All that he heard or read before was less.
Sad *Germany* can no such Trophy boast,
For all the Blood these twenty years sh' has lost.
Vast was their *Army*, and their *Arms* were more
Than th' Host of Hundred-handed *Gyants* bore.
So strong their *Arms*, it did almost appear
Secure, had neither Arms nor Men been there.
In *Hopton* breaks, in break the *Cornish* Powers,
Few and scarce Arm'd, yet was the advantage ours.
What doubts could be, their outward strength to win,
When we bore *Arms* and *Magazine* within.
The violent Swords out-did the Muskets ire,
It strook the Bones, and there gave dreadful fire:
We scorned their Thunder and the reaking Blade,
A thicker Smoak than all their Cannon made.
Death and loud *Tumults* fill'd the place around;
With fruitless rage; fallen Rebels bite the Ground,
The *Arms* we gain'd, were *Wealth*, *Bodies*, of the Foe,
All that a full fraught Victory can bestow.
Yet stays not *Hopton* thus, but still proceeds,
Pursues himself through all his glorious deeds.
With *Hertford*, and the *Prince*, he joyns his fate,
The *Belgian Trophies* on their journey wait.
The *Prince* who oft had check'd proud *W——* fame.
And fool'd that flying *Conquerours* empty name:
Till by his loss that fertile Monster thriv'd,
This Serpent cut in parts rejoyn'd and liv'd.
It liv'd and would have stung us deeper yet,
But that bold *Greenvil* its whole fury met.
He sold like *Decius* his devoted Breath,
And left the Common-Wealth Heir to his Death.

478

ON THE LATE CIVIL WAR

Hail mighty *Ghost*! look from on high and see
How much our *Hands* and *Swords* remember thee.
At *Roundway Heath*, our Rage at thy great fall,
Whet all our Spirits, and made us *Greenvils* all.
One thousand Horse beat all their numerous power;
Bless me! and where was then their *Conqueror*!
Coward of Fame, he flies in haste away,
Men, *Arms*, and *Name* leaves us the *Victors Prey*.
What meant those *Iron Regiments* which he brought,
That moving Statues seemd and so they fought.
No way for Death but by Disease appear'd,
Cannon and Mines a Siege they scarcely feared:
Till 'gainst all hopes they prov'd in this sad sight,
Too weak to stand, and yet too slow for fight.
The Furies houl'd aloud through trembling Air,
Th' astonish'd Snakes fell sadly from their Hair,
To *Lud*'s proud Town their hasty flight they took,
The Towers and Temples at their entrance shook:
In vain their Loss the' attempted to disguise,
And mustred up new Troops of fruitless lies:
God fought himself, nor could th' event be less,
Bright Conquest walks the Fields in all her dress.
Could this white day a Gift more grateful bring?
Oh yes! it brought bless'd *Mary* to the King!
In *Keynton* Field they met, at once they view
Their former Victory and enjoy a new.
Keynton the Place that Fortune did approve,
To be the *noblest Scene* of *War* and *Love*;
Through the Glad vail, Ten thousand *Cupids* fled
And Chas'd the wandring spirits of *Rebels* dead,
Still the lewd scent of Powder did they fear,
And scatter'd *Eastern smells* through all the Air.
Look happy Mount, look well, for this is she,
That Toyl'd and Travel'd for thy Victory,
Thy flourishing Head to her with reverence bow,
To her thou owest that Fame which Crowns thee now.
From far stretcht Shores they felt her spirit, and might:
Princes and *God* at any distance fight.
At her return well might sh' a Conquest have,
Whose very absence such a Conquest gave.

ABRAHAM COWLEY

This in the *West*, nor did the *North* bestow
Less Cause their usual gratitude to show;
With much of state brave *Cavendish* led them forth,
As swift and fierce as tempest from the *North*.
Cavendish whom every *Grace* and every *Muse*,
Kiss'd at his Birth; and for their own did chuse:
So good a *Wit* they meant not should excel
In *Arms*, but now they see't and like it well:
So large is that rich Empire of his heart,
Well may they rest contented with a Part;
How soon he forc'd the *Northern* Clouds to flight,
And struck Confusion into Form and Light!
Scarce did the Power Divine in fewer days,
A peaceful World out of a Chaos raise.
Bradford and *Leeds* propt up their sinking fame,
They bragg'd of Hosts, and *Fairfax* was a name.
Leeds, *Bradford*, *Fairfax* Powers are strait their own,
As quickly as they vote Men overthrown.
Bootes from his *Wain* look'd down below,
And saw our Victory move not half so slow.
I see the *Gallant Earl* break through the Foes,
In Dust and Sweat how gloriously he shows.
I see him lead the Pikes; What will he do?
Defend him Heaven, Oh whither will he go?
Up to the Cannons mouth he leads! in vain
They speak loud Death and threaten till they'r ta'ne.
So *Capaneu*'s two Armies fill'd with Wonder,
When he charged *Jove* and grappled with his Thunder.
Both Hosts with silence, and with terror shook,
As if not he, but they were thunder-strook:
The *Courage* here, and *Boldness* was no less,
Onely the *Cause* was better and *Success*.
Heaven will let naught be by their Cannon done,
Since at *Edghil* they sin'd and *Burlington*.
Go now your *silly Calumnies* repeat,
And make all *Papists* whom you cannot beat.
Let the World know some way, with whom you are vext,
And vote 'em *Turks* when they overthrow you next.
Why will you die fond Men, why will you buy,
At this fond rate, your Countreys slavery?

480

ON THE LATE CIVIL WAR

Is't liberty! what are those threats we hear,
Why do you thus th' *Old* and *New Prison* fill?
When that's the onely why; because you will?
Fain would you make *God* too thus tyranous be,
And *damn poor Men* by such a stiff Decree:
Is't property? why do such numbers then,
From God beg *Vengeance* and *Relief* from Men?
Why are the *Estates* and *Good's* seiz'd on of all
Whom *Covetous* or *Malicious Men* miscall?
What's more our own than our own Lives? But oh
Could *Yeoman's*, or could *Bourchier* find it so?
The *Barbarous Coward* alway's used to fly,
Did know no other way to see men die.
Or is't *Religion*? What then mean your Lies
Your Sacriledges and Pulpit Blasphemies,
Why are all *Sect's* let loose, that ere had Birth,
Since *Luther's noise* wak'd the *Lethargick Earth*,

The Author went no further.

APPENDIX.

Coolyes verses uppon my Lady Elisabeth *birth on Christmass even* 1635.

(From Harleian MSS. 6383: first printed by Dr Grosart in his Edition of Cowley.)

YOUR picture mighty P. ingrav'd in gould
    whiche from your picture doth more lustre hould
men to their frends for gratulation send
when Janus doth beginn the yeard and end:
Nature wch muche from your large hand receaves
for new-years-guift to thee thyne image gives
of farr more worth then thy goulds lovely print
both for the graver mettall and the mint:
what better auspice could the year beginn?
what richer crown for Janus head to beare?
well may we know yr spring time forward creeps
from th' fertile roote a new frenche lilly peeps:
go on wise nature, and with equall care
eache twelvemonth suche a new-years guift prepare.
Thou, whom 4. kingdomes for their father know,
art father only of 4. children now.
Oh lett the number of thy of-spring mount
till we thy children by thy citties count:
leave thy self with us diversly, or we
at the fear'd day shall envy heav'n to thee,
whiche mayst thou late enjoy and Nestor be
in years, as now thou art in prudency.
And when ould age that over Princes raignes,
hath scatterd could, and fayntnes through thy veyns,
and made thee weake such travaile to sustayn,
mayst thou be carried there in thine owne wayn.

                    A. COWLEY.

Upon the happie Birth of the Duke.

From Voces Votivae ab Academicis Cantabrigiensibus etc. MDCXL.

WHILST the rude North Charles his slow wrath doth call,
    Whilst warre is fear'd, and conquest hop'd by all,
The severall shires their various forces lend,
And some do men, some gallant horses send,
Some steel, and some (the stronger weapon) gold.
These warlike contributions are but old:

APPENDIX

That countrey learn'd a new and better way,
Which did this royall Prince for Tribute pay.
Who shall henceforth be with such rage possest,
To rouze our English Lion from his rest?
When a new Sonne doth his blest stock adorn,
Then to great Charles is a new Armie born.
In private births Hopes challenge the first place:
There's Certaintie at first in the Kings race;
And we may say, Such will his glories be,
Such his great acts, and, yet not prophesie.
I see in him his Father's boundlesse sprite,
Powerfull as flame, yet gentle as the light.
I see him through an adverse battel thrust,
Bedeck'd with noble sweat and comely dust.
I see the pietie of the day appeare,
Joyn'd with the heate and valour of the yeare,
Which happie Fate did to this birth allow:
I see all this; for sure 't is present now.
Leave off then, London, to accuse the starres
For adding a worse terrour to the warres;
Nor quarrel with the heavens, 'cause they beginne
To send the worst effect and scourge of sinne,
That dreadful plague, which, wheresoe're 't abide,
Devours both man and each disease beside.
For every life which from great Charles does flow,
And 's Female self, weighs down a crowd of low
And vulgar souls: Fate rids of them the earth,
To make more room for a great Princes birth.
So when the sunne, after his watrie rest,
Comes dancing from his chamber of the East,
A thousand pettie lamps spread ore the skie,
Shrink in their doubtfull beams; then wink, and die:
Yet no man grieves; the very birds arise,
And sing glad notes in stead of Elegies:
The leaves and painted flowers, which did erewhile
Tremble with mournfull drops, beginne to smile.
The losse of many why should they bemone,
Who for them more then many have in one?
  How blest must thou thy self, bright Mary, be,
Who by thy wombe canst blesse our miserie?
May't still be fruitfull. May your offspring too
Spread largely, as your fame and virtues do.
Fill every season thus: Time, which devours
Its own sonnes, will be glad and proud of yours.
So will the Year (though sure it weari'd be
With often revolutions) when't shall see
The honour by such births it doth attain,
Joy to return into it self again.

A. Cowley, A.B.T.C.

APPENDIX

On the Power of Love.

N.B. This is delivered down by tradition as a production of Cowley;
and was spoken at the Westminster-School election, on the following
subject:

"*Nullis amor est medicabilis herbis.*"—Ovid.

SOL Daphne sees, and seeing her admires,
Which adds new flames to his celestial fires:
Had any remedy for Love been known,
The god of Physic, sure, had cur'd his own.

The second and the third of the above poems were included in Dr Johnson's
editions of the works of the poets. The same collection includes two other
poems attributed to Cowley, but I have not been able to bring myself to
believe that the internal evidence justifies the inclusion of them and I have
therefore not printed them here. They are entitled *The Force of Love*,
Preserved from an old manuscript ('Throw an apple up a hill') and *The
Character of an Holy Sister* ('She that can sit three sermons in a day').

485

NOTES.

In the volume entitled *Poems By the most deservedly Admired Mrs Katherine Philips* (London, 1678), Cowley's commendatory verses 'On the Death of Mrs. Katherine Philips' (see the first volume of the present edition, p. 443) end with the following additional lines:

> To the glad world of Poetry and Love;
> There all the bless'd do but one body grow,
> And are made one too with their glorious Head,
>   Whom there triumphantly they wed,
> After the secret contract pass'd below;
> Their Love into Identity does go,
> 'Tis the first unity's Monarchic Throne,
> The Centre that knits all, where the great Three's but One.

(Ed. Saintsbury, *Caroline Poets*, Vol. I. p. 503, 1905.)

---

p. **1**. *Poetical Blossoms* was first published in 1633 : the title-page states that the book is ' By *A.C.*' The imprint is ' London, | Printed by *B.A.* and *T.F.* for Henry Seile, and are to | be sold at his shop at the Signe of the *Tygers-head* | in St. *Paules* Church-yard, | 1633.

A second edition was published when *Sylva* appeared in 1636. The third edition of 1637 has been followed in the present work. The following variations have been noted in a collation of the texts of 1633 (A) and 1636 (B).

In the folio edition of 1681, ' Printed by *Mary Clark*, for *Charles Harper*, at the Flower-de-luce in *Fleet-street*, and *Jacob Tonson*, at the Judges Head in *Chancery-lane*, near *Fleet-street*,' a ' Second Part ' was added, ' *Being what was Written and Published by himself in his YOUNGER YEARS*. And now Reprinted together.' The title-page describes the poems as in their ' *Fourth Edition*,' and they are prefaced by the following publishers' note :

The Book-sellers to the Reader.

THE following Poems of Mr. *Cowley* being much enquired after, and very scarce, (the Town hardly affording one Book, though it had been thrice Printed) we thought this Fourth Edition could not fail of being well received by the World. We presume one great reason why they were omitted in the last Collection, was, because the propriety of this Copy belonged not to the same person that Published those: but the reception they had found appears by the several Impressions through which they had pass'd. We dare not say they are equally perfect with those written by the Author in his *Riper Years*, yet certainly they are such as deserve not to be buried in obscurity. We presume the *Authors Judgment* of them is most reasonable to appeal to; and you will find him (allowing grains of modesty) give them no small Character. His words are in the 6th. Page of his Preface before his former Published Poems.

NOTES

You find our excellent Author likewise mentioning and reciting part of these Poems, *in his several Discourses by way of Essays in Verse and Prose, in the* 11th. *Discourse treating of himself,* page 143. These we suppose a sufficient Authority for our reviving them; and sure there is no ingenuous Reader to whom the smallest Remains of Mr. *Cowley* will be unwelcome. His Poems are every where the Copy of his mind, so that by this Supplement to his other Volume you have the Picture of that so deservedly Eminent Man from almost his *Childhood* to his *Latest Years,* The bud and bloom of his *Spring,* The warmth of his *Summer,* The richness and perfection of his *Autumn.* But for the Readers further curiosity, we refer him to the Authors following Preface to them, Published by himself. And to contribute all we can to our Readers satisfaction, we have endeavoured to make these Poems something more acceptable, by prefixing the Sculpture of the Authors Monument.

Your humble Servants,

C. H. J. T.

p. 3. *Not in* A.

p. 9, l. 9. A] Lover always followes them.

p. 10, l. 13. A] who with.

p. 11, ll. 24–27. A]
> Then from the Woods with sorrowful heart he goes,
> Filling with flowing thoughts his grieved minde,
> He seeks to ease his soule oppressing woes,
> But no refreshing comfort can he find:

l. 33. A] Which with.   l. 34. A] And Cupids.

p. 12, l. 3. A] By his.   l. 11. A] But either.   ll. 16–19. A]
> Whilst wandring thoughts thus guide her troubled Brain,
> Seeing a Lute (being farre from any cares)
> Shee tun'd this song whose musicke did transcende
> The pleasant harmony of the rowling Spheres;

p. 13, ll. 19–21. A]
> Such lines as I desire, that they may keepe
> Mee from sterne death, or when I leave my rime,
> They in my deaths revenge may conquer time.

l. 34. A, *possibly correctly*] any sweat.

p. 14, l. 5. A] and the fondling love.   l. 20. A] As th' Soul of Pylades and Orestes was.   l. 21. A] may wee.   l. 24. A] his fate as too. l. 26. A] teareth the.

p. 15, ll. 5–7. A]
> As if she strove to shew her miseries
> Were greater farre then his, and sweetly sings
> To out-reach his Sorrowes, by her sufferings.

ll. 9–14 (i. e. Stanza 35). A]
> His sadenesse cannot from Philocrates
> Be hid, who seekes all meanes his griefe to know,
> Seeing all mirth Philetus doth displease
> And Passion still pursues his conquered Foe:
> Hee therefore of his griefe did oft enquire,
> But Love with covering wings had hid the fire.

l. 17. A] to usurping.

p. 20, l. 11. 1637 *misprints*] impeachmeut.

p. 21, l. 7. 1637] power.

488

NOTES

p. 22, l. 36.   1637 *misprints*] Uulesse.

p. 29, l. 13.   1637 *repeats* of *incorrectly before* the.

p. 33, l. 17.   1637] fight.

p. 42, l. 4.   1637 *misprints*] appproaching.

p. 47, l. 5.   *A bracket has been added after* shoulders.   l. 11.   1637]
Parsalias.

p. 50, l. 7.   1637] Romor.

p. 61, l. 28.   1637 *omits number of stanza.*

p. 63, l. 27.   1637 *omits number of stanza.*

p. 64, l. 30.   1637 *misprints*] you.

p. 66.   The three-volume edition of Cowley's works published in 1711
contains, at the end of *Sylva*, the following verses :

To a Lady who desired a Song of Mr. Cowley, he presented this following.

COme, *Poetry*, and with you bring along
      A rich and painted Throng
Of noblest Words into my Song.
Into my Numbers let them gently flow,
Soft and pure, and thick as Snow,
      And turn thy Numbers still to prove
      Smooth as the smoothest Sphere above,
And like a Sphere, like a Sphere, harmoniously move.

Little dost thou, vain Song, thy Fortune know,
      What thou art destin'd to,
      And what the Stars intend to do.
Among a thousand Songs but few can be
Born to the Honour promis'd thee.
      Eliza's self shall thee receive,
      And a blest Being to thee give,
Thou on her sweet and tuneful Voice shalt live.

Her warbling Tongue shall freely with thee play,
      Thou on her Lips shalt stray,
      And dance upon the rosie Way.
No Prince alive that would not envy thee,
And count thee happier far than he.
      And how shalt thou thy Author crown !
      When fair *Eliza* shall be known
To sing thy Praise, when she but speaks her own.

p. 72, l. 13.   *Some copies print*] traversed.

p. 73, l. 9.   1638] Shepheads.

p. 75, l. 23.   *A comma has been substituted for a full stop at the end of this
line.*

p. 78, l. 13.   *Some copies print* humour *for* honor.

p. 79, l. 2.   *A bracket has been added at the beginning of the line.*

p. 80, l. 5.   1638 *misprints*] All.   l. 38.   *A full stop has been added at*

NOTES

the end of the speech here and in similar places elsewhere; also at the end of
the contracted names of the characters, instead of the commas of the text.

p. **81**, l. 23. 1638] blossomes?. l. 24. *Some copies read*] two needs
have. l. 25. *Some copies read*] lose't. *Some copies read*] speaking to?
l. 31. 1638] houest.

p. **82**, l. 3. *Some copies read*] salute them. l. 11. *Some copies read*]
open't hereafter.

p. **88**, l. 29. *Some copies read*] Ile cry.

p. **89**, l. 13. *Some copies read*] Recourse. l. 37. *Some copies read*] ô
would.

p. **92**, l. 1. *Some copies read*] She wall. l. 11. *Some copies read*] fat's.
l. 12. 1638 *misprints*] *Ball.* Weither. l. 21. 1638 *prints* ll. 18–27 *as one*
speech, but in the margin of two or three copies collated Cal. *is written where*
here inserted in square brackets.

p. **96**, l. 21. *A bracket has been taken away before* In.

p. **97**, l. 8. *Some copies read*] now many.

p. **99**, l. 18. *Some copies, and possibly correctly, read*] falt.

p. **103**, l. 39. 1638 *misprints*] hithet.

p. **106**, l. 1. 1638 *misprints*] scaudall.

p. **109**, l. 20. *A superfluous bracket has been taken away from the end of*
the line.

p. **114**, l. 29. 1638 *repeats the word* let.

p. **120**, l. 18. 1638 *misprints*] thuse.

p. **125**, l. 12. 1638 *misprints*] Malernus.

p. **133**, l. 29. 1638 *misprints*] wondcr.

p. **137**, l. 6. *A full stop has been added after* riddle.

p. **138**, l. 19. *A full stop has been taken away after* too.

p. **139**, l. 6. 1638 *misprints*] Shepheatdesse.

p. **145**, ll. 14, 15. *The last two words are possibly a stage direction.*

p. **146**, l. 1. *A mark of interrogation has been taken away after* sweetest.

p. **149**. There is a copy of this poem, signed 'Abr: Cowley,' among the
Burn MSS. in the British Museum, from which the following variants have
been taken. I am indebted to Mr G. A. Brown for a transcript of the MS.

p. **150**, l. 6. MS. *throughout to p.* 157 *except where otherwise stated*] and
so grow. l. 8. *Omits*] the. l. 9. goes. l. 20. scarce. l. 21.
their neat...have. l. 26. Ministers. l. 28. knew not. l. 31. Brain-
ford. l. 32. e're long.

p. **151**, l. 2. Nor vast. l. 4. In their own authors John Brown, Clever,
Parr. l. 5. what their. l. 6. Stroud. l. 8. maintain in liberty.
ll. 8, etc. *The square brackets are those of the original text.* l. 10. greatest.
l. 11. rout the. l. 13. *Omits*] gracious. l. 16. ne're. l. 17. th'
Estates of Subjects. l. 20. *Omitted in* MS. l. 22. of God. l. 24.
You've swore. l. 25. more. l. 26. swearings. l. 27. are so.
l. 32. prayers do say. l. 33. you doth ensue. l. 39. *Omits*] enough.
l. 40. in the.

p. **152**, l. 1. you would. l. 2. ye have...of Religion. l. 3. hope
to. l. 5. *Omits*] too. l. 9. Brainford. l. 13. your souls. l. 18.

NOTES

and punish. l. 20. That marry. l. 21. *Omits*] a *and* sacred. l. 23.
So great. l. 24. has. l. 25. you would. l. 27. men. l. 32.
Popish Invocation. l. 33. e're long you'l grant.

p. **153**, l. 3. proud lys to God himself you'l cant. *After* l. 4 *adds
following lines* :

> They simple fornications count no Crime
> Nor you in holy place and holy time,
> But wisely to Gods glory Sanctify
> Your fornication and Adultery,
> Zeal and the Spirit, so work among you then
> At all the meetings are begot new-men.

l. 7. doth. l. 14. Synods. l. 15. oth' earth you. l. 16. make.
l. 17. meat. l. 18. the Irish. l. 21. or Lent. l. 23. you'l.
l. 24. but your tongues. l. 25. *Omits*] few or. l. 32. will.
l. 35. backwards. l. 39. on the.

p. **154**, l. 1. 't' offend. l. 3. if your mind be rightly understood.
l. 6. bit by the. l. 12. have. l. 16. We hear of Divels. l. 20.
You've given to that Idiott 6. l. 21. there you begin. l. 25. have a.
l. 26. Kingdom. l. 27. *Omits*] not. l. 33. Parry. l. 34. He does.
l. 35. Lawry. l. 39. and men. l. 40. From Mr. Calumny.

p. **155**, l. 4. as well as. l. 5. you'l do't. l. 6. em to't. l. 7.
now her's twixt you the. l. 9. But what's. l. 10. or One Generall.
l. 14. I've. l. 20. them. l. 21. Excuse, Loans, Contribution.
l. 24. and your Synod hath. l. 25. Where's now the 20 part of all that
hath been. l. 27. Where all. l. 30. touch. l. 36. ha's.
l. 38. Would he be. *After* l. 40 *adds following lines* :

> One Groom for the close-stool again wou'd be
> Rather then still Groom of the close-Committee,
> Another for his Staff again doth itch
> Faith let him have it for another switch.

p. **156**, l. 2. They'd. l. 4. By's mothers. l. 10. Bishops not
their copes or. l. 11. Oh let us not. l. 16. tricks. l. 19. 1643
misprints] Tyrnnts. l. 22. About these men. l. 23. Iniquitys.
l. 26. or why. l. 30. Unjuster. l. 32. Gods. l. 33. Ye say...
Preferment. l. 36. *Omits*] will. l. 40. With pikes, Clubs, halbeards
sav'd.

p. **157**, l. 4. *Omits*] that. l. 10. assistance. l. 11. you enter'd
England. l. 13. their moneys. l. 18. 1643 *misprints*] mauy. l. 19.
Omits fats. l. 20. Stafford's. l. 22. good fine we.

p. **160**, l. 3. 1650 *misprints*] Öld. l. 11. 1650] and.

p. **161**. The *Prologue* and *Epilogue* to *The Guardian* were printed by
Cowley also in his *Miscellanies*. See *Poems*, 1905, pp. 31, 32. l. 4. 1650
misprints] Iis.

p. **164**, l. 1. 1650] you.

p. **169**, l. 1. 1650] three.

p. **170**, l. 31. *The central* d *is missing in the text of* 1650.

p. **171**, l. 11. *An exclamation mark takes the place of a mark of interro-
gation here and in one or two similar cases elsewhere.*

p. **187**, l. 4. 1650] you.

NOTES

p. 194, l. 10.   1650] Canundrums.

p. 196, l. 38.   1650 *misprints*] he he.

p. 201, l. 25.   1650] your.

p. 202, l. 23.   *A full stop has been added after* saw.   l. 30.   *A comma has been added after* corners.   l. 40.   1650] too.

p. 208, l. 6.   1650] i'm sure thon.

p. 212, l. 32.   1650 *misprints*] 'Siid.

p. 213, l. 3.   1650 *misprints*] ncv'r.

p. 216, l. 39.   1650] to.

p. 221, l. 2.   1650 *misprints*] malancholy.   l. 14.   1650] love, you

p. 226, l. 3.   *A full stop has been added after* true.

p. 230, l. 14.   1650 *misprints*] he.

p. 233, l. 22.   1650 *misprints*] Ralp.

p. 235, l. 9.   1650 *misprints*] knowlede.   l. 39.   1650 *misprints*] vety.

p. 236, l. 16.   1650 *misprints*] meeting.

p. 243.   *Some copies of the same date read*] A Proposition for the Advancement of Learning.   By A. Cowley.   Virg. O Fortunati quorum jam Mœnia Surgunt.

p. 248, l. 3.   1661] Londòn.

p. 255, l. 12.   1661] Schòol.   l. 19.   1661 *misprints*] well.

p. 256, l. 8.   1661] Nenesianus.   l. 16.   1661] Volumn.

p. 267, l. 7.   1663] Soveraing.

p. 271, l. 4.   1663 *misprints*] Tabith Baarebottle.

p. 275, l. 7.   1663 *misprints*] ye.

p. 282, l. 25.   1663 *misprints*] Madenhead.

p. 289, l. 3.   1663 *misprints*] dearh.

p. 291, l. 30.   1663] Their.

p. 295, l. 29.   1663] Wor.

p. 300, l. 21.   1663] their.

p. 317, l. 39.   1663] Similtudes.

p. 327, l. 9.   1663 *misprints*] cast.

p. 334, l. 1.   *The text gives this speech to* Wor.   *I have ventured to substitute* Pun.

p. 336, l. 7.   1663] him.

p. 341, l. 19.   1663 *misprints*] Earih.

p. 342.   Published in 1661.   I have not been able to see a copy of the edition of that year and I have therefore accepted the text of the folio of 1668. The title-page in the *Harleian Miscellany*, Vol. 5, reads: 'A Vision, concerning his late pretended Highness, *Cromwell* the Wicked : Containing a Discourse in Vindication of him, by a pretended Angel, and the Confutation thereof, by the Author, *Abraham Cowley*.—*Sua cuique Deus fit dira Libido.*— Virgil. *London*, Printed for *Henry Herringman*, at the *Anchor* in the *Lower-Walk* in the *New-exchange*, 1661.'   In the version of the tract

NOTES

given in the *Harleian Miscellany* the following *Advertisement* prefaces the text :

This Discourse was written in the time of the late Protector, Richard the Little *; and was but the first Book of three, that were designed by the Author. The Second, was to be a Discourse with the Guardian-angel of* England, *concerning all the late Confusions and Misfortunes of it. The Third, to denounce heavy Judgments against the three Kingdoms, and several Places and Parties in them, unless they prevented them speedily by serious Repentance, and that greatest and hardest Work of it, Restitution. There was to be upon this Subject the Burden of* England, *the Burden of* Scotland, *the Burden of* Ireland, *the Burden of* London, *the Burden of the Army, the Burden of the Divines, the Burden of the Lawyers, and many others, after the Manner of Prophetical Threatenings in the Old Testament : But, by the extraordinary Mercy of God, (for which we had no Pretence of Merit, nor the least Glimpse of Hope) in the sudden Restoration of Reason, and Right, and Happiness to us, it became not only unnecessary, but unseasonable and impertinent to prosecute the Work. However, it seemed not so to the Author to publish this first Part, because, though no Man can justify or approve the Actions of* Cromwell, *without having all the Seeds and Principles of Wickedness in his Heart, yet many there are, even honest and well-meaning People, who, without wading into any Depth of Consideration in the Matter, and purely deceived by splendid Words, and the outward Appearances of Vanity, are apt to admire him as a great and eminent Person ; which is a Fallacy, that extraordinary, and, especially, successful Villanies impose upon the World. It is the Corruption and Depravation of human Nature, that is the Root of this Opinion, though it lie sometimes so deep under Ground, that we ourselves are not able to perceive it ; and when we account any Man great, or brave, or wise, or of good Parts, who advances himself and his Family, by any other Ways but those of Virtue, we are certainly biassed to that Judgment by a secret Impulse, or, at least, Inclination of the Viciousness of our own Spirit. It is so necessary for the Good and Peace of Mankind, that this Error (which grows almost every where, and is spontaneously generated by the Rankness of the Soil) should be weeded out, and for ever extirpated, that the Author was content not to suppress this Discourse, because it may contribute somewhat to that End, though it be but a small Piece of that which was his original Design.*

  p. 346, l. 16. Folio] Men. l. 25. Folio] and and.

  p. 354, l. 23. Folio] again).

  p. 356, l. 17. Folio] and, Murderers l. 19. Folio] scource. l. 31. Folio *misprints*] refresh.

  p. 361, l. 31. Folio *misprints*] hamless.

  p. 362, l. 21. Folio] probably.

  p. 363, l. 15. Folio] danger.

  p. 364, l. 36. Folio] tell.

  p. 378, l. 6. *Should be* servitium. l. 36. Folio] Cataline.

  p. 379, l. 3. Folio] Cataline.

  p. 380, l. 14. Folio] frindships.

  p. 381, l. 6. Folio] Freind. l. 19. Folio] Incoveniences. l. 23. *A bracket has been added after* Atticus.

NOTES

p. 382, l. 8. Folio] Perithoam. l. 34. *The second* for *should have been left out.*

p. 383, l. 18. Folio] miseros. *Altered in errata.*

p. 384, l. 3. Folio] Autority.

p. 385, l. 25. *A comma has been substituted for a full stop after* Man.

p. 386, l. 32. *A semi-colon has been added after* Friend. l. 34. *A full stop has been added after* have.

p. 387, l. 15. *The reference* 2 *is not in the Folio.* l. 24. Folio] I a.

p. 389, l. 12. Folio] steam.

p. 390, l. 34. Folio] unwildly.

p. 391, l. 5. Folio] Morgage.

p. 392, l. 1. *The number* 2 *is not in the Folio.*

p. 393, l. 16. Folio] to.

p. 394, l. 29. *A semi-colon has been added after* Letters.

p. 396, l. 22. *A comma has been added after* pace.

p. 397, l. 3. Folio] the. l. 9. Folio] 18. l. 23. *A comma has been substituted for a full stop after* well.

p. 401, l. 1. *A semi-colon has been supplied after* City.

p. 402, l. 18. Folio] Materials,

p. 408, l. 28. Folio] non plenius, l. 30. Folio *misprints*] Fpistles.

pp. 409, 414, 416. Published earlier in the volume of 1663. See the first volume of the present edition, p. 462.

p. 419, l. 3. Folio] whom 'ere. l. 12. *For* described *read* desir'd. l. 14. Folio] Yeomen.

p. 420, l. 7. Folio] men.

p. 421, l. 22. *For* their *read* your.

p. 423, l. 3. Folio] T'had.

p. 424, l. 1. Folio] whisling.

p. 432, l. 19. Folio] auros. l. 20. Folio] Ætheria.

p. 433, l. 9. Folio] Table. *Altered in errata. The list of errata also indicates that for* moaths, mouths *should be read in* l. 8.

p. 434, l. 16. Folio] too, is, but.

p. 435, l. 22. *For* Title *read* Tide.

p. 438, l. 14. *For* their *read* the. l. 32. *For* their *read* your.

p. 441. Published earlier in the volume of 1663.

p. 442, l. 29. Folio *misprints*] himsef.

p. 443, l. 1. *Unnumbered in the Folio.*

p. 445, l. 25. Folio] Baffoon. *Altered in errata.*

p. 447. Published in 1663.

p. 449, l. 25. Folio] Vita. l. 26. Folio] incoare. l. 36. Folio] Melibæe. l. 37. Folio] Melibæus.

p. 450, l. 7. *A full stop after* him *in the Folio has been altered to a colon.*

p. 455, l. 4. Folio] selfs. l. 22. Folio *misprints*] wha.

NOTES

p. 460, l. 2.   Folio] beationem.

p. 461.   Published in 1663.   l. 20.   Folio] *The full stop after* free *has been altered to a comma.*

A list of errata is given at the end of the Folio of 1668.   *Some of the alterations were made in later editions and others not.   In the present edition the errata are included in the above notes, save a few to which effect has been given in the text.   It will be remembered that the Essays were posthumously published and that Cowley never saw them in print.*

p. 464, l. 2.   *A comma has been added after* betide.

p. 468, l. 4.   1679] Folishness *and* to.

p. 470, l. 32.   1679] many Headed-Rout.

p. 471, l. 21.   1679] Charle's.   l. 27.   *A full stop has been taken away after* above.

p. 474, l. 15.   Essex *was printed in the blank in later editions.*   l. 23.   *Later eds.*, W——n.

p. 475, l. 23.   1679] woulst.

p. 476, l. 24.   *Later eds.*, B——ks *and* H——ns.   ll. 30, 33, 35.   *Later eds.*, H——n.   l. 30.   1679] to.   l. 39.   *Later eds.*, Martyn.   l. 40.   *Later eds.*, Pym.

p. 477, ll. 14, 16.   *Full stops have been altered to commas after* Flood *and* fill.

INDEX OF TITLES

INDEX OF TITLES

INDEX OF FIRST LINES

INDEX OF FIRST LINES

INDEX OF FIRST LINES

CAMBRIDGE: PRINTED BY JOHN CLAY, M.A. AT THE UNIVERSITY PRESS.